A STEWARD'S
THE ROYA

(1943 — 1961)

Derek Hamilton Warner

ARTHUR H. STOCKWELL LTD.
Elms Court   Ilfracombe
Devon

ISBN 0 7223 2439-1

Printed in Great Britain by
Arthur H. Stockwell Ltd.
Elms Court   Ilfracombe
Devon

CONTENTS

INTRODUCTION

Let it be said, right from the start, I had little education. In fact you could say that I was backward and slow at learning.

This story is not written by a scholar, but straight from the heart of a steward who did his best to serve his country, and officers, in the Royal Navy. I ask the reader to follow the story day by day; starting from a boy of seventeen living each day in the Navy, never knowing what lay ahead; until reaching the rank of petty officer steward.

You will note that I have broken the story up into chapters; each chapter giving my life in the ship named.

The ships and dates are taken from naval documents which were given to me on leaving the Service.

CHAPTER 1

HMS *ROYAL ARTHUR*
(Skegness)

I volunteered for the Royal Navy and was called up on the 12th of July 1943; how thrilled I was at receiving my first orders. I was to report to the RTO at Skegness Railway Station. RTO, I soon learnt, meant Regulating Transport Officer. He was responsible for you while you were travelling on the railway; he could also give you food vouchers, if needed. If ever your train was late, he would stamp your draft sheet; this would then clear you if you arrived late at your destination. A draft sheet was a document which gave your name etc., the name of the ship that you were to join and where; the name of the ship that you were leaving and on what date; information on train times etc. If you were travelling in large numbers then there would be a petty officer in charge, then all you had to do was to follow his instructions.

This was my first time away from home and I am pleased to say that I managed to get to Skegness in one piece. At Skegness there were about one hundred chaps gathered outside the RTO's Office, all very excited. Soon I was to get my first taste of the Service, it was when a petty officer shouted at us to get into a waiting bus.

I had somehow imagined that I was going to be in a ship; I was:— HMS *Royal Arthur*, a shore establishment for the training of new recruits. It had once been a Billy Butlin's holiday camp, but I soon found out that I was in for no holiday, and the only SHIP that I saw was a boat secured in the swimming-pool, which was used for the training of seamen.

My first real taste of the Service was that everything had to be done at the double, and that the instructors never talked to you; they shouted. Being rather timid I found this hard to endure.

The accommodation in *Royal Arthur* was very good; two bunk-beds to a chalet, with a nice locker. The bathrooms and wash places were also good. The food was very nice but never enough, so we filled up with currant cake from the NAAFI (Navy, Army and Air Force Institutes).

At first I found it very hard to have my life run on a routine basis; for example, being awakened by a bugle call; going to meals when piped to do so, and the pipe — "Out Pipes" — which followed ten minutes after the pipe — "Stand Easy".[1] There was always a rush to get a cup of tea and a slice of cake from the canteen. Many times when it was my turn to be served — "Out Pipes" — would be given, which meant that I would rush back to my class; stuffing cake into my mouth as I ran. However; I very soon began to outrun my class-mates.

ORDERS AND ISSUES

All orders to the ship's company were given through a Tannoy system, preceded by a pipe whistle which was known as a Bosun's Pipe. The pipe was to call your attention to an order that was to follow. I was told that you should never whistle on board a ship before the mast. This was something to do with the wind carrying your whistle through the ship. It was a taboo that I respected whilst in the Service. Some orders were preceded by a bugle call; this was only on big ships or shore establishments that had Royal Marines aboard.

The day after I joined *Royal Arthur*, they took away all my clothes, which were sent home. In return I was issued with my kit (uniform). This was:—

1 Kitbag. 1 Hammock Kit (2 Hammocks, 2 Bed Covers, Mattress, Clews and Lashing). 2 Suits (Blue). 2 Suits (White) (Known as Duck Suits, when overseas). 3 Shirts (White). 2 Ties (Black). Underwear. 1 Pullover. 2 Prs. Pyjamas. 2 Prs. Boots. 3 Prs. Socks. 1 Overcoat. 1 Raincoat. 2 Towels. Shaving and Toilet Gear. 2 Peaked Caps. 2 Cap Covers (White) (Used when overseas). 1 Mug. 1 Small Case. 2 Cap Badges (Red Anchor with a Crown above it). Arm Badges (Red Star with OS in the centre — which told me that I was an Officer's Steward in the Supply Branch). 1 Housewife (Huzzif) — (A full sewing kit). 1 Lifebelt with red torch attached (To assist being seen in the night if you were unlucky and forced to abandon ship).

All this kit had to marked with your name. (Kitbag and hammock with your official number).

The same day, I was issued with a pay book, which contained my photo, official number, date of long leave and date of inoculations. (If you ever lost your pay book it would mean punishment). I was then issued with an identity disc, which had to be worn around the neck and finally with a station card. This contained your details: part of ship, duty watch, action station and pay number. This card was always given up when leaving a ship, as a new one was issued when joining a new ship. At this point I must say how disappointed I was with my uniform, having expected a sailor's uniform which was square rig.

Sympathy in the Navy whilst under training was never given. When I was being issued with my respirator, it was 'chucked' at me by a supply rating; it slipped through my fingers, breaking my glasses. I was at once sworn at, then sent off to the sick-bay (quarters), where my eyes were tested for a Service pair of glasses, which could be worn under your respirator.

The next month was hell; what with pipes, bugle calls, all followed by orders such as:—

Wakey Wakey	—	A call to rise in the morning.
Hands To	—	Breakfast, dinner, tea and supper.
Hands To Divisions	—	Only on Sundays, which was followed by a Church Service.
Hands Fall In	—	For evening quarters. To ensure that no one was missing.
Fire Party Fall In	—	Only if needed.
Pipe Down	—	Time to turn in.
Colours	—	This was a very important pipe, which I will explain later.
Stand Easy	—	(See Note 1).

The training consisted of divisions, evening quarters, parade drill, keep fit (PT — physical training) and games. There were also lectures on first aid, naval history and on what to do if you had to abandon ship.

Divisions, was when the ship's company (apart from those on duty) would march on the parade ground, in their divisions, to be inspected by the captain. Divisions meaning, seaman's, engineer's, supply, communications and miscellaneous branches, lead by the guard and RM band. But there was more to it, than just marching on to the parade ground.

First, each division (branch), would fall in on the roadway to be inspected by their divisional petty officer. He would then march them on to the parade ground to their allocated position. Then their divisional officer would march on to the parade ground to take over from the D.P.O.

The D.O. would then order the D.P.O. to "carry on". At this, the D.P.O. would give the order "open order march"; the front rank would take two paces forward, and the rear rank would take two paces backwards, the D.O. would then walk through the ranks, inspecting each person in turn; the order "close order march" was then given. The D.O. would then report to the captain or the senior officer in charge of the parade, that his division was correct and ready for inspection. The captain would then inspect the guard, then choose a division at random to inspect.

The order "off caps" would then be given, and the chaplain would then take over; after prayers, the order "on caps" would then be given, followed by the order "parade will march past, guard leading"; the RM band would then strike up and we would all march past the captain. As each division drew level with the captain, the order "eyes right" would be given; the captain saluted each division in turn. The divisions would then march off the parade ground, and after a pep talk by the D.O., would then be dismissed.

The same thing happened on all big ships, but on small ships, each division would fall in on the fo'c's'le, midships or the quarterdeck, and of course, there would be no march past. I never minded divisions, in fact, I always took part with some pride.

Evening quarters was when each division would fall in at an alloted place, so to be counted; the same practice on board a ship. This was to ensure that no one was missing.

In all these, there were also divisions of C.P.O.s, and P.O.s.

Your hammock was your best friend. The saying "I do not have a clew", meaning that you did not know, was very apt, for if you did not thread your clews in the right way, then you would soon tip out of your hammock. The lashing had to be in seven turns round the hammock, a good sailor could be indicated by the way he lashed his hammock, and I was told that a well-lashed hammock could keep you afloat. I am pleased to say that I never had to check this story out.[2]

I soon became used to the sayings such as:—

Aft	—	The stern, or the quarterdeck (QD) — back end of the ship.
Fo'c's'le	—	Bow or forecastle — front end of the ship.
Midships	—	Centre of the ship.
Port	—	Left side of ship.
Starboard	—	Right side of ship.
Up Top	—	Main deck or on the bridge — above the upper deck.
Below Deck	—	Under the main deck.

All these sayings came in very useful when I joined my first ship.

Colours, was the raising and lowering of the White Ensign (naval flag). Every morning at 0800 hours the ensign would be raised, then lowered at sunset. This ceremony was carried out by all ships in the Royal Navy at the same time — wherever they may be. When Colours were piped, everyone on the upper deck would stand to attention. Officers, chief petty officers and petty officers would salute. When a warship went into action, the ensign would fly from the main mast.

The QD, (quarterdeck) on a ship, was where the duty officer or officer of the watch could be found; at sea, he would be on the bridge. In a shore establishment, the QD was represented by two broad white lines at the main gate. You had to double over the QD and salute when stepping on it and when leaving it. This was always done under the beady eyes of the regulating staff, who were ready to pounce on you for your dress, etc. They were headed by the master of arms (equivalent to a sergeant-major in the army), who ruled with an iron fist and was always addressed as 'master', or else! On a small ship they were replaced by the coxswain, who may be only a petty officer.[3]

Whilst at Skegness, my mother came to see me. I was piped to report to the main gate. I remember my mother asking me why I had to run all the way. She little knew that I was under punishment for being late on parade. When she turned to go, I felt my first pangs of homesickness.

My dignity was soon lost, as when we showered or did our washing (dhobi-ing), we would all be naked; also before proceeding on draft, we always had a 'short arm inspection'. This meant lowering your trousers in front of the medical officer to ensure that we were clean. Then there were always those inoculations.[4]

After four weeks I passed out, gaining my first 'very good' (VG). A list was put on the notice-board, and we all crowded round it to see where we were to be posted. This first posting would be to a RN barracks at Devonport, Chatham or Portsmouth, and would remain as our home depot whenever we were not at sea. My name was under Dev; which was near Plymouth; had I only known, when I was given my official number I would have seen at once that I was to be a Devonport rating, as there was a "D" in front of my number. Devonport ratings were known as 'Guzz Ratings'.

On the 10th of August 1943, with a large party, we were given packed meals; these were always exciting — wondering what was in them — and you have guessed right, there was a piece of cake. I am sure that the Navy ran on navy cake. Under a petty officer, we travelled to Devonport; the land of the 'Oggies' (meat pasties).

I was to find out that we were only paid every other week, and 'what a to do' this turned out to be. You would fall in for pay parade; then when your name was called out, you would double up to the pay table with your hat in your hand and your pay book on top of your cap shouting out your pay number; the writer would shout out the amount of pay, then the paymaster would place the cash on the pay book and you would double away. All this was done under the eye of the master of arms or a regulating petty officer waiting to pick you up if you were slack etc. C. and P.O.s always saluted.[5]

On our way to Devonport we had to change at London; at Paddington we were given a hot meal and another packed meal. I shall always remember passing through London in an open truck and the way that the people waved to us and wished us luck.

While in *Royal Arthur*, I spent my evenings going to the camp cinema six nights a week, at 6d. (3p) a time; with a free live show on stage every Sunday. I only went ashore once as I never had very much money.[6]

CHAPTER 1

Footnotes:

1. The pipe "Stand Easy" — I'm sure you have guessed — meant tea-break.
2. Clews, were a number of small ropes, which were threaded into holes each end of your hammock. The clews were attached to an iron ring on the end of a larger rope, with which you slung your hammock. It was practice to use a piece of wood, called a hammock stretcher; you would place this between two end clews which would keep your hammock wide apart; so that you could easily climb into it.
3. The master of arms was a chief petty officer (C.P.O.), the regulating staff were petty officers (P.O.s) or leading hands. The regulating staff were responsible for the discipline and office work, such as making out draft chits, leave passes and patrol duties, they also carried out duties as wardens in naval prisons.
4. Draft was a posting to a new ship.
5. If you were ever short of cash you could get a casual payment. This was a small amount from your next payment.
6. While in *Royal Arthur*, I learned how to look after myself, doing my own washing etc.; I also learned to take orders. I must admit that the training that I received in *Royal Arthur* gave me much more confidence in myself, and I soon became a fit young man. I very soon fell into navy routine.

CHAPTER 2

HMS *DRAKE*

As soon as I arrived in *Drake* I was given a hot meal then sent to the stewards' mess, which was near to the officers' quarters. Our mess was full; I found myself in a large room where I had to fight for a 'slinging billet' so that I could sling (hang up) my hammock, which I had not yet mastered. There were no spare lockers, which meant that I had to live out of my kitbag — in all I was a bit depressed as the barracks were dismal and more like a prison.

Next morning I was given a 'pep talk' by the divisional officer (D.O.) a Lieutenant Franks; then sent to do a 'joining ship' routine. This meant to check in at the Regulating Office, Pay Office, Drafting Office, Sick-bay and Clothing Office where I had to lay out my kit for inspection. If ever I was short of any kit I would replace it by purchasing clothing from the clothing store known as Slops (kit).

The next day I was issued with a Steward's Manual (B.R.97), which I still have. I then started my training as a steward, this included:—

Laying tables for all meals, including lunch and dinner parties.

Table service, including mess dinner routine.

Marketing.

Composing of a menu.

Care of duties in the pantry. I was informed that a pantry needs and breeds a good steward.

Cleaning and storage of store-rooms.

There were also mess traps to learn about, these were divided into three groups:—

CONSUMABLES

All breakable articles. (Including teaspoons and tea-cloths, as these were easily lost).

13

PERMANENT

All silver — cutlery — galley gear — linen. (If there were any losses they had to be reported before they could be replaced).

STORED ARTICLES

Sieves — butter beaters — breadboards. (These could be replaced at any time).

All ward room crockery was edged by a blue line. Admirals' and captains' with a gold line.

All mess traps were entered in a book called a S.100 — known as a 'top line'. Whenever you mustered mess traps they had to correspond with the top line (this being the number of each article mustered at the last count — and giving the date of the muster).

Valeting covered the cleaning of cabins, care of officers' clothes and the laying out of them. Some of the uniforms that we had to know were:—

Number Ones	—	best uniform, with medals on parade etc. and sword.
Number Threes	—	working uniform.
Number Fourteens	—	action dress.
Mess Undress	—	with short waistcoat and minature medal ribbons, soft white shirt, bow-tie.
Mess Dress	—	with white waistcoat and minature medals, stiff fronted shirt, bow-tie.
Number Eights	—	full white uniform.
Number Thirteens	—	tropical uniform.

Then there were plain clothes and dinner suit, all these clothes had to be kept well pressed. There was also the cleaning of shoes and sword.

We were also taught how to address an officer, when calling him in the morning. A cheerful "Good-morning, Sir", tell him the time and what the weather was like, then ask him as to what uniform he would be requiring. A good valet soon came to know his officers, and also, just what to say to them.

Last of all there were wines to know about — the serving and storage of them and the wine books and wine steward duties, and care of a wine bar. All this training was crammed into one month, so you see how much I had to take in. However; I took to the training very well, so well that on passing out I received a 'superior'. Because of this I was detailed as a mess waiter in the ward room mess; with Wrens, who were very good because they had been given longer training. Perhaps I should point out that ward room (W.R.) was the term given to the officers' dining-room or officers' quarters.[1]

As I have already said the accommodation in *Drake* for stewards was very bad, we also had to walk over to the other side of barracks for all our meals, which was not very nice when it was raining. The food was good but still not enough, thank goodness for the currant cake which we could still get. The only drill that I had was on Sunday divisions, followed by 'Church Parade'. I was given an air raid shelter to make for in case of an air raid.

My first time in the W.R. as a waiter was very rewarding. I at once became used to serving officers, but even so, I was only allowed to serve on the long table which was for junior officers. The senior officers were placed on small tables around the W.R. The Wrens were very helpful. I partnered a Wren which meant that she would take the officer's order then send me to get the vegetables known as firsts and seconds; after I had served them the Wren would then serve sauces, etc. It worked out very well and I soon became confident. The chief steward was always in the background, watching every move we made.

There was only one pensioner in the W.R. who was an ex-steward; he was responsible for the cleaning of the W.R. and the laying of the tables. Sometimes I worked under him and I learned a lot. He remained in the W.R. right up to the time of my becoming a petty officer steward.

While I worked in the W.R. as a waiter, I soon became used to officers' ranks and branches which they served in. This was indicated by colours between their gold stripes. During my wartime service they were:—

One thin gold stripe	— Warrant-Officer
One thick gold stripe	— Sub-Lieutenant
Two thick gold stripes	— Lieutenant
Two thick gold stripes with a thin gold stripe	— Lieut.-Commander, or Number One[2]
Three thick gold stripes	— Commander
Four thick gold stripes	— Captain
One broad with a thick gold stripe above	— Rear-Admiral
One broad with two thick gold stripes	— Vice-Admiral
One broad with three thick gold stripes	— Admiral
One broad with four thick gold stripes	— Admiral of the Fleet

The branches were:—

No colour   —   Executive
Red   —   Engineer
Light red   —   Medical
Green   —   Electrical
Blue   —   Educational
White   —   Supply and Secretarial

These colours were abolished at the end of the war, also the warrant rank and mess.

Outside the Stewards' Regulating Office was a large notice-board — we were told to keep our eyes on it at all times — as we may find our names on it telling us to report to the Foreign Drafting Office (F.D.O.) or Home Drafting Office (H.D.O.); if it was the F.D.O. we would be issued with tropical kit, which was:—

Three white shirts
Three pair of white shorts
One pair of sandals

Petty officers and above were issued with two pairs of white shoes and socks. We would then be sent on foreign draft leave (F.D.L.).

One evening I saw my name on the board with eleven other stewards. We were told to report to our D.O. On reporting to him he told us to pack our kit and be on Pier 4 in the dockyard by 2000 hours. As it was now 1800 hours, this was known as a Pier Head Jump. We did not have to do a 'leaving ship' routine, owing to the short notice that we had been given. I was pleased to learn later that my mother had received a card from the Admiralty saying that I was safe, as I did not have time to write to her.

Up to now I had not seen a warship or any ship; so when I arrived at Pier 4, I was thrilled at seeing warships alongside and at buoys in the harbour. At 2100 hours we boarded a drifter (large boat for transporting stores and men to ships at buoy); this took us alongside a great ship that turned out to be HMS *Renown*, a battle-cruiser.

Again while I had been in *Drake*, I had spent most of my off duty time in the barrack's swimming-pool or in the cinema.

CHAPTER 2

Footnotes:
1. Although I have laid out the stewards' training programme in full, the only instruction that I received was to serve food from the left, drink from the right. If you were a wine steward, always give way to a mess waiter. Serve white wine with fish, and white meat — red wine with game and dark meat — and how to decant port. (This should be done twelve hours before use, leaving it in the room that it was to be served in — with the decanter, top off.) This was to ensure that the port would gain the right temperature. The rest of the training programme, I taught myself from the B.R.97.
2. Lieut.-Commander, or Number One, known as Jimmy, who was also the President of the W.R. Mess, in a small ship, but in a large ship the Commander was always the Mess President.

CHAPTER 3

HMS *RENOWN*

I joined *Renown* on the 10th of November 1943. I and the other stewards, were at once tumbled down into the stewards' mess, which was a box mess (enclosed), much better than an open mess, as we had more privacy. Alas! I did not have a 'slinging billet', but I soon found one in a quiet passage. I did not even do a 'joining ship' routine. I was soon informed that Prime Minister Winston Churchill was on board, and I was to be on his staff — I was amazed at this.

Soon I was looking for the toilets, known as 'heads'. These were kept clean by a sailor known as the captain of the heads — they were very much respected and did a fine job, especially in rough weather, if you know what I mean?

There were more pipes to get used to, such as:— Hands of the Mess for Mail. Up Spirits — the issue of a tot of rum. (I would not have this until I reached the age of eighteen.) Pipe for Shore Leave — to inform the ship's company of the time that shore leave was to be given.

At 2359 I heard more pipes:— Hands Fall in for Leaving Harbour, and many more; I was so excited I could not remember them all.

Then I felt the throb of the engines under my feet, I ran to a porthole but could not see very much as it was dark. I could only see the lights of other ships as we passed them. This was the first time of many to follow that I was to say goodbye to the 'Land of Tiddly Oggies', which I had come to like.

At first I was afraid of all the dials, levers, fans, guns and hatches that were all around me, but I soon settled down. The hatches were all numbered, as were the compartments, such as B.3; the letter giving the position of the compartment, while the number gave the deck level.

The first morning out I reported to the admiral's chief steward, as instructed, in the admiral's mess. The chief asked me my name, then asked me to lay the table for four courses — soup, fish, joint and sweet — this I did. The chief said "Well done" and instructed me on my duties; they were to clean shoes and scrub the pantry deck. What a come-down from a mess waiter!

Between my duties I managed to get on the upper deck. I was full of pride at being at sea and watching our escort of destroyers ploughing their way through the seas. It was also very nice to purchase duty-free cigarettes on board at 6d. for twenty.

I was fascinated with the pantry, with all its racks — for plates, saucers, glasses, etc., and hooks for cups — there was a place for everything. I learned that the rubbish known as 'gash' had to be tipped down the gash shoot, which was attached to the side of the ship. Gash could only be tipped when piped to do so — as floating rubbish could give away a ship's position to the enemy.

Whenever I heard the pipe — Attention on the Upper Deck and Salute, I knew that we were passing another ship. The custom was, the junior captain (Junior Ship) would pipe his ship to attention to the senior captain (Senior Ship). Merchant ships would dip their ensign (Red Duster). This was a courtesy always observed at sea and God help the officer of the watch if he slipped up.

After a couple of days at sea, the chief said that I was not experienced enough to remain on his staff and too good for scrubbing decks, so I was transferred to the W.R. as a mess waiter. There I found that we were carrying Wren officers and were they 'living it up'? Thus the saying "It's alright for some." Enough said.

While working in the W.R., I soon became more confident and was placed on the senior officer's table.

I had now learned the art of mess waiting, such as:— pushing condiments, butter, etc., in easy reach of an officer and advising an officer on the menu; also to push the side plate in front of the officer as he finished his sweet — then serve cheese, without the officer having to ask. These little points soon gained you respect from the officers.

A leading steward became my first 'Sea Daddy'. This was a shipmate, who kept you out of trouble. He warned me against 'Lower Deck Lawyers', these being big-headed people who thought that they knew everything, also 'Arse Bandits', these were dirty people who loved to pat your backside. Then there was the 'Buzz Spreader', he was a person who would give wrong rumours. Buzz meaning rumour.

This being my first time at sea I was soon drawn on to the upper deck, whenever I had the chance. I loved to watch the bow of the *Renown* dip into the sea then rise again, letting the seas fall back. I found it very fascinating. The destroyers looked so fine as they watched over us. Every so often we would all change course, this was to prevent any lurking U-boats from getting us in their sights.

One afternoon, feeling tired I turned in, when I was awakened by a rough shove; looking over the top of my hammock I saw a gold-braided peak cap, which turned out to be the commander. He asked me where my cruising station was. I replied that I did not have one. He then told me to report to the gunner's mate (G.I.). The G.I. gave me a station on the starboard midship guns as an ammunition feeder. I had been so honest to the commander that he had taken a fatherly attitude and I heard no more about it, although I was told I could have been given fourteen days' punishment.

On *Renown* I had my first fight, it was with our mess man, a seaman who kept our mess clean. He called me a bastard, so I hit him; this gave me some prestige amongst the stewards.

We passed Gibraltar, where I managed to get a glimpse of the Rock, then on to Malta but no shore leave was given, although the Maltese came alongside to sell fresh fruit and lace. The fresh fruit tasted divine. Malta looked very impressive with its high walls and white buildings.

We then set sail again; passing close to Algiers I noticed the white buildings all flat topped against a background of sand; this brought back memories of being at school learning Geography — how I wished my schoolteacher could see me now.

Up to now I had not seen Churchill, and I was informed that he slept all day and worked all night. I do not know how true this was, but I do know that a large part of the upper deck was out of bounds so that he could stretch his legs in private. I thought this very unfair, knowing how cramped the crew were below decks.

We arrived at Alexandria with our escorts, where Churchill left us. How I remember his leaving! As he drew away in the admiral's barge the ship's company manned the ships side to cheer him on his way. I did not cheer as I was still quite cross at all the space he had taken. I am afraid I just did not like him.

No shore leave was given; in fact as soon as Churchill left us we at once set sail for the UK, calling at Malta again; but this time shore leave was given. I purchased some lace for my mother and some bananas, which we were allowed to keep in the W.R. cool room. I also made my first visit to the Gut; the area where all the sailors made for to get their entertainment and 'you know what sailors are?' One night-club was run by a drag artist called Bobbie.

He left Danny La Rue standing, and he was always ready to buy a round of drinks for us.

We then set sail again, passing Gibraltar; then arriving at Devonport to the cheers of crowds on the Hoe and alongside the dockyard, till we reached our bouy. This was my first sailor's return, but I had not met the enemy. I was then drafted back to *Drake* with my cherished lace and bananas. The bananas were now ripe so I gave them to Mr Smythe, the pensioner, whom I have spoken of as working in the W.R. mess in *Drake*.

I must say at this point how interested I had become in my work as a steward — although I had only been a mess waiter, I was looking forward to carrying out further steward's duties.

I should point out at this stage that a naval rating's history sheet was always written up by his divisional officer, after he had completed his time in a ship. However, I found out later that this was not always the case, as there were times when I had been sent on loan to a ship for a short time and although I had done a good job this was not recorded — which meant that the duties I had carried out remained unnoticed. This was a bad slip-up on someone's part. Also on occasions the write-up was not true and biased; this I will point out as I go along.

Because I had only been aboard *Renown* for a short time, I did not receive a write-up in regard to the way I had carried out my duties while in her. This had been up to the D.O. in *Drake*, but he never even recorded that I had been sent to *Renown*. The only thing that I found out was that I did not suffer from seasickness.

CHAPTER 4

HMS *DRAKE*
(First Return)

I rejoined *Drake* on the the 23rd of November 1943, and was rated to assistant steward. I was placed in the W.O. mess as a mess waiter and valet. I must tell you of my stay in this mess as it remains one of my happiest memories. On Christmas Day, after we had served the W.O.s with their Christmas dinner, they then served the staff with our dinner. The W.O.s dressed up as Wrens and we had great fun. After our dinner, the W.O.s gave us the freedom of their mess for the remainder of the day. After Christmas I was sent on my first long leave.

My parents were very proud of me and interested in my sea tales. My mother was thrilled with her lace. Then my schoolteacher invited me to give a chat to my old class; this made me feel very important and much more a man.

When I returned from leave I found a draft chit waiting for me; I was to join HMS *Black Prince*, a cruiser waiting in Scotland; but before I tell you about this, I would like to give you some idea about naval catering:—

A large officers' mess found in big ships, or shore establishments, was run by a mess committee. This would be the president (Senior Executive Officer) (as the captain always had his own mess); a wine caterer and the catering officer, who would also be the D.O. The catering officer was responsible for the catering which, in most cases, included for the catering of the staff. He would be assisted by the chief steward and chief cook. The wine caterer was nearly always the medical officer or 'Doc', as he was known.

On small ships, the senior steward was responsible for the catering, receiving cash from the mess treasurer to do this duty with. He would be assisted by the senior cook.

There was also a mess man, usually a chief or P.O. steward, who catered for the officers and staff. Mess men were far and between. If I had been given chance to be a mess man in a large ship, I would have been pleased, as you could make a good profit. The Admiralty victualling allowance would be made to him at the end of each month by the paymaster, after deductions had been made for any stores that he had received from the ship's store. A.V.A. was paid to you when going on long leave. The mess man was also paid a mess subscription by the officers, which could be up to 40p per day. This was for fresh fruit, cakes and laundry, etc. He would then settle his accounts with the ship's canteen and ashore; then any money left over was his. If he had a good cook and a pantry steward, then he could be well in. He always paid a gratuity to those who assisted him, he was under contract and so responsible for his own debts.

The lower deck had two types of messing — these were general messing (G.M.) and canteen messing (C.M.). G.M. was catered for by the senior supply rating and senior cook, under the supply officer. They would make out a menu the same for all (apart from the W.R.). Canteen messing was done by each mess, other than the W.R., they catered for themselves — this was only found in small ships.

Now to go back to HMS *Black Prince*. I did not join her with the main draft, for when we arrived at Perth I was taken off the train with septic tonsillitis, then sent to an army hospital. I asked the P.O. in charge of us if I could have my kit, which was in the guard's van with the bulk of kits, but he said there was not enough time. So all I had was my small case and toilet gear.

During the time that I was in hospital, the nurses made a great fuss over me as I was the only sailor. I was then sent to Stirling Castle, which had been turned into a convalescent home — again I was made a fuss of. In fact, one day, the matron, who was a dear old lady, sent for me to have tea with her; we had quite a chat. I also received an American war parcel, which contained a bright red jumper that I gave away.

I was then sent on ten days' sick leave. As my parents were spending their holiday with my auntie and uncle at Lincoln, I had to join them. One night the men were going out for a drink, but my father said I was too young to join them, so I went out on my own and got drunk. This was the first time I had ever been drunk. My father let it pass, but my uncle thought it was a great joke. The next morning I had a head — which was not a joke. The reason that I got drunk was because I thought that if I was old enough to fight for my country, then I was old enough to get drunk.

Returning from sick leave, I was then sent to a shore establishment where they were training stewards. As I had been to sea, I was made into a bit of a hero and treated to drinks. This was not to last, as they found out where *Black Prince* was, and I was sent packing.

CHAPTER 5

HMS *BLACK PRINCE*

As the drifter took me out to the *Black Prince*, I at once noticed how grand she looked, like a large destroyer. I knew at once that I was going to like this romantic cruiser, as she was later known as.

It was the end of February 1944 when I joined her. The master at once pounced on me, asking me where the hell had I been? As the P.O. in charge of the draft had not reported my going into hospital, I had been listed as an absentee. On top of this, my kit had been lost. After being checked out, they accepted my story, but the pay commander was not very pleased at my loss of kit. In the end I was issued with another kit, but I was well out of pocket over this. The pay commander still thought that it was my fault, and that was that.

I was rated to steward, as I had now reached eighteen; so I was issued with a tot of rum (Grog). This was one-third rum with two-thirds water. Chiefs and petty officers had their tot neat. Officers were only issued with rum when it was 'splice the mainbrace'. Ship's company were then issued with a double tot. How I wished that I had remained a T.-man (Temperance) and had taken the extra pay instead.

I was in a box mess, which was very nice, with plenty of room and a good 'slinging billet'. The officers and staff were catered for by a mess man called Hains, a P.O. who was very good at his job. I met him later in *Drake* when he was a pensioner, working in the W.R. silver pantry.

In *Black Prince* I came to know even more Pipes:—
> Hands Prepare for Leaving Harbour.
> Hands Detailed for Leaving Harbour — Fall In.
> Hands to Cruising Stations.
> Hands to Action Stations.

Duty Part of the Watch — Fall In.
Close All Portholes.
Stores are Now Being Issued.
Darken Ship.
Men Under Punishment Fall In Outside the Regulating Office.

Then there was boat drill, which gave me a boat or a float to make for in case I had to abandon ship; all this I took in my stride.

The buzz (rumour) soon went round the ship that we were going north, as we were taking in stores and winter clothing. This proved to be true, as one night we slipped out to sea where we joined a convoy bound for Russia. As we joined the convoy the merchant seamen cheered us. I felt very proud at being a part of it all. As we steamed through the convoy to take up our position; the merchant ships dipped their ensigns and we answered their salute by dipping our ensign.

I was issued with anti-flash gear, which was a white balaclava and gloves. These had to be worn whenever we went into action stations — also a thick pair of long underpants and woollen jumpers and balaclava. These I found kept me nice and warm; the underpants I wore over my pyjamas. I also kept my lifebelt on all the time as this was a standing order.

We were to make for Murmansk. Being in a Russian convoy did not worry me too much, but I did not like my action station as it was down in X-magazine, at the bottom of the ship.

One night while we were closed up (at action stations), I kept looking at the bulkhead (ship's side) wondering what would happen if a torpedo hit us; and thinking of the cruel sea outside, I was brought to my senses by a slap in the face by the Royal Marine sergeant in charge of the magazine. His name was Webb; a name I will never forget, as he had done me a good turn. I never let my imagination stray again. I also soon became used to the bucket, dry biscuits and cocoa. The bucket was used when we wanted to pass water as we were not allowed to leave our station when closed up. I also got a taste for 'goffers', which was a soft drink that the canteen served up; it was very nice. Then there was the game called Housey-Housey, which is now called Bingo and I learned to play Crib and Ockers, which is known as Ludo. These games were played for a sip of our tot, or for cigarettes.

On our way to Murmansk, while closed up, we had removed the clips of the cordite shells, which was the practice as it was much easier to pull them out if needed, when suddenly the ship rolled over to starboard, causing the shells to fall all over the deck, just missing our feet. The captain gave out over the Tannoy that we had just missed a torpedo attack; was I thankful that we had a good skipper. The captain was called G. M. Lees, RN; he was always keeping us up to date as to what was happening — this proved most reassuring as it was not very nice being shut down in the magazine. A mention in dispatches (M.D.) was given to the youngest crew member, which I missed by a week; it went to a boy seaman.

My duties were as assistant wine steward to a Royal Marine called Reynolds, who was also the commander's valet. The commander was called Gregory, whom I met later in *Drake* when he was captain. Reynolds was made wine steward because the leading steward had been sent to hospital just before we sailed. This was the only time that I ever knew a Marine as a wine steward. Reynolds taught me a lot on the storage of wines, wine accounts, the care of wines and the mixing of drinks. If you could mix a good cocktail, then you were highly regarded by the officers. It was useful to know what each officer drank, as some officers would just nod to you — you then served him his drink.

It may be interesting to know just how duty-free drink came on board. The wine steward and wine caterer would make out the order for fresh stock; this was then passed on to the captain's secretary who would then make out a C and E90 (Customs and Excise Note), this was then sent to the wine merchants with a copy to the customs office. A date would be sent for delivery and a customs officer, known as a 'watcher', would be on the gangway to check the wines aboard. I never once saw a 'watcher'. It was always left to the wine steward to check them in. The stores were then entered into the gangway book, which was kept by the master. The wine steward would then enter them into the wine stock book.

Officers paid for their drinks by signing a chit; these chits were then entered into the rough book, then the wine book. The wine book was inspected by the captain once in a while to see if any officer was over-indulging. If an officer had a guest, then a red G was placed against his name. At times an officer would ask me to give him a red G when he had not had guests, to cover up that he had been drinking a lot.

As we sailed further north, I saw the Northern Lights; they were a fine sight caused by a luminescent display of colours in the atmosphere arising from electrical interactions between the Earth's magnetic field and streams of energetic charged particles from the sun. I also saw the Midnight Sun; these sights will always remain in my mind.

Life on board went very well, I had a good mess, good food and a drink whenever I fancied one — (wine stewards' perks) — as it was a responsibility looking after the wines, and I was always being asked by the crew to sell them a bottle; but I never did, as this could mean 'cells' if caught.

In those days your wine stock would always be up. This was because we were guided by our B.R.97 as to the measures that each bottle held. For instance, a bottle of gin contained 30 thirds; you were allowed 3 thirds spillage. Nearly all bottles contained more than 30 thirds, so if you were careful, then you could make up to 3 thirds out of each bottle opened; which meant that every ten bottles opened you would be up one bottle of gin. This was the same on all wines and spirits. All wine stewards had their own way of keeping their stock in order. I think I should say no more on this subject.

On crossing the Arctic Circle, I became a 'Blue Nose' and received a proclamation signed by the captain. This read as follows:—

> *Be it known that on this day of the 23rd February 1943. In a Latitude 66D.33N. and in a Longitude 2D.West. The Worthy and Esteemed Name Embarked in HMS* Black Prince *being bound for the Land of the Midnight Sun while in search of Divers, Scrap Metal and Stray Mermaids. Did with my Royal permission enter these Dark and Frosty Wastes. By crossing the Arctic Circle. And by Virtue whereof, I Neptune Rex Ruler of the Raging Seas, do hereby declare him to be a Loyal and Trusty Blue Nose. And I call upon all Icebergs, Sealions, Narwhals, Polar Bears and other Creatures of the Frigid North to show him Due Deference and Respect. Disobeyed under pain of my Royal Displeasure.*

I have given this proclamation in full, as it may be of interest to those readers who may be old salts.[1]

We arrived at Murmansk without any further bother. We were greatly welcomed by the Russians. Shore leave was given, but it proved most disappointing as there was nothing but snow — lots of snow — but I did manage to get some Red Star cap badges in exchange for cigarettes, and that was about all.

One night the officers entertained some Cossacks in the W.R.; after plying them with drink they soon broke out dancing and performing acrobatics. That night I turned in a bit under the weather, and I was not the only one.

A week later we set sail for home, leaving behind cheering Russians; we had done a good job. We had no contact with the enemy on our way home, and we arrived at Devonport to a hero's welcome and were then sent on leave. Before closing the story of the Russian convoy, I must point out that the Russians did all they could to make our stay one to remember. They had nothing to give us, only their appreciation, and this they did with their hearts.

Returning from leave, we soon sailed again; this time we slipped out of Devonport one night — heading a force of a British destroyer called *Ashanti* — with three Canadian destroyers called *Athabaskan, Huron* and *Haids*. Dawn had not yet broken when we engaged three German Elbing-class destroyers; they altered course and increased speed to try and reach Germany. We fired star shells to light them up, while the escorts opened fire, sinking one and damaging the other two. We had to take avoiding action to miss a torpedo attack; again I was thankful for a good skipper. Lord Haw Haw gave it out that we had been sunk. I found out later that a card had been sent to my mother from the Admiralty saying that I was safe. The sea battle was given out on the radio; so when we returned to Devonport, it was to more cheering crowds. I was now well-blooded.

This was the first time that I had returned to my port after action at sea. As we sailed into the Hoe, we fell in for entering harbour, which meant, standing all along the upper deck and on the signal bridge. As we moved up harbour at a slow pace, the crowds cheered us all along the side of the dockyard. Each time we drew level with another ship, we would be piped up, all that I could hear, was the cheering crowds and the sound of trumpets and pipes, the air was full of excitement; tears ran down my face; tears of joy and pride.

Up to now when returning to harbour, we had always gone to a buoy, this meant that you had to listen for the pipe telling you that a liberty boat would be leaving at a given time. You had to be ready, as sometimes there would only be short notice given; it also meant that you had to return aboard sober, or you may easily fall when climbing aboard. This time we went alongside, which was much better, as there would be a free gangway; which meant that you could go ashore at any time while the gangway was open — after first reporting to the duty officer, and again when you returned aboard.

By now we were building up for D-Day. On the eve of D-Day we sailed with HMS *Ramillies* and other ships and waited off the French coast. On D-Day we opened fire with *Ramillies* covering the USN Forces. What a sight this was, although we were covering the Americans, our lads went in. As they passed us in their landing-craft, we tossed them cigarettes; they were full of fight. I must tell you that the Americans, who we were covering, sent a signal to *Black Prince* which read as follows:— 'Wish you could see what your guns are doing. They are smashing enemy targets.'

We then steamed inshore where we fired on enemy batteries by map reference. The first to be destroyed was a howitzer battery, then many others. We were then ordered to return to Newcastle where the Geordies made us very welcome. Whenever we went into a dockyard club, they at once would buy us drinks; they even took us to their homes for supper; but this was not to last very long, as I was drafted back to *Drake*.[2]

I was very sorry to leave *Black Prince*, as I gained much experience in wines; also P.O. Hains had taught me a lot on carving and pantry work, as he was in the pantry at all meals. I did not receive a write-up from *Black Prince*; I think that this was due to the fact that we were at war, and your write-up may never be seen; if you know what I mean?

CHAPTER 5

Footnotes:
1. As we sailed further north, I noticed how the ice was forming on the bow, rails and guns. You had to wear gloves at all times, whenever you were on the upper deck, or you would get frost-bite. I also noticed how the small merchant ships sailed very close to us for protection. I saw two merchant ships go down; the survivors were picked up by our destroyers. My heart went out to the merchant ships, as they were sitting ducks for the U-boats.
2. As soon as we arrived at Newcastle, Reynolds the wine steward, got drunk, and so was sent packing. I then took over as wine steward. Most of the ship's company were also sent on draft; the remainder, including P.O. Hains, went on 21 days' leave. A leading steward took over Hains' duties, but he was not very good, and he put Hains in debt. Hains told me of this when I met him much later in *Drake*. I remained aboard as wine steward with the care and maintenance party (C. & M.P.) until Hains and the others returned from leave. As I have said, I then returned to *Drake*.

CHAPTER 6

HMS *DRAKE*
(Second Return)

I joined *Drake* again on the 22nd of July 1944, but I only remained in *Drake* for two months before I was drafted to HMS *Turtle*; however, while in *Drake* as a mess waiter, I was very lucky to take part in a mess dinner. That night I took it all in, which proved most helpful to me later on. The mess dinner routine was as follows:—

The chief steward (Mess Butler) would first inspect the table with a ruler, to see that the lay-ups were evenly spaced. Then he would inspect all the staff's fingers, nails, etc.; finally placing us into groups, each group under a P.O. These groups were allotted a part of the table for which they would be responsible. The table looked magnificent with the ship's trophies and silver candelabras all along the centre of the table. Drake's sword and goblet was placed in front of the president's chair. The candelabras were attached to wall plugs, where a steward would be placed. At the sound of the president hitting the gavel, when all the officers were seated, the W.R. lights were switched off, and the table lights switched on. If done correctly it would give a wonderful effect. The chief would then check with the chief cook that he was ready and see that the R.M. band was in place.

The chief would then report to the mess president that "Dinner was Served, Sir" then lead the officers into the mess accompanied by the music of the band (a March). When all the officers were seated he would report to the president:—

"Gentlemen Seated, Sir, Chaplain present" — The president would then hit the gavel and grace was said.

The dinner would be served, going right through the menu, till the last course.

The chief would then ask permission to clear the table:— The table would then be cleared and polished, leaving only the table decorations. The chief would then report:

"Table cleared, Sir" — Grace would be said again when the wine steward stepped in, placing decanters in front of the president and vice-president, with a wine glass to each officer. The chief would then report:

"Wines ready to pass, Sir" — The decanter tops would be removed by the president and vice-president; then the port would be passed from the right to each officer. The wine steward would change the decanter tops round, and after each officer had taken a glass of port, the wine steward would check that no officer had an empty glass; if he had he would be given water. The chief then reported:

"Wine passed, Sir" — The president would then say 'Mr Vice,' the vice would then say 'Gentlemen, the King'. This was the signal to place on the table dessert gear, followed by dessert, then coffee and cigars, etc. From a nod from the president, the chief then called the bandmaster to sit on the left of the president and take a glass of port. At another nod, the bandmaster would leave and the president, and vice would replace the decanter tops; this was the signal for the chief to ask:

"Permission to remove the wines, Sir" — The chief and wine steward would then remove the decanters from the table; which again was the signal that officers could leave the mess.[1]

As I have said, I was only in *Drake* for a short stay, but it proved to be a very busy period as I was soon to be taken off steward's duties, to be made the divisional officer's messenger. Now at this time a Lieutenant Franks had been catering officer and D.O., but he was relieved by a Lieutenant-Commander Woodward-Brown. Franks was sent to Lynam Camp, where the training of stewards took place. Brown had requested me to be his messenger, and at this, Franks took a dislike to me, which was proved later.

I had volunteered for submarines, and so Brown sent me to Lynam Camp to take a leading steward's course. At Lynam, I was put in charge of a stewards' dining hall, while a one badge steward was in charge of another S.D.H. One day we had a quarrel, and the steward reported me to Franks. Franks pointed out that if I could not respect a senior steward, I would never make a leading hand. At this, I was at once given the exam to take; before time, and was failed — but guess what on? — wine accounts. How could I have failed when wines were my pet subject. This proved the saying, "It's not what you know, it's who you know". I was then sent back to *Drake*, where a draft chit was waiting for me to join HMS *Turtle*. Although I had only been in *Drake* for under three months, all that Brown wrote was:— 'Failed in examination for leading steward on wine accounts.'

I feel that he was quite happy to leave the outcome to me. I did not receive a write-up from Franks.

Perhaps I should now explain that a steward was the same as a lance-corporal; a leading steward as a corporal; a petty officer steward as a sergeant and a chief as a sergeant-major; or in some cases a warrant-officer.

I had now formed an opinion of naval officers; they loved to be made a fuss over, but I found it hard to trust them as there was a barrier in regard to the Service; the W.R. mess. One had to be careful when choosing a friend. On a ship it was like living in a town. The canteen being shops; the regulating office the police station; the sick-bay the hospital and the chaplain as your church. There had to be a lot of trust in each other.

You should now know something about 'Request Men and Defaulters'. You could request to see the captain at any time, first you would put your request in writing as follows:—

Request to see the captain through the commander, through the divisional officer, then state your request. Each time you would be put before the officer by the master of arms etc.; salute, then your request was read out. After it had been granted, or turned down, you would salute again and leave the table. Defaulters were a lot different. You were doubled up to each officer, again by the M.O.A. etc.; when you were ordered "Off Caps". After you removed your cap, the charge was read out. Your divisional officer was there to speak up for you. The charge was then passed up to the commander and so on, until you reached the captain who would deal with it according to how serious it was. You were then ordered "On Caps" and you would double away. The punishments were many, but if it meant cells, then the captain would ask you if you will receive his punishment. If you did then he would deal with it right away. Good conduct badges could be taken away in place of cells, but if the crime was serious enough for you to be dis-rated, then the captain would send for a warrant from his flag officer — when the warrant returned, you would then be dis-rated in front of the ship's company.

c

This warrant should not be confused with the other warrant (a free railway ticket).

CHAPTER 6

Footnote:

1. I must point out that no plates were removed from the table until a signal had been given by the chief steward to do so; this meant that after each course was finished, when the signal was given, all plates would be removed at the same time. This would be followed by another signal from the chief to place a plate down in front of each officer for the next course. Each course would only be served when the signal was given by the chief to do so. This meant that there was a complete uniform routine throughout the dinner.

CHAPTER 7

HMS *TURTLE*

As I had volunteered for submarines, I thought that *Turtle* would be a training ship for submariners, but it proved to be a training ship (establishment) in Poole, near Bournemouth, for Combined Operations. This was sea and land forces training.

I joined *Turtle* on the 9th of September 1944, and what a ship it turned out to be. The captain was a lieutenant-commander retired, who had been brought back. The first lieutenant was lame, and the P.O. steward was also a pensioner who had been brought back, and was making a packet by running the ship's canteen. Alright, they were all doing their bit; but they seemed to have a chip on their shoulders. Also I got off on the wrong foot, as I had relieved a leading steward, this gave me reason to think that I had passed out as a leading steward; but the results came through that I had failed. Thus the P.O.s and stewards thought that I had been pulling a fast one, and I never did get on with them over this.

I was given the duties as captain's valet and mess waiter, but I never received the respect that was given to a captain's valet. The P.O. steward and the three stewards were Portsmouth ratings and the stewards all had G.C. badges, so I found that I was doing most of the scrubbing. I did not mind this so much, except that one of the stewards kept making advances to me, until I threatened to hit him.

The W.R. was a large house consisting of bedrooms, dining-room, lounge, kitchen and bathroom. The duties were quite good, as I was only on duty every other day. I would take over by serving lunch at 1300 hours; clean up then serve tea in the lounge at 1600 hours; lay up for dinner and serve it at 2000 hours; there would only be the duty officer, as all the officers lived ashore. Clean up after dinner and lay out the captain's uniform, ready for the morning; I was finished by 2200. The next day I would call the duty officer, serve

35

breakfast at 0800, clean up, then clean the captain's room and bathroom; then lay up for lunch. I was off duty then till noon the next day, apart from valeting the captain. The P.O. steward was always ashore shopping, or over in his canteen; so leaving the stewards to run the W.R.

One day the ship ran a cross-country race, in which I took part. The next morning the quartermaster piped "Wakey Wakey — stand fast ratings who took part in the cross-country race". At this I turned over and went back to sleep, only to be sent for by the P.O. steward who asked me why I was not on duty. I told him why, but he politely ran me in. The first lieutenant did not believe my story, and so I was given Captain's Report. The captain also did not believe me, and gave me fourteen days' punishment. I had it out with the Q.M. telling him that his joke had cost me; he gave me his tot and we remained friends.

There was only one nice thing that I can remember about *Turtle*. That was one evening, whilst visiting the YMCA at Bournemouth, I was given an address to go to where I was greeted by a parson and his wife, who entertained me to dinner. There were also two nurses and an army sergeant; we had a lovely night. The parson later told me that he had lost his son at sea, and he would pray for me. I found this very comforting and it made me feel good.

Although I was only in *Turtle* for four months, I did receive a nice write-up as follows:— 'Works well, should make a good steward with more experience.'

However; I was very happy when I was drafted back to *Drake*. While I was in *Turtle*, I must say that I did not learn a thing; only the experience of being a captain's defaulter.

None of the training of Combined Operations touched me. I shall never know why I was sent there. The catering staff were the only ratings in blues. The rest of the ship's company were in army battle dress with a Royal Navy flash on their shoulders.

CHAPTER 8

HMS *DRAKE*/HMS *FROLIC*

I had joined *Drake* on the 19th of December 1944, when I was sent on Christmas leave. On my return there was a draft chit waiting for me to join HMS *Frolic*; a minesweeper based at Dovercourt, Suffolk. There is not much that I can say about my short stay in *Drake*, only that I did get roped in for fire watching — which meant spending a night on the roof of the W.R. block — this proved very cold so I was pleased when I was sent on leave, then on to *Frolic*. However; for my short time in *Drake* my duty was in the serving room. This was a room off the W.R. mess, which acted as a pantry. The food was sent up from the galley by a hand lift, then placed into heaters ready to be passed out as requested by the mess waiters. The dirty dishes were sent down to the scullery; the silver to the silver pantry. You had to be on your toes, as there were only two hatches, one for passing out and one for receiving back. If there was a hot roast, then a chief steward would do the carving in the servery. There was a table with cold meats in the W.R. mess where a chief or P.O. steward would attend to the carving.

There were seven minesweepers in the flotilla, and we sailed each day to sweep the North Sea. We returned to harbour every night, and short week-end leave was given every week. Although my home was only sixty-five miles away, I could never take this leave, as I could not get back in time before the ship would sail on Monday morning; so I dipped out on this (missed out).

The *Frolic* was an American ship on loan to the Navy and I found that we had the luxury of bunks and nice lockers. I joined *Frolic* on the 6th of January 1945.

The leading steward in charge was called Connolly, whom I met later when he was a chief. Connolly was on compassionate leave most of the time, as his mother was very ill, so a one badge steward called Robinson was in charge. There were two other stewards and we were all Devonport ratings. My main duty was to valet the divisional officer, who was a very nice officer. I was also a mess waiter; as I was the junior steward, I found that I was doing most of the scrubbing, which I had now come well used to.

Again the duties were quite good; when on duty I would take over at noon, serve lunch, tea and dinner, then I would turn back the D.O.'s bunk. I was nearly always finished by 2200 hours. Next day I would rise at 4 a.m. and scrub out the W.R. mess and ante room, lay for breakfast, call my officer, then serve breakfast. After breakfast I would clean the D.O.'s cabin and lay for lunch; then I was off duty until noon the following day, apart from valeting the officer. The officers ran their wine bar and helped themselves to a drink as required.

When sweeping with the flotilla, all the decks were battened down; so this meant it was impossible to get to your bunk or locker. If you had been on duty you would have to sleep where you could.

Each sweeper has a device called a 'hammer', this was attached to the side of the ship on her bow. The hammer would send out vibrations which would set off a mine that lay ahead. The Germans, after learning of our device, then invented a type of mine that could be placed on the sea-bed astern of the other mine nearer the surface which; when the hammer exploded the first mine, would then explode the mine which would be beneath the ship. However; we soon mastered this, but not until we had lost a sweeper. I was on the upper deck at the time and I saw it happen. The sweeper went down with no survivors. I then realised just how dangerous our work was. We were paid extra pay while on sweepers.

Sweeping was very boring as we sailed at a very slow speed, which meant the ship would roll a lot. Sometimes if there was a bad swell we would have to fit 'fiddles' on the table; these were racks that had a hole for glasses, etc., and a space for the lay up. Fiddles had nothing to do with fiddles that meant rackets or swindles.

While sweeping in these bad swells, I managed to get a laugh; this was while washing my clothes (dhobi-ing) in the bathroom. You would find naked bodies slipping about, so you had to take care or you would get someone up your backside. Also, when using the 'heads', if the ship rolled right over, then you would get a backwash of sea water, which gave you a wet backside.

I had my first injustice in *Frolic*. One day while we were sweeping I was returning the pots and pans to the galley, which meant that I had to pass through two doors on the upper deck. As I passed through the last door, the boatswain shouted to me "Shut the door." I had my hands full so I replied "You must be kidding," he then slammed the door on me hurting my leg, so I swore at him; he then ran me in. I finished up at the captain's table and, after hearing my story, he told me I should have put a complaint in and not sworn at a P.O., so I was lashed up to twenty-one days stoppage of leave. However; the coxswain took pity on me and proved to be friend later on.

The very next day we were ordered to sail for Flushing in Holland. We left the ship there and the ship's company were all drafted back to their barracks; I to *Drake*. We travelled through Belgium, where I managed to visit Skipper Street, a well-known place where sailors made for. It was when I arrived back in *Drake* that I found that the coxswain had not recorded my punishment on my draft sheet, so I only lost one day; this was a very humane thought by the coxswain.

The write-up that I received was not too bad, it was as follows:—
'Commenced well, but the fact that he took a personal dislike to the leading steward reflected in his work so much that he was continually being checked by the W.R. officers. Quite capable of doing excellent work.'

I should point out that when I got into trouble with the boatswain, I had asked Robinson to stand up for me, but he refused. This caused me to lose respect for him.

CHAPTER 9

HMS *DRAKE*/HMS *F.D.T.13*

I joined *Drake* on the 6th of April 1945, where I served as mess waiter and valet; but only for three months, before I was drafted to *F.D.T.13*; so I did not receive a write-up.

I joined *F.D.T.13* on the 4th of August 1945; I found her to be an American tank landing-craft, which had been converted into a fighter director tanker. She had been given a false bow which proved the saving of the ship later on. The tank space had been fitted out with many radar rooms, which RAF personnel worked in; so we were a mixed crew, but we all got on well together. We again had the luxury of bunks and large lockers, and our quarters were nice and big and well fitted out.

My duty was captain's steward; all other duties were excused. This was my first sea captain to look after. I had to keep his clothes well pressed and lay them out as he needed them; all his meals, while a sea, were served to him on the bridge. If it was rough, then I would stand by his bridge chair and hold the tray as he ate. I loved this as I found it most interesting being on the bridge. I also saw that all his meals were well prepared, which he appreciated. I would also turn his bath on and lay back his bunk every night; I even filled his cigarette case for him. To be a good captain's steward you had to know his likes and dislikes, and when it was the right time to talk to him. In fact you were more like a 'gentlemen's gentleman', and you never made his desk tidy, you ALWAYS took care to touch nothing on his desk.

The P.O. steward in charge was called Knowles; he had passed out for catering officer and he taught me a lot about bookkeeping. There were four other stewards, but I did not spend much time with them, as I was kept busy looking after the captain.

After many exercises at sea with the RAF, we were ordered to sail for the Pacific; but on reaching the Red Sea we were informed that the Japs, had surrendered — was I pleased, as I had not been looking forward to meeting their suicide planes. We then received fresh orders to proceed to Norfolk, Virginia, to return their ship.

On reaching the Azores, we ran into a very bad storm. The destroyer, *Speaker*, which was escorting us, made for cover; our captain decided to ride the storm out by turning into it. This was when the false bow saved us. The dockyard had done a good job; without the false bow we would have been in trouble. We turned into the storm as we were flat-bottomed and could quite easily have turned over. I must say that I was too busy looking after the captain to be afraid. The captain had given me warning about the storm, so I had time to secure his cabin, which meant stowing everything away, such as picture frames, etc.

This was the first real bad storm that I had experienced. The pipe was given "The Upper Deck is Out of Bounds". This did not bother me as I could reach the bridge without going on the upper deck. When I managed to get on to the bridge I saw the seas break right over the bow, so the bow and the forepart of the ship was completely submerged. The seas then broke off as they hit the bridge; sending spray all over us. The wind and salt water hit my face, and somehow I felt as though we were challenging the sea to do its worst; it was a great feeling and I knew that I was meant to be a sailor, and that the sea was in my blood.

When the storm calmed down, we made for the West Indies and limped into Hamilton, where there was a dry dock. While in dry dock I could see the extent of the damage the sea had caused. The bow was twisted and there were large dents in the side and on the bottom of the ship. The dockyard workers did a fine job in fixing us up ready to continue our journey to America.

The people of Hamilton made our stay a nice one, and they were kind to us, but somehow I felt that they were not altogether for the British.

While in Hamilton I was fascinated by the noise of the grasshoppers at night. I also came to like their local drink of rum and Coke, which the sailors had made up a song about, which I will not repeat. One night while ashore, I climbed over the wall of a large house to pinch some bananas. It turned out to be the commodore's house. Next day, a signal was sent to all naval ships warning ratings on how to conduct themselves while ashore. I felt very silly as I had only done it for a dare.

After we had been given a clean bill of health, we continued on our journey to America, where I got into another spot of bother. A crowd of us went into the USN Club in Norfolk dockyard, which the American Navy called "Shit City". As I was having a drink at the bar, an American sailor slapped me on my back and said "Limeys give me the shits." I at once replied "It takes an Englishman to be a Limey, any silly bastard can be a Yank." At this all hell broke out and I finished up under the table. After a while the fight stopped and the Americans complimented us on a good fight and finished up buying our drinks for the rest of the night.

Leaving the ship at Norfolk, we travelled overland by ferry and rail to New York. When I saw the skyscrapers and yellow taxis, it at once brought to mind all the films that I had seen about America. Although the Americans were very kind, I am afraid that I was not impressed by them, as they seemed to think that they had won the war on their own. I did manage to purchase some perfumed soap and nylons for my mother. I could not get anything else, as I did not have the money.

We made our passage home on the *Queen Elizabeth*. This was the last trip that she made in war-paint. As we passed the Statue of Liberty everyone crowded to the side of the liner to see it. I did; but it did not do anything for me, so I set about to explore the liner. She was a wonderful ship; we were given cabins and we ate in her grand dining-rooms. The crew entertained us to dances and parties; they were very kind to us. All this time I had been responsible for my kit and the captain's.

We arrived at Southampton to the cheers of the crowds and the bands. The ship's company of the late *F.D.T.13* then broke up, each going to their barracks. I went to *Drake*, from where I was then sent on leave.

I am very sorry to have to say that I did not receive a write-up from *F.D.T.13*. I feel sure that this was a bad slip-up on someone's part, as I had done a fine job while serving in her.

CHAPTER 10

HMS *DRAKE*/HMS *ROYAL ALBERT* (NP. 1820)

Joining *Drake* on the 30th of December 1945, I was made senior steward of the stewards' mess, which meant that I was responsible for the running of the mess and the collection and issue of rum; but this cushy job was not to last very long as I received a draft chit to 'Naval Party 1820', which was in Germany. However; while in *Drake* I did manage to attend night-school to try to better my education, as I now realised that I would have to pass 'Educational Test Part 1' (E.T.1), before I could make a leading steward.

I should have gone to Germany on the 22nd of March 1946, but the night before, I was taken to hospital with appendicitis. I remember as I was travelling in the ambulance I could hear people singing, and it came to me that it was like an echo of VE night. After being discharged and sent on sick leave, I was then sent on to Germany, travelling to Harwich then across to Holland and then by train to Minden. The journey was very exciting and I was to meet the Germans face to face.

Joining *Royal Albert* on the 5th of May 1946, I found that we were under the German Control Commission (G.C.C.). I was issued with an army battledress, but this only lasted for three months when we went back into 'blues'.

Warrant-Officer Sparks was my divisional officer who gave me a pep talk on how to conduct myself and that I was not to fraternize with the Frauleins. The least said about that the better, as I soon found out that the Frauleins, were willing, for a bar of chocolate or a packet of cigarettes. I tell you this, not to prove my manhood, but to point out how desperate they were for food.

I soon came to know the Germans very well. I did in fact come to like them; they told me that they did not want to go to war against us. There were still some Nazis about — they stood out like a sore thumb. I was always giving the Germans cigarettes, chocolate, etc.,

43

as I felt sorry for the way they were surviving amongst the ruins. I was just sentimental towards them and they gave me respect and generally liked the British.

Living in Germany was bliss as all the catering duties were carried out by ex-German naval stewards, which meant that we had much in common. I had lots of spare time to learn horse riding, and visit places of interest. Every three months we were sent to the Black Forest where we were waited on hand and foot; we were also allowed to fraternize. These long week-ends were wonderful, and I shall always remember them.

At Minden, I was put in charge of a large house, fully furnished, just as the German family had left it. As I was a senior steward, I was given another steward to assist me. He was called Jimmy Lyntham, who turned out to be a good shipmate. I met him many times later on. I was also given two Frauleins to do the housework. All that Jimmy and I had to do was to valet the four commanders who were billeted in the house and collect the tea, coffee, etc. Jimmy and I shared a room in the house; everyone ate in the barracks.

One of the Frauleins was called Lola, she was a proper little Nazi whom I had to keep my eye on, but I soon won her over. The other Fraulein was called Anita, she was a good German who taught me a little German. She took me to meet her mother who gave me a bone china teacup and saucer, which I still have to-day. Anita's father died in a German camp.

Now the exchange was forty marks to the pound, so what with the black market and tips from the commanders of 100 marks a month, then my pay, I was soon becoming rich. I was also a drummer in the naval dance band, known as the Blue Anchors, which brought me in another 500 marks a month. Then we had an issue of fifty cigarettes and two bars of chocolate each week, which could be exchanged on the black market for about 2,000 marks. We were allowed to bank part of our pay. This was soon changed by a new currency being brought in, but it still did not stop the black market.

The ship was then transferred to Hamburg, but a captain took over the admiral's house in Minden, and I was put on his staff under a P.O. steward and a P.O. cook; they soon put their foot in it by getting drunk and so they were sent back to the UK, which left me in charge. Although I ran the house with the German staff and was responsible for the collecting of food rations from the Army, I never did get made acting leading steward, even though I was doing the duties of a P.O.; I thought this a bit unfair, but worse was to follow when I received another injustice.

My routine in the captain's house was to rise at 0630, supervise the calling of officers and their breakfast; report to the captain's secretary at 0900 hours to receive the daily orders then collect the rations; supervise lunch and dinner; and lock up at night. My duties were very light and I had plenty of time to myself. My main task was to teach the German stewards the naval way of doing things. I was also responsible for the feeding of a leading writer and two writers, the captain had his secretary, and one other officer billeted with him. I was also responsible for the captain's wines.

One day, the captain sent for me and informed me that the flag-officer Germany, was to pay him a visit and would be staying for dinner, and overnight, until after breakfast the following day. I was to look after the admiral. But a week before he arrived, I turned over a jeep that I should not have been driving and landed up in the army hospital. I requested to be discharged so that I could look after the admiral. You should have seen his face when he saw two black eyes and my arm in a sling, he just smiled. I little knew that I would be on his staff at a later date. When the admiral left, I too was sent packing, but not to UK. I was sent on to Hamburg to join *Royal Albert* again.

I arrived at Hamburg on the 12th of November 1946, to find that I was still under W.O. Sparks. I met Jimmy again and we talked over some good times that we had.

A P.O. Steward Walker was in charge of the W.R. mess staff, and he was a very heavy drinker and could be very cantankerous; so was best left alone when he was in drink. There was also a P.O. cook called Ford who was a fine P.O.; I met him later in *Drake* when he was a chief and I was a P.O. My only duty was to keep an eye on the German staff as they would steal anything they could get their hands on.

I had just settled in when a military police jeep drew up with two redcaps (Military Police), they had orders to take me back to Minden as the captain wished to see me. I was at a loss as to what it could be all about; this was to be the second injustice that I told you about.

On arriving at the captain's house, the leading writer told me that the captain's wine store had been broken into and all his wines had been stolen and that the German stewards had told him how I had been drinking. On meeting the captain he at once laid into me. I was so taken aback that I could not speak, but on leaving I informed the secretary that I was going to put in a complaint. He advised me not to do so and to forget it; this was hard to do as I had nothing to do with the break-in. So what was it all about? I then found out that the report that the captain had given me was as follows:— 'Slow and unreliable. Needs a good shake-up, for which he should be sent to sea. Not suitable for advancement.'

Now I ask you, was that fair? Why did he not praise me for the way that I had carried out a petty officer's duties, then say that I was inclined to drink too much. Then perhaps a good D.O. may have given me a pep talk. I must point out that I never touched a drop of his wines, I only drank what had been obtained on the black market.

I returned to my duties in Hamburg, but was then chosen by the C.P.O.s' mess to be their mess man and run their mess; keeping an eye on their German staff and also draw the chief's rum ration. This did not last very long as I reported the wine caterer for not paying for his drinks. This was hushed up as the wine caterer was a chum of the mess president. So once again I was sent packing back to the officers' mess. While with the C.P.O.s' mess, I was responsible for running their bar.

I remained in the W.R. mess for only a month, when I was sent out to the admiral's house just outside Hamburg. There I found that the admiral called Walker was the admiral that I had looked after in Minden (the captain's house), and I was also pleased to meet my old shipmate Jimmy again; but I found that he was not the same. He was quite big-headed as he was the admiral's valet. Somehow our friendship was not the same. There was an acting chief in charge who had a P.O. March as his second steward. The only German staff were gardeners and in the laundry. I was given the duty as valet to the admiral's secretary, who had his wife with him. This was my first dealings with an officer's wife but I soon found out that if she was pleased with your services then the officer would be satisfied.

I was to call them with morning tea; clean the bedroom, bathroom and commander's dressing-room; then assist in the cleaning of silver; serve lunch with the chief; clean up after lunch; serve tea and lay for dinner (if on duty); then assist in serving dinner. I was responsible for laying out the commander's clothes and laying back his bed at night.[1]

At one time the commander's wife fell sick. I looked after her, taking all her meals to her. The commander was so pleased that he gave me a bottle of beer; but very soon after, I began to get into trouble, I put this down to boredom.

It started while being ashore with one of the cooks. We came across the admiral's barge and the cook started to mess about on it. We were reported and as I was the senior rating (having a good conduct badge), I took 'the can' back. I was given seven days stoppage of pay. Then a month later I was reported for driving a naval bus; for this I was given seven days stoppage of pay and fourteen days stoppage of shore leave. By now I could do nothing right in the eyes of the commander.

Jimmy was sent on fourteen days' leave, and I took over his duties as admiral's valet. The admiral did a lot of horse riding, and Jimmy told me that the admiral was very particular about his riding boots; it used to take me up to two hours boning them.

One morning I called the admiral and turned on his bath for him, when I was caught short. When I returned I found the admiral was still in bed. I said "Sir," but was cut off by the admiral saying "Never mind about the Sir, turn the bloody water off or I shall be drowned." I had forgotten to turn his bath water off. When Jimmy returned I went back to my duties looking after the secretary and his wife, but somehow he had turned against me, so I was drafted back to *Drake*.

I never received one write-up from Sparks and the write-up that I received from the admiral's secretary was:— 'Unreliable and seems incapable of learning from his mistakes. He is slow and needs constant supervision. Unsuitable for duty on admiral's staff.'

This write-up was not true. I am sure that he was going by what the captain at Minden had written. In the beginning I had pleased him, so again, why did he not praise me for my steward's duties, then say that I was inclined to be mischievous? Still this write-up was proved to be wrong, as you will see later in the book.

Leaving Hamburg, I travelled alone to Holland, then across to Harwich and on to Plymouth, arriving in *Drake* on the 12th of July 1948; the same date that I had joined the Navy. I had served two years with 'Naval Party 1820', and five years in the Navy.[2]

CHAPTER 10

Footnotes:
1. Serving meals in an admiral's mess was always carried out as a mess dinner routine. The chief would not report but we still waited for his signals before removing plates, or serving each course. Meals were never rushed.
2. While I was serving in Hamburg, Jean Kent paid a forces visit to the Victory Club (our NAAFI) and I managed to have a dance with her. Ivy Benson and her band also paid a visit, and many other celebrities. They all did a fine job

CHAPTER 11

HMS *DRAKE*
and THE CAPTAIN of THE DOCKYARD HOUSE

Joining *Drake*, my first duties were to be a mess waiter and cabins; but soon after I was put in the wine bar as a wine steward, where I met my old mate Jimmy who had followed me from Germany. I was placed in the bar because I had caused a stir in the W.R. I had been given the duty as a mess waiter, so I had to wear a white coat. I complained to the chief that I was a senior steward, with a G.C.B., which I was proud of. The chief stood firm, so I pinned a red stripe on the arm of my white coat. The chief "took off", but I insisted that as I was being paid for a G.C.B.; then I was entitled to wear it. With that I was transferred into the bar where I could wear my blue jacket with my red stripe. In the afternoon I attended a leading steward's course and I continued with evening classes at night-school. So you see I was doing my best to get on in the Service. Nothing exciting happened until Lieutenant Davies, my new D.O., sent for me and informed me that I was to look after a captain R.N., and all other duties were excused. I met the captain and gave him my fullest attention, bringing his clothes and shoes up to scratch. After I had been looking after him for a week, he told me that he was to be the captain of the dockyard (King's Harbour-Master) and would I like to be his steward and look after him and his wife in their house. I jumped at this as it could mean an acting rate for me, as a captain was entitled to a leading steward, and when at sea, a petty officer steward. However, I was soon in for a shock.

When I arrived at the house I found that I had been given a room over his garage about a hundred yards away. The only water was a cold tap outside the garage and the toilet was over in the captain's house backyard; nevertheless it was a luxury to have a room to myself; but this did not last.

There was a leading cook, but he did not last very long as he lived ashore. He was replaced by Leading Cook White, and I was also given a seaman. There were now three of us in my little room — then later on I was given another seaman — this now meant four people in a room, which at first had been for me.

The captain's house was very large, it had five bedrooms; four flights of stairs; dining-room; lounge; a green-room, which was used by his son and daughter as a study; two bathrooms and toilets; five scullery rooms with another bedroom over them; then the outside toilets. I attended to the captain's bedroom, guest's bedroom and the stairs. The seamen cleaned the rest of the house and the shoes. To give you some idea of my duties I have set out the routine that I worked:—

0730   Call the captain and his wife with morning tea.
        Call the children — no tea.
        Turn the captain's bath on and lay out his clothes.
        Prepare the breakfast; they helped themselves from a hotplate.
0855   Be at the front door with the captain's cap and stick.
        Clean captain's bedroom and guest's bedroom (if any), and the stairs.
1100   Serve morning coffee.
        Clean the silver and lay for lunch. Place drink tray in the lounge.
1255   Meet the captain at the door.
1300   Serve lunch. Coffee in the lounge. Remove drink tray.
1355   Be at the door again to see the captain off to his office.
1600   Serve tea in the lounge.
        Lay out the captain's evening clothes. Lay for dinner.
1700   Meet the captain at the door again. Put the drink tray out.
2000   Serve dinner. Coffee in the lounge. Turn back beds.
        Then I would report to the captain that all was well and was there anything more that he required. If not, then I was finished for the day, so I could pop off to my local for a pint.

This routine was for seven days a week, although madam gave me and the staff every Sunday night off as they looked after themselves on that night; but there was always a load of washing-up to be met on Monday morning.

The captain then began to entertain and have guests to stay. By now, his daughter had left for college and his son went to Dartmouth as a cadet, but in their place we had the captain's nephew to stay with us. He had the bedroom over the scullery, and was no trouble. In fact he gave me·a lot of help in passing the 'Educational Test Part 1' (E.T.1). I had by now been made acting leading steward with pay.

D

I soon trained the seamen in stewards' duties, and the cook and I exchanged duties so that we could split into two watches; a seaman in each watch. This made things much easier and we all got on very well together.

To show how strict the captain was — one night after a dinner-party — I was awakened at 0200 hours in the morning by the captain shouting my name out to come down from my room. He was very angry and asked me why I had turned in. I said that I had understood him to say that he had finished with me. He then said that I was never to leave before the guests had departed.

Life went on much the same. I remember one day, the captain told me to give the staff a bottle of beer each and have one myself as it was his wedding anniversary. Then another night the commodore of *Drake* and others were entertained for supper, but the commodore was soon doing the entertainment by playing the piano and leading the singing.

On the 2nd of November 1949, I went into *Drake* and passed out for leading steward. I gained 83% and was given a V.G.; then on the 22nd of the same month, I passed the E.T.1; all I needed now was a sea recommend for advancement.

I must tell you about one of the seamen. He was called Ettlinger and came from a very good family. He was a National Serviceman and had been offered a commission but had turned it down. He kept the polished decks like glass. He made a pair of boots out of an old blanket, which he put over his shoes when he cleaned the decks. The captain did his best to get him to sign on but Ettlinger would have nothing to do with it.

Madam was very helpful, she taught me 'flower table decoration' and how to cook many simple dishes, and was most encouraging when I passed out for leading steward and the E.T.1. I also became very confident in the supervising of lunch and dinner parties.

One Saturday morning while I was cooking lunch, the captain returned after inspecting my room (which he had not given me notice of). He was waving a pair of socks in the air and demanded to know what they were doing in my room. I said they were not his; so he called his wife and asked her. She said they were not his. However; the captain still had doubts and this was proved when only three days later a leading steward arrived at the back door saying he was my replacement. Madam was as surprised as I was and she rushed off to the captain's office returning very upset. When the captain saw me he said that he wanted me to go to sea so that I could get a sea recommend for advancement. Who was he kidding? I packed my gear and returned to *Drake*. I was not even given transport. I lugged my gear through the dockyard into *Drake*;

this was on the 1st of February 1950.

For all my hard work the captain wrote me up as:— 'Honest and hard-working, but outside his duties has the intelligence of a child.'

Now this was well below the belt and hurt me very much. Later in *Drake* the chief steward let me read my history sheet and he asked me what went wrong. So I told him. He agreed that the write-up was not fair as the captain had not said anything about the way I had trained the seamen in stewards' duties, or anything about my cooking. Still, I was rewarded for his bad write-up of me when I met him much later.

Joining *Drake* I lost my acting rate; then only two months later I was drafted to HMS *Burghead Bay*.

When I returned to *Drake*, I was placed in the wine bar again. The write-up that Lieutenant Davies gave me was:— 'Hard-working, willing and honest. Occasionally he acts very stupidly, but has improved in this respect. With experience he should make an average leading steward.'

Most of the time I had been with the captain of the dockyard, but as you see the write-up was a little better than the captain's. I am sure the the chief steward had spoken up for me.

CHAPTER 12

HMS *BURGHEAD BAY*

I joined HMS *Burghead Bay* on the 4th of February 1950. She was a frigate attached to the local flotilla, which was based at Plymouth; although we went to sea quite a lot, we always returned to harbour every night.

There were four other stewards, a leading officers' cook and a cook. As I was the senior steward, I was made acting leading steward with pay. My duties were to run the officers' mess and cater for them and the staff. The leading cook was not much help, so I found the menus were left to me. As we were only at sea for short periods I could make out the menus twenty-four hours ahead. Sometimes I would be left ashore to do the shopping while the ship was at sea.

I made it my duty to serve breakfast, as this gave me a chance to find out if the officers had any complaints (which they never did). The officers could also see me to ask for any private shopping that they may need to be done. I always returned from shopping in time to supervise lunch, except when I was left ashore.

Like me, one of the stewards was waiting for his B.13 (notice of promotion) to come through, and as it happened our B.13s came through on the same day; so we were made leading stewards also on the same day. The other leading steward was drafted to *Drake* and I remained aboard *Burghead Bay*.

The captain was Lieutenant-Commander Storey. When at sea we did target towing for the RAF and for the 'Shore Gunnery School'. We also exercised off Portland with submarines. When we were exercising with submarines, we always returned to Portland. We paid many visits to Dartmouth, where we would take cadets to sea for the day, and we always acted as guard ship when they had their regattas.

At sea I was always in the pantry for lunch and dinner, and it was just as well, as we met some rough seas, and *Burghead Bay* had a bad habit of dipping her bow into the sea; then when she raised her bow, she would send sprays of sea water all over the bridge; she would then go into a roll. This caused me to be on my toes in the pantry. I had to judge just when to open the heater and the fridge doors or the contents would spill all over the deck. Food on the hotplate had to be watched or it would slide off. Talk about a pantry needing and breeding a good steward; it most certainly made a good seagoing pantry steward.

By now I had become well known with other senior stewards who went shopping. We would meet in a pub and have a good chat, as we had a good grape-vine (information).

Another one of my duties was to be the leading hand of the mess; with my staff, there was also a leading ship's cook and his mate. All that I had to do was to make out the duty roster as to who cleaned the mess, and to see that everyone was up in the morning. On the whole, we all got on very well together.

My main duty was the catering; it was now that I put to use all that P.O. Knowles had taught me on *F.D.T.13*. How to keep my books tidy by keeping a record of all goods purchased on one side, and a record of all monies given to me by the W.R. treasurer on the other side, so that, at the end of each month, I could quite easily balance my books out.

The only problem that I had was the laundry; as when returning from sea, I never knew exactly where we would berth; there being the five dockyards in Plymouth, or a buoy, or even Portland or Dartmouth. But I overcame this by asking the first lieutenant for the ship's programme, and was highly honoured when he gave it to me, as it gave the ship's movements up to three months ahead. The ship's company were always asking me where we were going, but I never told them as I respected the confidence that the first lieutenant had shown in me.

The Navy was now beginning to go into peace-time routine; this meant that we had 'captain's rounds' on Saturday and divisions in the week. Captain's rounds was when the captain would inspect all departments and messes; this gave him a chance to see that the ship was clean and the messes not overcrowded. During rounds I would report the stewards' mess to him, then nip round to the pantry and report that to him. I am very pleased to say that I was never picked up once. Divisions was always a good chance for the captain to meet members of his ship's company.

While in *Burghead Bay* my war medals came through and I was surprised to find that I had been awarded five medals, these were:— the Defence Medal, the 1939-45 Sea Medal (known as

Spam Medal), the Atlantic Medal, the German and French Medal, and the Victory Medal.

Three nice things happened in *Burghead Bay*. The first was when we took a party of Wrens to sea for the day. I was quite chuffed (pleased) at showing them our duties and they were very interested. Second we were invited by Teignmouth to spend a week as their guests during their summer fête. At night we lit the ship up; it looked very effective from the beach. We also ran boats for people to come aboard and look over the ship. Then we 'kidnapped' their beauty queen and held her for ransom. The ransom we paid over to the fête organisers. They made us very welcome, giving us a dance and free tickets to the cinema. We all had a fine time. The officers gave a cocktail party for the dignitaries.

The third, was when the first lieutenant sent for me to inform me that we were to take the C.-in-C. Plymouth to France (Admiral McGregor) and that he would be entertaining the French to a lunch party. As the admiral was only bringing his valet, the catering was left to me, so I produced a menu which the first lieutenant passed and off I went ashore, loaded with extra cash. While at sea the admiral was looked after by his valet. Then on arriving at France I was kept very busy with the lunch party, which I am glad to say was a success. We returned to Plymouth where the admiral left us, and the captain then sent for me and told me that I had done a fine job. I have a photograph of the table laid for lunch.

After nearly a year in *Burghead Bay* I was drafted back to *Drake*. The write-up that I received was:— 'A bit slow on the uptake. Poor power of command, but has improved in this respect. Should make a good leading steward.'

The remark about a poor power of command was not fair as I had kept the W.R. staff in order and also the stewards' mess. As we all got on so fine I could see no reason why I should go about shouting my head off. Still it wasn't a bad report, but no mention was made of the way I had catered for the admiral's lunch party.

MARKETING

I should now tell you that I had become very good at catering and marketing; this was helped by my ability at cooking.

When marketing, it was most useful to know the seasons; when it was best to purchase fresh vegetables, fish and salads. So to start with you would compose a menu remembering what seasons of the year you were in, the amounts that were required and the standard of the cook's cooking. A menu should never have pastry for a main course, followed by pastry for a sweet, or a thick soup followed by a stew. Fresh fish and fruit was always acceptable when at sea but you had to take pains in your purchases to ensure that they would remain fresh for as long as possible. A fresh salad was always nice to serve after being at sea for some time, and this was possible if you purchased well and stored well.

Fresh milk and daily papers I would arrange to be delivered, so it was important to know the ship's programme so that you could give details of where the ship would be after returning from sea.

If you always provided a well-balanced menu and took great pain in marketing and the storage of your supplies, then you would not go wrong.

The marketing book was kept as follows:—

Date	Debits	Receipt	£.p	Date	Credits	£.p
Feb.				Feb.		
3rd	Fisheries	1.	6.70	1st	Cash	30.00
"	Reynolds	2.	7.19	16th	"	35.00
"	Co-op	3.	4.20			
28th	Laundry	4.	15.30			
"	Dairies	5.	11.15			
"	Newsagents	6.	6.10			
"	Expenses	7.	2.30			
	Total Debits =		52.94			
	C/f Cash in Hand =		12.06			
	Balance =		65.00		Balance =	65.00

You always numbered each receipt, which gave full details of the purchases, then start the following month with your cash in hand.

To assist you in the catering, a mess book was kept; this was kept up to date by the duty steward, by asking each officer when in harbour, if he would be aboard for lunch, dinner, etc. This would give some idea of how many to cater for. The mess book was as follows (G. stands for guest):—

Breakfast — B,   Lunch — L,   Tea — T,   Dinner — D

Name	1st Feb.				2nd Feb.				and so on . . .
	B	L	T	D	B	L	T	D	
Lt. Brown	/	/	/	—	/	/	/	—	
Lt. White	/	/	/	/G	/	/	/	—	
Lt. Smith	/	/	—	—	/	/G	—	—	

Then there was a mess 'extra book', as follows:—

Name	Extras	Mess Sub.	£.p
Lt. Brown	Laundry £2.50	£5.00	= 7.50
Lt. White	Laundry £2.76 D.G. £2.00	£5.00	= 9.76
Lt. Smith	Laundry £2.95 L.G. £1.50	£5.00	= 9.45

These extras would be paid to the mess treasurer each month. The mess subscription was for a higher standard of living and varied on each ship. The Admiralty allowance was paid into the mess funds, after deductions had been made for stores from the ship. If the officers held a party then the full cost would be divided amongst the officers and entered in the 'extra book'.

CHAPTER 13

HMS *DRAKE*/HMS *VULTURE*/HMS *CURLEW*

Joining *Drake* on the 30th of August 1951, I was placed in the mess trap store; the mess traps were the responsibility of the chief steward; my duties were to keep a constant check on them, reporting to the chief any losses. While carrying out these duties I gained a great deal of knowledge, which turned out to be most helpful at a later date.

That summer the officers held a summer ball; this was another challenge for me as I was responsible for each private party in giving out the required mess traps. These parties were scattered all over the place, in the W.R. mess and in a large marquee on the lawn. Many trophies were used as table decorations; these and the mess traps had to be checked-in the following day; apart from one or two forks, etc., all was correct.

While in *Drake*, I passed an arithmetic exam for petty officers and I also qualified for petty officer steward by passing the exam on the 19th of November 1951. I was then drafted to HMS *Vulture*. The P.O. stewards' exam was a written exam, apart from the carving test, which was a practical and oral test taken by a lieutenant-commander and a lieutenant of the supply branch. The exam was as follows:—

Paper A — Valeting and Mess Duties. Maximum Marks 200.
(i)   Cleaning and Care of Store-room, Pantries and Dom. Fridges.
(ii)   Cleanliness and Care of Mess Traps and Utensils.
(iii)   Table Attendance.
(iv)   Valeting and Care of Cabins.
(v)   Duties of a Wine Steward.
(vi)   Keeping of Mess, Wine and Tobacco Accounts.
(vii)   Customs Regulations.

Paper B — Arithmetic. Maximum Marks 100.

Paper C — Catering. Maximum Marks 200.
(ix)   Elements of Cooking.
(x)   Preservation of Food.
(xi)   Systems of Catering and Knowledge of Books affecting Officers' Messing.
(xii)   Marketing.
(xiii)   Stocks and Stocktaking.
(xiv)   Official and Private Entertaining.
(xv)   Carving (see Carving Test).

(As you see, the above examination was no mean test.)

The carving exam was quite frightening. I entered a room and was faced with a long table, with all kinds of joints, fish and game spread out on the table. I then had to distinguish what they were and tell the examiners a bit about them. For instance there was a large salmon laid out on a dish. I knew that it was not the salmon season, so I explained that by sight and touch it must be a frozen salmon which had been imported; for this I received a V.G. The game foxed me, it turned out to be a small duck; I had said that it was a small chicken, this was the only mistake that I made.

The write-up that I received from Lt. Davies was:— 'Has tried hard but is below average as a leading steward. He is inclined to worry too much.'

Of course I had worried, it was my place to worry as I had been the responsible person and I had kept a good 'top line'. It would have been much better if Davies had praised me for the way that I had looked after the mess traps. I had only been employed in the mess trap store, so how could he say that I was below average? Anyway I proved him wrong as you will see later.

I joined HMS *Curlew*, which had been called *Vulture*, on the 26th of April 1952. *Curlew* was a Fleet Arm Station in Cornwall. The W.R. mess was run by Wrens. My duty was in the commander's house looking after him and his wife. They also had two small daughters. This was an easy task, as madam did the marketing and most of the cooking. My duties were to valet the commander, serve the meals, and clean the house. My daily routine was:—

0730   Call the commander and his wife with a tea-tray, and then the children. Lay out the commander's clothes and serve breakfast (never a cooked meal). Make the beds and clean through the house. Lay for lunch.

1100   Serve morning coffee.

1300   Serve lunch (the children ate at school). Clean up after lunch. Lay out the commander's evening clothes and lay for dinner.

1800   Assist madam to cook dinner.

2000   Serve dinner, coffee in the lounge. Clean up. Lay back the beds; then I was finished until next morning.

I had every other day off, also every other week-end. The bungalow consisted of three bedrooms, bathroom and toilet, lounge, dining-room, large hall and kitchen.

While I was with the commander, the late Princess Royal paid a visit to the station and lunched with the captain. I was then sent to assist the captain's leading steward, called Fryer, whom I met much later in *Drake* when he was a chief. The princess was a lovely person and I was very proud to have served her.

I was only with the commander for a short time before Fryer was made petty officer. As Fryer was drafted to *Drake*, I was informed I was to take his place.

The captain was called Webb; he and his wife were very nice to work under; they had one small daughter. The captain's house was the same as the commander's. The captain had a leading cook called Bexon; he was a wonderful cook who taught me much about cooking. Bexon and I worked 'watch about', and we had every other week-end off; we got on very well together. I made a good cook and Bexon a good steward.

The duties were much the same as they had been in the commander's house except, when I was on duty I had the cooking to do, and likewise Bexon would carry out my duties; but, of course, I looked after the captain's clothes.

I had made friends with an officer's cook; we used to spend all our off duties on the beach. It was great fun swimming in the sea, as the waves were very big. We took with us a packed meal, then we would spend the evening in a local, drinking 'scrumpy' (apple cider from the wood).

I have three nice memories while with the captain. The first was when I asked the captain if there was any chance of a flight. After only a week the captain told me to report to the control tower. They then sent me to be instructed on how to use a parachute. I was then given a parachute and assisted by a pilot's mate into the back seat of a Firefly. The pilot told me not to speak to him until he first spoke to me. I had also been instructed on how to use the mouthpiece in the helmet. I heard all the jargon that went on between the pilot and the control tower. It was very interesting. We then took off and did some aerobatics. When we landed, the pilot, a sub-lieutenant said that I had done very well. When I returned to the captain's house to serve lunch, the captain asked me all about it and was very interested in what I told him.

The second thing was, the captain told Bexon and I, that he would be entertaining four captains to lunch and we were to put on a good show. As the captains were to talk shop, madam ate out. Bexon put on a grand lunch. What did I do? I tipped soup all over the arm of one captain. I gave him another napkin, wiped the table and carried on as if nothing had happened, but expecting a good telling off from the captain later. In fact he congratulated me on keeping a cool head.

The last memory was when the captain informed me that he and his wife were to spend a week-end away, and would I live in and look after his daughter. As Bexon was on week-end, I had the lot to do, but all went well and when they returned madam praised me, saying that I had done a fine job.

Now I come to proving how wrong Lieutenant Davies had been when he wrote that I was below average as a leading steward. I had only qualified for petty officer on the 19th of November 1951, and now, only sixteen months later, I was to be promoted to P.O.; so you see how wrong those write-ups were.

I shall always remember the day that I was promoted. I had been informed by the master of arms that my B.13 had come through. It was two weeks later before I was informed that I was 'captain's request man' to be promoted. At the captain's table, he told me that he had no doubts about my ability to be a petty officer steward, as he knew that I knew my job, but he was concerned about my common sense in being a P.O. However; he had given it much thought and had decided to promote me. It was wonderful when the master of arms said "Request granted, carry on Petty Officer". This was the first time that I was called petty officer. The master then informed me that I had twenty-four hours to change rigs. Off I went to the supply store to collect my cap badges, arm badges and brass buttons. I took my uniforms to the station tailor, who said they would be ready by tea-time. I returned to the captain's house to serve lunch and the captain asked me why I was not in the rig of the day (meaning in P.O. uniform). I at once told him that I had twenty-four hours to change rigs, he said "Well done".

I moved into the P.O.s' mess and was introduced to the mess president. I had a room to myself; and being served my meals and having our own bar was great.

When I returned to the captain's house to serve dinner, madam remarked on how smart I looked.

That night was a monthly ship's company dance. I was treated to many drinks and congratulated on being made a P.O. I did not get drunk, although I felt very high that night. I had by now been awarded my second good conduct badge, so I was now a two-badge petty officer, ready to go forward for a chief's rate.

Only a week after being made P.O., I received a draft chit to join HMS *Decoy* which was at Glasgow. Before I left, the captain wished me luck and informed me that I was to be the captain's P.O. steward and that he knew the captain of *Decoy*, and that I was to watch my step as this captain was a real sea-dog.

The write-up that Captain Webb gave me was:— 'An honest and hard-working steward. Very competent, with considerable ability at cooking. Little initiative or common sense and has periods of stupidity. Weak at taking charge but has had little opportunity. Keen on Service life and making every effort to justify advancement.'

Not too bad a write-up, but still a bit personal. After all I was not aiming to become an admiral.

CHAPTER 14

HMS *DECOY*

I joined *Decoy* on the 9th of May 1953. I found that she was a brand-new Daring-class destroyer. There was a very up-to-date pantry which I was pleased with. She had completed her sea trials and was waiting for her sailing orders.

It was surprising to me that this was the third captain I had been given to look after and yet they were still saying that I was being stupid. I just could not understand this at all.

The captain was called Maurice and he was a gentleman. When meeting me, he at once got down to brass tacks, saying that he would advance me some cash, and I was to cater for him and the staff; which was a leading steward and a seaman. He wanted no meals from the W.R. and he would require grapefruit, eggs and bacon every morning, and plenty of fresh fish. He then surprised me by saying that he would pay me £2 and the leading steward £1.50 at the end of each month, and I was to remind him if he forgot to pay us. The only thing was that the captain did not go ashore very much, only for long walks, returning for dinner.

My main duty was the catering, but I always returned from shopping in time to serve him his lunch. When at sea I took him his meals on the bridge. The leading steward, called Taylor, valeted him and looked after his wines, which was quite easy, as they were only transferred from the W.R. mess. The captain would settle his wine account at the end of each month; the captain drank very little. Taylor also kept the captain's sea cabin clean, while the seaman cleaned the day cabin (which was also the captain's dining-room and office), the bathroom and pantry. The captain was no trouble as long as he was served with good food, which I ensured, as I had now become very good at marketing and producing fine menus. The captain also had his own P.O. cook, who was called Shilton, and he left the menus to me.

There was only one bad thing about Taylor, that was whenever he went on week-end leave he always came back adrift; this meant that I would be on duty for up to a week. Taylor always made it up to me (when he returned) by covering for me, as he was always given stoppage of leave.

By now I had come to know the seaman who was responsible for the issue of stores (Tanky) and the seaman who was qualified to issue meat (Butch). I had many a choice fillet for a little kindness shown to them, the least said about that the better.

Our sailing orders arrived — we were to join the fleet for exercising in the North Sea — this exercise was called 'Exercise Mariner'. We ran into a force 10 gale — *Decoy* being a new ship, caused us all to be a little worried as to how she would respond in such a gale. Each ship in the exercise broke off and went their own way; we nosed into the gale. I went on the signal deck as I always felt safer on the bridge in a storm. *Decoy* did very well; at times her bow, up to the forward gun turret, was completely submerged, but she just pushed her bow up again and shook the seas off with only a slight shudder. Then our sister ship, *Diamond*, somehow rammed the flag ship, which was HMS *Swiftshore*. The exercise was called off and we were ordered to escort *Diamond* back to Plymouth.

While at Plymouth, our captain invited the captain of *Diamond* over for dinner. I felt very sorry for the captain of *Diamond*; later on he was court-martialled, but he only lost some seniority.

We sailed again to pay a courtesy call on a French port — the name I do not remember, but it was close to a French Foreign Legion headquarters. They sent an invitation for our officers, chiefs and petty officers to pay them a visit; they did us proud. When we arrived at their headquarters' front gate, we were met by a guard of honour, band and general salute; they gave us the lot. We petty officers were then whisked off to the sergeants' mess, where there was a long wooden table loaded with food and wine; we had a fine time. I struck up a friendship with an American who took me on a tour of the arab quarters — it was all very interesting. I had somehow expected them to be dressed in uniforms that I had seen in pictures, but they were in uniform much the same as our army chaps. When we left they crowded the main gate and gave us a fine send off.

After returning to Plymouth for long leave, we then sailed for Lorient an ex-U-boat pen in France. The French made us very welcome, entertaining the ship's company to dances and a cocktail party; they obviously liked the British and made a fuss over us. When it was time to depart, the captain sent for a bottle of champagne and glasses; then on the bridge the French dignitary toasted us. I had never heard of this, but I was informed that it was a custom of the French; it was supposed to bring luck to the ship. I do not know how true this was. As we sailed away, the French cheered us until we were out of sight. Again we returned to Plymouth, I was then surprised when the captain informed me that we were to sail again to carry out more exercises, and that we were to be the flag ship as the admiral was to transfer his flag to *Decoy*, from *Swiftshore*.

The captain told me that the admiral would only be bringing his valet, and that the admiral would be a guest. I was to be responsible for the catering and I was to spare no expense. The admiral would take over the captain's sea cabin and eat in the day cabin. The captain would have all his meals on the bridge.

I was very pleased when Shilton rose to the heights of a chief cook and did very well. I had made out menus for the three weeks that we were to be at sea and I had stocked up with fresh fruit and fish, etc. When the exercise was over, we returned to Plymouth where the admiral left us, but not before he had thanked me, saying that his stay on board had been most pleasant. Again I was let down, as the duties that I had been carrying out while the admiral was on board, had not been recorded on my history sheet.

While in *Decoy*, the Royal Tournament was being held in London. I requested permission to keep a record of the field gun competition. This was granted, so I made out a fine chart, which I placed on the company's notice-board. To my surprise the first lieutenant arranged for signals to be sent to me after each run off, giving me the results. I was thrilled when the signalman reported to me with signals from London made out to me. I was even more thrilled as that year Devonport won the competition.

The highlight of my stay in *Decoy* was the Coronation Review at Spithead, on the 15th of June 1953, for which I received a certificate.

What a wonderful sight it was, seeing the fleet and ships from every nation assemble; each ship making for its alloted buoy; the air was filled with the pipes and bugle calls as each ship saluted one another, according to seniority. I saw my old ship, HMS *Black Prince*, which was now sailing under another flag.

We had a good buoy, next to HMS *Vanguard*. The postman and I went ashore to carry out our duties. It was great meeting all the chief and petty officer stewards doing their shopping. I felt very proud of being one of them.

I was kept on my toes by the calling of captains on our captain, and vice versa. When we dressed our skipper up to dine with the queen on HMS *Surprise*, I am sure that he felt very chuffed (happy).

We dressed the ship with flags and lights. The highlight came when the fleet lit up; it was a wonderful sight. I will give a copy of the daily orders of that day as I am sure that it will be of interest to any reader who was there.

DAILY ORDERS — MONDAY, JUNE 15th 1953

Officer of the Day	Lt. Knight
P.O. of the Day	P.O. S. H. Millford
Duty P.O.	P.O. Cordon
Duty E.R.A.	E.R.A. Dunnet
Stand by P.O.	P.O. Mitchell
Duty L.S.M.	L.S.M. Thomas
Duty Watch	Port
Duty Elect.	R. E. Partridge
Duty Part	2nd

Dress of the Day — No. 8s. until 1400 hrs.
the No. 1s. or 2s. with medals.
Dutymen No. 2s.
Boatmen No. 3s.

0730	Hands Fall In, Stand Fast Guard. Detail for Dress Ship. Taut and Illuminate Ship Jackstay.
0800	Dress Ship.
1315	Hands Fall In, Square off Upper Deck. In Gash Chute.
1400	Hands to Clean.
1450	Out Pipes.
1500	Hands Fall In, Stand by to Man and Cheer Ship.
1710	(Approx.) Secure. Hands to Tea.
1800	Duty Watch Fall In, Rig Boat Ropes, etc. Gunnery Division Rig Firework Screens
2045	Duty Party Fall In, Detail for Undressing Ship.
2100	Undress Ship.
2200	Darken Ship. Darken Ship Screens need not be used.

Laundry. 8.9.14 and 15 Messes.

Cheer Ship. The Cheer should be a Hur-R—AH. In order to achieve the best noise, take a deep breath during the Hips.

Chin Stays. Chin Stays should be lightly stitched in the top of the Cap.

J. T. Gillespie, Lt.Cdr. R.N.
First Lieutenant.

E

Review Day Routine

0730	Hands Fall In, Clean Ship.
0800	Dress Ship.
1200	Dinner.
1315	Hands Fall In, Final Square Off. Both Motor Cutters proceed to Boat Anchorage.
1400	Hands to Clean.
1445	Hands Fall In, Stand by to Man and Cheer Ship.
1500	HMS *Surprise* leaves Harbour. Royal Salute to be Fired.
1550	HMS *Surprise* enters Review Area.
1600	(Approx.) Ten Minutes Stand Easy.
1640	Man Ship. Royal Salute followed by Three Cheers.
1710	HMS *Surprise* Anchors at end of E. Line. Secure, Hands to Tea.
1730	Fly-past of Naval Aircraft.
1800	Duty Watch Fall In, Rig Boat Ropes, etc. Rig Illumination Circuits.
2100	Undress Ship.
2200	Darken Ship. Darken Ship Screens will not be used.
2240	Firework Display.
2250	Illuminate Ship.
2350	Illuminate Ship ends.

(Signed) *First Lieutenant.*

After the review, the queen gave the order to 'Splice the Mainbrace'; this was the only time that I heard this order given.

We then sailed with our sister ships, *Diamond, Duchess* and *Dainty*, to carry out 'officer of the watch exercises'. This was the same as parade drill, the ships being the bodies. The senior captain would give an order, this order would then be hoisted from the main mast. When all the ships had read the order, they would hoist a flag, the senior captain would then give the order to execute, by his order being pulled down. The ships would then carry out the order, which would mean a change of course. All the ships would change course at the same time. This was most interesting to watch. We had one or two close shaves but no mishaps. The officer of the watch, coxswain and signalmen really had to be on their toes, as some of the manoeuvres were very tricky. We broke off and then returned with the fleet to the North Sea to carry out oiling at sea exercises.

We were ordered to refuel at the same time as *Vanguard* and I must say that it was a bit rough; there were some high waves. We pulled alongside on the port side of the tanker, while *Vanguard* went alongside the tanker's starboard side. We connected our hoses

OK, but we had a few frights as one moment the hoses would be submerged, then as we rolled away the hoses would become tight. Just when we thought the hoses would part we would roll towards the tanker again. On completion, the tanker sent our mail across. After another week at sea we returned to Plymouth.

At Plymouth the captain went into a R.N. hospital to undergo an operation. I visited him every day to report to him what was happening, as by now I was a true 'Captain Tiger', a nickname given to captain's stewards.

While the captain was in hospital, the first lieutenant did his best to get me to do a duty watch in the W.R., but the skipper said I was not to do so. Then the first lieutenant told me that the W.R. mess was to hold a dinner-party, and that the guest of honour was a supply captain, and he wanted me to act as mess butler (in charge). I knew that the W.R.P.O. steward was not up to being the mess butler and he proved this by falling down a ladder and going sick; so the skipper consented to me being the mess butler.

On the night of the mess dinner, the first lieutenant told me to go by the book. Now I knew that the book (B.R.97) stated that the dessert gear was to be placed on the table at the same time as the port and wine glasses, but it was always the practice to place the dessert gear on the table after the toast had been made, but I did as the first lieutenant had said — "Go by the book."

After dinner, the captain (guest) sent for me and said that I had made a boob. I at once replied that I had gone by the book. He asked to see my B.R.97. When he read it he complimented me and said that he would amend the book. I never did know if he did so.

A new captain then arrived. He was very dashing, bringing with him his golf clubs, tennis gear, cricket gear and diving equipment. I knew that I was in for a busy time.

It started off by the captain wishing to hold a ship's company dance so that he could get to know the ship's company. I was to organise it. I did, ordering and booking a band and dance-hall — I did the catering. I must say that I came out at the end of the day in pocket. I was also asked to present flowers to the captain's wife. I must admit that I was very pleased when I received a draft chit to return to *Drake*.

Captain Maurice gave me a very good write-up, which read as follows:— 'Has served me well and with great loyalty. He knows his job and would benefit by being given experience in charge of a larger staff.'

At last, I may now get the chance to prove that I had power of command, but I was disappointed as I was soon to find that I was to be given another captain to look after.

CHAPTER 15

HMS *DRAKE* and HMS *GAMBIA*

I joined *Drake* on the 3rd of September 1954, and only carried out duties as duty mess butler, before being drafted to *Gambia* a month later.[1] Although the captain had recommended me for a larger staff, I soon found out that I was to have another captain to look after, but this time I was to be the captain's mess man, which I have already explained meant using my own money; this was to be a new experience.

It was on the 22nd of October 1954 when I joined *Gambia*, which was alongside in the dockyard. The captain was called Evershed and he was indeed a fine gentleman.

Gambia had just returned from taking the Emperor of Ethiopia home, after his state visit to England. The captain's quarters, which the emperor had used, were still in fine condition. There was a very large cabin; the captain's office was at one side, which also acted as his lounge; while at the other side was his dining-room. The sleeping cabin and bathroom led off from the office side of the day cabin, and there was a nice big pantry.

I found that I also had to valet the captain as I only had a seaman to assist me, but the captain did have his own P.O. cook.

The routine was to call the captain in the morning and serve breakfast. The captain loved 'Scotch' porridge every morning, which I used to cook overnight, and then heat up for his breakfast. This was the way that the captain liked it and he was very particular about his porridge.

I would then go ashore shopping, returning in time to serve lunch. The seaman cleaned all the quarters, pantry and silver. This was not a hard task as the captain was very tidy. I would then serve him tea, lay out his evening clothes and serve dinner. The seaman always finished at 1700 hours. I was always finished by 2100, so it wasn't too bad. The only entertaining that the captain did was to have his wife stay with him every Sunday. The captain's wife was a lovely person who always found time to have a chat with me. Every Sunday, I would prepare a cold lunch, which was always requested; then a high tea before madam left about 1800 hours.

The seaman was not victualled with the captain, so I only had to cater for the captain and myself, which was quite easy. The first month I used my own money, then the paymaster would pay me our admiralty victualling money the following month; so after the captain had settled up with me for his extras I found that I was well in, but this was not to last, for four months later I was drafted back to *Drake*. I was sorry to leave the captain as I was not only happy but I was fast becoming rich.

I used to get a night off twice a week by preparing a cold supper for the captain. As I had never taken a short or long week-end, the captain gave me seven days' long leave before I joined *Drake*.

Although I was only with the captain for four months he gave me a good write-up, which read as follows:— 'This petty officer has done a very good job and has done well. He is not gifted with a great brain but is most thoughtful and makes the best use of what he has. He is really keen on his job and takes great pride in it. Deserves a larger staff.'

Now this was the second captain to recommend me for a larger staff, but did you notice the remark about my brain? This was really too much as I was trying hard to better myself in this field. But at least he did not say I was stupid.

I returned to *Drake* on the 25th of February 1955, where I was given the duties of mess butler and P.O. in charge of the public rooms. I was given twelve stewards, whom I supervised in the cleaning. I must have done well in that short time as the D.O. wrote me up as:— 'A loyal, hard-working and conscientious P.O. He has tried hard to please and give of his best with this, and usually succeeds. Very interested in his work and the stewards' branch.'[2]

As I have said, it was only a short time, four months in fact, before I was sent for by the D.O. who informed me that I had been appointed as second steward on the staff of Flag Officer Aircraft Carriers (F.O.A.C.), who was at Malta. A chief steward and chief cook had also been appointed with me. Now, as I have said, this proved that the write-up of the admiral's secretary in Germany was a farce, because, here I was only six years later, being appointed to the staff of a very important admiral. So you see, the write-up from Germany must have been biased.

The chief steward and chief cook travelled with me to London, where we stayed overnight at the airport, before flying out to Malta on the following day. We passed the time away on the flight by drinking and talking about our appointments . . . I said to the chief steward that I had served under him in the wine bar in *Drake* when he had been a P.O., but he could not remember it. I also said that I was a little nervous at my appointment, but he assured me that all would be well and that he knew that four sets of P.O. stewards' papers had been sent to the F.O.A.C. secretary and that I had been chosen because of my experience of looking after so many captains. I explained to the chief that I had been hoping to get a larger staff so that I could make chief, but he said that I was now on the stepping-stone to become an admiral's chief steward and that was much better than serving in a W.R.

CHAPTER 15

Footnotes:
1. Perhaps I should give you some idea of the duties of a mess butler. In *Drake* there was a 'pool', consisting of C.P.O. stewards and cooks, and P.O. stewards and cooks, who would be waiting for a posting. The mess butler would be a chief steward, assisted by a P.O. steward during breakfast and lunch. The time spent in the W.R. mess depended on the number of N.C.O.s in the 'pool'. The chiefs never carried out duties after 1630, unless there was a large function, so the mess butler duties after 1630 were carried out by the duty P.O. steward. A good mess butler would acquaint himself with the menu, see that the table was laid correctly and that the mess waiters were well turned out. He would also ensure that the servery was ready and that the plates, etc. were nice and hot. From the moment that dinner commenced, he would ensure that no officer was kept waiting and that the stewards did not group up and chat. This, of course, was during a running dinner; dinner routine I have already explained in an earlier chapter.
2. The interest in the stewards' branch which he mentioned was the fact that I had spoken to him of an idea, of a C.P.O. steward working very close with the C.P.O. supply branch and the C.P.O. ship's cook, to improve the lower deck menus. The D.O. suggested that I write to the supply branch in the Admiralty, so I did. I shall never know what good it did, but I do know that the lower deck meals did improve much later.

CHAPTER 16

HMS *EAGLE* and HMS *ALBION*

We knew that F.O.A.C. was to fly his flag on *Eagle*. As we arrived over Malta, I had my first glimpse of *Eagle*; she looked very grand laying at her buoy in the harbour, surrounded by many other warships.

We landed at the airport, where there was transport waiting to take us to the 'Grand Harbour'; we were then taken out to *Eagle*. Drawing alongside, I saw how big she was and a little panic came over me as I wondered if I would come up to the admiral's expectations; but it soon passed.

I at once felt resentment as I did my 'joining ship routine'; the ship's company were very wary of admiral's staff. The two chiefs had a cabin between them. I had a locker in the petty officers' mess, but no 'slinging billet', so I had to sleep on a camp bed in the pantry flat. The remainder of the staff managed to get a billet in the W.R. stewards' mess. I was very disappointed at my accommodation as there was a three-berth cabin meant for the two chiefs and myself, but it had been taken over by two C.P.O. air crew and they would not give it up — as I have said, we were not welcomed.

The admiral was still living ashore with his wife, so I had time to prepare his quarters which had been used by the captain of *Eagle*. There was a nice big pantry and store-room, but the store-room was three decks down; this was where I was to stow all the empty packing cases and trunks, and as the *Eagle* captain's trunks were there also, it was a tight fit — I also had to stow the admiral's wines there.

The admiral's quarters were back aft, under the quarterdeck. They consisted of a very large dining-room, a day cabin-cum-office, which led off to his sleeping cabin and bathroom. There was also a pantry, day cabin and sleeping cabin on the bridge.

71

I had three leading stewards and a steward, the admiral's valet, also a leading steward who was to come later with the admiral. We all got stuck in, getting his quarters up to scratch. I also unpacked the mess traps and bedding, checking them with care; they had all been waiting for me in the store-room. The leading stewards also prepared the cabins for the admiral's chief of staff, secretary and flag lieutenant. They were to mess with the admiral; making four in all.

After two days, the admiral, who was still ashore, sent for the two chiefs and myself. When I stepped into his office I was at once impressed with the admiral; he looked very smart in his 'whites', seated behind a large desk, with a fan whirling over his head. He greeted me, then said I was to look after his wines, trophies, mess traps and bedding. I was also to be in charge in the absence of the chief steward.

The admiral then came aboard with the three members of his staff and his valet; also came his trophies and wines. These I checked, then stowed away until needed.

The admiral then asked me to go ashore to assist his wife in the packing of their private possessions, which were to be sent home. Some time later, while at sea, the admiral informed me that his possessions had arrived home without any breakages. He said that I had done a fine job.

As soon as the admiral came aboard, the captain of *Eagle* became flag captain; he had his own P.O. steward and valet. They shared my pantry but the F.C. never dined with the admiral, only at lunch or dinner parties that the admiral gave.

In harbour, the chief steward was always ashore shopping; but he always returned in time to serve lunch. My main duty was to keep an eye on the staff. My routine was to supervise breakfast — this was put on a hotplate, as they helped themselves; then supervise the staff in their duties; the valets would go away and attend to their officers, and the stewards and I cleaned the pantry and laid for lunch. I insisted that all the staff met in the pantry at 1100 hours to clean the silver. I would then prepare the drinks tray. If the admiral had any callers then I would serve drinks or coffee, according to their needs. Once a week I would inspect the cabins, but they were always clean as the staff knew their jobs.

In harbour, I was always in the pantry for all the meals to ensure that all was ready for the chief, who as I have said served lunch. After lunch the duty watch would take over. This was myself, a leading steward and a steward in one watch; while in the other watch were three leading stewards. When I was on duty, I also valeted the admiral. At sea the chief would move up to the bridge mess with the admiral, leaving me back aft, where the secretary and flag lieutenant dined. The chief of staff was not with us very much, as he was away preparing the admiral's programme; as the C.O.S. never took his valet with him, I had one extra staff.

We sailed for 'flying exercises'; I managed to get on the flight bridge to watch these exercises (we were called Goofers). Just try to imagine an air station at sea; there was so much to see, and when I looked up at the admiral's flag flying from the mast, I felt very proud of being on his staff.[1]

Our first call was at Gibraltar. As soon as we arrived, the Flag Officer Gibraltar, paid a courtesy call on our admiral. And who did it turn out to be? My old captain of the dockyard. You should have seen his face when he saw me. He overcame his surprise by saying "Hello, Warner, what have you got on your arm now?" I turned and let him see. He then said "Well done". As the chief had been ashore, it had been up to me to serve drinks. The following night the F.O. Gibraltar and his wife came to dinner, and madam asked me to call on her; but I never did. That night the chief allowed me to serve dinner, and I noticed that madam watched my every move. I had proved to my old captain that his write-up of me was another farce, and I was not a child.

After more exercises, we returned to Malta to find HMS *Albion* and *Centaur* (aircraft-carriers) waiting for us. The secretary then informed me that the admiral, whom I should have told you was called Pedder, was to transfer his flag to *Albion* and that I was to supervise the packing and transfer of all the gear, but not the mess traps, as there were new ones waiting on board *Albion*.

We transferred to *Albion* on the 9th of January 1956. The admiral and his staff were transferred by helicopter while at sea. With the *Centaur*, we then sailed for the Far East, going through the Suez Canal; then on to Bombay, Colombo, Singapore and Hong Kong. All this time we had been exercising flying planes from one carrier to another; I found out the reasons for these exercises later.

In *Albion*, I had quite a job getting the admiral's quarters up to my standard, as they were not too clean; also the flag captain's P.O. steward was not very co-operative. The secretary pleased me when he said that I was doing a fine job. I wish he had put it in writing.

When we arrived at Suez, it was given out that we were not to take any notice of what we may see or hear as we sailed up the canal. This was at the time of the Suez flare-up. As we sailed through the canal, the natives showed us their backsides and hurled abuse at us, but this was overcome by the cheers from the British as we sailed past them at their stations along the canal.

Arriving at Bombay, we went alongside; but only for two days, as we then sailed again with *Centaur* to carry out a flying demonstration; this is why we had been exercising so much.

We sailed with twenty-seven V.I.P.s aboard, and we were to entertain them to lunch on the quarterdeck. I had never heard of entertaining at sea before, and I found it most instructive. We had the assistance of W.R. staff.

The chief's party was:—

Pandit Jawaharial Nehru.	Prime Minister of India.
Mrs Indira Gandhi.	Prime Minister's daughter.
Dr K. N. Katju.	Defence Minister.
Dr Harekrushna Mahtab.	Governor of the Bombay State.
Shri Morarji Desai.	Chief Minister of the Bombay State.

My party was:—

Sandar Surjit Singh Majithia.	Deputy Defence Minister.
Shri B. S. Hiray.	Minister of Revenue Bombay State.
Shri S. K. Patel, M.P.	President of Bombay State.
Captain Fenwick.	
Group Captain R. Dutt.	

There were five other parties. I still have a copy of the programme. This took place on the 21st of February 1956. We returned the V.I.P.s then sailed for Colombo and Singapore.

At Singapore, the chief took me ashore, the treat being on him for the way that I had been carrying out my duties. We visited the local market, which was quite an experience. At this stage I must admit that the chief steward knew his catering, and the chief cook turned out some fine dishes, which I noted. We then sailed for Hong Kong, where I made an ass of myself.

One night I booked a room in a hotel to sleep it off, only to find that I overslept. In a panic I rushed down to the dockyard, jumped into a boat and told the chap to take me out to my ship. I boarded the ship and reported to the officer of the day, who smiled at me, then told me that I was on the wrong ship. I was; in my panic I had boarded *Centaur*. The *Albion* sent a boat over for me. This time I reported to the officer of the day, who at once put me on 'commander's report'. The commander then put me on 'captain's report'. At the captain's table he heard what I had to say then dismissed the charge. They all had a good laugh at my expense, even the secretary pulled my leg. While in *Albion* I was awarded my third good conduct badge.

We sailed for Bombay again, where this time, leave was given. The petty officers were invited to a midnight supper by the nurses of a local hospital. We travelled by coach to the opening of a forest. I remember sitting on a wall and looking over it. I saw shining lights like cat's-eyes. The nurse who I was with, told me that they were alligators. I soon shifted. On the whole we all had a good time. We then sailed for Malta.

At Malta the *Eagle* was waiting for us, and on the 8th of May 1956, we transferred back to her, but without the chief steward and cook, as they were to remain in *Albion* from where they would return to Plymouth, then proceed on long leave; afterwards they would fly back to Malta again to join *Eagle*.

The secretary then informed me the Admiral Pedder was to be replaced by Admiral Powers on board *Eagle*, and I was to supervise the turnover of all the gear again. I even had to look after the two chiefs' gear. This meant that not only had I to attend to the transferring of Admiral Pedder's gear ashore, but also the settling in of Admiral Powers and his staff in *Eagle*.

The write-up that I received from Admiral Pedder was:— 'Hard working, willing and trustworthy. Has kept my wines, trophies and bedding most ably. In the absence of the chief steward, he has coped with a young and inexperienced staff quite adequately.'

This was a very good write-up and it was written by the admiral himself.

On joining *Eagle*, I found that the flag captain's P.O. steward had been replaced by a P.O. whom I knew, and never did get on with. Admiral Pedder's secretary had said that I was to be in charge while the chief was on leave, but this P.O. pulled rank of seniority on me and insisted that he should do the shopping. I agreed with this as I had my hands full unpacking mess traps, etc., again, and supervising the staff.

While I was getting things shipshape, the new secretary sent for me and said that he was not satisfied with the cleanliness of the cabins and store-room. I at once replied that the staff were doing their best and that he should remember that we had only joined *Eagle* two days before him. For that he took an instant dislike to me, as I had stood up to him; after that I could do no right in his eyes.

I had been told that a leading steward called Dance, was to be flown out. When he arrived he told me that he had been with the admiral before. Dance had left the Service then rejoined again to be with the admiral. He was a very quiet man who kept himself to himself, but I was sure that he was keeping the secretary up to date as to what was going on.

Admiral Powers loved to go on 'banyans'. This was going out in the barge and taking packed lunches and cold drinks. The admiral used to swim under water, exploring underwater caves; while the secretary went water skiing. One time Dance and I went with them; it was then that I found that Dance could not swim. This was against Admiralty regulations, as they state that leading rates and above, must pass a swimming test. As the old saying goes — 'It's not what you know, it's who you know.'

One day, Dance surprised me by asking me if I could take over as chief. I replied 'Yes, if our chief agreed on this.' I heard no more about it, but when the chief returned I was informed that Dance was to be rated P.O. and I was to be transferred to the W.R. in *Eagle*. At this I put my foot down and told the chief that as I had completed my time on the admiral's staff, then I wished to be sent back to *Drake* and I was willing to fight for it. I didn't have to, as they agreed to my wishes. The chief was sorry to see me go and I never saw him again until much later.

The write-up that I received from the admiral's secretary was:— 'Very willing and hard-working, but over-anxious and appears to be emotionally unstable at times. His dress and appearance are not always up to standard. Does not control his opinions very well, but keeps his pantry clean. He has performed his duties well on the whole, but with supervision. Should benefit by a change of employment.'

Now this write-up that was given by a lieutenant-commander did not agree with what Admiral Pedder had said. Was this lieutenant-commander implying that Admiral Pedder did not know what he was saying? — How could I have changed in only three months? — The only emotion I had shown, was when I had stood up for the staff, and yes, my opinion could not be controlled. I saw no reason for not letting him know how I felt at this complaint of the cabins and store-room. As for supervision, the chief had left it to me right from the start to organise the staff, and on Pedder leaving and Powers arriving, the chief had been on leave. My dress was the same as when I had been with Pedder, and he had not complained. So what was it all about? It just did not seem fair that a lieutenant-commander could give such a write-up so soon after the good write-up that I had received from Admiral Pedder.

I was flown home on twenty-eight days' leave, with orders to join *Drake* on completion of my leave. I must point out that I did not know about this write-up until much later. If Powers' secretary had shown me what he had written, as Pedder's secretary did, I would have had it out with him.[2]

CHAPTER 16

Footnotes:
1.   Serving in an aircraft-carrier was most vigorous. HMS *Eagle* had been modernised with a flight deck, which could allow for planes to fly off and land at the same time. It was a wonderful sight when flying was taking place. The hangar lifts would be going up and down, bringing planes up on the flight deck. Planes would be warmed up, then catapulted off at two at a time; then landed and sent down below into the hangars. While all this was happening, the carrier would be sailing at top speed, and the destroyer escort would be sailing close to the carrier, with a helicopter flying just on our stern ready to pick up a pilot should he crash into the sea. I regret to say that we did lose one plane and the pilot, although he was picked up, he died later.

     When serving the admiral and his staff meals, etc., one had to close one's ears as to what was being conversed about. I felt a trusted man when in the admiral's presence.
2.   During the 'crossing of the line ceremony' in *Albion*, I was carrying out my duties back aft, so I did not take part; but I still received my certificate.

CHAPTER 17

HMS *DRAKE* and HMS *OCEAN*

I joined *Drake* on the 20th of September 1956, then, only a month later, on the 26th of October, I was drafted to *Ocean*, a fleet carrier that only had squadrons of helicopters aboard. She was to sail for the Suez, carrying the 52nd Royal Marine Commandos and army troops, which were to be landed at Port Said.

On joining *Ocean*, I found that there was only one chief steward and a P.O. steward, who was a wine steward. The chief was assisting the catering officer so this left me to run the officers' mess and pantry. I had quite a large staff to supervise, but I did not mind this, as this was what I had always wanted, a large staff.

The W.R. mess soon filled up with extra officers, but I was given R.M. orderlies to assist in the table waiting; so things were not too bad. In fact this gave me an even larger staff. I had a very good pantry steward, but he let me down later on.

We sailed for Malta, where shore leave was given. While I was ashore, I met the pantry steward, whom I have spoken about, and bought him a drink. I remained in his company and told him that he was doing a fine job. The very next morning I caught him eating a grapefruit after breakfast. I told him that they were extras for the officers only, he then said "Get stuffed", so I at once put him on report for insubordination; he went all the way to the captain's table. The captain asked me if he was my friend? I said that he had been, but until he respected my rank I would not befriend him. The captain said, "Well done". He then told the steward that as we were under sailing orders he could give him a dismissal from the Services and a prison sentence. This really put the breeze up the steward. The captain then gave him twenty-one days' stoppage of leave. When the steward left the captain's table, he apologized to me, which I accepted, and we did in fact remain friends.

One day in the W.R. mess, the commander came up to me and said

"You are doing a fine job P.O., and it has not gone unnoticed." But this was not put in writing.

At Suez, our lads were flown in and I was taken aback by the amount of wounded being flown back to us. There were wounded all over the place. To me this was a silent war and we should never have pulled out, as the Americans had requested. Still, I suppose the government at that time knew what they were doing.

After we had been ordered to pull out, we returned to Plymouth, where the wounded were sent to hospitals; but there were no cheering crowds. It was all very gloomy, although we had been winning, we all felt let down; the troops were very disgruntled. Nothing was reported of our wounded in the Press or on the radio, and we had fought a good fight.

Again, after only serving three months in *Ocean*, the report did not agree with what the commander had said to me, the write-up was:— 'Hard working and anxious to please, but still lacks power of command. Would probably do better in a smaller ship, in charge of a smaller staff.'

I wish they would make up their minds on what to do with me — first not suitable for admiral's staff — then appointed to one. Then deserves a larger staff — and now a smaller staff in a small ship. In *Ocean* I had been in complete charge of the W.R. mess, and I had gained the respect of my staff. Still, I must have done well, as my name was put forward for the Suez Medal, which was not given to everyone. I did not know about the medal until it was presented to me in HMS *Wave*.

On returning to Plymouth, the P.O. wine steward was disrated for selling a bottle of brandy to a chief. This was where I was slow, as I should have requested to remain on board *Ocean*. However; I was not to know at the time.

I was drafted direct to HMS *Royal Arthur* on the 10th of January 1957.

CHAPTER 18

HMS *ROYAL ARTHUR*
(Bath)

When I joined *Royal Arthur*, near Bath, I found that it was a shore establishment for the advanced training of chiefs, P.O.s and leading rates. This included, power of command by parade drill and was most interesting, as we were allowed to take turns on divisions by acting as the captain, commander and D.O., etc. This training gave me much confidence.

We were all treated the same, no matter what our ranks were. Physical training was made interesting, as we were all given the chance to take the class. In P.T. we would first demonstrate to the class the exercise, then give the order to carry it out, correcting anyone who was not doing it right.

We were given lectures on first aid, naval history and damage control. We were also given a chance to lecture to the class on a chosen subject. I chose life saving. This lecture was on tape. When my tape was played back to me I found that I sounded very much like John Mills.

Then there was 'get back exercise'. This was when part of the class were taken out in a covered transport about fifteen miles; we would then be dropped. Then we had to find our way back to the main gate without being caught. The rest of the class were the guards who would try to catch us. I managed to get back, but was outside the given time.

To me the most interesting part of the course was to play out a court martial. Each of us would act as the president of the court, prosecuting officer, defence and the defendant. I was the defending officer and I lost my case, but it was great fun.

The Duke of Edinburgh had once been a lieutenant instructor there; there was a picture of him in the dining-room. The meals were first class, and on the whole it was all very instructive. The course lasted for six weeks; my class was 521.

The lectures on naval history proved most interesting. First I learned that the Royal Navy had first been called Navy Royal. This was when the monarch had been responsible for the upkeep of the Navy, in James' time; but it was then agreed that the country pay for the upkeep, so the name was then changed to Royal Navy. In those dark days the ships flew the Union Jack, so this was changed to the White Ensign.

I was also informed that the gold braid cord (egglets) that were worn around the shoulders of flag rank, went back to the days when officers used to ride horesback. The egglets were used to tether their horses by pressing the peg into the ground.

The 'dragging of the sword', I was told, came from Queen Victoria's time, when a naval officer upset her. So she gave the order that naval officers should drag their swords. The only time that they could hitch it was if riding, or when wearing an overcoat.

Then, of course, why naval officers can toast the monarch while seated; this was because of the low deck heads in earlier ships.

How true these tales were I do not know, but this is what I was told. On the completion of this course, I returned to *Drake* a much more confident petty officer. On the course I had to have my boots repaired three times.

F

CHAPTER 19

HMS *DRAKE*
(Mess Traps)

I joined *Drake* on the 21st of February 1957, where I completed a two-day course on civil defence and light rescue. I was also put in charge of the mess traps and trophies. I was known as the 'mess trap king'.

The trophies consisted of large oil-paintings and pictures, also Drake's sword and goblet, and a large amount of silver trophies. One of these was insured for over £2,000. The knowledge that I had received, when I had been working in the store as a leading steward, proved a great help to me and, of course, while I had been on the admiral's staff.

While carrying out this duty, the officers had many dinner-parties, a guest night and a summer ball, so I was kept on my toes. The silver pantry was staffed by ex-stewards who were now pensioners. That was when I met my old P.O. who had been in *Black Prince* with me. They kept the silver lovely and clean. However; I was in charge, overall, and it was my duty to see that all was correct and accounted for.

I would muster the cutlery once a week; the trophies and pictures twice a week. Although I had been given this responsibility, I was still expected to carry out a duty in the W.R. mess and be duty P.O.

As duty P.O., I would take over the watch at 1300 hours in the W.R. mess; complete lunch, then supervise teas, followed by supervising dinner. At dinner there may be two sittings — first a running dinner, which was for officers who did not wish to change, followed by mess dinner, where officers must change into mess undress. This dinner routine I have already set out earlier in the book. After dinner I would report to the duty supply officer; we would then do the rounds of the stewards' and cooks' quarters. I would then lock all the doors in the W.R. mess at 2200 and pipe 'down the staffs' quarters' at 2230. Next morning, call the hands at

0630, supervise breakfast until I was relieved at 0800. Then report any incidents to the chief steward; muster the hands in the W.R. mess at noon; supervise lunch until I was relieved at 1230; then I was off duty until 0800 the next morning. The duty roster for P.O.s was according to the number of P.O.s on *Drake*.

When the officers held their summer ball, there were over twelve P.O. stewards in *Drake*. I had been duty P.O. the day before the ball, so I should have been off duty. However; the chief said that all P.O.s were to be on duty. I explained to the chief that there were ample P.O.s to do the job, but he said that he still needed me, although I had the mess traps to see to. He did give me the afternoon off, saying I was to report for duty at 1900 hours. I had a couple of pints over in the P.O.s' mess, and when I reported for duty, the chief said I was drunk; now I was not drunk. I said that I was tired. Anyway, he sent me home. Next morning the D.O. sent for me and said that I had let the side down. I explained how hard I had worked and that I had accounted for all the mess traps, so he said no more. I took a few bad remarks from the other P.O. stewards, but I did not mind as I knew that I had done my share of work.

Later I found that the D.O. did not give me the write-up that I deserved for looking after the mess traps. He wrote:— 'Very loyal and tries hard to please most desperately, but his capabilities on occasions fall short of his enthusiasm. Entirely trustworthy and has a pleasant disposition. His ability to direct and organize his staff is improving.'

CHAPTER 20

HMS *WAVE* and HMS *DUNCAN*

I joined HMS *Wave* at Portsmouth, on the 17th of December 1957. I should now point out, that the practice of sending ratings from Devonport, Chatham and Portsmouth to join ships from their own ports, had stopped. This meant that ships now had a mixed crew of ratings from various ports. I think that this was a bad move, as I knew that each port took a great deal of pride in its own ship, such as paintwork and drills; this pride was lost with a mixed crew.

HMS *Wave* I found, was a frigate, which was the flag ship of the Fisheries Protection flotilla. The 'Cold War' (known as the Cod War) had now started. So it was up to us to keep an eye on what was happening out in the fishing grounds. We were to keep watch over our fishing boats, which were fishing off Iceland, making sure that they were inside the fishing limits and to protect them from interference from any Icelandic gunboats.

The captain was called Anderson. He was made acting commodore. The captain had his own P.O. steward who, in turn, had his own pantry. However, although the commodore had his own quarters, he and his P.O. steward were catered for by me. In the W.R. there were seven officers and a midshipman. On my staff were two leading stewards; three stewards; and a leading cook and his mate; so in all, I was catering for eighteen people.

This catering had to be done with great care, as we were to spend as long as seven weeks at sea at once. This was the longest period I had ever catered for, so when purchasing my stores I had to keep in mind the time that we would be at sea, the cold weather that we would come up against, and the small storage space that I had. I was able to stock up with fresh milk and fresh vegetables, as I was given a veg locker on the upper deck; but I had to ensure that it was well covered when at sea.

We set sail for the fishing grounds in the North Atlantic, just on the border of the Arctic Circle. When we arrived, the fishermen waved to us. I really felt sorry for them as the weather was always very bad, with high winds and rough seas. One moment they could be seen, then they would disappear into a deep trough, out of sight. HMS *Wave* stood up to this bad weather very well. While in these storms I was always in the pantry at every meal. It was a masterful task being on the hatch as I had to time the opening of the heater and fridge with the movement of the ship, or I would have food and dishes spilling all over the deck. I had also to place wet tea-cloths over the face of the polished top to stop things from sliding about. I really had to be on my toes. On top of this, many of my staff were seasick, so at times I was short handed. It was a blessing that I never suffered from seasickness.

Whenever I could, I always made for the signal bridge, where I could watch the ship plough her way through the high waves. As a large wave would start rolling towards us she would dip her bow, then it would rise high out of the water as the wave rolled beneath us. Her bow would then slide down into the bubbling seas, leaving her stern up out of the water; she would then slide down until the sea was well over her bow; then just as you thought she would dive to the bottom, her bow would rise again, shaking the seas off like a woman shaking her head when stepping out of a shower. The sprays that she shook off would come right over the bridge, that was when you had to duck, if you didn't then you would receive a slap in the face from the cold icy waters. At times she would roll right over till the lifeboats were nearly in the water; then she would roll back again, after she had given you a fright. She would then dip her bow into an oncoming wave. Many times she would give a shudder as her bow came up out of the water, and many times I patted her and said "Good old girl". HMS *Wave* was a grand old ship; she rode out a storm much better that *Decoy* or *Duncan*. I was very sorry when the time came to leave her.[1]

I became a firm friend of the canteen manager. He would order by signal on our way home; fresh vegetables, milk and salads; so that they would be waiting for us as soon as we docked. If we went to a buoy, then the canteen boat would bring my stores out to me. The canteen service proved a great help. As always the only headache that I had was the laundry, but I managed to keep topside of this.

While at sea on these long trips, the leading sick berth attendant and I ran a ship's request programme. This turned out to be very popular. I also became friends with a seaman P.O. who trained me to take the wheel. One day he said that he was satisfied and would I like to take over the wheel. I said "Yes", so he requested the bridge if I could take the wheel; the bridge gave me permission. What an experience this was! As soon as I had the wheel I reported to the bridge the ship's course and speed. Then the bridge said "Very good". After a short time, the bridge gave me a new course. I changed course then reported to the bridge the new course that I was now on; again they said "Very good". When it was time for me to leave, I requested permission to hand over the wheel. This was given and "Well done P.O." was added. I felt very chuffed. I took the wheel many times while on these patrols, and I soon came to know *Wave's* little tricks — such as when she hit a large wave she would dip her bow, roll over and go off course; if you left her alone she would come back on course, but if you tried to steer her back on course she would go further off on the other side. She was, in fact, a very good ship to handle.

The first time out, we met the Norwegian ship called *Albert*. She was interfering with a fishing ship. I well remember how the commodore sailed right alongside of her, just on the fishing limit. It was a lovely bit of seamanship; the *Albert* moved off, not wishing to start anything.

On the same trip we went into Reykjavik. I had been informed by the pay officer that the rate of exchange was forty krona to the pound, and that they were after our sterling as the banks had been closed on them.

On going ashore, I found a ships' store that was run by a German; this was when my bit of German helped me. The German made quite a fuss over me, giving me a glass of brandy and a cigar. He then surprised me by offering me 100 krona to the pound. I at once stocked up with many cheeses, meats and fresh potatoes. Returning to the ship, I reported my good fortune to the first lieutenant, who was also the catering officer (mess treasurer).

Next morning, the commodore sent for me and said that he had heard that I was a bit of a diplomat ashore, and that I was getting 100 krona to the pound. I replied that it was in the officers' interests, quite expecting a telling off. Instead he gave me some money to change for him. The rest of the officers did the same. I found out that they wished to purchase some leather goods, etc. The first lieutenant then told me that all the ship's potatoes had frost-bite and could I manage to purchase some with a promissory note. This was a note that could be sent to the Admiralty pay office; they would then settle the account with the named person. So off ashore I went with the supply P.O. to see what the German could do for us. The German took us out to a Laplander's farm, where he arranged for the purchase of a large amount of potatoes. He even arranged for the transport of them to the ship. After a couple of brandies he gave me a box of cigars, and wished me luck. It was quite a thrill to see the Laplanders in their clothing, all the transport was on a sledge drawn by reindeers. We then set sail for Scotland.

On our return the officers decided to give a mess dinner, with the commodore as the guest of honour. The cook and I got our heads together and I composed a fine menu:—

Iced Melon
With Lemon and Ginger
                    -o-   Sherry
Consommé a L'Italienne
With Fairy Toast
                    -o-   White Wine
Boiled Turbot
Dutch Sauce
                    -o-   Red Wine
Tournedos of Beef
Jardiniere
                    -o-
Duchess Potatoes
French Beans
                    -o-
Rum Trifle
                    -o-
Devils on Horseback
                    -o-   Port Passed
Dessert
                    -o-
Coffee

For the centre-piece, the cook made a model of *Wave* in sponge, covered with icing. He used shoe eyes as portholes and the model had lifeboats, guns, etc. He even had lights on the mast, bow and stern; these were attached to a switch where the commodore would be seated. When the quartermaster reported to the officer of the day that it was sunset, the commodore was requested to switch on the model lights. The commodore was very impressed and very pleased.

After dinner, the cook was sent for, was praised and given a drink. The first lieutenant then arranged for the cook to take the model to a children's home the following day, where he had his photograph taken for the local paper with a write-up. In all everything went to plan; I also received a "Well done".

We set sail again for the fishing grounds to join the fishing fleet.

This time a new fishing boat came out, and they brought us fresh fruit and magazines — compliments of the fishing boat owners. This was to happen many times and was greatly appreciated by the ship's company. The fishing boats were always sending lots of fresh fish over to us. We had fish on the menu most days. This transfer of fish was made whenever we sent our medical officer to inspect their nets. This was always a good excuse for such a transfer.

We returned to Scotland again and were sent on fourteen days' leave. On returning the officers decided to hold a cocktail party. As my birthday would be spent at sea, the petty officers also decided to give me a party in the mess on the same night. So after I had arranged everything for the officers' cocktail party, I informed the staff that I would not be on duty that night. But alas the leading wine steward got drunk and so I was sent for. I also being under the weather, was put on a charge with the leading steward, for being drunk on board. The D.O., Lieutenant Smith, did his best to tie me in with the leading steward; so much, that I said I wanted a court martial. The commodore sent for me, telling me that I was too good a P.O. to be disrated, so would I accept his punishment. I agreed, so a warrant was sent for. As I have said we were at sea on my birthday and it was on that day that the warrant arrived back, so it was read out to me in the petty officers' mess. It was so funny, as all around the mess were my birthday cards. I lost one good conduct badge.

Lieutenant Smith was not very happy over this and from then on he kept a close watch on me; I had a feeling that he was out for me.

This time we returned to Portsmouth, where we were informed that we could make arrangements for our relations to be on board when next we sailed. When we were five miles out, they would be returned by a lighter; and we would then carry on to join the fishing fleet.

My mate, the P.O. seaman, lived in Portsmouth, so he at once suggested that my mother could stay with his wife, and so make the sea trip with us. The day we sailed will always remain one of my nicest memories. We left harbour with all our relations on board. My mother was thrilled at all she saw and she did not miss a thing. I let her inspect my pantry and I know that she was very proud of me. I also took her into the petty officers' mess and showed her where I slept. She took it all in, then I lost her, only to find her on the bridge talking to the commodore. He told me afterwards that my mother was a very interesting person. The relations were then transferred onto the lighter and they escorted us off on our way. As the lighter turned to return back to port we waved to them; it was all very touching.

This time the commodore took us right up to the pack ice and on to the Arctic Circle. While on *Wave*, I received another 'blue nose certificate'. We also sailed through the fiords; sailing over where the *Tirpitz* had been sunk. We received more fresh fruit and magazines, before returning back to Portsmouth. This was when we were informed that we were to pay off *Wave* (meaning that *Wave* was to be taken out of commission) and that if we wished we would be joining a brand-new frigate called HMS *Duncan*. I requested to join *Duncan*.

I must tell you that before we left *Wave*, I was ashore one night when I bumped into the divisional P.O. On returning aboard I invited him into the pantry for a hot drink. While he was explaining the duties of a D.P.O., Lieutenant Smith opened the door and asked us what we were doing. We explained; but he sent the D.P.O. off then asked me for the pantry keys, telling me to report to the first lieutenant the next morning. I know that he expected us to be drinking — not a hot drink. After explaining to the first lieutenant, he returned the keys to me; but as I have said I knew that Lieutenant Smith was out to catch me.

I joined *Duncan* with a new leading steward, and this time a P.O. cook. The P.O. cook and I did not get on right from the start, as he was T.T. and against my drinking. He also insisted that he would make out the menus, and he would have done the shopping, if I had let him, but I insisted that shopping was my duty. I joined *Duncan* on the 11th of October 1958.

We also had a new first lieutenant and an engineer officer. The engineer officer took over the duty as catering officer, he knew nothing about catering, but he always wanted to see my books at the end of each month. He would pick me up for such silly things as a decimal point, which I need not have shown in any case. He also teamed up with Lieutenant Smith, so now I had two officers watching over me. The commodore and his P.O. steward also remained on board.

We sailed again to join the fishing fleet, but this time the first lieutenant took over as acting captain, as the commodore had to go to the Admiralty for talks.

This time out we ran into a very bad storm, the worst one that I had experienced. We lost two lifeboats and the bow was badly damaged. As this was *Duncan's* maiden voyage, we were all a bit worried; also most of the time the acting captain was in his bunk with seasickness. It was the navigating officer, a Lieutenant-Commander Weir who pulled the ship through; he was a fine officer. We had to make for Oslo where shore leave was given.

The people in Oslo made us very welcome; we had some fine

G

times. One night I was stand-by duty P.O. I was in the mess putting away a couple of cans of beer; if you know what I mean? When Lieutenant-Commander Weir, who was duty officer, sent for me and told me to get a patrol together and report to the local police station to see if all was well. This proved quite an experience, as I had never been a patrol P.O. I returned aboard and was ordered to report to the duty officer on the fo'c's'le that I had completed my patrol. On returning to the P.O.s' mess my mate told me that I had been reported for drinking, so the patrol was a put up job to see if I was drunk. I felt that Weir was in fact being helpful to me, in stopping me from getting drunk.

On returning to the fishing fleet, I had a bust-up with the P.O. cook; it had to happen. He threw out a challenge for me to lay on a buffet for the officer on the next Sunday night. I accepted his challenge, although we had been at sea for three weeks and all my fresh supplies had been used up. It was a known thing in the Navy that when at sea the officers always had a cinema show in the W.R. every Sunday, after supper. So the next Sunday I laid a buffet, as follows:—

Vegetable Soup	Served in a silver tureen.
-o-	
Sardine Royale	Sardines laid out on a silver salver, garnished with tinned carrots, cabbage and hard-boiled egg.
-o-	
Salmon	Tinned salmon mashed and laid out on a flat dish shaped as a salmon, garnished with tinned peas and carrots and covered with pink salad-dressing.
-o-	
Cold Meats	Corned beef, spam laid out on a flat dish, garnished with chopped cabbage, tinned beetroot and egg.
-o-	
Russian Salad	
Mixed Vegetable Salad	
Jacket Potatoes	Served in silver foil, opened like a flower.
Baked Beans	Served in a silver side-dish.
-o-	

| *Mixed Fruit Salad* | Served in a glass bowl. (Tinned.) |
| *Whipped Cream* | Served in a silver sauce-boat. (Tinned.) |

-o-

Assorted Cheeses
Biscuits

-o-

Coffee

I must admit that when the P.O. cook saw the lay-out, he did say that it was very good. Somehow though things were never the same between us, so much so, that when we returned to Scotland I was so depressed with the P.O. cook, Lieutenant Smith and the engineer officer, that I requested to be drafted back to *Drake*. When the commodore saw me at his table as a 'request man', he granted my request, but he said he was sorry that I felt as I did, and that he would be sorry to lose me. I was then drafted.

I received two write-ups; the first from Lieutenant Smith, who wrote:— 'Has proved a moderate P.O. steward; most sincere and tries hard to please his officers, almost to a non-fault. Does well on special occasions. Not very good supervising routine work. Works hard.'

I feel that this was not a good write-up as he did not say how well I had catered for such long periods at sea.

The second write-up was given by the engineer officer, who had only known me for a short time, this read as follows:— 'Not a good power of command but has the ability to produce better results, when spoken to often and kindly. Poor bookkeeping and untidy figures let him down.'

Again nothing said about my catering. As for my bookkeeping I never once ran them into debt. On the whole the recommendations that the commodore and the officers had given me did not show up in either of the two write-ups. The engineer officer had obviously been influenced by Lieutenant Smith; both these reports only gave my bad points, and not my good ones.

I should have told you that while in *Wave*, I was surprised when on divisions, the commodore presented me with the Far East Suez Medal. This had been recommended to me by the captain of *Ocean* for the part that I played in that Suez War.

CHAPTER 20

Footnote:
1. You may be interested to learn why a ship was always called "she". This was because a ship wore an apron; this was a guard to protect a lead screw on a lathe and also, the iron part across the bow for strength.

CHAPTER 21

HMS *DRAKE* and HMS *APOLLO*

I joined *Drake* on the 10th of April 1959, carrying out general duties until the end of May, when I was sent for by the D.O., who informed me that he was sending me to HMS *Apollo* on the following day, which was Thursday. It was a 'pier head jump', owing to the fact that the W.R.P.O. steward had been rushed to hospital with a breakdown. The D.O. also said he was confident I would do a good job, and that I would only be aboard *Apollo* for a short time.

HMS *Apollo* was a minelayer, based at Devonport. I joined her on the 22nd of May 1959. As soon as I put my foot in the pantry, I knew that something had gone wrong. It was filthy and all the silver was tarnished. I went into the W.R. mess and again could see how dirty it was. I then looked into a couple of cabins and found them to be dirty and untidy. While I was inspecting the cabins, the D.O. on *Apollo* came up to me and said that I had a difficult task ahead of me. On top of the mess being dirty, the officers were not too happy with the standard of meals that they had been given. The D.O. told me that he would back me up all the way in getting the mess and the staff up to scratch. He also informed me that as we would be spending some time at sea, I would be given unlimited sums of cash to purchase fresh stores and improve the standard of the meals. Then he dropped a bomb by saying that a rear-admiral would be joining *Apollo* on the Saturday, and we would be sailing on the Sunday. Then to top it, he said that the captain would be carrying out 'ship's rounds' on Saturday morning. As I have said this was already Thursday, the same day that I had joined *Apollo*. So you see I had my work cut out.

I called the five stewards together, along with the three seamen who were also on my staff. I said that I would be responsible for the pantry, but they had to get the W.R. mess and cabins up to my standard. I added that I would be inspecting their officers' cabins on Friday afternoon.

One of the seamen assisted me in the pantry while the other two seamen cleaned the officers' heads and bathroom; they were very good, so I left them alone.

That afternoon I got cracking in the pantry; it was an old-fashioned pantry and very big. The seamen and I worked very hard until I was satisfied. When the stewards saw us working hard, they too got stuck in. That night I made out a week's menus and made a list of the stores that I required.

Friday morning I went ashore to do my shopping, leaving orders that I wanted all the silver cleaned before I returned aboard. I returned aboard to attend to lunch and was pleased to see that the pantry and silver was nice and clean. Over lunch I heard the officers remark how nice the silver looked. After lunch I inspected the cabins and found them also to be much cleaner.

On the Saturday morning, the captain did his rounds, finishing in the W.R. mess. When he stepped into the pantry, he remarked, "A good improvement". He was then invited into the W.R. mess and he did not miss a thing. As he left he said "Well done Petty Officer".

Saturday morning the admiral came aboard and took over the captain's mess. He brought with him his own C.P.O. steward and valet, so I had nothing to do with them, although his flag lieutenant and secretary dined in the W.R. mess. I then went ashore to stock up for the coming sea period of two weeks' exercising.

I can honestly say that I do not know very much about the exercises as I was most of the time working in the W.R. and keeping an eye on the staff. I also must admit that the staff responded very well to my work routine. After two weeks at sea, we returned to Devonport, where long week-ends were given. We then sailed again on the following Monday for more exercises. I just had time to stock up again. At this point the D.O. informed me that the officers were pleased with the improvement of meals. On completion of exercises we sailed for London.

On our way to London, the captain held 'request men'. I put in a request to be given back the good conduct badge that I had lost in *Wave*. My request was granted and the captain added "Keep up the good work". This is where I made a bad slip, as I should also have requested to remain in *Apollo*. I feel sure that the captain would have granted this, and I may have received a superior, which I badly needed to be made chief.

When we arrived at London, it was a great experience sailing up the Thames to a buoy, which was just abreast of the Tower of

London. Long week-end leave was given and the admiral with his staff left us. Also the captain and most of the officers went on leave.

Then I had a nice surprise; on the Saturday morning, just after lunch the officer of the day came into the pantry and told me that there were some people waiting on the jetty who were asking to see me and did I want a boat to take me ashore to see them? I accepted his kind offer and went ashore where I found my mother, sister and her family waiting to see me. They were thrilled when I told them that they could come aboard *Apollo*. I gave them a conducted tour round the ship, then tea in the pantry. I was then given another boat to take us all ashore, where I spent the rest of the day with them until they went home, and I returned aboard *Apollo*. It had been a wonderful day.

We sailed on the Monday for Devonport, where I was returned to *Drake*. I joined *Drake* on the 4th of July 1959 and carried out general duties again until the following October. I was greatly disappointed with the write-up that I received from the D.O. in *Drake*. It was as follows:— 'Above remarks still apply, he tries hard to please but is below average in ability.'

Now the write-up that he was referring to was the one that I had received from *Duncan*. How could this be true? The D.O. on *Apollo* had not given me a write-up, owing to the short time I had been in *Apollo*. I felt that something could have been recorded about the good work I had carried out in her. This was to me, a bad let-down, which gives further proof that all write-ups do not record an up-to-date report on a rating's conduct or ability.

CHAPTER 22

HMS *ORION*

After a further short stay in *Drake*, I was then drafted to HMS *Orion*, which was in the reserve fleet in Devonport dockyard. I joined her on the 27th of October 1959. In *Orion*, there were two C.P.O. stewards; one was the mess man, while the other was responsible for the regulating and officers' accommodation. His name was Nicholas, a very fine man, who had gone to chief from a two-badge petty officer. There was also another P.O. steward, but he left very soon after I joined.

My duties were to supervise the running of the pantry and act as the mess butler at lunch-times; I was also given the mess traps to look after. I just could not get away from mess traps. One good thing about being in *Orion* was that the chiefs and I did not do a duty watch. We finished each day at 1630 hours and with every week-end off, Saturday noon until Monday 0800 hours.

My time in *Orion* was quite nice, although there were about sixty officers aboard, most of them lived ashore, rationed ashore (R.A.). My duty would commence at 0800 when I would supervise the end of breakfast, the cleaning of the W.R. mess and the pantry. After a cup of coffee I would then supervise the laying of lunch, type out the lunch menus, then take over as mess butler, till the completion of lunch. After lunch I would check part of the mess traps and type out the dinner and breakfast menus, then attend to any duty that Nicholas gave to me, such as inspecting a cabin, etc. At 1630 I was off duty until 0800 the following morning. As you can see, I was not overworked, I expect you could say this was a rest cure, after spending so long at sea. In any case, I was very happy in *Orion*.

Having had my good conduct badge restored, I was now awaiting for my good conduct medal (Blue Peter), given for fifteen years' service. With this medal was given a gratuity of £25, which was a lot of money in those days.

However; the week before my G.C.M. was to be awarded to me, the officers held a summer ball. The W.R. mess was turned into a dance-hall, while the cold buffet was served on the quarterdeck. Then there were private parties in the captain's cabin, the commander's cabin, commander (S) (supply), and the engineer's cabin; all went off very well. We all worked until 0200 hours the following morning. I well remember Nicholas saying to me that he was pleased that I did not have a drink. As you may have guessed I was now beginning to drink rather heavily, but I must say never while on duty. Nicholas was the only man that ever spoke to me about my drinking and he gave me a lot of encouragement. Saying that if I controlled my drink I should get a superior; the D.O. and commander (S) also encouraged me.

Going back to the summer ball, I was off duty from noon the following day, but instead of going home to catch up on my sleep, I called in a pub for a drink. When I came out I was picked up by the shore patrols for having my jacket undone; they asked to see my pay book, but because I did not have it on me, they brought me back to *Orion*, where I was confined to the P.O. mess until 1800 hours. I was then allowed home, but next day the captain put me on a month's 'stand over', which meant that I had to keep my nose clean. At the end of the month, the captain presented me with my G.C.M.; I was very proud that day and I did not get drunk.

The write-up that I received from commander (S) was very good, it read:— 'A very willing P.O. steward, who makes great efforts to "please", as has been written before. In *Orion*, however, he has made a determined effort to improve his power of command, which has been a weak spot in the past. He has made good progress in this respect and deserves every encouragement to improve further. His heart is in the right place, and responds to encouragement.'

You will note that this write-up was given by commander (S) and not my D.O.

CHAPTER 23

HMS *ROYAL ARTHUR*
(On the Staff)

After only nine months in *Orion*, I was drafted direct to HMS *Royal Arthur*, this was on the 12th of July 1960, just seventeen years to the date that I joined the Navy. You will remember that *Royal Arthur* was a training establishment for N.C.O.s, which I have told you about in chapter 18; well here I was, now finding myself on the staff in this establishment (ship). Things were really looking up, for to be on the staff in *Royal Arthur*, one had to be good at their job, above reproach and to be able to set an example to those N.C.O.s who were on a course of training.

When I stepped into the officers' mess, I was met with the same situation that I had met when joining *Apollo*. The whole of the W.R. mess, pantry and cabins were in a terrible state, and believe it or not, when I opened the safe which I had in my office, I found a set of false teeth and a shaving mug. I could not believe my eyes.

The comanding officer turned out to be the engineer officer who had served in *Duncan* at the same time as myself. When he saw me, he said that he expected great things from me. I did not know what he meant until I saw the D.O. later on.

After getting over the shock at seeing the state that the W.R. was in, the D.O. came into my office and sat down. He then told me that the P.O. steward had been sent to hospital with a breakdown, just as the P.O. in *Apollo*; he went on to say that things had really got out of hand. I was to start from scratch and get the place running as best I could. He also said that if I wanted to stop the staff's leave, then he would back me up. He explained that a large number of officers passed through and that I would be responsible for making out their mess accounts and receiving the cash for the same; that was the reason that I had a safe in my office. I would be given transport to do my shopping and a free hand in the catering. This was at last the job that I had been waiting for and I made up my mind that there would be no drinking.

I had a nice big office and desk, but there was nothing on the walls or notice-board, as to what staff I had or their duties, or anything about the officers' accommodation. So the first thing that I did was to muster all the staff together and give them a good talking to. I had one leading steward, who was a wine steward, and eight stewards. I told them that if they got the W.R. mess, pantry and cabins up to my standard, I would not stop their leave. They had been working 'watch about'. I put them in three watches until I was satisfied that the place was cleaner. This meant that the duty watch and stand-by watch would serve lunch. After lunch, the stand-by watch would clean the silver, and serve teas. They would then be off duty until 0730 the following morning. The duty watch would serve dinner, then lay back the beds of the officers who were sleeping aboard. They were then off duty until 0630 the following morning. Next morning, the duty watch would call the officers, lay for breakfast and serve breakfast until 0900 hours, assisted by the stand-by watch at 0730. After breakfast, all the staff carried out their own duties until noon, when the stand-by watch took over as duty watch; and the off duty watch took over as stand-by watch. The off duty watch were off from noon until 0800 hours the following morning. The wine stewards worked 'watch about', and I left the leading steward to carry out his own routine. The 'watch bill' was as follows:—

RED WATCH Off Duty	BLUE WATCH Duty	GREEN WATCH Stand-By
(Noon — 0800)	(Noon — Noon)	(Noon — 1700)
Steward 1	Steward 3	(0730 — Noon)
Steward 2	Steward 4	Steward 5
Wine Steward	Wine Steward	Steward 6
Seaman 1	Seaman 2	Seaman 3

This 'three watch bill' was accepted by the stewards and everyone worked quite well. There was a P.O. cook and three cooks. The P.O. cook assisted me in the menus and the making out of the shopping list, he proved a great help. I always returned from the shopping in time to supervise lunch; this also helped me to be on hand should an officer wish to settle his account. Sometimes I was requested to forward on an officer's account to his ship or home.

Of the three seamen, one of them worked in the pantry, the other two were responsible for the cleaning of the officers' 'heads' and bathrooms. They were very good and did not need much supervising. Five of the mess waiters were also valets, the sixth mess waiter was responsible for cleaning the W.R. mess, while the two wine stewards were also responsible for cleaning the ante room. I was overall responsible and, of course, did the catering. I also kept an eye over dinner. I was, in fact, working seven days a week. The accommodation and duty list was as follows:—

Cabin	Valet	Cabin	Valet	Cabin	Valet
1 Captain	Steward 1	5 Officer	Steward 3	9 Spare	Steward 5
2 First Lt.	Steward 2	6 "	Steward 4	10 "	"
3 Officer	Steward 3	7 "	"	11 "	"
4 "	"	8 "	"	12 "	"

All stewards will act as mess waiters.
Steward 6 will clean the W.R. mess.
Wine stewards will clean the ante room.
Seamen will join up in their watch and work in the pantry at lunch and dinner.

Although I had only eight officers in the mess, I would always have as many as twelve officers for lunch, and up to four officers who would stay overnight. I would say that my most important task was to ensure that the mess books were up to date, and to collect monies from the visiting officers.

I soon had charts on my office wall, which gave me the officers' accommodation, the stewards' place of duty and the 'watch bill'. I was surprised to see how interested the officers and staff were in my charts. I have gone into detail about this, to show that I did have the ability to run a large staff.

After two weeks, which up to then I had not taken any shore leave, the D.O. sent for me to tell me that the officers were delighted with my work and the interest that I was showing in the W.R. mess; if I kept this up, I would be given a superior. At last I thought that I had made it, but fate was to step in.

I went on my first week-end, but while I was on leave, the Sunday that I was due to return to *Royal Albert*, I was involved in a road accident. I was rushed to the R.N. hospital with a fractured pelvis and upper femur, also a broken nose and ankle. I was to remain trussed up in bed for two months. I was then sent to *Drake* on P.R.7 (unfit for sea service). I was taken into hospital only thirteen days after first joining *Royal Arthur*, so all my good work had come to nothing; for later I found that nothing had been recorded on my history sheet about my work in *Royal Arthur*. Now this was the second time that this had happened; the first in *Apollo*. I felt badly let down that twice I had achieved great results, and although officers had recommended me verbally for a superior, nothing had been recorded. This proves my point, that these write-ups did not give a true account of a rating's work. I know that I have said this before, but I still feel very strongly about this subject, and I can only hope that these write-ups have now improved in the Service, because they can be so important to a rating.

CHAPTER 24

HMS *DRAKE*
(The School)

While in hospital, I was under a Captain Latterman, who was a fine surgeon. He was so pleased at the way I had learned to walk again, that he asked me if he could help me in any way. I at once asked him if there was any chance of returning to *Royal Arthur*. He promised to do his best, but as I have said I was sent to *Drake*.

I joined *Drake* on the 21st of December 1960. While in *Drake* on P.R.7 I was using a walking-stick, as my leg was still weak. Also I was excused all duties as there was not much I could do while I was limping about.

In *Drake* there was a P.O. steward called Griffiths; he was in charge of the catering officer's food store. I also noticed that he took the stewards and the cooks on division every Wednesday. I did not think very much of this at the time, but one day while I was in the mess, which comprised of all the C.P.O. stewards and cooks, also P.O. stewards and cooks, the P.O. stewards were calling Griffiths for not taking a turn in the W.R. mess, or of being duty P.O. Now I had been relieving Griffiths at lunch-time in the store while he went for his lunch, and I had become a firm friend of his; so at the P.O.s' remarks, I at once said that Griffiths was taking divisions every Wednesday and in any case, I think that he and the P.O. in charge of mess traps should be excused doing a duty in the W.R. mess, or as duty P.O. As I turned round I saw 'Griff' standing in the doorway, and he just turned and left.

On the following Saturday morning, 'Griff' offered me a lift home; but on our way home he stopped at a pub for a drink. He was surprised when I told him that I was still on the wagon; however, he bought me a lemonade and himself a gin and tonic. He kept rubbing his finger round the top of his glass and then he asked me if what he was doing meant anything to me. I said "No". He then shook me by asking me if I was still a 'Buffalo'. Now not many people knew this, and that I was in fact a K.O.M. in the R.A.O.B. I said that I was still a member. He then went on to ask me what I thought about the 'Freemasons'. I said that I did not agree with the way that they stuck together, explaining that if a Mason was interviewing two people for a job and one of them was a Mason, then he would get the job, even if the other one was much better and more suitable. He then took me home and taking me upstairs, he opened his wardrobe and there hanging were two officers' uniforms, each with one gold stripe. He then told me that he had passed out for a sub-lieutenant and was only waiting for his appointment, which would be very soon, but I was not to say anything. He then said that he had heard what had been said in the mess and that he would help me all he could if ever I needed his help. Now I have brought this point up, as there was an occasion which came about six weeks later. Also, I am convinced, that had I requested to become a Mason he would have put my name forward, but this is another chance that I missed.

I shall never know if 'Griff' had anything to do with it, but ten days later, I was sent for by the D.O. who informed me that the chief steward, who was instructing Wrens and stewards for advancement, had been sent for by an admiral and that he would be away for a short time, so would I like to take over his school and carry out instructing. I at once said "Yes".

This was wonderful, as I was getting bored doing nothing while on P.R.7. I at once purchased a brand-new brief-case and got stuck into my B.R.97, so that I would be ready for my first class. This class consisted of four Wrens and a steward.

I really got down to the job of instructing, using all my experience in teaching them. I went right through the B.R.97, leaving nothing out; even such points as when officers were entertaining ladies, they should ensure that there was a powder-room, with all the necessities, if required.

After about four weeks, one of the Wrens was very upset. The Wrens were stationed at a Wren establishment. I took her to one side and asked her what the trouble was. She said that she had been given an officer to look after whom she did not like. That lunch-time, I phoned the Wrens' establishment and asked to speak to their D.O., and who did it turn out to be? Yes, Sub-Lieutenant Griffiths, who was also the catering officer. After congratulating him, I told him about the Wren's trouble and added that she was doing so well and I would like her to pass out. 'Griff' at once said that he would see into it. The next morning the Wren came in smiling and said that she had been given another officer to look after. She said that she did not know what happened or what I had done but she was very happy. She little knew what a true friend could do, this was a case of 'it's not what you knew, it was who you knew'.

I was still on the wagon, and it became quite a joke when I walked over the quarterdeck with my walking-stick and brief-case. The sentries used to nickname me 'the commander', but it was all taken in fun.

After six weeks, the class was passed out by a lieutenant-commander (S). The class presented me with a cigarette-case, which I showed off to the chief steward. He remarked that it was more than my predecessor had been given.

Then the chief steward did a strange thing, he took me into the chiefs' mess and introduced me to some other chiefs, saying that I had a bright future. I shall never understand what he meant, but I had a strong feeling that my B.13 had come through.

The second course that I had, consisted of eleven stewards and three Wrens. This course was passed out by a commander (S), who afterwards congratulated me on turning out such a good class. They also passed for leading rates. I had a photo taken of my two classes, which I still have to-day.

Just before I was to start a course for leading stewards for advancement to P.O., the chief returned, so he took over his school once more. I was rather disappointed, but after all it was his school and I had only stood in for him. He did thank me and said that he had heard that I had done a fine job.

While still in *Drake*, my old chief, Nicholas, came to see me. He informed me that he had been appointed as mess man to a new cruiser called *Tiger*, and that he would like me to put in for her as he wanted me to be wine steward. I asked him if he was sure. He replied that I had proved myself and he was confident that I would do good. I told him that I had a feeling that my B.13 had come through, but he said that I must have a 'sea recommend' and that he would see that I got it. But up to now my ankle was still giving me a lot of pain; so after seeing the medical officer, I was again sent into the R.N. hospital.

The write-up that I received from *Drake* was:— 'Average ability. He has worked well and I believe has made good progress. He has been beset by personal problems, which when fully clear, should allow him to produce better results.'

Now again nothing was recorded as to the way that I had taken over from a chief and had instructed two classes with 100 per cent passes. I was now really becoming to think, that write-ups were 'a load of tripe'.

CHAPTER 25

R.N. Hospital and HMS *HERMES*

While in hospital, Nicholas came to see me and said that he still wanted me as the wine steward in *Tiger*. I told him that I was still in pain but I would think it over. At the same time the chief steward in *Drake* came to see me and he said that there was a draft chit waiting for me to join HMS *Hermes*, an aircraft-carrier, and that I would be in charge of the mess traps, and work as duty P.O. in the W.R. mess. He added that my chief's rate would be waiting for me. I was at a loss just what to do; after much thought I requested to be returned to sea duty. I returned to *Drake* and was drafted to *Hermes* on the 4th of October 1961.

Hermes was at Portsmouth, she had just returned from the Med flying the flag of F.O.A.C., on whose staff I had once served. I found that the catering officer, who had just been made up, had only joined her a week before me, and that the chief steward and P.O. steward had left her. A new chief joined the day after I joined, and I knew him; he also had just been made up (promoted). There was one other P.O. steward, but as he lived ashore; he left me to do duty P.O. almost every day.

I gathered from the stewards that as the officers had been entertaining so much, the stewards were upset at having so much shore leave stopped, and that they had been tossing mess traps over the side. I passed this information to the catering officer. The catering officer then asked me to do a full muster of the mess traps. After finding the S.100, I could see at once that it had not been kept up to date. I informed the catering officer that it would be impossible to do a muster with the S.100; so he told me to do a complete check on what mess traps I could muster and make out a new top line.

This meant that I had to go right through the *Hermes*, the captain's mess, galley, and even on the mess decks, where I found cutlery, plates, etc. I got them all together and mustered them, only to find great losses. I cannot go into detail, but out of twenty silver tops to entreé dishes, I could only muster four, and out of five hundred dinner forks, there were only about three hundred. I went right through the S.100 and found out that all these shortages had not been recorded in the S.100. I reported my findings to the catering officer, who was very pleased with me; then said that an enquiry would have to be held. This meant that someone's head would be on the block. The chief steward had a chat with me, and again I was given to understand that my chief's rate was on board. How true this was I shall never know, because the amount of pain that I was now getting caused me to report sick.

The medical officer in *Hermes* put my ankle in plaster, but then took it off and sent me to the R.N. hospital for X-rays. The result was that I was sent back to the R.N. hospital in Plymouth.

I entered hospital at Plymouth on the 27th of October 1961, and after a full examination they found that I had osteo-arthritis in my left ankle and that I was to be given a discharge from the Sevice on medical grounds. I was sent back to *Drake* and then I was discharged in December 1961.

I could write one more chapter, but I have decided to end my book on a happy note. I must thank the Service for educating me and teaching me such a fine catering trade and, of course, for allowing me to see the world. I feel that I served my country well and perhaps any officer who may read this book may remember me and agree that I served them to the best of my ability.

To any stewards still in the Service, I would recommend that they request to see their history sheet at the end of each year — which they can do — then they can judge for themselves.

To any young man who feels that he would like to serve as a steward, then I hope that my book will assist him to make up his mind, and I would add that it takes a special kind of man to make a good steward.

To any officer who is still serving, please respect the steward, and should they have to give a write-up, then *BE FAIR*, and bring out the steward's good qualities.

I dedicate this book to
the many good stewards who have lost their lives at sea.
May they Rest in Peace.

THE END

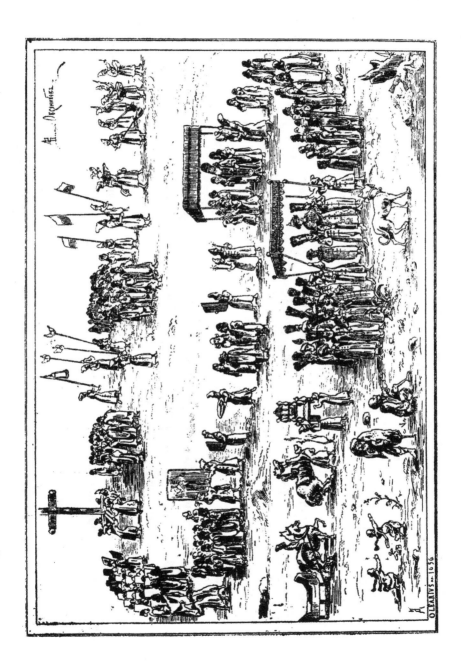

1) TSAR'S CARRIAGE OF THE 17TH CENTURY. One of those conserved in the Armory Palace. The first carriages and coaches were introduced to Russia from abroad in the 16th century. By the 17th century they were being manufactured in Moscow. The cabin was painted with decorations and upholstered with carpeting on the interior. The windows were isinglass. It was suspended by stout straps from a sturdy wooden chassis.

2) TSAR'S PAINTED, ENCLOSED SLEIGH, also with isinglass windows. It was placed on runners.

3) TYPICAL PROCESSION OF THE TSAR from the Kremlin to monasteries. A single horse was attached to the sleigh, covered with a horsecloth, and adorned with a plumed harness; it is led by the halter, by a boyar guide. Four boyars stand on the sleigh as guards fore and aft. Musketeer guards proceed on foot surrounding the sleigh. Both the boyars and the musketeers are without headgear. The tsar proceeds at a walking pace – any other speed for important personages and officials was considered improper.

FORMAL RELIGIOUS PROCESSION ON THE DAY OF THE EXALTATION OF THE CROSS. Drummers are in the van to signal people that they should make way. Following the drummers are sweepers to sweep the road. After them come the secretaries, gonfalon-carriers and clergy with sacred objects. The tsar and metropolitan proceed, attended by boyars, under their own separate baldachins. After the tsar there are more boyars and close stewards, and following them are servitors carrying the tsar's chair. The procession concludes with the tsar's riding horse and sleigh.

FORMAL MEETING OF A FOREIGN EMBASSY AND ITS ENTRY INTO MOSCOW. Foreign emissaries were usually met a few versts from the city by boyars dispatched by the tsar. They would seat the emissary in a royal carriage harnessed to six horses. In front of the carriage were detachments of musketeers, mounted and on foot, as well as mounted boyar cadets and court nobles. Trumpeters would blow their trumpets and drummers would beat their drums. A line of troops in full armor was posted in a single rank all along the road to the city.

TSAR'S RECEPTION OF AN EMBASSY IN THE GOLDEN PALACE during a session of the Boyar Duma. The tsar sits on his throne in full royal finery, which the tsars wear only on the most formal occasions. Near the throne and to the side stand *ryndy*, honorary royal guards, with silver poleaxes on their shoulders. The boyars sit around the walls, on benches. The emissary presents his monarch's greetings to the tsar while the Duma secretary receives gifts and documents from his suite. There is a silver washstand in the corner so the tsar can wash his hands after receiving a foreign document from the emissary's hands.

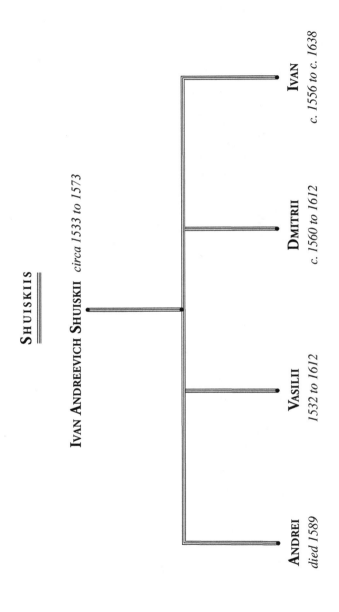

SHUISKIIS

IVAN ANDREEVICH SHUISKII *circa 1533 to 1573*

ANDREI
died 1589

VASILII
1532 to 1612

DMITRII
c. 1560 to 1612

IVAN
c. 1556 to c. 1638

GODUNOVS

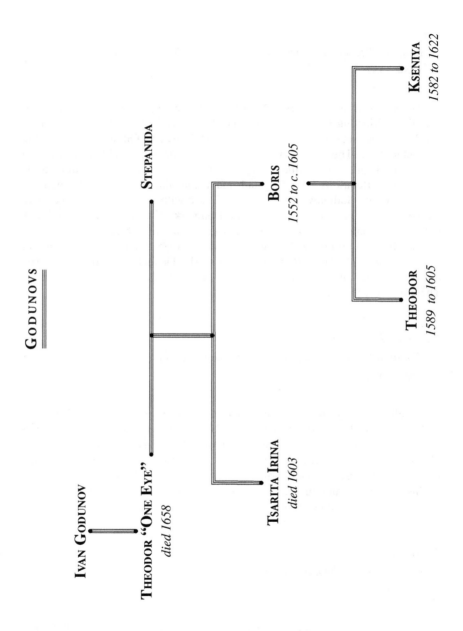

IVAN GODUNOV

THEODOR "ONE EYE"
died 1658

STEPANIDA

TSARITA IRINA
died 1603

BORIS
1552 to c. 1605

THEODOR
1589 to 1605

KSENIYA
1582 to 1622

KARAMZIN'S
TABLE OF CONTENTS

CHAPTER *IV*

Reign of Tsar Boris Godunov
1598-1604

CHAPTER *V*

Conclusion of the Reign of Boris
1604-1605

REIGN OF THEODOR IVANOVICH

AND

REGENCY OF BORIS GODUNOV

1584-1587

Theodor's characteristics. Members of the Supreme Duma. Popular agitation. Meeting of the Great Duma of the Land. Crown Prince Dimitrii and his mother set out for Uglich. Mutiny in Moscow. Godunov's power and characteristics. Theodor crowned tsar. Various favors. Godunov as ruler of the realm. Pacification of the rebellion of the Cheremisi. Second subjugation of Siberia. Relations with England and Lithuania. Plot against Godunov. Comparison of Godunov with Adashev. Truce with the Swedes. Embassy to Austria. Resumption of friendship with Denmark. Crimean affairs. Embassy to Constantinople. Iberian, or Georgian ruler a Russian subject. Dealings with Persia. Internal affairs. Arkhangelsk founded. Construction of the White, or Tsar's Town in Moscow. Beginnings of Uralsk. Dangers for Godunov. Exile and execution. Piteous death of the hero Shuiskii. Fate of Magnus's family. Theodor's idleness.

"The first days following the death of the tyrant," says the Roman historian [Tacitus], "were the happiest for the people." This is because the end of suffering is the most vivid of human pleasures.

| 1584 |

However, a cruel reign often sets the scene for a weak one. A new monarch fears to be like his hated predecessor and wants to gain general popularity, but he easily goes too far to the other extreme, and his weakness is injurious to the country. True friends of the nation might fear this all the more, since they knew of the unusual meekness of Ivan's successor.* In him this was joined with a timid mind, unbounded piety and an indifference to worldly grandeur. On the imposing former throne of the cruel torturer, Russia now saw a man devoted to fasting and silence, better suited to the cell or the cave than born to sovereign power. In moments of sincerity, Ivan would say as much, in speaking of Theodor,** while mourning his beloved elder son.

THEODOR'S
CHARACTERISTICS

The new tsar had neither inherited an administrative mind, nor his father's majestic appearance, nor the manly handsomeness of his grandfather and great grandfather. He was of short stature with a flabby body and a pale face; he was always smiling, but without animation. He moved slowly with an uneven gait, due to a weakness in the legs. In brief, he exhibited a premature exhaustion of natural and spiritual powers. Surmising that this 27 year old sovereign, condemned by nature to a permanent mental immaturity, would be dependent on nobles or monks, many did not dare to rejoice at the end of tyranny so that they would not regret it in future days of anarchy, boyar intrigue and discord, albeit less lethal to the populace, but more harmful to a great power organized around the strong and unitary power of a tsar. Fortunately for Russia, Theodor, fearing power as a dangerous enticement to sin, entrusted the helm of state to a skilled hand, so that this reign, although no stranger to lawlessness, and darkened by the most terrible crimes, seemed to contemporaries, by God's grace a prosperous, golden age, for it followed Ivan's!

MEMBERS
OF THE
SUPREME DUMA

The new pentarchy, or Supreme Duma, constituted by the dying Ivan of five nobles, was an object of general attention, hope and fear. Prince Mstislavskii, who was distinguished solely by his eminent lineage and rank, was the senior boyar and voivode. Nikita Romanovich Yuriev, esteemed as the brother of the unforgettable Anastasiya and uncle of the sovereign, was loved as a good-humored noble who had not been besmirched, even by gossip, in those calamitous, bloodthirsty times. Prince Shuiskii was respected for the glory of his great

* [Ivan is Ivan IV, or Ivan the Terrible
** [Karamzin uses the pre-Revolution orthography. Nowadays Theodor would be rendered as Fedor, Feodor or Fyodor.]

military exploits, for his courage and heartiness. Belskii, sly and flexible, was hated as Ivan's foremost favorite. Godunov's rare gifts were already known, and he was feared all the more, since he had also been able to gain the tyrant's special favor. He was the brother-in-law of the vile Malyuta Skuratov and an in-law and friend (although hardly sincere) of Belskii. After receiving sovereign power, the Supreme Duma on the very first night of 28 March expelled from the capital many known servitors of Ivan's ferocity and imprisoned others. The in-laws of the widowed tsaritsa, the Nagois, accused of evil schemes (probably, of intending to declare young Dimitrii as Ivan's successor) were placed under guard.

Moscow was in an uproar, but the boyars quieted the disturbance. They solemnly swore allegiance to Theodor, along with all the officials, and on the following morning made a

> POPULAR
> AGITATION

written announcement of his accession to the throne. Detachments of troops marched from street to street and cannons were positioned in the squares. Heralds were immediately dispatched to the districts with orders to pray for Ivan's soul and for Theodor's felicitous reign. The new administration summoned the Great Duma of the Land: the most distinguished clergy, court nobles and all eminent people to take some general measures for the organization of the national government. The tsar's coronation date was set and a con-

> MEETING
> OF THE
> GREAT DUMA
> OF THE LAND

ciliar letter confirmed these holy rites. They also discussed the welfare of the state and means to lighten the burden on the people.

They then sent the widowed tsaritsa, her son, father, brothers and all the Nagois to the town of Uglich, giving her royal servitors: stewards, clerks, boyar cadets and musketeers for a guard. The kindly Theodor tenderly bid farewell to young Dimitrii, weeping bitter tears, as if unwilling to perform a duty that pained his heart. This removal of the tsarevich, the only heir to power, might have seemed like

> CROWN PRINCE
> DMITRII AND HIS MOTHER
> SET OUT
> FOR UGLICH

a glittering exile. Dimitrii's guardian Belskii wanted no part of it and remained in Moscow. He had hoped to legislate with the Duma, but perceived the threat hanging over him.

Meanwhile, as Russia praised the good intentions of the new government, envy and illegitimate hunger for power schemed in Moscow. At first, dark rumors spread of great danger threatening the young monarch, and soon a man was named who was ready to astonish Russia with his criminality. It was said that Belskii had apparently poisoned Ivan and was now scheming to kill Theodor as well, to murder all the boyars and raise his friend and advisor Godunov to the throne! The secret perpetrators of this calumny were thought to be the Shuiskii princes, while the Lyapunovs and Kikins, Ryazan nobles, were stirring up gullible people. The latter, accepting this as the truth, fervently wished to save the tsar and the country from the schemes of this monster.

| MUTINY IN MOSCOW |

The cry of mutiny resounded through Moscow's quarters and 20,000 armed men, rabble, citizens and boyar cadets, rushed the Kremlin. Inside, they barely managed to shut the gates, gather some musketeers for defense and summon the Duma to council in the suddenly perilous circumstances. The rebels gained control of Kitaigorod with heavy artillery and turned the Tsar-cannon on the Florovskie Gates, trying to destroy it and break into the fortress. Now the sovereign sent Prince Ivan Mstislavskii, the boyar Nikita Romanovich and the secretaries Andrei and Vasilii Shchelkalov out to them to ask the cause of the rebellion and what did they want.

"Belskii!" the people answered. "Turn the criminal over to us! He is plotting to exterminate the tsar's family and all the boyar lineages!" Thousands of voices were crying, "Belskii!"

That unfortunate noble, bewildered by the accusations and frightened by the people's malice, sought safety in the sovereign's bedchamber, shaking and praying for help. Theodor knew of his innocence, and so did the boyars, but, whether sincerely or hypocritically frightened of bloodshed, they entered into negotiations with the rebels. They persuaded them to be satisfied with the exile of the supposed criminal and quickly expelled Belskii from Moscow. The people exclaimed,

"Hail to the tsar and his loyal boyars!" Then they quietly dispersed to their homes, while from then on Belskii was a voivode in Nizhnyi Novgorod.

W hat should one have expected from such shameful humiliation, such abasement of autocratic power? Intrigue in the Duma, willfulness in the populace and anarchy in government. Belskii was gone, but Godunov remained as an object of vengeance. The rebels did not demand his head, nor mention him by name, out of respect for the fact that he was the tsaritsa's brother. Yet he sensed the schemes of the calumniators, he saw that the brazen instigators of this insurrection were preparing his doom and gave thought to his own safety. Up till now, the tsar's uncle, in accordance to the ancient respect given the senior relative, could consider himself foremost among the nobles. So thought the court and the people, and so did the cunning state secretary Andrei Shchelkalov, who was trying to gain the trust of the boyar Yuriev, hoping to run the Duma with him.

They knew the power that Godunov had over his sister, the tender and virtuous Irina, whom the chroniclers likened to Anastasiya (for there was now no one else comparable among virtuous women). They also knew the power Irina had over Theodor, who in this world perhaps loved only his wife. But it seemed that Godunov had betrayed his friend and rejoiced at his impotence and fearfulness. Apparently Belskii did not guess that Boris was feigning his friendship, but inwardly fearing him as a secret rival, and was using this opportunity to consolidate his power.

The tender hearted Theodor, burdened with the state, frightened by the rebellion, saw the need for strict measures to govern the state, and having neither an incisive mind nor a firm will, was seeking more than an advisor and helper – he wanted someone on whom he could place the whole burden of government, who would be answerable only to God, and so he completely surrendered to this bold and ambitious man who was so close to the heart of his dear wife. Without any cunning, but following only her feelings, knowing Godunov's mind, but not his secret evil propensities, she cemented the alliance between a tsar incapable of ruling and a subject qualified for power. This eminent man at 32 was in the full bloom of life and at his prime both physically and mentally. Majestically handsome, of commanding mien, swift and deep of thought, this smooth-tongued seducer

GODUNOV'S POWER
AND
CHARACTERISTICS.

excelled over all the other nobles, as the chroniclers say. Boris was lacking only in . . . *virtue*. He wished to do good, and knew how, but this was due solely to his love of glory and power. He saw virtue not as a goal, but as a means to attain his goals. If he had been born to the throne, he would have earned the name as one of the best monarchs in the world, but he had been born a subject with an unrestrained passion to rule. When evil seemed more profitable he was unable to overcome his temptations, and so the condemnation of the ages has darkened Boris's reputation.

Godunov's first action was to punish the Lyapunovs, the Kikins and the other chief instigators of the Moscow masses: he exiled them to distant towns or locked them up in prison. The people either praised the tsar's justice or were silent. The royal court surmised the cause of this legal harshness and regarded Boris with unease: his decisive imperiousness had not been in evidence prior to Theodor's coronation, which had been deferred until 31 May for six weeks of prayer following the Ivan's death.

THEODOR CROWNED TSAR

Right at dawn on this day there was a terrible thunderstorm and pouring rain that flooded many streets in Moscow like a portent of looming disaster. Superstition was calmed, however, when the storm passed and the sun shone again in a clear sky. A countless crowd of people gathered in the Kremlin Square and the soldiers could barely make way for the sovereign's confessor when he left the tsar's palace for the Cathedral of the Dormition, to the pealing of all the church bells, carrying a relic of Monomakh, the life-giving cross, crown and the royal cloak (Godunov followed the confessor, carrying the scepter). Despite the unexampled press of people, everything became quiet when Theodor emerged from his palace with all the boyars, princes, voivodes and officials.

The sovereign was dressed in sky-blue raiment, the courtiers in gold, and the amazing silence accompanied the tsar all the way to the cathedral doors, which were likewise filled with people of all ranks, since all Russians were permitted to see Russia's sacred ceremony, as one family under the power of the Father-Tsar. During the church service, okolnichie and church officials went through the church, quietly telling the people to "Venerate and pray!" The tsar and the metropolitan Dionisii sat in the places prepared for them by the western doors, and in the general silence Theodor declared to the archprelate,

"Priest! Our father, the autocrat Ivan Vasilievich has left this earthly realm, and, taking angelic form, has gone to the Kingdom of Heaven. He blessed me with power and all the gonfalons* of the realm and ordered me, pursuant to ancient law, to be anointed and crowned with the tsars' crown, diadem and cloak. His will and testament has been made known to the clergy, the boyars and the people. And so, by the will of God and the blessing of my father, do perform the sacred ceremony, so that I shall become tsar and anointed sovereign!"

The metropolitan, holding the cross above Theodor, replied, "Lord, beloved son of the Church and of our humility, chosen of God and raised to the throne by God! You have been given to us by the blessing of the Holy Spirit for us to anoint and crown, so that you may be titled Autocrat of Russia!"

Dionisii placed Monomakh's life-giving cross and cloak on the tsar and the crown on his head with a prayer that the Lord might bless his rule, then took Theodor by his right hand and placed him in the special spot for the tsar, gave him the scepter and said,

"Guard the gonfalons of Great Russia!" Then the archdeacon at the ambo and the priests at the altar and in the choir shouted long life to the newly crowned tsar, who was now greeted by the priesthood, the officials and the people with a display of vivid joy. The metropolitan made a short speech reminding Theodor of the chief duties of a monarch: the obligation to preserve the faith and the realm, to be spiritually obedient to the prelates and have faith in the monasteries, sincere friendship towards his brother, respect for the boyars based on their hereditary seniority, and charitable towards his officials, soldiers and all the people.

"We have tsars in place of God," continued Dionisii. "The Lord entrusts the fate of humankind to them. May they may guard not only themselves, but others from evil; may they may save the world from unrest and may they fear the heavenly scythe!

---

* [A gonfalon is a banner suspended from a horizontal crosspiece.}

Without the sun, gloom and darkness rule the earth; so without instruction, souls are in darkness. Love wisdom and follow the wise. Be virtuous, for only virtue adorns a tsar, only virtue is immortal. Do you wish the favor of Heaven? Then favor your subjects . . . Do not listen to evil calumniators, O Tsar, born to goodness! . . . May justice flourish during your reign, may our homeland be tranquil! . . . And the Lord will lift your right hand above all enemies, and your realm will be ever peaceful from generation to generation!"

Then, with tears of emotion, all the people shouted, "Many, many years to you!"

Now Theodor, in full royal raiment, wearing Monomakh's crown and a rich cloak, and holding a long scepter in his hand (made of precious narwhal tusk), heard the liturgy, and appeared fatigued. Before him lay the crowns of conquered realms, and on his right stood Godunov, as a close noble, while Theodor's uncle, Nikita Romanovich Yuriev, stood with the ranks of other boyars. According to eyewitnesses, nothing could have ever surpassed the splendor of this ceremony. The ambo, where the sovereign and the metropolitan were sitting, the lectern, where lay the tsar's regalia and the places for the priesthood were all covered with velvet, and the church dais was covered with Persian carpets and red English fabrics.

The costumes of the nobles, especially Godunov and Prince Ivan Mikhailovich Glinskii, shone with diamonds, rubies and pearls of amazing magnificence, so that foreign writers value them in the millions. But greatest of all was the exultation in the faces expressing joy and ardent love for the throne. After the cherubimic hymn, the metropolitan at the Tsar's Entrance placed Monomakh's chain of Arabian gold on Theodor, and at the end of the liturgy, anointed him with sacred myrrh and partook of the holy sacrament.

During this, Boris Godunov was holding the scepter, and Yuriev and Dmitrii Ivanovich Godunov (Irina's uncle) were holding the tsars' crown on a golden dish. Blessed by Dionisii and showered with coins at the southern entrance of the cathedral, Theodor went to bow at the tombs of his ancestors, praying that he might inherit their administrative virtues. Meanwhile, Irina was sitting, wearing her crown, surrounded by her boyars, beneath an open window in her palace and was greeted by a thunderous acclamation from the people:

"Hail to the tsaritsa!"

In the throne room, the nobles and officials kissed the sovereign's hand; in the dining hall they dined with him, along with all the eminent churchmen. Feasting, merrymaking and popular amusements continued for a whole week and were concluded with a military display outside the city, where, on a broad meadow, bronze cannons thundered before eight ranks of musketeers dressed in fine cloth and velvet. A large number of horsemen, equally richly dressed, accompanied Theodor.

A fter giving the metropolitan and the prelates gifts and receiving the same from all the ranking people, from Russians, | VARIOUS FAVORS

Englishmen and Dutchmen, rich merchants and tradesmen, the newly crowned tsar announced various favors. He lowered taxes and restored liberty and property to many distinguished people who had been in prison for nearly 20 years. He executed Ivan's will by freeing all prisoners of war and named certain princes boyars: Dimitrii Khvorostinin, Andrei and Vasilii Ivanovich Shuiskii, Nikita Trubetskoi, Shestunov, the two Kurakins, Thedor Sheremetev and three Godunovs, junior relatives of Irina. He also awarded the hero, Prince Ivan Petrovich Shuiskii, all the revenue from the city of Pskov, which he had saved.

But these personal favors were nothing in comparison to what Theodor showered on his brother-in-law, to whom he gave everything that a subject might have in an autocracy. He not only gave him the old, distinguished rank of equerry, which no one had held in 17 years, but also the title of Privy Grand Boyar, and made him deputy the territories of Kazan and Astrakhan. His unprecedented rank went with unprecedented wealth. Godunov was given, or took for himself, the best lands, estates and the revenue of the Vaga district in the [Northern] Dvina region, and all the beautiful meadows along the Moscow River, with their forests and apiaries, as well as various governmental revenues from Moscow, Ryazan, Tver and Severskii, in addition to his salary.

The result was that these sources, combined with the revenues of his family patrimonies in Vyazma and Dorogobuzh, brought him a yearly income of no less than 800,000 or 900,000 of today's silver rubles, wealth such as no noble had had since Russia's beginnings up till this time, so much that Godunov could personally support upwards of 100,000 troops in the field! He was no longer just a favorite, but in fact the ruler of the country. Although confident of Theodor, Boris still feared enviers and enemies, and tried to astound them with his majesty, so that they would not dare even consider deposing him from such a lofty rank, one that was inaccessible to ordinary ambitious noble courtiers.

These enviers and enemies were indeed overwhelmed, but occasionally would feel embittered and would silently and secretly plot a blow against him, while Godunov, hungry for glory, would zealously press towards his great goal: to justify the tsar's trust, and to earn the people's trust as well, and the gratitude of the nation by his achievements of common benefit. The pentarchy established by Ivan vanished like a shadow, and the old Tsar's Duma remained, where Mstislavskii, Yuriev and Shuiskii now sat in judgment right along side the other boyars, following the ruler's beck and call, for that is what contemporaries called Boris, who, in the eyes of Russia, boldly handled the tiller of state alone. He commanded in the name of the tsar, but acted according to his own mind; he had advisors, but no rivals or comrades.

GODUNOV AS RULER OF THE REALM

At times, Theodor, fatigued by secular splendor, sought rest in piety. He would interrupt his glittering amusements and feasts and in the guise of a humble pilgrim, proceed on foot from monastery to monastery, to the Sergeiev Monastery and other holy cloisters, along with his wife, accompanied by the most eminent boyars and a whole legion of her personal bodyguards. (This magnificence was a novelty invented by Godunov, to implant in the people a greater respect for Irina and her line.)

The administration was ever vigilant now, occupied with important governmental affairs, correcting misuse of power and ensuring internal and external security. As in the happy days of

Prince Ivan Belskii and Adashev, all over Russia, bad deputies, voivodes and judges were replaced by better ones. Punishment was threatened for injustice and officials' salaries were doubled, so that they might live decently without taking bribes. The army was reorganized and sent wherever the honor of arms or the peace of the nation needed restoration. They began with Kazan. Russian blood was still being spilled on the banks of the Volga and rebellion was brewing in the Cheremis lands. Godunov pacified the rebels using his mind more than his sword. He assured them that the new tsar would forget past crimes, and like a good father, show mercy even to the guilty if they were sincerely repentant. The locals sent elders to Moscow and pledged their loyalty. Boris now ordered fortresses be constructed on both the low and high sides of the Volga, at Tsyvilsk, Urzhum, Tsarev-Gorod on the Kokshaga, Sanchursk and other places and settled them with Russians, thereby establishing peace and quiet in this land that had been troublesome to us for so long.

> PACIFICATION
> OF THE REBELLION
> OF THE CHEREMISI

After pacifying Kazan, Godunov completed the conquest of Siberia.* As yet unaware of Yermak's death, but knowing his diminution of power due to illness and hunger, he immediately sent the voivode Ivan Mansurov there with a detachment of musketeers, and others after them later: Vasilii Sukin, Ivan Myasnoi and Danil Chulkov with a considerable number of troops and some artillery. Sukin encountered our Siberian knights, the ataman Matvei Meshcheryak, with the remnants of Yermak's comrades-in-arms on the river Tura.

> SECOND
> SUBJUGATION OF
> SIBERIA
> 1585

"The valiant Cossacks were reanimated with joy," says the chronicler. They had not feared new perils and battles, but only of arriving in their homeland as miserable fugitives with news of the lost conquest. Filled with valor and hope, they returned to

---

* [At this time Siberia denoted a relatively small territory just east of the central Urals. The Cossack Yermak had initiated the Russian conquest of this territory in the time of Ivan the Terrible.]

the mouth of the Tobol, but were unable to take Isker,[*] where old Kuchyum no longer ruled, but the young, hearty Prince Seidyak, who had defeated him. When he had learned of the Cossacks' flight, he gathered Nogai and Siberian Tatars loyal to him and expelled Kuchyum.

When he heard of the new Russian approach, he stationed himself on the banks of the Irtysh with a large number of troops, prepared for a tough fight. The Cossacks proposed that Mansurov sail farther on the Irtysh, despite the autumnal cold and frosts. There, where this river joins the Ob, they disembarked and built a wooden fort. It is written that the Ostyaks were planning to take it and brought their famous Belogorskii idol, or Shaitan. They began to pray to it beneath a tree, but fled in horror when a Russian cannon volley destroyed their revered idol.

The voivodes Sukin and Myasnoi halted on the banks of the Tura and founded today's Tyumen on the site of the town of Chingii. Chulkov, however, either found no resistance or overcame it, and founded Tobolsk, building the first Christian church there in 1587. After informing the voivode Mansurov and the ataman Meshcheryak of this, he linked up with them and defeated Prince Seidyak, who had dared to assault the fort at Tobolsk. Wounded, he was taken prisoner, along with all his baggage train and his wealth. With this victory, which cost the life of Yermak's last voivode, Nikita Meshcheryak, the fall of the Nogai Irtysh kingdom was complete. Isker was abandoned and Tobolsk became the new capital of Siberia.

Another, less reliable tradition, praises not the courage, but the cunning of the voivode Chulkov, but it was hardly praiseworthy. It is written that he learned that Seidyak, his friend, the Kirghiz prince Uraz-Mahmet and Murza-Karacha had departed Isker with 500 troops and were enjoying bird hunting on the Prince's Meadow, near Tobolsk. Supposedly, the voivode invited them over, seized them and sent them to Moscow. The fugitive Kuchyum was still with some bands of Nogai of the Taibugin Ulus[**] in the Barabin steppes, burning settlements and killing people in the Kurdatskaya and

---

*   [Also known as Qashliq and Sibir.]
**   [Ulus: a Tatar camp or settlement.]

Salynskaya volosts* right in the vicinity of the Tobol. To suppress this brigand, the new Siberian voivode, Prince Koltsov-Mosalskii, went deep into the Ishim wilderness near Lake Chili-Kul, and on 1 August 1591 destroyed a large part of his cavalry, captured two of the khan's wives and his son, Abdul-Khair. Wishing to establish tranquility in his new, distant realm, the sovereign offered Kuchyum a salary, towns and districts in Russia, but in vain. He even promised to leave him ruler of the Siberian lands if he would come to Moscow to show his obedience. The prisoner, Prince Abdul-Khair, wrote to his father, praising Theodor's magnanimity: the tsar had given him and Prince Mametkul rich lands, loving and giving life to mortals and mercy to the convicted. Abandoned by his two sons, his Nogai allies and the eminent Chin-Murza (who came over to us with Prince Mametkul's mother), Kuchyum proudly replied to Theodor's offer,

"I did not yield Siberia to Yermak, even though he took it. I want peace, and the banks of the Irtysh."

But Kuchyum's impotent ill will did not hinder the Russians from continuing to consolidate their position in Siberia, building new towns from the Pechora to the Ket and the Tara to facilitate secure communications with Perm and Ufa, which had now been constructed, along with Samara, to restrain the Nogai. In 1592, during the administration of the Tobolsk voivode Prince Theodor Mikhailovich Lobanov-Rostovskii, Pelym, Berezov and Surgut were founded, Tara in 1594, and Narym and Ketskii Ostrog in 1596. These forts were impervious to the primitive Ostaks, Voguls and all the former residents of Kuchyum's uluses who still occasionally contemplated resistance. They were rebellious and did not want to pay tribute. The tsar's letters mention the rebellion of the Pelym prince Ablegirim, whom our voivode was ordered to seize by stealth or force and execute along with his sons and five or six of the principal Vogul rebels.

In addition to troops, musketeers and Cossacks, Godunov sent farmers to Siberia, from Perm, Vyatka, Kargopol and even from the Moscow districts to settle the wilderness and establish agriculture in suitable places. By prudent, well-thought-out

---

* [A volost is a low-level administrative unit subordinate to an uezd, which in turn is subordinate to a district [oblast].]

instructions, he permanently consolidated this important acquisition for Russia without great effort, to the enrichment of the state through new revenues, new commercial possibilities and folk industries. In about 1586 Siberia furnished the treasury with 200,000 sable pelts, 10,000 black fox and 500,000 squirrels, not counting beaver and ermine.

I n foreign policy, Boris followed the principles of the best periods of Ivan's reign, displaying prudence and decisiveness, as well as caution with respect to Russia's aims, dignity and greatness. Two emissaries had been in Moscow for Theodor's coronation: Elizabeth's and Lithuania's.

RELATIONS
WITH ENGLAND AND
LITHUANIA
1584-1587

"Ivan's passing," writes [the English ambassador Jerome] Bowes, "changed my circumstances and placed me in the hands of the chief enemies of England – the boyar Yuriev and the secretary Andrei Shchelkalov, who took control of the Supreme Duma on the first day of the new reign. For a while they would not let me leave my house, fearing a rebellion in Moscow, and Shchelkalov ordered me to say, as a joke, 'The English tsar has died!' Boris Godunov, our benefactor, had not yet been able to gain power at this point."

At the beginning of May, Bowes was told he might return to England; he was presented to the tsar and sent off with honors, gifts and a friendly letter in which Theodor told Elizabeth,

"Although the matter of a wedding and a close alliance with England ended with the death of my father, I sincerely wish your good will, and London merchants will not lose the advantages granted by the last letter of preference."

But Bowes, in an irrational pique, would not accept either the tsar's letter or his gifts; he left them in Kolmogory* and departed Russia with the physician Robert Jacob. Astonished by such impertinence, Theodor sent the herald Bekman to the queen to complain about Bowes. He once again offered her friendship and promised favor for English merchants, provided ours could also freely trade in England. The herald stayed a long time in

---

* [Later, Kholmogory.]

London without seeing the queen; finally he saw her in a garden and handed her his sovereign's letter.

"Why does the new tsar not like me?" asked the queen. "His father was my friend, but Theodor expels our merchants from Russia."

When she heard from Bekman that the tsar was not persecuting them, but complaining that they paid the treasury only half that of other foreign merchants in Russia, Elizabeth wrote a reply to Theodor:

"Beloved brother! It was with inexpressible grief that I learned of the passing of that great sovereign of glorious memory, your father and my very dear friend. In his time bold Englishmen opened a sea lane hitherto unknown to your distant land and enjoyed important rights there. If they have enriched themselves, Russia has been enriched no less; they gratefully praise Ivan's protection. However, I have solace in my sorrow: your herald assured me that the son is worthy of his father and has inherited his principles and friendship towards England. All the more do I regret that my emissary Bowes incurred your displeasure: he is a man experienced in affairs of state, both here and in other countries, and is always modest and prudent. I am surprised, although I believe your complaints, which may be explained by the provocations done him by a member of your Duma Council {the secretary Shchelkalov}, who is clearly partial to German merchants. However, our mutual friendship is unchanged by this unpleasantness. You request free trade for Russian merchants in England. This is something that has never existed, being incompatible with our interests. However, we will not object, provided you issue a new letter of preference giving exclusive trading rights in your country for the company of English merchants that we have established, but not allowing other English merchants to partake of these benefits."

Not very pleased with Elizabeth's reply, nor with Bekman's cold reception in London, but desiring to preserve the beneficial ties with her country, in September 1585 the tsar ordered the English merchant Jerome Horsey to travel to the English queen to explain [our position] more satisfactorily to her, and the choice of such an emissary would show her the sincerity of our favorable disposition [towards her].

"Russia's borders," Theodor wrote Elizabeth via Horsey, "are open for free commerce by all peoples, whether by land or sea. Merchants travel to us from the sultan, the Kaiser, Germany, Spain, France, Lithuania, Persia, Bukhara, Khiva, Shemakha [in Azerbaijan] and many other lands, so that we could manage without the English and will not close the roads to our land to please them. With us, everyone is equal, but you listen to the greedy London merchants and do not wish to equate them with the rest of your subjects. You say that you have never had our tradesmen. This is true, for they trade profitably at home. Consequently they might not travel to England in the future, either. We should be happy to see London merchants in Moscow, provided you do not insist on exclusive rights for them, for such are incompatible with the laws of my country."

Theodor's concept of free trade amazed the English historian Hume, who found in it greater truth and perspicacity than in Elizabeth's ideas of commerce.

But Elizabeth was persistent: she made excuses to Theodor that important affairs of state had interfered with her getting further clarification from Bekman, and that she had only seen him in the garden where she was accustomed to stroll and converse with the people closest to her. The queen no longer demanded a monopoly for the London merchants and only tried to persuade the tsar to exempt them from the payment of onerous duties. After she learned all the circumstances of the Moscow court from Horsey, she wrote especially to the tsaritsa and her brother, calling the former her dearest blood sister and Godunov her own dear friend. She praised the tsaritsa's intellect and virtue, and informed her that out of friendship for her, she would again send her physician Jacob to Moscow; he was especially skilled in curing women's disorders and complications of childbirth. She thanked Godunov for his good will toward the Englishmen and hoped that he, as a man with a penetrating mind, would also be their benefactor in the future, as much as a favor for her as for the genuine benefit of Russia.

Thus did Elizabeth scheme, and not without results. The tsaritsa received her flattering letter with amicable feelings, and Godunov read his with great pleasure. In 1587 he gave the English the right to trade without duties (thereby depriving the treasury of more than 2,000 pounds Sterling annually), but with the obligations:

1) not to import foreign products to us;

2) not to dispatch buyers to various cities, but to exchange goods locally;

3) not to sell anything at retail, but only wholesale: cloth, damask, velvet by the bale, wine by the cask, etc.;

4) not to send their people to England by land without informing the sovereign;

5) in lawsuits with Russians, to rely on the tsar's treasurers and the secretary for embassies.

The ambitious Boris did not hesitate to inform the queen that it was he who had gained these rights for the London merchants; he perceived her favor and wished always to guard them with his own hand, in hopes that they would conduct themselves quietly, honorably and without deceit, and would not interfere with trading by Spaniards, French, Germans or other Englishmen trading in our harbors and cities, "for the ocean lanes belong to God, and are universal and unbounded." We see here for the first time a Russian noble in correspondence with a foreign monarch, something the cautious policies of the tsars had heretofore not tolerated.

At the same time, Godunov received a document from Elizabeth's ministers concerning various immoderate demands of their merchants; he ordered the secretary Shchelkalov to write in reply that everything possible had already been done for England, that nothing further would be, that it was shameful to trouble such a great man with empty words, and that it would be improper for the tsar's brother-in-law, an eminent boyar of the great state of Russia, to personally reply to such an indiscreet document. While valuing highly the good will of the famous queen, and sensitive to her charms, there were limits on Godunov's attempts to please her. The English were trying to get rid of Shchelkalov, whom they hated, but Boris respected his experience and abilities; he entrusted him with all foreign affairs and gave him the new title of privy secretary.

Relations with Lithuania were much more important and more difficult for us. Stefan [Batory], as if he had a premonition of his approaching death, was impatient to finish what he had started: he wanted to increase his state's power by subjugating Russia, and considered Livonia only a down payment and peace merely a respite; he dreamt of reestablishing Vitovt's old boundaries on the banks of the Ugra. When [Lew] Sapieha, his emissary in Moscow, learned of Ivan's death, he told the boyars that in the absence of new instructions from his king, he would be unable to see the new tsar or discuss affairs with them. After waiting three months for his instructions, he was presented to Theodor on 22 June, and disclosed to him the secret, supposedly as a token of his sincere good will, that the sultan [Mehmet III] intended to attack Russia. That is, Batory wanted to frighten Theodor and make him pliable with regard to Lithuania. During this lavish but routine audience, the tsar was sitting on the throne with his orb and scepter. Next to him stood his bodyguards in white uniforms with gold chains. Only Godunov was next to the throne – all the other nobles sat farther away. The emissary was shown respect, but not kindness; Theodor did not invite him to dine, and he left for his lodgings in anger and would not admit an official with dishes from the tsar's table.

When their negotiations began, Sapieha demanded that Theodor give the king 120,000 gold pieces for our prisoners, that he free the Lithuanian prisoners without payment, satisfy all complaints of his subjects against the Russians and not call himself prince of Livonia in state papers, if he did not want war. Batory believed that Ivan's death had nullified the Zapolskii treaty.[*] Sapieha was told that Theodor, moved solely by humanitarian feelings, had already freed 900 prisoners of war on the day of his coronation: Poles, Hungarians and Germans, and that we expected a similar Christian deed of Stefan. Lithuania's justified complaints would not go unsatisfied, but Ivan's son had inherited the state and also his father's title, which included of Livonia. As a result of many discussions, Sapieha concluded a truce with the boyars, for only 10 months. The tsar sent the boyar prince Thedor Mikhailovich

PLOT AGAINST
GODUNOV

---

[*] [The Yam-Zapolskii Treaty, one of the diplomatic actions that concluded the Livonian War of 1558-1583.]

Troekurov and the Duma noble Mikhail Beznin to Warsaw to persuade the king to make a genuine peace. However, Stefan wanted war more than ever and expected success, since he knew what was going on in Moscow, and had additional malicious insinuations.

Godunov was trying to gain the gratitude of the nation through energetic and sagacious governance, and with the kindly good will of the principal boyars, ruled peacefully for 16 or 17 months. He scorned ill-wishers, since he had the sovereign's heart in his hand, and gained the special friendship of two eminent nobles, Nikita Romanovich Yuriev and Prince Ivan Theodorovich Mstislavskii. He ruled alone, but consulted with them, thereby gratifying their moderate ambitions. This happy bond was broken with Yuriev's death. The weak-willed Prince Mstislavskii, although called Boris's father [as an endearment], was deceived by Boris's enemies: the Shuiskiis, Vorotynskiis and Golovins. He joined them, and if we are to believe the chronicler, became a participant in a vile plot: they wanted him to invite Boris to a feast and deliver him into the arms of his assassins! That is what Godunov's frightened friends told him when they learned of the evil plot, and that is what Godunov told the tsar. It is not known whether there was a legal investigation or inquiry; we only know that Prince Ivan Mstislavskii was involuntarily tonsured and exiled to the Kirillovskii Cloister, while the Vorotynskiis and Golovins were sent to remote places and others were imprisoned. The Shuiskiis were left untouched, either because charges could not be brought, or else out of respect for the intercession of the metropolitan, who had friendly ties with them. Overall, not a single man was executed. Perhaps Godunov feared a bloodbath would recall Ivan's hated reign; perhaps, and more likely, he punished only those who personally wished him ill and had spread rumors of an imaginary criminal plot. Even Mstislavskii's son, Prince Theodor Ivanovich, was left in the Duma as the first, or senior boyar.

Despite such moderate punishment of real or imagined crimes, the capital and court were frightened. Relatives and friends of those disgraced feared further vengeance, and the distinguished official Mikhailo Golovin abandoned his patrimony in Medyn and went over to Batory. This seemed to vindicate Godunov, since this fugitive-traitor was favorably received in Lithuania and advised the king not to make peace with Russia, assuring him that Moscow and Russia were in anarchy and disorder because of dimwitted Theodor and dissension amongst the nobles. He said that the king had only to march in and take anything he pleased in our miserable, orphaned country, where no one wanted to fight for or serve their sovereign. Batory believed him, and after coldly receiving Moscow's emissaries, told them that he might condescend to give us a truce for 10 years if we would return Novgorod, Pskov, Luki, Smolensk and the Severskii lands. He added, "Theodor's father did not care to know me, but he dealt with me. The son will do likewise."

The emissaries tried to demonstrate the absurdity of the king's demands, but he would not listen to them. They then employed cunning: firstly, they artfully leaked that Mikhailo Golovin was a spy sent to Stefan by the boyars, and secondly, they proposed to the crown nobles and the Lithuanian nobles a close alliance between their country and Russia in order to destroy the Crimean khan. Both schemes were effective. In Warsaw, they stopped believing Golovin, judging that eminent Russians might naturally have left their homeland during Ioann's cruel reign, but not during charitable Theodor's. They figured that this supposed refugee was spreading money around, doubtless given him from the tsar's treasury to bribe people, and was absurdly deprecating Russia, which was supposedly going to fall at Stefan's feet, and thereby expose its pretensions. The king had been seduced by David Belskii and lost many troops beneath terrible Pskov and must not become the victim of gullibility again. He was getting old and sudden death might snatch away the sword from this indefatigable warrior, even if he were victorious. The noisy Sejm* would quarrel over the choice of Stefan's successor while a powerful enemy laid waste to Lithuania. It would be better, therefore to take advantage of Theodor's known weakness to establish with the boyars a sincere, permanent alliance between the two states, one that was not dependent on the life or death of their monarchs. This opinion gained the upper hand in the King's Council, so that

---

* [The Polish parliament.]

not only did Troekurov and Beznin return to Moscow with a new truce document, good for two years, but the king also sent his extraordinary emissary with a proposal so unexpected that the tsar's council was astounded.

This emissary was the distinguished Mikhailo Garaburda, who had been long known and welcome in the Moscow court because of his complete knowledge of our language, his flexible mind, his courtliness and even more for his ardor for the Greek faith. He handed the boyars a pacific, flattering letter from the king's nobles, and told them in secret conversation,

"I have the complete trust of my sovereign, our clergy and all the men of the King's Duma and the Lithuanian Duma. I declare that we sincerely want an indissoluble alliance with your country and are eager to stand shoulder-to-shoulder with you against all mutual enemies. To that end we shall forget all vain disputes over cities and volosts that neither we nor you would yield without bloodshed. Let each rule forever that which it rules now! We demand nothing, and neither should you. Hear me further: we and you are brothers of a single Slavic tribe, and also to some extent of the same faith – why should we not have a single ruler? May God prolong the years of both monarchs – but they are mortal. In the event of Stefan's death, we are prepared to join the Grand Principality of Lithuania and Poland to Theodor's state (so that Krakow would be considered equal to Moscow, and Vilnius to Novgorod), and in the event of Theodor's death, you would be obliged to acknowledge Stefan as the sovereign of all Russia. This would be the most reliable method – and there is no other – to establish peace and a firm, genuine friendship between our countries."

The boyars reported to the tsar and after formally notifying the Duma and eminent clergy gave the following reply,

"We do not even allow ourselves to think of the death of our great autocrat; we would not even want to speculate on Stefan's. Your custom is different, and hardly praiseworthy. Is it proper for an emissary to come to a foreign land to speak of the death of his monarch? Eschew this impropriety and we shall declare our sovereign's agreement to a permanent peace."

However, Garaburda did not want to hear of this without a treaty unifying the two powers, and added,

"Otherwise, give us both Novgorod and Pskov, for Stefan is not satisfied with Smolensk and the Severskii district."

"Our sovereign," the boyars told him, "would not even give you shingles for a roof. We can manage without a peace. Russia is not old [and feeble] now – you should guard not just Livonia and Polotsk against its hand, but Vilnius as well!"

Expressing his regret that our nobles and churchmen would not listen to reason with regard to this great and good idea, Garaburda took his leave of the tsar, and later of the boyars, who had especially invited him to a reception at the shoreline hall, where they seated him on a bench (where Boris had taken the fourth seat, having yielded precedence to the princes Mstislavskii, Ivan Petrovich Shuiskii and Dimitrii Ivanovich Godunov). They gave him their hands and a respectful letter for the king's nobles, saying, "You have been amongst us for important matters, but accomplished nothing. The tsar hates bloodshed and will communicate with your king through his own emissary." Garaburda departed on 30 April and Prince Troekurov was again dispatched to Stefan on 28 June with new instructions.

There is no doubt that Batory would have immediately drawn his sword against Russia had not the noble pans, especially the Lithuanian ones, who feared the destruction of their land, resisted his love of glory and threatened the king with the Sejm's refusal to provide men and money. Seduced by his successes in war against Ivan, he was only dealing with us for appearances' sake and to keep his nobles happy. Seemingly wanting peace, he had absurdly proposed to the Tsar's Duma to hand over Russia to him on Theodor's death, while at the same time requesting money from the Pope in order to march on Moscow, to conquer our land for himself, and our Church for Rome. The Jesuit Antonio [Possevino] was his eager intermediary (for he hated Russians because of the failure of his embassy to Ivan), and Sixtus V promised to give Stefan 25,000 scudi a month for such a great enterprise! In this frame of mind, Stefan would not think of following Theodor's example of charity. He praised Theodor's unselfish release of the

Lithuanian prisoners, but demanded immoderate ransom for ours. He took 54,000 rubles from the tsar and freed some, but kept the most eminent, and did not want to return the silver he had taken from Muscovite merchants in Lithuania who were travelling to Greece with alms for the memory of Ivan's son, nor did he control his voivodes who were sending gangs of brigands from Livonia, Vitebsk and other places into the districts of Pskov, Velikie Luki and Chernigov. In brief, he was openly testing the patience of Russia in order to provoke a war.

Troekurov found Stefan in Grodno and handed his pans the letter from our boyars. After reading it, the pans expressed their strong displeasure, and said,

"Desiring tranquility, in spite of our king, we proposed conditions of sincere brotherhood to you, consonant with the welfare of both countries, but you, without replying to this important proposal, write that it would please the tsar to gratify the king with peace if we were to yield you Kiev, Livonia and everything that had been an ancient Russia possession! That is, we would feed the Muscovite nobles bread, and the Muscovite nobles would toss us a stone! What is the cause of such hauteur? Do we really not know of the current pitiable condition of your country? You have a tsar, but what sort? He can barely breathe and is childless – he can only pray. Your boyars are in confusion, your people in unrest, your state in disorder and your army lacks spirit and good voivodes.

"We know that you are in secret contact with the German emperor's brother. What is your intention? How will you find a protector in the Kaiser when he cannot even protect himself? Many European sovereigns now have their sights on you. The sultan demands Astrakhan and Kazan; the khan is in Russia's bowels with fire and sword; the Cheremis people are in rebellion. Where are your boyars' wits? Their homeland is in bad shape and yet they scorn our good will and insist that the tsar is ready to stand against all enemies. We shall see. Up till now we have restrained Stefan from fulfilling the oath he made when he took the throne, an oath to take from Russia all the Lithuanian territory it had conquered since the time of Vitovt. We do not now wish to irritate him by repeating your idle words, rather, we shall say, 'March on Russia, to the banks of the Ugra. There is our gold; here, take our arms and heads!'"

Prince Troekurov had listened coolly, and now replied with some heat,

"It is not we, but you, noble pans, who engage in idle talk that is impudent and absurd! You call a godsent reign a misfortune and a calamity for Russia. You see the wrath of God where we seen only Heaven's favor. How can the future be known to mortals? You have not conversed with the Most High. Woe to him who maligns our monarch. We have a tsar sound in mind and body, wise and fortunate, and worthy of his great forebears. Just as Theodor's father, grandfather and great grandfather, so does he judge his people and develop our country. He loves tranquility, but is ready to defeat enemies. He has an army the like of which has never before existed in Russia; he is gracious to his people and rewards them generously from his treasury. There are valiant voivodes, eager of the glory of dying for their homeland.

"Theodor knows how to pray, and thanks to his divine faith, the Lord will surely grant him victory, and peace, prosperity and beloved sons, so that the line of St. Vladimir will rule throughout the ages. Let traitors broadcast their shameless lies about dissension among our nobles and disorder in our country: the wind will blow these calumniators away. We do not want to resemble you in brazenness, and in truth we shall be silent about what we see in Lithuania and Poland, for we were not sent to cause dissension."

Troekurov further stated that the Russian nobles know only their own tsar and do not deal with foreign princes; that the sultan had not demanded Astrakhan or Kazan, but had requested our friendship; and that the khan, recalling the year 1572 and Prince Mikhail Vorotynskii, would not dare even to look at our Ukraine.* He said that Russia was everywhere at quiet and we ruled peacefully even in remote Siberia – on the Konda, in the Pelym state, in the land of the Pega Kalmyks and on the Ob, where 94 towns were paying us tribute. Our emissary concluded with these words,

---

*   [The prince routed a 120,000-man Tatar army at Molodi.]

"So why do you call Russia troubled? We desire peace, but we will not buy it. But do you wish war? Go to it! Do you wish good relations? Then speak up!"

They began negotiations. The tsar agreed not to ask for Kiev, Volhynia or Podolia. For a peace he only wanted Livonia, or at any rate Derpt,* Neuhaus, Atsel, Kirempe, Marienburg and Tarvastu.

"Why such magnanimity?" the pans asked sarcastically. "We authorize you to seek all of Lithuania – conquer it and take it!"

Once again they suggested a permanent union of both powers, and that to this end, Moscow's nobles and the king's should meet at the border. However, Troekurov explained to them that the tsar could not decide such an important matter without a general Duma of the Land [Zemskaya Duma], and that it would take some time to summon all the government people to Moscow from Novgorod, Kazan, Astrakhan and Siberia – and that this would require a longer truce.

"There is no tradition in Russia of consulting with the land," the pans rejoined. "The tsar thinks of something, the boyars say *Da*, and the deed is done."

They argued for several days and established a truce for two more months (from 3 June to August 1588), during which time the grand emissaries of both sides were to meet at the river Ivat, between Orsha and Smolensk to reach an agreement on:

"1) how the tsar would live in fraternal affection with Stefan;

2) how their countries would be unified in the event of the death of Theodor or Stefan; and

3) which cities Lithuania and Russia would indisputably rule, if they did not want to unify."

Although the third item removed the force of the second, and although in fact we had yielded nothing and had not harmed our honor or national security with these conditions, yet this agreement was signed by Troekurov under duress when the pans gave him leave to depart. We wanted to prolong things in hopes of the

* [Also known as Dorpat or Tartu.]

future, and could see the strong sentiment for peace in our enemy's land. The archbishop of Gniezdo himself, in a conversation with an official of the tsar (Novosiltsov, who had been sent to Vienna), told him that Russia had but one irreconcilable enemy in Lithuania and Poland: Batory, who had not long to live. A dangerous sore had been found on his leg and his doctors were afraid to treat it lest they hasten his death. Stefan was unloved by the people because of his limitless love of glory and his bad treatment of his wife. The archbishop also said that the nobles and the courtiers would prefer to be under Theodor's hand because they knew of this Christian monarch's virtue, the intellect and kindness of the tsaritsa and the wisdom and great merit of the ruler, Boris Theodorovich Godunov.

COMPARISON OF GODUNOV WITH ADASHEV

"This eminent man," continued the archbishop, "fed and comforted our prisoners of war when they were still in confinement, and after he released them, he graciously entertained them in his palace and gave each of them cloth and money. His fame has spread everywhere. You are fortunate to have now a ruler like Aleksei Adashev, that great man who administered Russia [early in] Ivan's reign."

Not yet comfortable with such a comparison, Novosiltsov assured him that Godunov surpassed Adashev in his distinguished rank and in the profundity of his intellect. To summarize, sound policy obliged us to put off war as long as possible. Stefan, still sound in mind and body as he sent off Troekurov, was stately and proud in his greeting, and with a stern look, took his hand and instructed him to convey his salutations to Theodor. With this he concluded his efforts with regard to Russia, which hated and honored him, for he, while hostile to us, was fulfilling those legitimate duties prescribed to a sovereign for the benefit of his country, and he, better than the gullible pans, knew the impossibility of peace and the difficulty of uniting their kingdom with the Muscovite state. Batory had already set the date for the Sejm in Warsaw to assure the future destiny of the kingdom by the timely selection of his successor; with sincerity and eloquence he fanned patriotism into their hearts, love of glory and finally wrested their consent for war with Russia. However, fate did not favor the plans of this great man, as we shall see in the next chapter.

In this final intercourse with Batory, our government had another, secret goal: it wished to repatriate the exiles and refugees from Ivan's reign, less out of charity than for the benefit of the nation. Hearing that some of them wanted to return to Russia, but were afraid, the tsar sent them letters of leniency, especially to Prince Gavrilo Cherkasskii, Timothei Teterin, Murza, Kupkeev, Devyat Kashkarov, and even to the traitor David Belskii (a relative of Godunov by marriage), promising them amnesty, rank and salary if they would appear in Moscow, repentant and eager to provide us with all requisite knowledge of the internal conditions in Lithuania, and the goals and capabilities of its policies. Theodor forgave all the fugitives, except for the unfortunate Kurbskii (it is likely he was no longer among the living), and except for the recent turncoat, Mikhail Golovin. Batory had found out many secrets about Russia from him, and also had his own spies among Lithuanian merchants, which is why Theodor had ordered them to do business only in Smolensk and had forbidden them to travel to Moscow.

Striving to put off a breach with Lithuania, but expecting it momentarily, the tsar showed all the more conciliation and indulgence with regard to relations with the Swedish

TRUCE WITH THE SWEDES

king, so as not to suddenly have two enemies. However, he did not forget Russia's dignity and felt the necessity to atone for its shame by the return of the ancient territories that had been stolen by the Swedes – he was only delaying war until a more convenient time. When the Estonian deputy De la Gardie* learned of Ioann's death, he asked the Novgorod voivode Prince Vasilii Thedorovich Shuiskii-Skopin if we intended to adhere to the treaty concluded on the banks of the Plyussa, and would our emissaries be coming to Stockholm to discuss terms for a lasting peace? Yet in his letter, as if he were trying to irritate the tsar, he called the king Grand Prince of the Izherskaya and Shelonskaya Pyatinas in Russia**.

He was told in reply that Russia had never heard of a Swedish grand prince of the Shelonskaya Pyatina, and that he (De la Gardie) might only excuse himself by reason of ignorance of national cus-

---

*   [Field Marshal and Count Jacob Pontusson De la Gardie, 1583-1652.]
** [A pyatina was an old territorial division in the Novgorod area.]

toms, being a foreigner and a stranger, far from the court and the affairs of the state council. The tsar was fulfilling the terms of his father's treaty, he was not fond of the calamities of war, and he was expecting the Swedish emissaries, while being unable to send his own to Stockholm. Sharp words led to invective. In a new letter to Shuiskii, De la Gardie spoke of the ancient ignorance and irrational pride of the Russians, who had still not been brought to reason by the deleterious consequences thereof.

"Know," he wrote, "that I have not been called a foreigner in the very laudable kingdom of Sweden. It is true that I have often been absent from the court, but only to teach you humility. I believe you have not forgotten how often my banners have met with yours, that is, how often you have taken yours and fled before me."

The response to this impropriety was a scornful silence. More prudent and praiseworthy, Theodor entered into personal relations with King Johan [III]. In a letter to the tsar, Johan proposed to us not to renew ruinous bloodshed, using the following expression,

"Your father, tearing up his own land and feeding on the blood of his subjects, was an evil neighbor both for us and for all other monarchs."

Theodor returned this letter to the king, ordering his herald to tell him that he should not tell a son such things about his father! Words did not interfere with deeds, however. On 25 October 1585 near Narva at the mouth of the Plyussa, the boyar Prince Theodor Dimitrievich Shestunov and the court noble Ignatii Tatishchev met with Klas Tott, De la Gardie and other distinguished Swedish officials. The Swedes demanded Novgorod and Pskov, and we, the cities they had taken, and all of Estonia, as well as 700,000 rubles. These demands were softened and both sides yielded somewhat, but an agreement could not be reached. The Swedes threatened us with an alliance with Batory and the hiring of 100,000 mercenaries. We menaced them with the strength of Russia alone, adding,

"Unlike you, we do not need to mortgage our cities and hire mercenaries; we shall act with our own arms and heads." The last of our conditions for peace, which were rejected by the Swedes, was that the king return Ivangorod, Yam and Koporye to us for 10,000 rubles, or 20,000 Hungarian chervontsy. They said, "Let there be war!"

But then they had second thoughts, and in December 1585 established a truce for four years without any conditions except the obligation to have emissaries of both sides meet again in August 1586 to reach an agreement on a permanent peace. During these negotiations, the haughty De la Gardie drowned in the Narova.

T wo more European powers began relations with Theodor at this time: Austria and Denmark. After notifying Rudolf of his coronation, the tsar proposed friendship and free trade between both countries. The Muscovite

EMBASSY
TO
AUSTRIA

official Novosiltsov was honored in Prague, where the emperor lived. Not only the Austrian ministers, but also the Roman legate and the Spanish and Venetian emissaries gave dinners for him. They quizzed him on the East and North, about Persia, the Caspian lands and Siberia. They praised the might of the tsar and the intelligence of his envoy (who really was intelligent, as evidenced by his papers). He reported to the Boyars' Duma that Rudolf was more concerned with his splendid stables than with administration; he yielded his burdensome power to the wise noble, Adam Dietrichstein.

The emperor, with a scanty treasury, was not ashamed to pay tribute to the sultan if only to delay temporarily the threat of the Ottoman sword. Europe's situation was pitiable: Austria was poverty-stricken during peacetime, and France during a civil war. Philip II, suspecting his son Carlos of plotting against his life, was considering declaring Ernest, the Kaiser's brother, the Spanish successor. In these reports, Novosiltsov, carrying out the instructions of the curious Godunov, also described aspects of civic life, progress in public education and useful or agreeable institutions that he had seen and that were unknown in Russia, including gardens and hothouses. The Austrian ministers secretly disclosed to him their desire to establish an alliance with Russia to depose Batory and divide up his kingdom. This plan was too audacious for weak Rudolf, however, and remained inoperative. The emperor intended to send a special noble to the tsar, but after sending just a polite letter to Theodor with Novosiltsov, failed to keep his word.

<table>
<tr><td>RESUMPTION
OF FRIENDSHIP WITH
DENMARK</td></tr>
</table>

King Frederik of Denmark had been openly hostile to Ivan, but hastened to assure the new tsar of his good wishes. He sent an eminent official to Moscow with a letter to him stating that Theodor's universal reputation for Christian justice and sentiment had given him hopes of putting an end to all the old unpleasantness and renew amicable governmental and commercial ties with Russia. These ties were in fact renewed and Denmark no longer schemed against our northern sea trade; it merely wished to participate in its profits.

Russia was at peace with Christian Europe, at least temporarily, and tranquil internally, and although not frightened, kept a constant eye on the Taurid. Mahmet-Girei, while promising alliances with both the tsar and with Lithuania, had been

<table>
<tr><td>CRIMEAN
AFFAIRS</td></tr>
</table>

in secret contact with the Cheremisi and was brazenly sending gangs of brigands into our southeastern marches. He was overthrown by his brother, Islam-Girei, who had come from Constantinople with a Janissary unit and the title of khan. Having succeeded to the throne and the policies of his predecessor by murder, Islam wrote to Theodor,

"Your father purchased peace with us for 10,000 rubles as well as valuable furs, which you sent to my brother. Give us still more and we shall crush the Lithuanian enemy. We shall assault their land from one side, the sultan from another, the Nogai from the third and your legions from the fourth."

The Crimean gangs, together with those from Azov and the Kazyev ulus* of the Nogai were currently torching settlements in the Belyov, Kozelsk, Vorotynsk, Meshchovsk and Mosalsk uezds. The Duma noble Mikhailo Beznin engaged them near Sloboda Monasterskaya on the banks of the Oka with light cavalry. He soundly defeated them, took prisoners and received a gold medal from the tsar for his valor. The Crimeans, numbering 30,000 to 40,000 twice more made depredations in the Ukraine: in June 1587 they captured and burned Kropivna. Moscow's voivodes struck at them and pursued them, following the ashes and blood. They did

---

* [Ulus: a Tartar camp or settlement.]

not leave the banks of the Oka, staying in Tula and Serpukhov to await the khan himself.

To us, the Taurid seemed like a poisonous reptile, which, although dying, could still deliver a lethal bite: it was spewing fire and death in our borderlands, despite the exhaustion and misery of which it was now a victim. Mahmet-Girei's sons Saidet and Murat, who had been expelled by their uncle in 1585, returned with 15,000 Nogai, dethroned Islam-Girei, seized his wife and treasury and laid waste to all the uluses. Saidet declared himself khan, but Islam, who had fled to Kaffa, once again chased out his nephews, overcoming them with 4,000 of the sultan's troops in a bloody battle. They killed many princes and mirzas,* whom they accused of treason. They surrounded themselves with Turks, whom they permitted to rape, kill and plunder. Taking advantage of the circumstances, the tsar offered asylum to the exiles Saidet and Murat: he permitted the former to wander with his Nogai bands in the vicinity of Astrakhan; he summoned the latter to Moscow. There the tsar honored him and got an oath of allegiance, then sent him with two voivodes to Astrakhan, where he was obliged to become an instrument of our policy, and where he was received as a distinguished sovereign prince. His troops remained under arms: their cannons roared in fortresses and harbors, *they beat on tocsins and tambourines, they sounded trumpets and pipes.* In this ancient city, filled with Eastern merchants, Murat appeared in tsarish splendor; he formed a magnificent court and formally received neighboring princes and their emissaries. In his hand he had a charter with a golden seal from Theodor and called himself ruler of four rivers: the Don, the Volga, the Yaik [Ural] and the Terek, and of all free Cossacks and men of the uluses. He boasted of crushing Islam and humbling the sultan, and said,

"By the grace and friendship of the Muscovite tsar, we shall be rulers: my brother of the Crimea, and I of Astrakhan. That is why the great Russian people have done me this service."

That is what he told his coreligionists, but he secretly tried to persuade the voivode of Astrakhan, Prince Thedor Mikhailovich Lobanov-Rostovskii, to exempt him from strict and obvious

---

* [Mirza: a Tatar aristocratic title, and incidentally the origin of the second component of Karamzin's surname.]

supervision, so that the Nogai and Crimeans would have more trust in him and not view him as a Muscovite pawn – for Lobanov and the other voivodes, while preserving decorum, where observing all of Murat's movements. Glorying in the symbols of external respect, he would ride to the mosque through ranks of numerous musketeers, but was unable to talk to anyone without witnesses being present. Meanwhile, he served us diligently: he persuaded the Nogai to be quiet and obedient, assuring them that the tsar had built cities on the Samara and the Ufa rivers solely for their safety and to restrain predatory Cossacks. He threatened the rebellious Prince Yakshisat of that horde with fire and sword for his enmity towards Russia. Together with his brother Saidet, he prepared to strike at the Taurid with the Nogai, Cossacks and Circassians, awaiting only the Theodor's permission, cannons and 10,000 musketeers promised for this undertaking.

But the tsar dallied. He feared Stefan far more than he did Prince Islam. Having no faith in peace with the former, he wrote to Murat in February 1587,

"A propitious time to conquer the Taurid has not yet come. We must first pacify another, stronger foe. Make ready to march on Vilnius with your loyal Nogai and Cossacks; there you will join up with me, and when we will have dealt with my Lithuanian enemy, then we shall easily destroy yours. We shall send our greetings to Saidet-Girei, khan of the Crimean uluses."

At the same time, the sovereign instructed Islam:

"Khan Saidet-Girei, Prince Murat and the Nogai, Circassian, Shavkal,* Tyumen and mountain region princes are all entreating us for permission to dethrone you. I am still restraining them temporarily; I still could forget your brigandage if you sincerely intend to provide troops to attack Lithuania when the truce expires. Although we concluded it with a bloodthirsty ruler, we are still keeping our word and our agreements. I myself will lead my army from Smolensk to Vilnius; you are to march with your main force on Volhynia, Galicia and farther. I have ordered another army to march on Putivl, where it will join with our Severskie forces to lay

---

* [Shavkal or shamkal was a ruler's title in Daghestan. Karamzin seems to use the term ambiguously to refer to their territory, their title or as a personal name.]

siege to Kiev. They will have my Astrakhan army on their right, which is also to invade Lithuania with Prince Murat. You have experienced bad consequences from your invasions of Russia – now experience the good fortune of an alliance with it."

Theodor foresaw that after Saidet overthrew Islam, like him, he would become another brigand ataman for us, and that we would have only exchanged one barbarian for another, so he tempted Mahmet-Girei's sons with the Crimean khanate, and he used them to frighten the khan so as to have more forces for his war with Batory. This cunning was not without effect: Islam, fearing his nephews, tried to assure him that the Crimean invasions of Russia had been perpetrated by certain willful mirzas, who had been punished without mercy. He said that he was waiting for Moscow's emissary with a sworn document and would invade Lithuania with all his forces. Islam in fact did announce to his uluses that for the time being it was better to pillage Stefan's lands than Theodor's!

Preoccupied with Batory, Sweden and the Taurid, we also saw danger from a different direction, and since we were neighbors with a power that was frightening all of Europe, we certainly did not need the Austrian court's warning to expect a threat from the banks of the Bosporus. The sultan's trophies in our hands, Suleiman's schemes on Astrakhan and the flight and destruction of Selim's army in the Caspian wastes could not remain without consequences. All the stratagems of Moscow's policies had to be directed so as to delay the beginning of the unavoidable, terrible struggle until a time more propitious for Russia. We needed to strengthen ourselves with external acquisitions and internal development before entering into a deadly fight with the destroyers of the Byzantine Empire.

Thus did Ivan the Great,[*] his son and grandson act. Sometimes they had friendly sultans to restrain both the Crimea and Lithuania: this is what Theodor also wanted when in July 1584 he sent his envoy Blagov to Constantinople to inform the sultan of his accession to the throne. He was to

EMBASSY TO CONSTANTINOPLE

_____

[*]   [Ivan III, 1440-1505.]

explain Russia's peace-loving policy with respect to Turkey and to persuade Murad to have friendly ties with us.

"Our great-grandfathers {Bayazet and Ivan}," Theodor wrote to the sultan, "and grandfathers {Vasilii [III] and Suleiman} and our fathers {Ivan and Selim} called each other brothers and had friendly correspondence with each other. Let there be friendship between us as well. Russia is open to your merchants, without any restriction on goods and without duties. We request no more than that this be mutual."

However, the envoy was ordered to tell Murad's pasha the following:

"We know that you have complained about the depredations of the Terek Cossacks, who are disrupting your communications between Constantinople and Derbent, where the sultan now rules after taking it from the Persian Shah. Ivan, our sovereign's father, founded a stronghold on the Terek for the safety of the Circassian prince Temryuk, but pulled out his troops to please Selim. Since that time, Volga Cossacks have lived there, disgraced fugitives, without our sovereign's consent. You also complain of the oppression of the Mohammedan faith in Russia, but whom are we oppressing? In the heart of Moscow's territories, in Kasimov, stand mosques and Moslem monuments – to the ruler Shig-Alei and Prince Kaibula. Sain-Bulat (now Simeon), the Grand Duke of Tver, accepted the Christian faith voluntarily, and in his place Mustafalei, a Moslem and son of Kaibula, was made ruler of Kasimov. No, we have never, and do not now, persecute those of other faiths in any way."

Blagov did not have instructions to enter into further discussion. He was honored in Constantinople on a level with the Wallachian sovereign, and more than the Venetian emissary. With some difficulty he convinced Murad to send his own official to Moscow. The pashas told him,

"The sultan is a great autocrat and his emissaries travel only to eminent monarchs: to the Kaiser and to the kings of France, Spain and England since they have important state dealings with him and send him funds, or rich tribute, but with you we have only commercial dealings." Blagov replied,

"The sultan is great among Moslem sovereigns; the tsar is great among the Christian. We do not send funds or tribute to anyone. Trade is important to nations: they may also deal with other important matters. But if the sultan does not send an eminent official to Moscow with me, then his emissaries would never see the tsar's eyes."

The sultan ordered Blagov to be dressed in a velvet caftan with gold trim, and that his official, Adziya Ibrahim travel with him to Moscow. The official was met on the banks of the Don by Russian voivodes who had been sent to assure his safe journey. In December 1585, after handing the sultan's letter to Theodor, Ibrahim declined any negotiations with boyars, but [in his letter] the sultan, calling Theodor *King of Moscow* expressed to him his gratitude for his kind wish to be a friend to the Ottoman Empire, confirmed free trade for our merchants in Azov and in Eastern style, praised the blessings of peace. However, he demanded, as proof of sincere friendship that the tsar hand over to Ibrahim the traitor Murat, Mahmet-Girei's son and immediately suppress the Don ataman Kishkin, a criminal brigand on the Azov border. Theodor could see that the policy of the Constantinople court had not changed with regard to Russia, that the sultan was not thinking of concluding a friendly treaty with him and that he just wanted free trade between both powers until the first opportunity to declare himself our enemy. The tsar sent Ibrahim off with the reply that the depredations on the Don were more due to Lithuanian Cossacks than Russian, that the ataman Kishkin had been summoned to Moscow and his comrades ordered not to menace the people of Azov, and that Mahmet-Girei's son, who was our servitor and vassal, would be ordered to travel to the sultan with the tsar's new emissary. However, in the course of the next six years we sent no one to Constantinople and even operated openly against the Ottoman Empire.

On the very day of Ibrahim's send-off (5 October 1586), the sovereign formally entered into an obligation that might oblige him to become quite hostile to the sultan. We have not mentioned Georgia for about a century. In

> IBERIAN
> OR GEORGIAN RULER
> A RUSSIAN SUBJECT

this unhappy land, oppressed by the Turks and the Persians, Prince Alexander ruled; he had sent to Moscow a Circassian priest who was both a monk and a horseman; he tearfully implored Theodor to take ancient and renowned [Caucasian] Iberia under his supreme hand, saying,

"Terrible times have come for Christendom; times foreseen by many divinely inspired men. We, of the same faith as our brother Russians, groan under the infidels. You alone, Orthodox monarch, can save our lives and our souls. I kowtow* to the ground before you, with all my people. Let us be yours, for ever and ever!"

Russia was being offered, plaintively and persuasively, a new realm, one that had been invincible before the ancient militaristic Persians and Macedonians, but gloriously conquered by Pompey. It was a dangerous gift, but we took it! With dominion on the banks of the Kura,** we had placed ourselves between two powerful warring powers. The Turks now controlled western Iberia and were disputing the eastern part with the Shah, who was demanding tribute from Kakhetia, where Alexander was ruling, and from Kartaliniya, where his brother-in-law, Prince Simeon, had dominion. But the matter was more one of our honor and reputation than of substantive rule in places so remote and barely accessible to Russia, so that Theodor, having declared himself supreme ruler of Georgia, still did not know the way to this land. Alexander offered to build him a stronghold on the Terek and sent about 12,000 troops against the mutinous prince of Daghestan, Prince Shavkal (or Shamkal), to conquer his capital, Tarki, and from the shores of the Caspian Sea to open communications with Iberia through the district of his tributary, the princeling Safurskii. This would have taken considerable time and preparation – they took another, surer route through the land of Prince Avarskii [or, possibly, the prince of the Avars].

Moscow heralds were sent first, to get an oath of allegiance to Russia from the ruler and his people, and following them, the eminent official, Prince Simeon Zvenigorodskii was sent with a letter patent. Alexander kissed the cross and swore, along with

---

* [From the Chinese kòutóu, literally meaning to bang the head. The Russian word literally means to beat the forehead. It is not clear whether this was originally a Mongol or a Chinese custom.]
** [Georgia's largest river.]

his three sons, Heracles, David, George and his whole land, to be Theodor's permanent, steadfast subjects; likewise for his *future* sons and successors. He should have the same friends and enemies as Russia, serve him diligently *until exhausted*, and send to Moscow annually 50 pieces of gold-braided Persian silk and 10 carpets with silver and gold, or products of Iberia of the same value. For his part, Theodor promised all the inhabitants an intrepid presence in their defense – and he did what he could.

To please the sultan, the town we had abandoned on the Terek, which had indeed served for some time as a haven for free Cossacks, was immediately set to rights and occupied by a musketeer unit under the command of the voivode, Prince Andrei Ivanovich Khvorostinin, who had been sent to establish Russia's dominion over the Circassian and Kabardian princes. They had been Russian vassals since Ivan's time and were to join with the prince to guard Iberia. Other troops from Astrakhan pacified Shavkal and conquered the banks of the Koisa. Theodor furnished Alexander artillery and promised to send to him masters skilled at casting cannons. Reassured by his hopes in Russia, Alexander increased the size of his own army: he collected about 15,000 cavalry and infantry, took them into the field, formed them up and drilled them. He gave them a banner with a cross on it as well as bishops and monks to instruct them. He said to the prince of Zvenigorod,

"Glory to the Russian monarch! These are not my troops, but God's and Theodor's." The Ottoman pashas now demanded provisions from them for Baku and Derbent, which they did not give, saying,

"I am a slave of the great Muscovite tsar!"

To the retort that Moscow was far, but the Turks were near, he answered, "Terek and Astrakhan are close enough." But the Tsar's Duma prudently advised him to deceive the sultan and not to provoke him until a general European uprising against the Ottoman Empire. Frightened by rumors that Prince Murat, Shavkal's brother-in-law was planning to betray us and was secretly corresponding with his father-in-law, with the Nogai and some perfidious Circassian princes to quickly conquer Astrakhan, but not to turn it over to the sultan, Alexander urged the sovereign not to believe the Mohammedans, and added,

"If that happens to Astrakhan, I shall forsake my poor kingdom and flee *to wherever my eyes carry me.*"

But the prince of Zvenigorod calmed him, saying, "We are not taking our eyes off Murat and are taking hostages from all the Nogai princes and the Kazyev and Zavolozhskie uluses. The sultan shamefully fled with the khan {in 1569} from Astrakhan, and it is now even more strongly fortified and filled with troops. Russia can stand up for itself and for you as well."

Meanwhile, we were busy ensuring Iberia's security and diligently aiding it in religious matters by sending learned priests to correct its church rituals, as well as artists to decorate its cathedrals with holy icons. Alexander kept repeating, with feeling, that the tsar's letter patent had "fallen from Heaven and led him out of the darkness and into the light," and that our priests were angels for the Iberian clergy, who had been clouded by ignorance. In point of fact, while boasting of the antiquity of Christianity in their land, the unfortunate priesthood had forgotten the chief principles of the Ecumenical Council and the rituals of the holy mass. Its churches, mostly in the precipitous mountains, stood solitary and vacant. Inspecting them with curiosity, Moscow's priests found in some of them remnants of rich antique utensils from the year 1441. Alexander explained to them,

"At that time, Iberia was ruled by the great despot George. It was then a single kingdom. Unfortunately, my great grandfather divided it into three principalities, so that it became a prize for the enemies of Christ. We are surrounded by infidels, but we still praise the True God and our Orthodox tsar."

In the name of Russia, the prince of Zvenigorod promised liberation for all of Iberia and the renovation of its churches and towns, which he saw everywhere in ruins. In his reports, he mentioned two miserable towns, Krym and Zagem, and some settlements and monasteries. From this time onward, Theodor included in his title *Sovereign of the Iberian land, the Georgian rulers, the Kabardian lands, and the Circassian and mountain princes.*

The renovation of the Terek stronghold and the annexation of Georgia riled the sultan, and we aroused his displeasure still further by our friendship with Persia. Shah Khodabanda [ruled 1576-1587] had informed

Theodor of his alleged victories over the Turks and proposed to him to expel them from Baku and Derbent. He promised to yield us these cities, which had long been Persian, in perpetuity, should he take them. In order to conclude an alliance under these conditions, Theodor sent the court noble Vasilchikov to the Shah in 1588. He found that Khodabanda had been imprisoned: his son, Mirza Abbas [Abbas I], had overthrown his father to become ruler. This change did not interfere with a good agreement between Russia and Persia, however.

The new Shah received Theodor's official in Kazbin with great honor and sent two nobles, Butakbek and Andibei, to Moscow to explain to the tsar that he would yield us not only Derbent and Baku, but also Tabriz and all the Shirvan lands [in Caucasian Albania] if, with our diligent cooperation, the Turks could be pushed out. They said that the sultan wanted peace with them and wished to give his daughter in marriage to his [Abbas's] nephew, but that Abbas did not want to hear of it; he rather hoped for an alliance with Russia and the Spanish monarch, whose emissary was then in Persia. In a special audience with Godunov, the Shah's nobles told him,

"If our sovereign had a genuine friendship [with Theodor], what might we not do with our combined forces? At the least, the Turks might be expelled from Persian possessions, and Constantinople might also be conquered. Such great deeds are accomplished by men with great minds. What great glory there will be for you, an eminent man and worthy of our ruler's favor, if your wise counsel saves the world from Ottoman violence!"

In reply, they were told that we were already in action against Murad. Our army was already on the Terek and blocking the sultan's route from the Black Sea to Persian territory, while another, yet more powerful army was in Astrakhan. Murad had been about to order his pashas to march to the Caspian Sea, but he had been thwarted when he learned of the new Russian strongholds in these dangerous places, and of the union of all the Circassian and Nogai princes, who were prepared to strike the Turks beneath Moscow's banners. The emissaries were dismissed after being told that ours would follow them to the Shah, but they had not yet left Moscow when they learned that Abbas had made peace with the sultan.

These were the actions of Russia's peaceful but ambitious foreign policy during the first years of Theodor's reign, or Godunov's rule. It was not without cunning, nor without success

INTERNAL
AFFAIRS

– more cautious than bold – threatening and enticing, and not always sincere. We did not go to war, but we prepared for it by fortifying and increasing our army's strength everywhere. Theodor seemed to wish to have an invisible presence in the army's camps – he organized general inspections, and chose military court nobles for this. They were able and seasoned, and travelled from legion to legion to inspect the conditions of each, their arms, men and organization, and report to the sovereign. The voivodes, who were obstinate in harmful squabbling amongst themselves over hereditary precedence, submitted without protest to the judgment of these courtiers, stewards and boyar cadets who in these inspections represented the person of the sovereign.

ARKHANGELSK
FOUNDED

Within the country, all was quiet. The administration was occupied with drawing up a new census of people and arable land, equalization of taxes, settlement of the wilderness and building towns. In 1584, Moscow's voivodes Nashchokin and Volokhov founded Arkhangelsk on the banks of the [Northern] Dvina near the site of the monastery of this name and the English merchants' court. Astrakhan, threatened by the sultan and so important for our commercial and governmental dealings with the East, and for restraining the Nogai, Circassians and all their neighboring princes, was fortified with stone walls.

CONSTRUCTION
OF THE WHITE, OR
TSAR'S TOWN
IN MOSCOW

In Moscow in 1586, the White, or *Tsar's Town*, was founded around the Great Suburb [*Bolshoi Posad*], starting from the Tver Gate. In the chronicle, the architect is named as the

Russian artist Konon Thedorov. Many government buildings were constructed in the Kremlin: the Monetary Court, the ministries for embassies and estates, the treasury and the Kazan Palace.

We also mention here the start of today's town of Uralsk. Around 1584, 600 or 700 Volga Cossacks chose a dwelling site on the banks of the Yaik [Ural] River in places open to fishing. They surrounded it with earthen

> BEGINNINGS
> OF
> URALSK

fortifications and became a terror to the Nogai, especially Prince Urus, Izmail's son, who constantly complained to the tsar about their brigandage. The tsar would always reply that they were fugitives and vagabonds who had settled there on their own. Urus did not believe it and would write to him,

"How could such a sizable town exist without your consent? Some of these pillagers that we have captured call themselves the tsar's men."

We note that this was the most flourishing time in the history of our Don and Volga Cossack-knights. Word of their audacity resounded from Azov to Isker:* they aggravated the sultan, menaced the khan, pacified the Nogai and established the Muscovite monarchs' power over northern Asia.

In these circumstances, which were propitious for Russia's greatness and integrity, when everything evinced the wisdom and energy of its administration, which is to say, Godunov, he was the subject of hatred and evil

> DANGERS
> FOR
> GODUNOV

plots, despite all his artful attempts to beguile the people. He personally corresponded with the monarchs of Europe and Asia, exchanged gifts with them and received their emissaries in his home. Boris was haughty, but tried to appear modest, yielding the foremost places in the Council to other, more senior nobles. He sat in the *fourth* place in it, but with a single word, a single glance and the movement of a finger, he silenced opposition.

He invented honors, tokens of the tsar's favor to captivate the vanity of the boyars, and to this end introduced the custom of din-

---

* [Also known as Qashliq and Sibir.]

ners for the men of the Duma, in the inner rooms of the palace. There Theodor would entertain the Godunovs and the Shuiskiis, but would never invite Boris. It was a futile ruse, since whomever the great boyar invited to his table on such days would incur the envy of the tsar's guests.

Everyone knew that the ruler had left Theodor only the title of tsar. It was not just many of the foremost people of the nation, but also the citizens of the capital who expressed their dislike for Boris. Unlimited power even in the most worthy of nobles is repugnant to the people. Adashev once had power over Ivan's heart and Russia's fate, but stood humbly behind a monarch who was intelligent, fiery and energetic, seeming to vanish in his glory. Godunov ruled openly as an autocrat and magnified himself before the throne while covering the monarch's pale shadow with his arrogance. There were complaints about Theodor's nullification and Godunov was viewed as a usurper of the tsar's rights. The Mongol tribe of Prince Chet was mentioned, and there was shame at the abasement of Ryurik's sovereign descendants.

His flatterers listened to this coolly, but his enemies paid attention, and easily believed that the son-in-law of Malyuta, Ivan's favorite, was a tyrant, although still a timid one! By the very social progress and success of his rule, he strengthened this hatred and sharpened its sting, so that he prepared for himself the calamitous necessity of instituting terror. He kept trying to delay this necessity, however, and attempted to make peace with the Shuiskiis, who had friends in the Duma and partisans among the people, especially among the tradesmen. They were incessantly and even openly hostile to Godunov. The archprelate Dionisii undertook to be peacemaker and brought the enemies together in his Kremlin halls. He spoke in the name of the country and of the faith; he touched and convinced, so it seemed, even Boris, who warmly gave his hand to the Shuiskiis. They swore to live in fraternal love, to sincerely wish the best for each other and together to benefit the nation. Prince Ivan Petrovich Shuiskii left the metropolitan's with a happy expression and went across the square to the Faceted Palace to inform the curious of this happy peacemaking. This is evidence of citizens' active involvement at this time in the affairs of society – they had now had time to recuperate after Ivan. Everyone was listening in speechless silence to the beloved and respected hero of Pskov, when two merchants emerged from the crowd and shouted,

"Prince Ivan Petrovich! You have made peace with our lives: both you and we will perish because of Boris!"

That same night these two merchants were seized and exiled to an unknown place on Boris's orders. He had wanted peace so as to disarm the Shuiskiis, but soon saw that they, who were as crafty as he, had remained his fierce enemies behind a mask of a fictitious new amity, and that they were acting in concert with other important and heretofore secret enemies of the Great Boyar.

The Russian clergy had never displayed a strong love of worldly power, always acting more to please than to resist the sovereigns' will even in regard to ecclesiastical matters, and our metropolitans had since the time of Ivan III on various occasions solemnly repeated that they were engaged only in conducting services, in Christian education, in the conscience of the people and in the salvation of souls. However, they did attend the Councils of the Land and were summoned for important governmental decisions, and although they did not legislate, they approved or affirmed civil laws. They had the right to advice the tsar and the boyars, to explain the precepts of the Heavenly Kingdom to them for the people's worldly welfare. These churchmen participated in governmental affairs commensurate with their abilities and the character of the sovereign – less in the time of Ivan III and Vasilii, more in Ivan IV's childhood and youth, and again less during the years of his tyranny. Theodor, with the soul of a child, surpassed his elders in piety, participated in the affairs of the Church with more ardor than in the affairs of state, and conversed more willingly with monks than with boyars. Without Godunov's leadership, might this have given the senior clergy some importance in the government, if they had an ambitious, intelligent and smooth-tongued metropolitan? For such was Dionisii, who was dubbed the wise grammarian.

But Godunov had not wanted the ruling power just to give it to the monks. He honored the priesthood as he did the boyars, with merely the tokens of respect. He lent his ear to the metropolitan and deliberated with him, but acted independently and irritated him with his unbending will. This explains Dionisii's hostile disposition towards Godunov and his close ties with the Shuiskiis. They knew that the ruler was more powerful than the tsaritsa, and believed that the weak-willed Theodor could not have strong affections for either Godunov or Irina. They thought that the effects of a sudden scare would easily tilt him towards extraordinary actions.

Accordingly, the metropolitan, the Shuiskiis and their friends made a secret pact with Moscow's merchants and some civil and military officials to formally petition Theodor in the name of all Russia to divorce his infertile wife, pack her off, like a second Solomoniya,* to a monastery and take another, so as to have heirs, essential for the peace of the state. This plea by the people, supposedly frightened by the thought of the end of Ryurik's line on the throne, was intended to increase the agitation of the masses.

It is written that a bride was chosen, the sister of Prince Theodor Ivanovich Mstislavskii, whose father had been brought down by Godunov and died in the Kirillovskii Monastery. A document was drawn up and ratified by kissing the cross. Boris, however, who had many people devoted to him, not to mention spies, found out about this dangerous conspiracy in time, and acted, it seemed, with rare magnanimity. Without anger or reproach, he tried to appeal to the metropolitan's conscience; he argued that divorce would be illegal and that Theodor still might have children by Irina – she was in the flower of youth, beauty and virtue, and in any case, the throne would not be without an heir, since Prince Dimitrii was alive and well.

Deceived, perhaps, by this mildness, Dionisii made excuses for himself and also tried to excuse his coconspirators on the grounds of their ardent, fearful desire for the peace of Russia. He gave his word for himself and the others to give no more consideration to divorcing the young wife, while Godunov promised not to take vengeance on the guilty parties and participants in this plot. He would be satisfied with just one victim, the unfortunate Princess Mstislavskaya, who, as a dangerous rival of Irina, was ordained as a nun.

---

* [First wife of Grand Prince Vasilii III, canonized as St. Sofiya of Suzdal.]

Now all was quiet in the capital, in the Duma and at the court, but not for long. In order not to openly break the promise he had given, Godunov, with hypocritical conscientiousness, sought another means of vengeance, which he justified in his own mind by the malice of his irreconcilable enemies, the security of the state and himself, and all the services he had furnished Russia, and those he planned, out of ardor for its welfare. He did not hesitate to resort to base means: employing that old instrument of Ivan's tyranny, he sought false denunciations. The Shuiskiis' servants, we are assured, sold their honor and conscience to him. They appeared in court with the accusation that the Shuiskiis were in a plot with the Moscow merchants and were planning to overthrow the tsar. The Shuiskiis were arrested, and their friends as well: the Tatev princes, the Urusovs, the Kolychevs, the Bykasovs, and many courtiers and rich merchants. A trial was arranged; witnesses and the accused were interrogated. Eminent people and officials were not touched physically, but merchants and servants were tortured, pitilessly and uselessly, since none of them corroborated the calumnies of the delators. So said the people, but the court did not vindicate the accused.

Amidst boasting of mercy and gratitude to the hero of Pskov, the Shuiskiis were exiled. Prince Andrei Ivanovich, convicted of being the principal perpetrator, was sent to Kargopol; Prince Ivan Petrovich, supposedly lured by

EXILE AND EXECUTION

Andrei and his brothers, went to Belo-ozero; the eldest of them, Prince Vasilii Thedorovich Skopin-Shuiskii, was deprived of his Kargopol estate, but since he was innocent, was permitted to live in Moscow. Others were confined in Bui-gorodok, Galich and in Shuya. Prince Ivan Tatev was sent to Astrakhan, Kryuk-Kolychev to Nizhnyi Novgorod, the Bykasovs and many courtiers to Vologda, to Siberia and to various other places in the wilderness. The Moscow merchants (who had participated in the plot against Irina), and Thedor Nagoi and six of his comrades were beheaded in the square. The metropolitan had not yet been touched, but he did not want to be a timid spectator to this disgrace. With courageous audacity, he solemnly called Godunov a calumniator and a tyrant to Theodor's face and argued that the Shuiskiis and their friends were ruined solely due to their good intention to save Russia from Boris's greedy hunger for power. He likewise boldly denounced the ruler and the Krutitskii [Sarai] archbishop Varlaam, threatening him with heavenly punishment. Having no fear of worldly punishment, he reproached Theodor for his weakness and shameful blindness. Both Dionisii and Varlaam were dethroned (without a trial, it seems). The former was confined to the Khutynskii Monastery, the second in Antoniev Novgorodskii,* and Archbishop Iov [Job] of Rostok was ordained as the new metropolitan.

Fearing the people, but unafraid of God, the ruler (so the chroniclers assure us) ordered the two chief Shuiskiis strangled in prison: the boyar Andrei Ivanovich, of outstanding intellect, and the eminent Prince Ivan Petrovich, the savior of Pskov and our martial honor, a man immortal in history, whose great exploit has been described by contemporaries in various European languages to the glory of the Russian name. His laurel-crowned head was consigned to a shameful noose in a stuffy prison or pit! His body was buried at St. Kirill's Monastery.

PITEOUS DEATH
OF THE
HERO SHUISKII

Thus began Godunov's misdeeds and thus was his heart revealed; he was drunk on the charms of power, aggravated by the intrigues of his enemies and embittered with his own vengefulness. He hoped to restrain his ill-wishers through fear, multiply his adherents through favors and silence malicious gossip through his wisdom in governmental affairs. Boris now ventured a perfidious deceit and a new cruelty.

The miserable Magnus, known only to history as the fictive king of Livonia, had ended his life in Pilten back in Ivan's time, where his widow Mariya Vladimirovna and her two year old daughter Evdokiya were left without property, without a homeland and without friends. Godunov invited them to Moscow, promising a rich appanage and a distinguished husband to the young widow Mariya. However, foreseeing the future, and fearing that in case of the death of Theodor and Dimitrii, this great granddaughter

FATE OF
MAGNUS'S FAMILY

---

* [St. Anthony's Monastery in Novgorod.]

of Ivan the Great might think of declaring herself the successor to the throne (which he already had designs on), although this was unexampled and contrary to the laws of our country, Boris, instead of an appanage and a groom, presented her with the choice of monastery or prison. As an involuntary nun, Mariya requested a single comfort: not to be separated from her daughter. But she was soon to mourn what was thought to be her daughter's *unnatural* death and would live for about eight more years, recalling the fate of her parents, husband and daughter with bitter tears. These two victims of a suspected crime, Mariya and Evdokiya, lie at the Trinity-Sergiev Monastery near the place where, outside the cathedral, we may see the humble, as if disgraced, grave of their persecutor, who was not saved by his majesty or glory from the just vengeance of God.

Yet this vengeance was in abeyance pending future crimes. After subduing the court with the Shuiskiis' disgrace, the priesthood with the deposing of a metropolitan, and the citizenry of the capital with the execution of eminent Moscow merchants, and after surrounding the tsar and controlling the Duma with his closest kin, Godunov no longer perceived any sort of protest, no kind of significant danger to himself prior to Theodor's death – or arousal from his somnolence. For such might this pathetic monarch's meek idleness be called, which contemporaries described in the following manner.

"Theodor would usually arise at the fourth hour of the morning to await his confessor in his bedchamber, which was

> THEODOR'S
> IDLENESS

filled with icons and illuminated by lamps day and night. The confessor would come to him with a cross, a blessing, holy water and an icon of the saint who was being celebrated that day in church. The sovereign would bow to the floor and pray aloud for ten minutes or more, then go to Irina, into her own room and they would proceed together to matins. On returning, he would sit in an armchair in a large chamber and be greeted "Good Morning" by monks and those closest to him. He would go to mass at nine and dine at eleven. Afterwards he would nap no less than three hours, then proceed again to the church for vespers. He would spend the rest of the time before supper with the tsaritsa, jesters and dwarves, watching their antics or listening to songs. Sometimes he would admire the work of his jewelers, goldsmiths, tailors or painters. At night, getting ready for bed, he would again pray with his confessor and lie down with his blessing. In addition, every week he would visit monasteries in the vicinity of the capital, and on holidays he would amuse himself with bear-baiting. Occasionally petitioners would surround Theodor as he was leaving the palace. *Avoiding worldly vanity and annoyances*, he would not listen to them, but rather to Boris."

While inwardly rejoicing at the tsar's humiliating idleness, the cunning Godunov tried all the more to elevate Irina in Russians' eyes. Only in her sovereign name, without Theodor's, would he dispense charitable instructions – forgiving, favoring, and comforting the people, so as to employ her general popularity, joined with the people's respect and gratitude to her, to consolidate his present majesty and prepare for future greatness.

REIGN OF THEODOR IVANOVICH
AND
REGENCY OF BORIS GODUNOV

1587-1592

Death of Batory. Important negotiations with Lithuania. Truce. Relations with Austria and the Taurid. Swedish War. New truce with Lithuania. Godunov's Greatness. Patriarchate established in Russia. Godunov's Scheming. Murder of Crown Prince Dimitrii. Conflagration in Moscow. Invasion of the Khan and Battle before Moscow. Godunov's New Rank. Donskii Monastery. Calumny against the Ruler and his Revenge. Godunov's Charity and Glory. Irina's Pregnancy. Birth and death of Princess Theodosiya

O n 12 December 1586, Stefan Batory died (either from poison or from the ineptitude of his doctors, it is thought). He was one of the most eminent monarchs in the world and one of Russia's most dangerous malefactors, whose

> DEATH OF
> BATORY

death overjoyed more than it distressed our country, for we tended fearfully to see him as a new Gedimin, a new Vitovt,* while Poland and Lithuania ungratefully preferred cheap peace to expensive eminence. If Batory's genius and life had lasted beyond Godunov's death, then Russia's glory might have faded forever in the very first decade of the new century. Thus do the fates of nations depend on personality and chance, or on the will of Providence!

O n 20 December the Boyar Duma received the news of the king's death from various sources, although these reports were not yet completely credible. Our voivodes on the Lithuanian border wrote to the tsar, treating it as a rumor, and adding that the

---

* [Gediminas and Vytautas, former rulers of Lithuania; hostile to Russia.]

noble pans were considering selecting as their sovereign Stefan's brother, the prince of Sedmigrad,* or the Swedish king Sigismund, or himself, Theodor.

<table>
<tr><td>IMPORTANT
NEGOTIATIONS WITH
LITHUANIA
1587</td></tr>
</table>

The honor and benefit of this possible union of three powers seemed obvious to Godunov and he immediately dispatched the court noble Elizarii Rzhevskii to Lithuania. He was to verify Stefan's death, express sympathy to the pans at their loss and propose they choose the tsar as their king. Rzhevskii returned from Novgorod with a letter of thanks from the Lithuanian nobles, but they were unwilling to enter into negotiations, saying that a matter so important would have to be decided by the Sejm in Warsaw, to which the tsar should send his emissaries.

However, Rzhevskii was secretly given to feel that Theodor and the Moscow boyars had written to them in a rather chilly manner and had not followed the example of the [Holy Roman] emperor or France and Sweden, who showered the pans not only with flattering words, but rich gifts as well. Meanwhile, Poland and Lithuania were powerfully agitated and passions boiled. The nobles and the court were divided: some took the side of Zamoiskii, who had been Stefan's comrade-in-arms, others sided with the Zborovskiis, enemies of Stefan to the extent that in formal meetings they drew their swords against those who ardently honored his glorious memory. Both sides anticipated the sessions of the Sejm as if they were battles. They took up arms, hired troops, posted guards and had camps in the field.

But Lithuania, which was adjacent to us, feared Russia, and so, on 6 April, distinguished emissaries, the nobles Chernigovskii and Prince Oginskii, arrived in Moscow to entreat Theodor to ratify a newly written truce with their orphaned state, to be valid till the end of 1588. The boyars willingly concluded a treaty with them and told them that the good or bad fortune of their homeland would depend on the king's and Lithuania's nobles: good fortune if they yielded to the great Russian monarch, bad if they once again turned to the Sedmigradskii barbarian or to that wraith of a Swedish kingdom.

---

* [Historically part of Transylvania.]

"You have had Batory on the throne," they said, "and with him war, destruction and dishonor, since with his own hands your monarch paid tribute to the sultan. How can you expect magnanimity from a stranger who is base both in birth and spirit, who is eager only for gain and is ruthless towards Christendom? Does holy love abide in his heart, without which even the power to move mountains, as the apostles say, is as nothing? Is it not to please the Ottomans that you want to choose a Swedish prince? By all means please them, for they rejoice in strife between Christians, and bloodshed will be unavoidable if Sigismund, with his hatred of Russia, sits on the Jagellonian throne.

"You already know our monarch, who is equally great and charitable; you know that the first act of his reign was to altruistically release your prisoners of war. This magnanimity was incomprehensible to Batory, who continued to haggle over his Russian prisoners until the end of his days. Batory is now in his grave, but Theodor does not rejoice or think of vengeance; instead he expresses his sympathy and offers a way to facilitate permanent peace for Lithuania and Poland. He wants the kingship not to enlarge the power and wealth of his state (for Russia is already powerful and rich), but to defend you from the infidel – he seeks no sort of advantage. He will yield to the pans and the knights all that the land now pays to the king. In addition, he will give them estates in the new Russian territories, and with his own treasury he will build fortresses on the banks of the Dnieper, Donets and Don so that Ottoman and Crimean feet do not trample the districts of Kiev, Volhynia and Podolia. Their infidel rulers will lose heart: confined within their borders, they will barely be able to hold out. Russia will take Azov, Kaffa and the Crimean khanate for itself and the Danubian lands for you. Vast numbers of troops are awaiting the sovereign's words to launch an assault, but at whom?

"You must decide: at the enemies of Christendom, if you have the same monarch as we, or at Lithuania and Livonia if you prefer the Swedes over us. Do not think of friendship with the sultan, for what sort of agreement can there be between light and darkness, what sort of intercourse between true believers and infidels? Think instead of glory and victory. What is interfering with our confraternity? Among your other sins, it is your ingrained hatred of Russia. Turn instead to friendship. Everything depends on beginnings, and a small fire can produce a great flame. The Russian sovereign promises you security and greatness, and asks nothing of you but friendship."

The emissaries prevailed upon the tsar to send one of his nobles to the Sejm, and two boyars, Stepan Vasilievich Godunov and Prince Fedor Mikhailovich Troekurov and the eminent secretary Vasilii Shchelkalov. They immediately left Moscow for Warsaw with the full trust of the sovereign and 48 letters for clergy and laity as well as royal officials and Lithuanian officials, but no gifts. Theodor proposed the following conditions to the Sejm:

" 1) That the Russian sovereign become the Polish king and the grand prince of Lithuania and that the people of both powers join in permanent, unbroken amity.

2) The Russian sovereign is to personally do battle, and with all his strength, against the Ottoman Empire, depose the Crimean khan and replace him with Saidet-Girei (a Russian servitor). After concluding an alliance with the Kaiser, the Spanish king and the Persian shah, he will liberate Moldavia, Wallachia, Bosnia, Serbia and Hungary from the sultan's yoke and unite them with Lithuania and Poland, whose troops will cooperate with the Russians in this effort.

3) The armies of Moscow, Kazan and Astrakhan will always be ready for the defense of Lithuania and Poland without mercenary contracts or payment.

4) The sovereign will not change these rights and liberties in any way without ratification by the Council of Nobles, which will make outlays independently from its treasury and all its national revenues.

5) Russians in Lithuania and Poland, and Lithuanians and Poles in Russia, are to be free to live there and to intermarry.

6) The sovereign will award lands near the Don and Donets to impoverished Lithuanian and Polish court nobles.

7) To those military men to whom Stefan Batory remains in

debt, the sovereign will pay up to 100,000 Hungarian gold pieces from his own treasury.

8) Funds which have heretofore gone for the maintenance of fortresses no longer needed between Lithuania and Russia shall be used by both powers to make war on the infidel.

9) After expelling the Swedes and the Danes from Estonia, Russia will yield all its towns and cities to Lithuania and Poland, with the exception of Narva.

10) Lithuanian and Polish merchants are to be free to travel in all Muscovite territories, and through them to Persia, Bukhara and other eastern lands; likewise to the mouth of the Dvina by sea, and to Siberia and to the great empire of Cathay, where precious stones and gold are to be found."

In the written instructions given to the emissaries, it is worth noting one concerning Prince Dimitrii, which says,

"If the pans mention the sovereign's younger brother, explain to them that he is still a child and cannot sit on their throne – he should be brought up in his own native country."

The ruler was preparing another fate for him!

There is no doubt that Theodor, like his father and grandfather, sincerely wanted the title of king in order to join these long-hostile powers with bonds of brotherhood. He was offering the Council of Nobles advantageous terms, attractive promises and glittering hopes. He would be sacrificing millions of today's rubles and, contrary to Ivan's chief demand, would agree to be an elective king with limited powers and without any right of inheritance for his sons or his line. Did the tsar, or the ruler, really plan to take up arms against the sultan and conquer the rich Danubian territories so as to strengthen Lithuania and Poland, which might in the future have their own rulers and once again turn against Russia?

For such an important enterprise, he made one of the conditions an alliance with the Kaiser, Spain and Persia. He did not enter into a decisive obligation, but rather enticed the pans' imaginations with this bold and grand plan. Theodor was prepared to seem yielding and indulgent to further his quest, but he showed cold-blooded inflexibility when the Sejm rashly demanded of him sacrifices incompatible with Orthodoxy or the dignity and welfare of Russia.

On 12 July our boyars, Stepan Godunov and Prince Troekurov, were stopped in the name of the Polish Duma in the village of Okunev, 15 versts from Warsaw, and told that there was no safe place for them in the capital, which was full of frenzied troops, mutiny and dissension. Such was indeed the case. The clergy, nobility, the knights and the gentry were unable to agree on the choice of a king. To please Batory's widow, Zamoiskii and his friends proposed the Swedish prince Sigismund, her sister's son. The Zaborskiis wanted the Austrian Duke Maximilian; the Lithuanian pans and the primate, the archbishop of Gniezdo, wanted Theodor, while the sultan, supporting Stefan's brother, threatened war if they were to choose Maximilian or the Muscovite tsar, enemies of the Ottoman Empire, instead. The so-called Knights' Circle, a place of noisy meetings, sometimes had the appearance of a battleground, with crowds of armed men shooting at each other. At last they prudently agreed to put an end to the civil strife and erect three banners in the middle of a field: the Russians', the Kaiser's and the Swedes', in order to see, by the constituencies beneath each, which had the majority. On Theodor's banner was a Muscovite hat, the Austrians had a German hat and the Swedes had a herring. The first achieved a majority: so many people crowded beneath it that when the partisans of Austria and Sweden saw their own small numbers, they were ashamed and joined us. Nevertheless, the Russian side's glittering triumph seemed fruitless when the matter came down to terms.

On 4 August the clergy, senators and nobility of the two conjoined powers received Godunov and Troekurov with great honors in the Knights' Circle. They listened to Theodor's proposal and wanted further elaboration. To this end, they chose 15 nobles, churchmen and laymen, to meet with our emissaries in the village of Kamenets, near Warsaw. There, to Godunov's and

Troekurov's surprise, these deputies met them with the following unexpected questions:

"Will the Muscovite sovereign unite Russia with the kingdom in the same manner as Lithuania is joined with Poland, permanently and inseparably? Will he take up the Roman faith? Will he obey the apostolic deputy? Will he be crowned and take communion from the archbishop of Gniezdo in the Latin church in Krakow? Will he be in Warsaw in 10 weeks? And in his title, will the Kingdom of Poland come before the Muscovite Empire?"

The boyars replied:

"1) The sovereign wishes to permanently unite Lithuania and Poland with Russia so that they can use all their power to help each other in the event of enemy attack, and so that their inhabitants may freely travel from one country to another: Lithuanians to us, and Russians to Lithuania, with the sovereign's permission.

2) The sovereign was born, and will continue to live by the Greek Orthodox faith and follow its sacred rites. Coronation as king should take place in Moscow or Smolensk in the presence of your government officials. He promises to respect the Pope and not to interfere with his authority over the Polish clergy, nor will he permit him to interfere in the affairs of the Greek Church.

3) The tsar will come to you if he can manage it.

4) *Yagailo's crown will be beneath Monomakh's* and Theodor's title will be: *Tsar and Grand Prince of all Russia, Vladimir and Moscow, King of Poland and Grand Prince of Lithuania.* If both Old Rome and New Rome – the ruling city of Byzantium – join with us, the sovereign still will not put these ancient and glorious names before Russia in his title."

"So Theodor does not want to be our king," rejoined the pans. "He decisively refuses and makes insincere promises. For example, he writes that his army is prepared to defend us from the sultan. Turkey frequently attacks our lands from Moldavia and the Danube region, from Transylvania and Belgorod. However, Moscow's troops are far away, and Astrakhan's and Kazan's are even farther. The sultan, the Kaiser and the Swedes each threaten us with war if we choose a king not to their liking. What will the tsar give us, and how much money will he provide annually to maintain the army? We have enough men of our own, and are not requesting Moscow's. Money is also needed to strengthen your partisans in the Sejm. Are you aware that the emperor is promising to send the Council of Nobles 600,000 gold pieces immediately on the selection of Maximilian and the same amount annually for six years, while the Spanish king promises 800,000 and the same annually for eight years?"

Our emissaries said,

"Our tsar has a great number of light troops ready for your defense: Volga and Don Cossacks, and even Crimeans, since their khan will be Saidet-Girei, a vassal of our sovereign. The tsar intends to assist you with his treasury, but without any obligation. You boast of the generosity of Austria and the Spanish king, but consider that the Orthodox tsar wants the king's crown not for his own benefit and glory, but only so that you may have peace and greatness.

"For how many years has Christian blood been spilled in battles between Russians and Lithuanians? Our sovereign is planning to put a permanent end to this misery, but you, pans, are not thinking of that as you weigh Spanish and Austrian gold! Let it be as you wish, and if money is dearer to you than the peace of Christendom, then know that the tsar does not wish to be a merchant and does not need to buy friends nor your kingdom with money. He does not want to feed the cupidity of people insensitive to their national welfare nor to arm them against each other in the mutinous strife of the Sejm, since he has no love of fighting or lawlessness!"

This firmness provoked a strong reaction from the deputies. They stood up and quietly discussed things amongst themselves for a few minutes, then finally, indignantly declared to the emissaries that Theodor would not be on the Jagellonian throne. When Godunov and Troekurov proposed that they delay the selection of a king and send nobles to Moscow for new clarifications with the tsar, Cardinal Radziwill and the other deputies replied,

"You are making fun of us. We have gathered in Warsaw from every corner of Lithuania and Poland. We have been living here for eight weeks as if in a war, losing our peace of mind and our money, and you want another [session of the] Sejm! We shall not adjourn without making a choice."

Theodor's emissaries now advised them to choose Maximilian, who was well disposed towards Russia.

"We have no need of your exhortations," they rudely rejoined. "God instructs us, not the Russian tsar."

They wanted to at least conclude a peace treaty, but could not agree on its conditions either: Lithuania demanded Smolensk and the Severskii territory, while Theodor wanted Derpt. Dissatisfied, they broke up, but this did not end the negotiations.

O n this same day and the following few, there were heated debates in the Sejm amongst its government officials and the friends of Austria, Sweden and Russia. The former, especially the clergy and all the bishops, said that their consciences would not permit them to have a king of a different religion – a heretic. Their partisans, the lay nobility, added,

"[A heretic] who is the natural, inveterate enemy of Lithuania and Poland, who will sit on our kingdom with Russia's ponderous might in order to stifle our liberty, all our rights and laws. You complained of oppression when Stefan brought several hundred Hungarian guards to us. What will happen when you see the terrible Oprichnina* here, countless thousands of grim and haughty Muscovites? Do you believe that they in their pride would wish to unite with us? Would they not sooner wish to annex our state to Muscovy, as the sleeve is joined to a caftan?"

Others deprecated Theodor, calling him weak-minded, incompetent to guard their nation, to restrain willfulness or to infuse the royal power with strength, adding that he would scarcely be able to arrive in less than six months, while the Turks, irreconcilable foes of the tsar and conquerors of two or three Moslem powers, could successfully take Krakow in the meantime. The nobles who were taking our part retorted,

"The first principle of a state is security. By choosing Theodor, we will reconcile a powerful enemy, Russia, and find it to be a

---

* [Ivan the Terrible's system of secret police, among other things.]

defense against another, no less dangerous – the Turks. The sultan forbids us to elevate Theodor to the royal throne, but should we obey an enemy? Should we really not do something he does not want us to? As for matters of faith: Theodor was christened in the name of the Holy Trinity and we know there is a Greek church in Rome, so evidently the Pope has not condemned this faith and surely permits it to remain, although perhaps with some conditions. Theodor magnanimously freed our prisoners of war, pacified rebellions in his own country and defeated the khan twice. In a spirit of love he wishes to unite powers whose mutual animosity has produced so much misery. He rules in the name of law over a free people as an autocrat. Where is his feeble-mindedness? Do we not see in him a monarch who is humane and wise? Could he rule the Russians, inconstant and crafty, if he were weak minded? As far as that goes, a weak-minded ruler is less perilous to a nation than internal discord. We are contemplating nothing new: how many of you after Henri's election and subsequent flight, wanted the Muscovite tsar, believing that Ivan would leave tyranny behind in Russia and would come to us only as a powerful savior? Has anything changed since then? It has been for the better, actually, since Theodor does not tyrannize even in Russia, but loves his subjects and is loved by them in return."

This argument obliged the Sejm to renew negotiations. Its deputies again met with Moscow's emissaries in Kamenets. They wanted the tsar to immediately give the Council of Nobles 100,000 gold pieces for military expenditures and to build fortresses not on the Don, where they would benefit only Russia, but on Lithuania's southwest border, and also to pay a salary to the Dnieper Cossacks out of his own treasury. They wanted him to allot lands for the Polish gentry not in the remote, wild steppes, like many of those in Lithuania beyond Kiev, but in the Smolensk and Severskii districts.

Our emissaries made some concessions: they agreed to give the pans 100,000 gold pieces, nor did they reject other requests. They proposed that Theodor include in his title *Tsar of all Russia, King of Poland and Grand Prince of Vladimir, Moscow and Lithuania.* The principle obstacle with regard to religion was minimized when the voivodes Christofor Radziwill of Vilnius and Jan Glebowicz of the Troitskii district secretly told our emissaries that Theodor might remain in the Greek faith, despite the reproaches of their clergy if he only would ask for the Pope's blessing and give him hope of unifying the Churches.

"For his own benefit and ours," they said, "he should be indulgent, for in the event of his obstreperousness, we shall choose an enemy of Russia – a Swede, and not Maximilian, whom no one in Lithuania wishes to hear of because he is cupidinous and indigent. He will get us into a war with the sultan but will not assist our kingdom with either men or money. The emperor himself is great solely in his title and rich only in his debts. We know that it is the Austrians' custom to eradicate rights and liberties in the lands that submit to them, and they everywhere burden residents with taxes. In addition to that, it is written in our books and has become a proverb that Slavs will never see anything good from a German!"

However, Theodor did not want to seek the Pope's favor, nor deceive him with a false promise about uniting the Churches. Nor did he want something that the Lithuanian pans kept demanding, that he be crowned king in Poland by a Latin prelate – he feared the thought of thus betraying Orthodoxy or the dignity of a Russian monarch. And so our emissaries learned on 13 August, as they were having a friendly meeting with deputies of the Sejm, that Chancellor Zamoiskii and a few pans had chosen the Swedish prince, while the Poznan voivode Stanislav Zgurka and the Zborovskiis had selected Maximilian. The Lithuanian nobles tried in vain to convince our boyars that since this choice was illegal, it would remain inoperative. They said that if Theodor sincerely wished to be king and wasted no time in deciding to come to them, then they would all immediately head for Krakow and would not give the crown to the Swede or the Austrian.

> TRUCE

With sword and the gold of widowed Queen Anna, Zamoiskii gave the throne to Sigismund, nullifying the selection of Maximilian. Our emissaries succeeded in only one thing: they concluded a truce with Council of Nobles, without any concessions or gains, for just 15 years with the sole condition that each power continue to rule what it then ruled, and that whomever was chosen king would ratify this agreement in Moscow through his plenipotentiaries. After hearing the report of Stepan Godunov and Troekurov, Theodor still hoped at least that Lithuania would not acknowledge Sigismund as king, and to this end wrote flattering letters to its nobles, agreeing to be a special grand prince of Lithuania, Kiev, Volhynia and Mazovia and promising them independence and security. Godunov also wrote to them, sending them each expensive gifts (worth 20,000 of today's rubles). But it was too late: the court noble Rzhevskii returned from Lithuania with the news that on 16 December Sigismund had been crowned in Krakow and that the Lithuanian nobles had concurred in this choice. Rzhevskii had already known of this when he presented the gifts to them. They took them, expressing their gratitude and desire that the tsar would always favor coreligionist Lithuania!

The tsar expressed his vexation, not at their rejection of his conditions at the Sejm, but at their choice of Sigismund. We have seen that Theodor, like Ivan, would have willingly conceded the kingship to the archduke – he had no rivalry with Austria, but a close alliance of Sweden with Poland strengthened both our enemies, and Zamoiskii had gotten the significant promise from Sigismund that, like his father King Johan, he would take up arms against Russia. He would conquer Moscow or at least Smolensk and Pskov, while the Swedish Dvina fleet took the harbor of St. Nikolai to wipe out our maritime trade. It seemed the spirit of Batory was still alive in Zamoiskii, and hostile to us. Theodor all the more wanted an agreement with Austria on the plans and actions of our policies.

RELATIONS
WITH AUSTRIA
AND THE TAURID
1587-1591

From 1587 to 1590 we sent herald after herald to Vienna, trying to persuade the emperor to provide Maximilian with every means to obtain the Polish crown, if not by election, then by force. We offered to provide him with money for arms, assuring him that we would prefer to yield this state to Austria than to annex it to Russia. We vividly described the joys of the peace that would then be established in northern Europe and which would permit it join in the great enterprise of expelling the Turks from Byzantium.

We boasted of our power, saying that he could depend on Russia to launch countless throngs of Asiatics at the sultan and that the Persian shah would field 200,000 troops, the ruler of Bukhara, 100,000, of Khiva, 50,000, of Iver, 50,000, of Shavkal, 30,000, while the princes of Circassia, Tyumen and Okutsk would field 70,000 and the Nogai, 100,000. Russia would easily pacify the Swede and would then have no other enemies; it would join its crusading legions with the armies of Austria, Germany, Spain, the Pope, France and England – and the Ottoman barbarians would become but a memory!

Moscow's heralds were being detained in Lithuania and in Riga, so we opened a route to Austria through the Northern Ocean and Hamburg. We wanted Rudolf and Maximilian to immediately dispatch plenipotentiaries to Moscow for a parley on where and how to act. However, when Theodor learned that Zamoiskii had pursued the fleeing Maximilian, invaded Silesia, gained a decisive victory over him, taken him prisoner, and tortured and dishonored him in confinement, the tsar shamed Rudolf with Austria's unprecedented abasement. But this was all futile: in his replies the emperor merely expressed gratitude for the tsar's favorable disposition. In June of 1589, instead of an important noble, he sent the insignificant official Varkoch to Moscow, blaming lack of time and the inconvenience of communications between Vienna and Russia. Concerning war with the Turks, he wrote that it would be necessary to get an agreement with Spain, while keeping such important plans secret from France and England, since they were seeking favors of the sultan. War with Poland was essential, but first Maximilian must be freed. The tsar later learned that the emperor, while entreating for the release of his brother, had sworn to consider the Polish crown no longer and to live in perpetual peace with that power.

"You are beginning an important undertaking, but you do not control it," wrote Boris Godunov to the Austrian ministry. "For our part, our Orthodox tsar does not want to hear any sort of amicable proposals from the sultans or the khans. We are on the outs with them and with Lithuania, while you, disregarding your own honor, make peace with the sultan and with Sigismund!"

To sum up: we had wasted both time and money in our relations with Austria in an effort that was utterly futile.

Much more zealous with regard to our policies, were the actions of a barbarian, the new khan of the Crimea, Kazy-Girei, the brother and successor in 1588 of the late Khan Islam. When he arrived from Constantinople with a letter patent from the sultan and 300 Janissaries to rule over the ruined uluses, he found it necessary to send them out to search for loot, since they knew no trade but brigandage. It was necessary to decide on either Lithuania or Russia as a theater for murder and arson. The khan preferred Lithuania, placing his hopes on its anarchy and the weakness of its new king. He prepared his forces to lay waste to Sigismund's territory, hoping to charm rich gifts from Theodor. He wrote to the tsar that he was better disposed towards him than toward any of his predecessors; he had convinced the sultan to stop contemplating the future conquest of Astrakhan and said that Moscow and the Taurid would always have the same enemies. At the end of 1589, Kazy-Girei informed Theodor that the Crimeans had torched many towns and villages in Lithuania and Galicia. Praising the khan's valor and good will towards us, the tsar, as a token of his gratitude, honored him with moderate gifts but maintained a strong army on the banks of the Oka; evidently he did not trust him very far.

However, Batory was no more. The sultan was not taking up arms against Russia and the khan was harassing Lithuania. These circumstances seemed propitious to the tsar for a significant exploit, one that Russia's honor had long demanded. We boasted of our might, and indeed had the largest army in Europe, and yet part of ancient Russia was now Swedish territory. The period of the truce we had concluded with King Johan had expired at the beginning of 1590, and another meeting of emissaries on the banks of the Plyussa in September 1586 had been fruitless, since the Swedes would not agree to return their conquests to us, and without that, we did not want to hear of peace. They only suggested an exchange: they would trade

SWEDISH
WAR

Koporye for the outpost of Sumersk and the territory across the Neva. Johan was complaining that Russians were harassing Finland with raids, raging like tigers there. However, Theodor reproached the Swedish voivodes for their depredations in the Zaonezhskaya and Olonetskaya districts, and on Lake Ladoga and the Dvina.

In the summer of 1589 they arrived from Kayani to plunder the volosts of the Solovetskii and Pechenskii monasteries, as well as Kola, Keret and Kovda, taking loot amounting to a half-million of today's silver rubles. In an attempt to get the king to make concessions, the tsar wrote to him about his great allies, the emperor and the shah. The king replied ironically,

"I am glad that you now realize your impotence and are expecting help from others. We shall see how much my in-law Rudolf helps you, while we shall deal with you without allies."

Despite this rudeness, Johan was still desirous of a third meeting of the emissaries when Theodor ordered him to be told that we would want neither peace nor truce if the Swedes did not yield us Revel and all Estonia in addition to the Novgorod territory they had seized. In other words, we declared war.

Up to now Godunov's intellect had been conspicuous only in internal and external politics, and had always been cautious and peace-loving. He did not have a martial spirit, nor was he greedy for military glory. However, in the event that bloodshed could not be avoided without shame or clear violation of the sacred obligations of power, he wanted to show that his pacifism was not cowardly timidity. In fulfillment of this important duty, he employed all means to guarantee success. If we are to believe the testimony of our ministerial papers of this time, he summoned into the field about 300,000 troops, both cavalry and infantry, along with 300 light and heavy cannons. This included all the boyars, all the princes (Mametkul of Siberia, Ruslanei Kaibulich and Uraz-Mahmet Ondanovich of Kirghizia) and all the voivodes from towns and cities near and far, where they had been living in peace. They were to appear at a designated time beneath the tsar's banners.

Quiet Theodor, not without regret, left his devotional exercises behind and mounted his warhorse (this is what Godunov wanted) to inspire his army with enthusiasm while the senior officers restrained ridiculous quarrels over precedence within it. Prince Theodor Mstislavskii, most eminent among the old noble houses, commanded the main legion, while Prince Dimitrii Ivanovich Khvorostinin, renowned for wisdom and valor, led the van. Godunov and Theodor Nikitich Romanov-Yuriev (the future eminent [Patriarch] Filaret), the tsar's cousin, were with him and were known as *court*, or *privy voivodes*. The tsaritsa Irina traveled after her husband from Moscow to Novgorod, where the sovereign was marshaling his legions: he ordered one of them to battle Finland, beyond the Neva; another to drive through Estonia to the sea. On 18 January 1590, the tsar set out for Narva with the main force. The march was difficult because of the severe winter cold, but exuberant due to the troops high morale: Russians were marching to take back their own, and on January 27th they captured Yam. Near Narva 20,000 Swedes, cavalry and infantry under the command of Gustav Baner encountered Prince Dmitrii Khvorostinin, who defeated them and broke into the city, which was full of people but had few provisions.

This was why Baner, after leaving the requisite number of troops in the fortress, had fled by night to Wesenberg, pursued by our Asiatic cavalry, after jettisoning all his baggage and cannons, to be left as booty. Some distinguished Swedish officers were numbered among our prisoners. On 4 February the Russians invested Narva. They destroyed the walls in three places with a powerful barrage and demanded that the city surrender. The local voivode, Karl Horn, grandly invited them to attack, and bravely repulsed them on 18 February. Our voivodes Saburov and Prince Ivan Tokmakov were killed in the breach, along with many boyar cadets, musketeers, and Mordvi and Circassian troops. This brilliant Swedish feat was unable to save the city, however: the barrage continued and the walls kept falling, while the large besieging army prepared for a new assault (on 21 February). Meanwhile, Russians continued to lay waste to Estonia all the way to Revel itself, and to Finland as far as Åbo: King Johan had more pride than power. Negotiations commenced. We demanded Narva and all of Estonia before we would leave the Swedes in peace.

However, the tsar, *satisfying Godunov's Christian entreaty* (as it says in our ministerial papers) was content to restore the old borders. On 15 February Horn concluded a truce for a year in the king's name, yielding the tsar Ivangorod and Koporye in addition to Yam, with all their provisions and artillery, and agreed to resolve the fate of Estonia at a future meeting of Muscovite and Swedish emissaries. He even promised to give Russia all of the Korela territory, along with Narva and other Estonian cities. We boasted of our moderation. Leaving voivodes in three captured fortresses, Theodor hurried to return to his wife in Novgorod and thence with her to Moscow to celebrate victory over one of the European powers that his father had advised him not to fight out of fear of their superior martial skill. The sovereign was met by priests with crosses outside the capital and the archprelate Iov made a pompous speech comparing him to Constantine the Great and Vladimir [Monomakh], and in the name of the country and the Church thanked him for chasing the infidel out of the bowels of holy Russia and for restoring the altars of the True God to the city of Ivan III and the ancient territory of the Ilmen Slavs.

Swedish perfidies soon provided peace-loving Theodor's forces with a significant new success. King Johan reproached Horn for faint-heartedness and declared the agreement that he had concluded to be a crime. He reinforced his army in Estonia and sent two nobles, the deputies of Uppsala and Västergötland, to a meeting at the mouth of the Plyussa with Prince Theodor Khvorostinin and the Duma noble Pisemskii, not to hand over Estonia to Russia, but to demand the return of Yam, Ivangorod and Koporye. It was not only Theodor's emissaries who were displeased, but also the Swedish troops, who, standing on the opposite bank of the Plyussa, shouted to us,

"We do not want a bloodbath!"

They compelled their emissaries to be indulgent, so that they at last ceded us the Korela district, without demanding anything but peace. The emissaries adjourned, but we still wanted Narva. That same night, the Swedish General Johan Boe perfidiously laid siege to Ivangorod while the Narva agreement was still in effect. The courageous voivode Ivan Saburov, however, trounced the Swedes in a powerful sally, defeating both General Boe and the Duke of Södermanland, who had joined up with him. The main Muscovite army, based in Novgorod, did not arrive in time for the battle; they found the city already liberated and only saw the enemy's flight from a distance.

While he was fighting the Swedes, Theodor wanted to keep the peace with Lithuania, and while Moscow's legions were sacking Estonia, Godunov informed all the mayors in Polish Livonia that they might rest easy: we would not touch their districts and would fulfill the provisions of the Warsaw treaty exactly. Sigismund remained silent, however. To ascertain his disposition, the Moscow Duma sent a herald to Vilnius with a letter to its local nobles informing them of the khan's intention to once again march on Lithuania, adding,

"Kazy-Girei has been trying to convince our sovereign to join with him to make war on your land and has offered him permanent peace in the sultan's name, but the sovereign has refused, since he is sincerely favorably disposed towards you. We are warning you because we believe that sooner or later you will see the necessity of joining with Russia for the common security of Christians."

This ruse did not fool the pans: when they read the letter, they laughed, and expressed their gratitude in a very courteous letter, saying that they had heard a different rumor: that Theodor himself, if Crimean prisoners were to be believed, had been trying, with promises and gifts, to persuade the khan to invade Lithuania. Meanwhile, 600 Lithuanian Cossacks were pillaging Russia's southern border. They had torched the new town of Voronezh and murdered its governor, Prince Ivan Dolgorukii. We demanded satisfaction and ordered Prince Araslan-Alei, Kaibul's son, to march on Chernigov with his troops. Finally, in October 1590, Sigismund's emissaries Stanislav Radominskii and Gavrilo Voina arrived in Moscow to discuss peace and an alliance. However, in the first exchange with the boyars, they declared that Russia had violated the truce by taking Swedish towns and was obliged to return them. We replied that Sweden was not Lithuania, and that kings' ties of kinship are not respected in politics – we had captured our own so as to punish injustice and perfidy. There was a protracted discussion about a permanent peace.

Feigning magnanimity, Sigismund renounced Novgorod, Pskov, the Severskii towns, etc., but did not want to make peace without Smolensk. Moscow's boyars were firm:

"We will not give you a single village of the Smolensk uezd."

For about two months both sides waxed magniloquent as to the advantages of a close Christian alliance of all the European powers. Our boyars vividly represented to the Lithuanian nobles that the king had certainly been quite insincere about wanting this alliance, since we knew that at the same time he was seeking the sultan's favor. Sigismund could expect the same fate as Batory – shame and futile abasement before Ottoman pride. Batory had tried to ingratiate himself with Murad with the criminal murder of the most renowned of the Lithuanian knights, Podkov*, but did not succeed; for the rest of his life he continued to fear the angry sultan and to pay him servile tribute. Only Russia, which out of a sense of its own majesty, had rejected the false friendship of the infidel, would be a reliable shield for Christendom. The khan, who was so terrifying to Sigismund's state, would not dare to offend Theodor by word or deed – and more than 200 Crimean princes and mirzas were serving in the tsar's army. Although the Lithuanian emissaries no longer manifested the arrogance and rudeness of Stefan's time, they did not accept our lenient condition: that both powers continue to rule what they ruled at present. After exhausting all arguments, on 1 January 1591, the tsar summoned the clergy, boyars and officials to council and resolved only to ratify the truce concluded in Warsaw

> NEW TRUCE
> WITH
> LITHUANIA

for 12 more years with the new condition that neither we nor the Swedes would fight each other for a year. In fulfillment of the ancient custom, Theodor swore to observe the truce and sent the okolnichii Morozov to get the same from Sigismund.

Russia now enjoyed peace such as heretofore had only existed in the ruler's mind. We shall now set aside foreign policy to speak of interesting and important internal events.

---

* [Karamzin's endnote has this surname as Podkop.]

Boris Godunov now had the eye of Russia and all the other powers dealing with Moscow. He now stood on the highest rung of majesty as master of the realm and he saw nothing around himself except silent servants, or those loudly praising his great merits. Not only in the Kremlin palace, but in parts of Russia near and far, and even outside it, before foreign sovereigns and ministers, the tsar's eminent emissaries expressed themselves, in accordance with their instructions:

GODUNOV'S GREATNESS

"Boris Theodorovich Godunov is the ruler of the land. This is all at the autocrat's bidding, and so it is now arranged, so that the people marvel and rejoice. The military, businessmen and the people are all flourishing. Cities are being beautified with stone buildings without taxes or involuntary labor, out of the tsar's abundance, with rich payment for labor and artistry. Farmers live well, knowing no tribute. Justice is respected everywhere: the strong do not hurt the weak. If a poor orphan goes boldly to Boris Theodorovich to complain of his brother or cousin, this true noble will press charges against close relatives, even without trial, for he is partial to the defenseless and the weak!"

Immodestly boasting of his power and virtue, Boris, equally sly and hungry for glory, thought to give new glory to his reign by a significant innovation in the Church.

PATRIARCHATE ESTABLISHED IN RUSSIA

In ancient times, the term *patriarch* only meant a humble preceptor of the faith, but since the fourth century it had become a grandiose and high-flown title for the chief pastors of the Church in three parts of the world, i.e., in the three most eminent cities of the universal empire at that time: in Rome, Alexandria and Antioch. Places of sacred memory, Jerusalem and Constantinople, the capital city of the triumph of Christianity, were likewise honored with their own grand patriarchs. From the time of St. Vladimir till Theodor, Russia had not sought this honor. Byzantium, majestic and proud, had not consented to equate its hierarchy with Kiev's or Moscow's. Constantinople, in thrall to the Ottomans, might not have refused this to Ivan III, his son or grandson, but these rulers had kept silent, either out of respect for the pristine statutes of the Church, or because they feared to strengthen ecclesiastical power with this grand title to the detriment of the monarchical.

Boris thought otherwise, however. After deposing the metropolitan Dionisii for intrigue and effrontery, he did not hesitate to elevate humble Iov, who was devoted to him, for he wanted his valuable cooperation in his important plans. Back in 1586, when Patriarch Joachim of Antioch had come to Moscow for alms, the tsar had expressed to him his desire to establish a Russian patriarch. Joachim gave his word that he would propose this to a synod of the Greek Church, and he presented it with fervor, praising the purity of our faith.

In July 1588, to Theodor's great pleasure, the patriarch Jeremy of Constantinople also came to Moscow. The whole capital was in a commotion when this chief prelate of Christendom (the throne of the Byzantine archpriest had long been considered foremost), an elder distinguished by misfortune and virtue, viewed with interest its great population and the beauty of its churches. He blessed the people and was touched to the heart by their joyous greeting. He rode on a donkey past Moscow's streets and squares to see the tsar, followed on horseback by Hierotheos, the metropolitan of Monemvasia and Archbishop Arsenios of Elassona [anciently Oloosson, in northern Greece].

When they entered the Golden Palace, Theodor got up to receive him a few paces from the throne, seated him next to himself, and lovingly received his gifts: an icon commemorating the passion of our Lord, with a drop of Christ's blood and a relic of St. Constantine. He then bade Boris Godunov to converse with him in private. The patriarch was escorted to another room, where he told Boris of his life. After leading the Church for about 10 years, Jeremy had been accused by a certain evil Greek and exiled to Rhodes. The sultan, despite Mehmet II's formal promise not to interfere in the affairs of the Christian spiritual authority, had illegitimately given the patriarchate to Theoleptos. Five years later the rank of hierarch was restored to the exile, but Allah and Mohammed were now glorified in the ancient cathedral of the archprelate – the church had become a mosque.

"Weeping," said Jeremy, "I implored the cruel Murad to permit me to travel to Christian lands to gather alms to consecrate a new cathedral to the True God in the ancient capital of Orthodoxy. Yet where, except in Russia, might I find zeal, compassion and generosity?"

Later, in conversation with Godunov, he praised Theodor's idea of having a Russian patriarch. The wily Godunov offered this distinction to Jeremy himself on condition he live in Vladimir. Jeremy consented, but wanted to live where the tsar was, i.e., in Moscow. Godunov did not want this, and argued that it would be unjust to remove Iov, a holy man, from Moscow's Cathedral of the Virgin. Jeremy, who did not know Russia's language or customs, could not be a preceptor for the monarch without an interpreter, and it would be improper for such to fathom the depths of the sovereign's soul.

"Let the tsar's will be done!" replied the patriarch. "Empowered by our Church, I will bless and ordain whomever Theodor chooses, for he is inspired by God."

There was no doubt as to the choice, but the Russian prelates nominated three candidates for the ceremony: the metropolitan Iov, Archbishop Aleksandr of Novgorod and Varlaam of Rostov, and submitted their report to the sovereign, who chose Iov. On 23 January 1589, after vespers, the archprelate-elect, in stole, scapular and chasuble, celebrated mass in the Cathedral of the Dormition with all the bishops and in the presence of the tsar and countless numbers of people. He left the altar and stood at the ambo, holding a taper in one hand and a letter of thanks to the sovereign and the priesthood in the other. Now one of the eminent officials approached him, likewise with a burning taper, and intoned loudly,

"The Orthodox tsar, the ecumenical patriarch and the holy synod elevate you to the throne of Vladimir, Moscow and all Russia."

Iov responded, "I am but a sinful slave, but since the autocrat, the ecumenical lord Jeremy and the synod are awarding me this exalted title, I shall accept it with gratitude."

He humbly bowed his head, turned to the clergy and the people and with feeling intoned his promise to diligently guard the flock bestowed upon him by God. This completed the ceremony of selection; the formal ordination was performed on 26 January during the liturgy, as with the usual installation of metropolitans and bishops, and without any new rituals. In the main cathedral on a dais, a depiction of a two-headed eagle had been made in chalk, as well as a stage with 12 levels and 12 candle-bearers.

Now the most senior pastor of Eastern Orthodoxy blessed Iov as a coregent with the great Christian fathers, placed his trembling hand on him and prayed that this archpriest of Jesus would be an inextinguishable lamp unto the faith. With a miter on his head and with cross and crown, the newly ordained patriarch of Moscow celebrated mass with the Patriarch of Byzantium, and then, after the liturgy, the sovereign took off his robes and with his own hands entrusted him with the precious cross, with the life-giving tree, a green velvet mantle with strips of texts sewn to it with pearls, and a white cylindrical hat with the sign of the cross. He then presented him with the crozier of St. Pyotr the Metropolitan, and in a speech of welcome ordered the [new] chief bishop to be called Father of Fathers, Patriarch of all the northern lands, by the grace of God and the will of the tsar. Iov blessed Theodor and the people, and the masses wished long life to the tsar and to the two archprelates of Byzantium and Moscow who were sitting in chairs next to him. After leaving the church, Iov, accompanied by two bishops, boyars and many officials, rode around the Kremlin walls on a donkey beneath a cross, sprinkling holy water and reciting prayers for the preservation of the city. He then dined with Jeremy along with all the clergy and the council.

To confirm the dignity and privileges of the Russian hierarch, an authorizing document was written, explaining that Old Rome fell because of the heresy of Apollinaris; New Rome – Constantinople – was conquered by the godless tribes of Hagar; and the Third Rome was Moscow. Instead of the false pastor of the Western Church, darkened by a spirit of vain philosophizing, the first ecumenical prelate was the patriarch of Constantinople; the second, of Alexandria; and the third, of Moscow and all Russia; the fourth, of Antioch; and the fifth, of Jerusalem. In Russia, one must pray for the Greek patriarchs, but in Greece, for one of ours, who will henceforth, until the end of the epoch, be chosen and consecrated in Moscow independent of the others' consent or approval. The following was added regarding the outward external honors of the archpastor of our Church:

"His appearances must always be accompanied by an icon lamp, hymns and bells. For his vestments, he is to have an ambo with three steps; on weekdays he is to wear a white cylindrical hat with embroidered seraphim and crosses, with watered silk gown and everything else in stripes; he is to proceed with a cross and crozier, and to ride in a six-horse carriage."

The sovereign and these two patriarchs decided that Russia should have four metropolitans: for Novgorod, Kazan, Rostov and Krutitsy; six archbishops: for Vologda, Suzdal, Nizhnyi Novgorod, Smolensk, Ryazan and Tver; and eight [sic] bishops: for Pskov, Rzev, Ustyug, Belo-ozero, Kolomenskoe, Seversk and Dmitrovsk.

Jeremy, the metropolitan of Monemvasia and the archbishop of Elassona participated in these ecclesiastical arrangements more *pro forma* than in fact. Meanwhile, they traveled to the Sergiev Monastery, where, just as in Moscow's cathedrals, they were astounded by the richness of the icons, vessels and the chasubles of the officiants. In the capital, they dined with the patriarch Iov and praised his intelligent conversation. They also praised Godunov's exceptional merits and the rare intellect of the elder, Andrei Shchelkalov. But most of all they praised Russian generosity, since they kept getting gifts of silver goblets, ladles, pearls, silken fabrics, sable pelts and coins.

Presented to the tsaritsa, they were delighted with her sanctity, humble majesty, angelic beauty and mellifluous speech as much as with her outer splendor. She wore a crown with 12 pearl-encrusted points, a diadem and a golden chain on her breast adorned with precious stones. Her dress was velvet, long and studded with large pearls, and her gown was no less rich. Next to the tsaritsa stood the tsar, and on the other side, Boris Godunov, bareheaded, modest and reverent. Farther off were many eminent women in white dresses and with arms folded. Irina implored the Greek prelates to pray God that He would grant her a son, an heir to the throne. The archbishop of Elassona writes in his description of his journey to Moscow:

"And all of us were touched to the depths of our hearts, and, weeping along with her, with one voice called upon the Most High to grant such a pure, fervent prayer from this devout soul!"

Finally, in May 1589, the sovereign sent Jeremy off to Constantinople with a letter to the sultan urging him not to oppress Christians. In addition, he sent 1,000 rubles, or 2,000 Hungarian gold pieces, for the construction of a new patriarchal church. This greatly gratified all the Greek clergy, who had approved, in a consiliar letter, the establishment of the Muscovite patriarchy. In June 1591 they provided Theodor with a charter via the metropolitan of Trnovo, along with holy relics and two crowns, for the tsar and tsaritsa.

In this way we established another upper rung in our church hierarchy, one that for 110 years the great autocrats had rejected as unnecessary for the Church and harmful for their autocracy. However, the prudent man who established this did not thereby give the priesthood any new governmental powers, and although changing his title, left the high priest completely dependent on the monarch. Pyotr I [Peter the Great] knew the story of Nikon and divided up the spiritual power so as to weaken it. He would also, if only during his reign, abolish the rank of patriarch, so that as in Ivan's time, or more anciently, only one metropolitan directed the Russian Church. Pyotr ruled as a tsar, and wanted only servants.

Godunov was still a subject, and sought support, since he could foresee circumstances in which the tsaritsa's friendship would not be sufficient for his love of power – or to save him, either. He restrained the boyars, but read the malicious envy in their hearts, justifiable hatred for his murder of the Shuiskiis. He had friends, but they would either stand by him and fall with him, or betray him, depending on the vicissitudes of fate. He benefited the people, but they had little faith in his natural inclination to do good. Boris knew that in crucial circumstances the people would turn their perplexed gaze towards the boyars and the priesthood. In Pyotr's place, Godunov might also have abolished the rank of patriarch, but being in different circumstances, he wanted to flatter Iov's ambition with a lofty title so as to have him as a more enthusiastic and eminent accomplice. The crucial hour was coming: would a rebellious noble at last dare to raise the veil of the future?

If, with everything except Theodor's crown, Godunov had not wanted anything further, how could he have quietly enjoyed his majesty while contemplating the imminent death of Theodor, who was weak not only in spirit, but in body as well? He also would be thinking of the tsar's legitimate successor, who was being raised by his mother and kinfolk, in public, although honorable exile, and would have vengeful and malicious feelings towards the ruler. What would await Irina in such an event? A nunnery. And Godunov? Prison or the executioner's block for him who moved the realm with a single nod, upon whom rulers from east and west fawned!

> GODUNOV'S
> SCHEMING
> 1591

Boris's soul had already been bared by his deeds. Those whom the ruler feared had died in the pit or at the execution place in Red Square – and who could be more dangerous to him than Dimitrii?

Godunov still suffered from a hunger of the soul and wanted that which he did not have. He was prideful from his distinctions and merits, from glory and flattery, and intoxicated by his good fortune and power, which were enchanting to such a noble soul. Boris circled heights to which no subject of the Russian state had heretofore ascended, and looked still higher, with bold desire. He ruled without demur, but not in his own name, for he shone only by reflected light. In his pride, he had to burden himself with a mask of humility, and solemnly abase himself before this shadow of a tsar, kowtowing with the other slaves. The throne seemed to Godunov not only a sacred, effulgent site of true primordial power, but also a place of paradisiacal peace, which the arrows of the hostile and the envious could not reach, and which a mortal could possess as if by divine right.

This dream of the charms of supreme power became more and more vivid to Godunov, and roiled his heart more and more, so that it ultimately preoccupied him constantly. A chronicler relates the following curious, albeit doubtful, event:

"Although he had a rare intellect, Boris believed in the fortune-tellers' art. He summoned a few of them in the quiet hour of the night and asked what awaited him in the future. The supposed wizards or astrologers answered, 'The crown awaits you...' But then they suddenly fell silent, as if frightened by a more distant vision. The impatient Boris ordered them to continue and heard that he would reign only seven years. He joyously embraced the fortunetellers and exclaimed,

"Although it might be for only seven days, at least I will reign as tsar!"

With such immodesty did Godunov appear to reveal the depths of his soul to these phony wise men of a superstitious age! At any rate, he no longer concealed his ambition from himself: he knew what he wanted! While awaiting the death of the childless tsar, he had the tsaritsa's confidence, filled the Duma, court and ministries with his relatives and friends, and had no doubts about the devotion of the grandly titled hierarch of the Church. He likewise relied on the brilliance of his rule and kept scheming to conquer the hearts or the imaginations of the people. Boris did not quail before a chance unexampled in our country from the time of Ryurik to Theodor's: an effectively vacant throne, the end of the ruling line and the roiling of passions in selecting a new dynasty. He was firmly convinced that after the scepter fell from the hand of the last monarch of Monomakh's blood, it would be entrusted to him who had ruled long and gloriously without the title of tsar. This power-hungry man saw only a defenseless child between himself and the throne, as a hungry lion views the lamb.

Dimitrii's doom was ineluctable.

In embarking on the realization of his horrifying plan, Boris first schemed to have the ill-fated tsarevich declared illegitimate, as the son of Ivan's sixth or seventh wife. He commanded that no prayers be given for him, nor his name mentioned at mass. However, he reasoned that this marriage, although in fact illegitimate, had been affirmed, or at least tolerated by the ecclesiastical powers. If they were to formally annul it, they would there by acknowledge their human failings and would doubly tempt Christians into error.

He also saw that Dimitrii, despite this, would remain tsarevich in public opinion and Theodor's sole successor. Accordingly, Godunov resorted to a more reliable means to get rid of his rival, justifying himself by a rumor, no doubt spread by his friends about a fictitious early precocious disposition on the part of Dimitrii towards evil and cruelty.

In Moscow they said openly (evidently without fear of offending the tsar or the ruler) that this child, when he was not more than six or seven years old, supposedly was completely like his father, that he loved torture and blood, that he was happy to watch animals being killed and even killed them himself. They wished to arouse hatred in the people against Dimitrii with this tale. They also concocted another story for eminent officials: they said that one time the tsarevich was playing on the ice with other children and ordered them to make 20 snowmen. He positioned them next to one another and named them after the foremost men of the country, then started slashing at them with a saber. He cut off the head of the one named Boris Godunov and the arms and legs of others, saying, "So much for you when I rule!" Contradicting this absurd slander, many insisted that the young tsarevich showed intelligence and qualities worthy of a ruler-to-be. They said this with compassion and fear, for they surmised the innocent child's peril and perceived the aim of this calumny. They were not deceived: if Godunov had been wrestling with his conscience, he had now conquered it; he had prepared the gullible to have no pity when they heard of the crime. He held poison or a knife in his hand for Dimitrii and only needed someone to perform the murder.

Can trust and candor be part of such a vile scheme? Yet Boris had need of accomplices and disclosed it to those closest to him. One of them, the butler Grigorii Vasilievich Godunov, wept, showed compassion, humanity and fear of God – and was banished from the council. All the rest thought that Dimitrii's death was necessary for the ruler's safety and the good of the nation. They began with poison. The tsarevich's nanny, the boyar's wife Vasilisa Volokhova and her son Osip sold their souls to Godunov and served as his instrument, but according to the chronicler, the potion did not harm the child, either in his food or drink. Perhaps a conscience still operated in the perpetrators of this hellish scheme; perhaps a trembling hand poured the poison carefully, lessening its effect – and angering the impatient Boris, who decided to use other, bolder villains.

The choice fell on two officials, Vladimir Zagryazhskii and Nikifor Chepchugov, who were indebted to the ruler for his favors, but both dodged the proposal. They were ready to die for Boris, but were revulsed by murder. They merely promised to be silent, and were banished from this time on. Then Boris's most enthusiastic calumniator, the tsar's uncle, the okolnichii Andrei Lupp-Kleshnin brought forth a reliable man: the secretary Mikhail Bityagovskii, whose face was distinguished by the stamp of brutality, and thereby vouched for his reliability as a criminal. Godunov sent gold, promising more, as well as complete safety. He ordered the miscreant to Uglich to manage the widowed tsaritsa's farms and household. He was not to take his eyes off the doomed victim and not to overlook the first favorable opportunity. Bityagovskii gave his word, and kept it.

R iding together with him to Uglich were his son Danilo and nephew Nikita Kachalov, who likewise had Godunov's complete trust. Success appeared easy: they were able to be with the tsaritsa day and night, busying themselves with her domestic duties, supervising her servants and managing her table, while Dimitrii's nanny and her son helped them with advice and deeds. Dimitrii, however, was protected by his tender mother. She was warned, either by some secret well-wishers or by her own heart, and doubled her efforts to care for her dear son. She stayed right with him, day and night, and left her rooms

> MURDER
> OF CROWN PRINCE
> DIMITRII

only to go to church. She fed him with her own hands, entrusting this neither to the evil nanny Volokhova nor to the diligent wet-nurse Irina Zhdanova.

Considerable time passed, and at last the assassins, seeing no possibility of performing the crime secretly, dared to do it openly. They hoped that Godunov, cunning and powerful, would find a way to conceal it for his own honor in the eyes of his mute servants. They were thinking only of men, and not of God! The day of the terrible event with its long-term consequences arrived. On Saturday, 15 May, in the sixth hour of the day, the tsaritsa returned from church with her son and was getting ready to eat. Her brothers were not in the palace and the servants were bringing the food. Just then the boyarinya Volokhova called Dimitrii to come and walk in the yard. The tsaritsa was going to go with him, but stopped due to some unfortunate distraction. The wet-nurse held onto the tsarevich without knowing why. Suddenly the nanny forcefully took him out of the room and into the hallway, and then to the lower porch, where Osip Volokhov, Danilo Bityagovskii and Nikita Kachalov were. The first took Dimitrii by the hand, saying,

"Sovereign! You have a new necklace." With an innocent smile, the boy raised his head and answered, "No, elder..."

The assassin's knife flashed above him, just missed his throat and fell from Volokhov's hand. Screaming in horror, the wet-nurse hugged her royal charge. Volokhov ran away, but Danilo Bityagovskii and Kachalov seized their victim, stabbed him and threw him down the staircase at the same moment as the tsaritsa was coming out of the hall onto the porch. The nine year old holy martyr lay bloody in the embrace of the one who had raised him and tried to protect him with her breast. He *quivered like a dove*, gasped, and expired, no longer hearing the despairing cries of his mother. The wet-nurse pointed at the godless nanny, who was rattled by the crime, and at the murderers, fleeing through the courtyard to the gate. There was no one to stop them, but the Almighty Avenger was present!

A minute later, the whole town presented a spectacle of inexplicable uproar. The sacristan of the main church – who, it is written, either saw the murder himself or was informed of it by the tsaritsa's servants – sounded the tocsin, and the streets filled with alarmed and bewildered people. They ran toward the sound of the bell; seeing smoke and flames, they thought the palace was on fire and broke through its gate, where they saw the tsarevich dead on the ground. His mother and wet-nurse were lying senseless next to him, but they had already named the perpetrators. These monsters, marked by the Unseen Judge for righteous punishment, were unable, or afraid to hide, lest they thereby reveal their crimes.

In the confusion and frenzy, frightened by the tocsin and the noise and the efforts of the people, they ran inside the Cabin of Ranks, and their secret leader, Mikhailo Bityagovskii, rushed towards the bell tower to grab the bell-ringer, but was unable to break through its locked door.

He fearlessly appeared at the scene of the crime and approached the body of the victim. He tried to calm the people's agitation, and dared to tell the citizens (he had previously concocted this lie with Kleshnin or Boris) that the boy had killed himself with a knife during an epileptic fit.

"Murderer!" cried the crowd, and showered stones upon the villain. He tried to find refuge in the palace with one of his minions, Danilo Tretyakov, but the people seized and killed them. They broke in the door of the cabin and killed Mikhailo's son and Nikita Kachalov as well. The third assassin, Osip Volokhov, escaped to Mikhailo Bityagovskii's house, but was seized and brought to the Church of the Savior, where Dimitrii's coffin was. He was killed there before the eyes of the tsaritsa. Also killed were Mikhailo's servants and three tradesmen guilty or suspected of collaboration with the assassins, and a deranged woman who lived at Bityagovskii's house and had often gone into the palace. The nanny, however, was left alive to give important evidence. It is written that as the murderers were dying, they unburdened their consciences with sincere confessions, and named the chief conspirator in Dimitrii's death – Boris Godunov. It is likely that the frightened nanny was not placed in hellish fetters, but the judge of this crime was the criminal himself [i.e., Boris].

Vengeance had been exacted illegally, although justifiably: civil laws had been forgotten due to hatred toward the villains and love for the royal bloodline. Exculpable due to their fervor, but guilty before a government court, the people came to their senses. They became silent, waiting uneasily for an edict from Moscow – the city leaders had sent a courier there with a frank report of the calamitous event, addressed to the tsar. But Godunov was vigilant: officials loyal to him were posted along the Uglich highway and all travelers were stopped, questioned and inspected. The courier was arrested and brought to Boris. The evil desire of the power-lover had been realized! It was only necessary to cover the truth with a lie, which if not completely credible to impartial people, would at least preserve appearances and propriety.

The letter from Uglich was taken and rewritten: it now said that the tsarevich, in a convulsive paroxysm, had stabbed himself with a knife. This was allegedly due to the negligence of the Nagois, who in covering their culpability had shamelessly and falsely accused the secretary Bityagovskii and his men of Dimitrii's murder, inflamed the people and criminally slaughtered these innocent men. With this forgery, Godunov hastened to Theodor and hypocritically expressed his heartfelt grief. While trembling and looking to the heavens, he related the terrible tale of Dimitrii's death, mixing his crocodile tears with the older brother's genuine ones. According to the chronicler, the tsar wept bitterly, was silent for a long time and then said, "Let God's will be done!" He believed it all, but Russia required something more. Diligence needed to be shown in investigating all the circumstances of this misfortune. Wasting no time, two eminent officials were immediately dispatched to Uglich. And who were these? One was the okolnichii Andrei Kleshnin, Boris's chief accomplice in the crime! This choice was no surprise. What was surprising was the second choice: the boyar Prince Vasilii Ivanovich Shuiskii, whose elder brother, Prince Andrei, had been killed by Godunov, and who during several years spent in disgrace, had expected the same fate.

But the cunning Boris had reconciled with this ambitious and flighty prince, who was intelligent, but lacked virtuous principles. Godunov had also reconciled with Vasilii's younger brother Dimitrii, and had married him to his young sister-in-law and given him the rank of boyar. Godunov knew men, and he was not mistaken in the case of Prince Vasilii; by this choice, he manifested a bogus intrepidity and a phony impartiality. On the evening of 19 May, Prince Shuiskii, Kleshnin and the secretary Vyluzgin arrived in Uglich with the metropolitan of Sarai and went straight to the Church of the Transfiguration.

Dimitrii's bloody body was still lying there, and on it, the assassins' knife. His ill-fated mother, relatives and all the good citizens were weeping bitterly. With a sensitive expression Shuiskii approached the coffin in order to see the face of the deceased and inspect the wound, but when Kleshnin saw that angelic, peaceful face, with the blood and the knife, he began trembling, froze in place, and began weeping. He still had a conscience and was unable to say a word. Dimitrii's deep wound, with his throat cut by a powerful hand – not his own, not a child's – testified to the certainty of murder. This is why they hastened to commit the sacred remains of this innocent to the earth. The metropolitan performed the funeral services and Prince Shuiskii began his enquiries. They are a monument to his remorseless mendacity, preserved by time as if in justification of the calamities which fell a few years later on the now-crowned head of this weak, if not ungodly prevaricator! After assembling the clergy and the citizens, he inquired of them,

"How did Dimitrii, because of the Nagois' negligence, stab himself?" Unanimously and with one voice, the monks and priests, men and women, old and young, replied,

"The tsarevich was murdered by his slaves, Mikhailo Bityagovskii and his accomplices, by order of Boris Godunov."

Shuiskii would hear no more, and dismissed them. He resolved to make a special, secret investigation, not open to the public, using threats and promises. He summoned whom he wanted, wrote what he wanted, and finally, with Kleshnin and the secretary Vyluzgin, composed the following report to the tsar, supposedly based on the testimony of the city officials, the nanny Volokhova, the tsarevich's boyar cadets, Dimitrii's wet-nurse Irina, the chambermaid Mariya Samoilova and two Nagois: Grigorii and Andrei Aleksandrov, as well as the tsaritsa's stewards and scriveners, plus some citizens and church people:

"On Wednesday, May 12th, Dimitrii became ill from epilepsy, but Friday he was better and walked with the tsaritsa to mass and strolled in the courtyard. On Saturday, again after mass, he went out to stroll in the yard with his nanny, wet-nurse, chambermaid and some young boyar cadets. They started to play with him in a game employing a knife, and in a new attack of his illness, he stabbed himself in the throat and writhed a long time on the ground before dying. Dimitrii had previously been affected by this illness: he had once wounded his mother, and another time he bit the arm of Andrei Nagoi's daughter. When she learned of her son's misfortune, the tsaritsa ran up and started hitting his nanny, saying that Volokhov, Kachalov and Danilo Bityagovskii had stabbed him, but none of them were present.

The tsaritsa and her *drunken* brother, Mikhailo Nagoi, however, ordered them to be killed, and also the innocent secretary Bityagovskii, solely because this diligent secretary was displeased by the Nagois' cupidity and would not give them money exceeding what the sovereign had instructed. When he learned that the tsar's officials were coming to Uglich, Mikhailo Nagoi ordered that some handguns, knives and iron cudgels be brought, smeared with blood and placed on the dead bodies to implicate them in an imaginary crime."

This absurdity was attested to by the Voskresenskii archimandrite Theodorit, two abbots and the Nagois' confessor, due to timidity and cowardice, while testimony of the truth, which was secular and unanimous, was covered up. Only the response of Mikhailo Nagoi was recorded, as a supposedly brazen slanderer, who stubbornly insisted that Dimitrii had died at the hands of malefactors.

Shuiskii returned to Moscow, and on 2 June presented his reports to the sovereign, and the sovereign sent them on to the patriarch and the prelates, who in joint session with the Duma, ordered the scroll to be read by the eminent secretary Vasilii Shchelkalov. After hearing it, the metropolitan Gelasii of Sarai stood up and said to Iov,

"I declare to the Holy Synod that on the day of my departure from the widowed tsaritsa summoned me and tearfully tried to persuade me to mollify the sovereign's wrath at those who killed the secretary Bityagovskii and his comrades. She herself sees the criminality of that deed and humbly prays that the sovereign not execute her poor kinfolk."

The sly Gelasii, who had probably misrepresented the unhappy mother's words, submitted a new document in the name of the bailiff of the city of Uglich, who wrote that Dimitrii had indeed died of the black disease [epilepsy] and that the *drunken* Mikhailo

Nagoi had ordered the murder of the innocents. The synod (a sorry memory for our Church!) submitted a report to Theodor with the following contents:

"May it be the sovereign's will! We have ascertained that there is no doubt that the tsarevich's life was cut short by divine judgment, that Mikhailo Nagoi is the perpetrator of a ghastly massacre, acting out of personal malice and the counsel of evil soothsayers, Andrei Mochalov and others. The citizens of Uglich and he merit death for their *treachery* and criminality. This, however, is a secular deed, known to God and the sovereign; disgrace or mercy is in the hands of the ruler. Our duty is simply to pray for the tsar and tsaritsa and for the tranquility and prosperity of the people!"

Theodor ordered the boyars to resolve the matter and punish the guilty. The Nagois were transported to Moscow, along with Dimitrii's wet-nurse and her husband and the supposed soothsayer Mochalov, in heavy fetters. They were interrogated once more and tortured, especially Mikhailo Nagoi, but they were unable to force him to lie about Dimitrii's alleged suicide. Finally, all the Nagois were banished to a remote town and imprisoned. The widowed tsaritsa was forced to take vows and taken to the wilderness of St. Nikolai at Vyksa (near Cherepovets). The bodies of the criminals Bityagovskii and his comrades, which the people of Uglich had cast into a pit, were removed for funeral services and committed to the earth with great honors. The citizens of Uglich who were declared murderers of the innocent were executed, about 200 of them. Others had their tongues cut out and many were imprisoned. The majority were sent to Siberia and settled in the town of Pelym. The result was that ancient and extensive Uglich, which if we believe tradition, had 150 churches and no less than 30,000 residents, was permanently abandoned and became a memorial to Boris's terrible wrath against those bold enough to accuse him of this deed. The ruins remain, and cry to Heaven for vengeance!

While punishing courage, Godunov rewarded criminality with the same audacity. He gave rich lands and estates to the vile nanny Volokhova and to Bityagovskii's widow and daughters. He also showered rich gifts on the men of the Duma and all the eminent officials. He flattered them and entertained them at sumptuous dinners, but was unable to calm Kleshnin, who was torn by his conscience and died some years later as a monk. Yet in the silence of the court and the Church the murmuring of the people could be heard. They were not deceived by Shuiskii's investigation, the prelates' verdict or the boyars' judgment. Godunov's spies heard muttering about a terrible immolation and its secret perpetrator, the tsar's regrettable blindness and the shameless connivance of the nobles and the clergy. They also saw the crowds of sorrowing faces.

Boris was disturbed by these rumors, but found a way to calm them when a great calamity befell the capital. On the evening before Whit Sunday, after the sovereign had gone with his boyars to the Monastery of St. Sergei, the Kolymazhnyi Court caught fire. In a few hours the following streets were consumed: Arbatskaya, Nikitskaya, Tverskaya and Petrovskaya as far as Truba. All of Belyi Gorod burned and beyond it, the Court of Emissaries, the

| CONFLAGRATION IN MOSCOW |

musketeers' towns and the whole Zaneglinnye. Homes, stores, churches and a great number of people were incinerated. The Kremlin and Kitaigorod, where the upper nobility lived, were left intact, but the citizens were left without shelter and some had lost their possessions. Moaning and wailing reverberated across the vast expanses of ashes, and crowds of people hurried down the Troitskaya Road to see Theodor and ask for his charity and assistance. Boris did not let them get near the tsar: he appeared before them with an expression of love and compassion. He heard everyone out, made promises to them all, and kept those promises. Godunov rebuilt whole streets and distributed money and letters of preference. He showed unprecedented generosity, so that Muscovites were consoled and amazed by his good works, and began to praise him enthusiastically. Did he just happen to take advantage of the capital's calamity to gain popularity, or was he its secret perpetrator, as the chronicler asserts, and as many contemporaries believed? Right in the Book of Ranks it says that a miscreant torched Moscow, but Boris tried to turn suspicion onto his enemies. He arrested Athanasii Nagoi's people and his brothers, interrogated them and declared that they were guilty. However, he did not punish them and the affair remains murky to posterity.

Soon another event, seemingly favorable to Godunov, roiled Moscow and all Russia. A great and unexpected peril distracted the people from the horror of Dimitrii's death: a barbarian invasion. While deceiving Theodor with assurances of friendship, Khan Kazy-Girei had contacted the Swedish king, requesting gold from him and promising to rock Moscow with a powerful attack. Carrying out the orders of our enemy, the sultan, and displeased with Russia himself, the khan had indeed been preparing for this. In the first place, he had learned that we had secretly informed the Lithuanian pans that he intended to invade them once again and had proposed to join forces with them to make war on the Taurid. He probably learned this from King Sigismund. In the second place, Theodor had not released Prince Murat to go to the khan. The latter had promised amnesty to this nephew and to make him *kalga*, or chief noble of the Taurid Horde. Murat was living in Astrakhan as Russia's ever-diligent vassal, restraining the Nogai. He died suddenly, to Theodor's genuine regret, done in, it was thought, by malefactors sent against him from the Crimea. The khan maintained, however, that the Russians had poisoned him and swore vengeance. The third reason for Kazy-Girei taking up arms against Russia was his princes' idea that every good khan was obliged to carry out the ancient commitment to one day see the banks of the Oka for martial honor. That is, he wanted Russian booty and believed the Swedish emissary who was with them that our entire army was engaged in warfare with his king.

> INVASION
> OF THE KHAN
> AND BATTLE
> BEFORE MOSCOW

We had always had friends and spies in the Crimea so that we could learn not just about the khans' operations, but also his intentions. There were also Muscovite heralds there at this time, so that the khan could not hide his extraordinary mobilization from us. Yet he was still able to deceive us: he assured our vigilant ruler that he was going to ravage Vilnius and Krakow. He also dispatched a distinguished embassy to Moscow to conclude a treaty with us and asked that the tsar immediately send one of our foremost officials to him. Meanwhile, all the uluses were mobilizing – all able bodied men, both young and old, mounted up. Legions from Kazy's Nogai uluses and the sultan's joined them from Azov and Belgorod, with artillery.

Spring had begun, always a dangerous time in southern Russia, but the tsar's Duma was not intimidated: at the beginning of April they sent some distinguished voivodes to our customary army on the riverbanks in Serpukhov, Kaluga and other places. These were the princes Mstislavskii, Nogotkov, the Trubetskiis, Golitsyn and Thedor Khvorostinin. The month of May arrived, but our mounted patrols had still not encountered a single Tatar on the banks of the Northern Donets or Borova; they saw only traces of the winter migration and abandoned yurts.

On 26 June, however, couriers galloped into Moscow with the news that the steppes were covered with masses of the khan's troops. No fewer than 150,000 Crimeans were heading for Tula, by passing our forts. They were not dallying anywhere, nor were they dispersing to pillage. Godunov was obliged to summon all his energy to make up for his negligence. That same hour he sent orders to all the steppe fortifications to speed to Serpukhov and link up with Prince Mstislavskii in order to engage the khan in the field. Unfortunately, our main army was then stationed in Novgorod and Pskov, keeping an eye on the Swedes; it would not be able to arrive in time for a decisive battle, and this was not under consideration. Moscow was declared under siege. Defense of the sovereign's palace was entrusted to Prince Ivan Mikhailovich Glinskii, of the Kremlin to the boyar Prince Dimitrii Ivanovich Shuiskii, of Kitaigorod to Golitsyn, and of Belyi Gorod to Nogtev-Suzdalskii and Musa Turenin. On 28 June they learned of a rapid enemy drive on the capital and became convinced of the impossibility of joining up with any of the legions on the Oka before the khan's arrival.

We modified our dispositions: Mstislavskii was ordered to march to Moscow to do battle with the infidel before its sacred walls, in view of the Kremlin palaces and cathedrals, before the eyes of the tsar and tsaritsa, for faith and fatherland. To cheer the people, word was spread that we had withdrawn from the banks of the Oka and were luring the enemy into a trap, an also that we intended to utterly exterminate him inside Russia. This with-drawal indeed united the riverbank army with several thousand of Moscow's best troops, the sovereign's noble guard, eminent court nobles and boyar cadets, as well as its armed citizens. It gave us a significant preponderance of forces and the advantage in a battle beneath those invincible walls, and under the thundering of our heavy artillery, which was terrifying to the barbarians. All that was needed was to take measures to prevent the khan from visiting fire and destruction on the bowels of the capital, as Devlet-Girei had in 1571.

Accordingly, the suburbs* across the Moscow River were fortified with amazing speed with wooden walls and gun emplacements. The Danilovskii, Novospasskii and Simonov monasteries were turned into strongholds and an army camp was established about two versts from the city, between the Kaluga and Tula highways. A moveable fort on wheels was constructed there of wooden planks, and a Church of St. Sergei containing the icon of the Virgin that had been with Dimitrii at the Battle of the Don. They sang hymns, circumambulated all of Moscow with crosses and impatiently awaited Mstislavskii. That voivode had departed Serpukhov on 29 June, leaving a small guard force on the Oka. He spent the night in Lopasna amidst lofty kurgans, glorious memorials to the unforgettable victory of 1572.

The same enemy was coming, but Russia no longer had a Vorotynskii! In the evening of 1 July our legions took up positions on the meadows by the Moscow River, opposite the village of Kolomenskoe, while the voivodes hastened to the sovereign to bring reports and receive advice. They returned on the following morning, leading the legions into the camp prepared for them opposite the Danilovskii Monastery. That same day the sovereign himself came out to inspect the troops and *rewarded* the voivodes and men-at-arms *with gracious words and inquired after their health.* He showed no timidity, but declared his hope in God and in his good Russians.

On 3 July Theodor was informed that the khan had crossed the Oka below Teshlov, had spent the night at Lopasna and was now marching directly for Moscow. The enemy's vanguard encountered the valiant voivode Prince Bakhteyarov, who had been dispatched to Pokhra with 250 boyar cadets. They defeated him and pursued him, cruelly wounded, to the settlement of

---

* [The word "suburb" has disconcertingly modern connotations, but unfortunate there is no better word in English.]

Bittsa. Our army was now ready for battle; every legion took its position and did not leave its fortifications. Towards evening the tsar's entire guard unit came to them, and Boris Godunov finally showed up in full armor, on a warhorse, beneath the ancient banner of the grand princes. He who was the heart and soul of the nation and the Council now also had to inspire the troops in a battle for their country.

Theodor gave him all his court nobles and his bodyguards, who had heretofore been inseparable from the person of the monarch. He had gone to a separate hall with his wife and confessor for prayer. He did not fear danger, since he feared for his sins, and had done all that he could for the salvation of the country. With angelic calm, he committed himself and his nation to the will of the Most High. The boyars all rode behind the ruler as if behind the sovereign. However, when he was met and greeted by the voivodes, he did not take command from the most eminent and experienced officer, Prince Mstislavskii. He was satisfied with second place within the main legion and formed himself a war council from six officers, which included that noted turncoat, Bogdan Yakovlevich Belskii, a knight decorated with tokens of distinction and glory, who through Godunov's power, had been reconciled with the court and the people.

The army was stationed beneath their banners all night long, and Godunov was awake the whole night, walking through the ranks, strengthening the morale of the voivodes and the troops, giving and taking counsel. He asked for their trust, and got it, using his great mind to make up for his insufficient military experience. The enemy was known to be close; noise could be heard in the distance, and the clatter of horses' hooves. When dawn came the dense formations of the khan's troops could be made out. Kazy-Girei moved cautiously and halted opposite Kolomenskoe village. From the Poklonnyi Hill he surveyed the scene and then ordered his princes to strike the Muscovite army.

Up till now, all had been quiet, but as soon as the numerous enemy cavalry charged down from heights and into the plain, all our gun emplacements thundered: from the camp, monasteries and Kremlin walls. Companies of crack troops from each legion, with select commanders, *Lithuanian* units and Germans with their captains, set out from their fortifications to engage the Crimeans, while the voivodes with the main force remained inside the moveable wooden fort awaiting their hour. The battle commenced suddenly in many locations, since the enemy had dispersed under a rain of cannon fire. They were shooting arrows, and in skirmishes were more effective than we with their sabers. But we had the advantage, and fired skillfully from small arquebuses, halting and attacking in unison.

The sandy plain was covered with more Moslem bodies than Christian: it could be viewed by both the khan and the Muscovites, whose walls, turrets and bell towers were covered with people, both armed and unarmed, full of curiosity and fear, for this was a battle for Moscow, which would either fall or be saved by the victors. The people would alternately be silent and cry out, attentively following all the movements of the sanguinary struggle – a novel spectacle for our ancient capital, which had seen assaults on its walls, but up till now had never seen a field battle on its plains. There was no need of messengers: one's own eyes determined the emotions of fear and hope. Others did not want to watch any of it, and looked only at the sacred icons, dampening the daises of the cathedrals with their tears, where the priests' hymns were drowned out by the noise of cannon fire and the smell of incense, by gunsmoke. It was a tale barely believable: in this solemn, fateful moment when hearts were shuddering even in aged Moscow elders, there was one man who enjoyed the peace of an unperturbed heart: it was he whose name and God's had summoned Russians to the slaughter, and for whom they were dying beneath the walls of the capital – the sovereign! Exhausted by long prayer, Theodor was taking his ease at the noon hour. He was standing and looking impassively upon the battle from his lofty chamber; behind him stood his good boyar, Grigorii Vasilievich Godunov, weeping. Theodor turned to him, saw his tears and said,

"Be at peace! Tomorrow the khan will be no more." These words, says the chronicler, seemed prophetic.

The battle was not decisive. Both sides were reinforcing their troops, but the main forces had not yet entered the fray.

Msistlavskii and Godunov, with the tsar's banners and the better half of the army were holding their positions, waiting for the khan, who, with his most reliable guard units, occupied the village of Vorobyevo that evening. He did not care to descend from his hill, from which his greedy eyes devoured the capital, with its enviable, but not easily acquired booty. The earth groaned from the thunder of Muscovite cannons and the Russians fought manfully on the plain until nightfall, which at last gave respite to both armies.

A great many Tatars had been killed in the struggle, and a great many were wounded, including Crown Prince Bakhti-Girei and some great princes and mirzas. A considerable number of eminent officers had been taken prisoner as well. The morale of the khan and the Crimean nobles was falling. They took counsel as to what to do and were more frightened than cheered by their estimation of the consequences of another, potentially decisive battle. They heard the constant barrage and saw the large movements between our camp and Moscow. Godunov, unstinting of gunpowder, had ordered the cannons to keep firing at night, as well, to terrify the enemy.

After the day's battle, citizens had come out to the camp in crowds to greet the heroes, see their living friends and relatives and learn of the dead. Russian prisoners of war, loyal to their homeland even in shackles, answered the khan's questions by telling him that fresh troops were coming to Moscow from Novgorod and Pskov, that we were shooting as a token of high spirits and had no doubt of victory, and would strike with all our might before dawn against the Crimeans . The khan was unable to believe them, but he now saw the Swedish king's deceit: that Russia had a sufficient number of defenders and would not hesitate to wage war against Sweden. An hour before dawn he fled.

After the sovereign learned of this, his voivodes, while all the church bells of Moscow were rejoicing, set out with all their legions after the khan, who in mindless flight had left horses, provisions and odds and ends along the road as booty for us. He could hear our cavalry's hooves behind him and, without stopping to rest, reached the Oka a full day later. At sunrise he could see the Russian vanguard and plunged into the river, leaving his own royal carriages on the banks. Many of his men drowned, while he continued his flight. Mstislavskii and Godunov spent the night in Bittsa. They kept pursuing the enemy with their light detachments, which caught up with the khan's rear guard near Tula and defeated them, taking 1,000 prisoners, including some eminent mirzas. They trampled and destroyed the Crimeans in the steppes and chased them out of our territory, which Kazy-Girei had been unable to plunder. During the night of 2 August he sped into Bakchiserai by cart with a wounded arm in a sling. No more than a third of the Crimeans made it back, on foot and hungry, so that the khan's expedition appeared to be the Taurid's least successful and the one least harmful for Russia, where everything was still intact: towns, villages and inhabitants.

The chief voivodes did not proceed farther than Serpukhov. The tsar, perhaps on the advice of the wise Irina, wrote to them that they should pursue and try to annihilate the enemy in the steppes. Prince Mstislavskii replied to him that it was not possible to catch the khan. In this letter he named only himself and received a strict dressing down from Theodor for not mentioning Boris's *great* name in it, for it was to him that the court ascribed the honor of victory. However, parity was observed in the distribution of awards. On 10 July the steward Ivan Nikitich Yuriev arrived in Serpukhov with gracious words and the sovereign's emolument. He inquired after the troops' health and gave medals to the voivodes. Mstislavskii and Godunov got gold portugals; the others, korabelniks and Hungarian chervontsii.* After ordering some of the junior commanders to remain on the banks, the sovereign recalled the rest to Moscow and gave them new favors. He gave Boris a Russian fur coat off his own shoulders, gold buttons worth 1,000 rubles (or 5,000 of today's silver ones) and his own valuable chain. He also awarded him Mamai's golden drinking vessel, a famous trophy from the Battle of Kulikovo, as well as three towns in the Vaga district as hereditary property, and the title of *Servitor* – the most distinguished boyar rank.

GODUNOV'S NEW RANK

This title had been only given three times over the centuries: to Prince Simeon Ryapolovskii, whose father saved young Ivan III

---

* [Apparently these were all gold coins.]

from Shemyaka's malice; to Prince Ivan Mikhailovich Vorotynskii for the victory at Vedrosha, and to his son, the immortal Prince Mikhailo, for defeating the Crimean princes on the Donets and the conquest of Kazan. Theodor gave Prince Mstislavskii, also from his own shoulders, a fur coat with gold buttons, a goblet and a gold cup, and the suburb of Kashin with its uezd. The other voivodes, chiefs, court nobles and boyar cadets were awarded fur coats, drinking vessels and estates, or coins, damask, velvet, satin, sable and marten. The musketeers and Cossacks got taffeta, broadcloth and money.

In short, none of the warriors was left without a reward, and there was no end to the sumptuous banquets at the Faceted Palace, which were more in Godunov's honor than the tsar's, since Theodor had formally announced to Russia and other lands that God had granted him victory *through Boris's zeal and enterprise.*

DONSKII MONASTERY	

In this manner, a new aura illuminated the ruler's head, the aura of military glory – the most brilliant kind for men of a military state that was still surrounded by so many dangers and enemies. On the site where the troops had been stationed in fortifications against the khan, a stone church was built, and a monastery, named *Donskii*, after the holy icon that was with Dimitrii* at Kulikovo Field and with Godunov at the Battle of Moscow. In case of another barbarian attack on the capital, all its suburbs were fortified by wooden walls with high towers.

CALUMNY AGAINST THE RULER AND HIS REVENGE	

However, Boris's triumph, the feasts at court and in the army, the favors and awards of the tsar, all concluded with tortures and executions! Reports reached the ruler that a rumor defaming him was spreading in the uezd towns, especially in Aleksin – a rumor spread by his enemies, and absurd in any case. Godunov was alleged to have caused the khan to come to Moscow in an attempt to quiet the outcry in Russia over the tragic death of [the tsarevich] Dimitrii. The people – and it was only the people – heard and repeated this slander. With courage and innocence, Godunov

---

* [Now known as Dmitrii Donskoi. Karamzin gives his name as Dimitrii Donskii.]

might have disdained this malignant gossip, spread on the wind, but his conscience was not clean and he boiled with anger. He sent out officials to various places to seek out, interrogate and torture the poor people who had, with their simple minds, echoed this calumny, and with fear and torture, the slanders fell upon the innocent. Some of them died from torture or in prison; some were executed or had their tongues cut out, and many places, according to the chronicler, were depopulated in the Ukraine, in addition to ruined Uglich.

This cruelty, worthy of Ivan's era, seemed to Godunov to be necessary for his safety and honor, lest anyone dare to say or think anything against him – this was the sole condition that could not be violated if one wished to have a peaceful and happy life during Theodor's reign. Terrible only to those who defamed him, in all other cases Godunov wished to shine with rare charity. If someone merited disgrace, but could be excused by natural human weakness, he would be pardoned and the following would be written in an edict [for example]:

> GODUNOV'S CHARITY AND GLORY

"The sovereign pardons, out of respect for the intercession of his servitor, the equerry boyar."

Even to traitors, even to Mikhail Golovin, living in Lithuania, Boris offered a peaceable return to his homeland, a distinguished rank and a better estate, as if in requital for a vile betrayal! For someone sentenced to death, however, the following would be written in the order: "Such is the sentence of the boyars, Prince Theodor Ivanovich Mstislavskii and his comrades." Of Godunov, there would be no mention. For friends, flatterers and sycophants there was nothing sacred except the supreme authority, reserved for Godunov's hands alone. Every day he increased their numbers and the more he earned reproach, the more he sought praise, which he heard everywhere, whether genuine or hypocritical. He read about it in books composed by the semiliterate, both clerical and lay. In brief, with skill and power, fear and good deeds, he produced a thunder of praise around himself that would have deafened him – if not to the inner voice of his conscience, then at least to the voice of truth in the populace.

However, he was sacrificing the thought of Heaven and the reality of earthly happiness itself: tranquility, the inner enjoyment of virtue, the legitimate greatness of a national benefactor and his clean reputation in history. Godunov was almost deprived of the desired fruits of his intrigues due to an event natural but unexpected. News spread suddenly from the Kremlin palace to the farthest corners of the realm, and everyone, from monarch to farmer, except Boris, was filled with happy hope: Irina was with child! Never, according to the chronicler, had Russia manifested greater genuine joy. It seemed as if Heaven, irritated at Godunov's criminality, but mollified by the secret tears of Russia's fine sons, had reconciled itself with the nation and planted a new royal tree on Dimitrii's grave that would embrace Russia's coming age with its branches. It is easy to imagine the emotions of the people, who were devoted to the monarchical line of St. Vladimir; it is much harder to imagine Boris's feelings. The vilest of murders had been rendered useless to the murderer. His conscience tore at him, and his hopes were eclipsed forever, or at least until another crime. Even more terrible for this malefactor, he would have to tolerate the general rejoicing and show active participation in it, to deceive the court and his sister.

IRINA'S PREGNANCY

After several months of impatient expectation, Irina gave birth to a daughter, which eased Boris's heart. The parents were just as happy as if they had not desired a successor to the throne. The problem with infertility had been settled, and their tenderness might be crowned by new fruit, in fulfillment of the general desire. Not only the sensitive mother, but the quiet and cool Theodor ecstatically thanked the Most High for their darling daughter. She was named Theodosiya and was christened on 16 July at the Chudovskii Monastery.

BIRTH AND DEATH OF PRINCESS THEODOSIYA

All those disgraced were pardoned, even the worst criminals, who had been condemned to death. Orders were given to open the prisons and strike off the fetters. Rich alms were distributed to monasteries and a great deal of silver was sent to the priesthood in Palestine. The people rejoiced as well, but those who were inclined to suspicion guessed what was hidden in Boris's heart and secretly transmitted their doubts to one another. Might Godunov have exchanged infants if Irina had given birth to a son, and falsely presented Theodosiya, taken from some poor new mother? Later we shall see the effects of this improbable idea. From another quarter the curious asked,

"Should Theodosiya, if she has no brothers, succeed to the state? Might such an event, heretofore unprecedented, serve as an example for the future? Russia has never had a female monarch by succession, but might it not be better to promulgate a new law than to leave the throne orphaned?"

It is likely that these vexing questions roiled Godunov as well. To his relief, they were resolved the following year with the death of Theodosiya. Despite all the consolations of faith, Theodor was unable to dry his tears for a long time. The capital wept with him as they buried the young tsarevna at the Devichyi Voznesenskii Monastery, and it shared in the anguish of the young mother, who had been forever disillusioned with worldly happiness by this blow. While gloating in the depths of his heart, Godunov no doubt was able to feign despair (for it is easier to show false grief while secretly pleased than it is to pretend pleasure while secretly sad).

But this cruel lover of power was once again under suspicion: it was believed that he, who was guilty of Evdokiya's death, had also murdered Theodosiya. God knows the truth, but he who was incarnadine with Dimitrii's sacred blood had no right to complain of malicious rumors and gullibility. It all served as a just punishment for him – even the most incredible calumny!

Chapter III

Conclusion of Theodor's Reign.

1591-1598

War and peace with the Swedes. Correspondence with Lithuanian nobles. A Crimean raid. Embassy to Constantinople. Willfulness of the Don Cossacks. Building towns. Peace with the khan. Assistance for the emperor. A distinguished Austrian emissary. Legate of Clement VIII in Moscow. Theodor's friendship with Shah Abbas. Campaign against the Shavkal. Relations with Denmark and England. Law about peasant and servant contracts. New fortress in Smolensk. Incendiaries. Moscow court. Tsar Simeon blinded. Greek prelates in Moscow. Destruction of the Pecherskii Cloister. Theodor's words to Godunov. Theodor's death. Oath to Tsaritsa Irina. Irina takes vows. Selection of Godunov as tsar.

In foreign affairs, Russia might have boasted, as heretofore, of its successes and prudent policy. King Johan of Sweden abrogated the truce that Theodor had given him in order to please Sigismund – he hoped to join with the khan. His general, Morits Grip, invaded the Novgorod district and torched many settlements near Yam and Koporye. Our voivodes, bewildered by this unexpected attack, sent a herald to ask if he was aware of the treaty signed in Moscow. "No," Morits replied, and marched farther. He was now 50 versts from Novgorod. When he learned that large Russian legions were waiting for him ahead, he declined battle, and turned back, but almost without an army: it had been nearly wiped out by winter cold and illness. In the summer of 1591, as the khan

	WAR AND PEACE WITH THE SWEDES 1591

was moving on Moscow, the Swedes appeared again, near Gdov. They defeated our detachment and captured its voivode, Prince Vladimir Dolgorukii. Other units of theirs invaded northern Russia from Kayani, through wilderness and forests. They took

Sumskii Ostrog on the White Sea, aiming to gain control of all its harbors. However, this grand strategy to deprive us of the benefits of sea trade demanded an effort impossible for weak Sweden. The tsar sent the princes Andrei and Grigorii Volkonskii from Moscow with units of musketeers. The former occupied the Solovetskii Monastery, which was being threatened by the enemy. The latter destroyed the Swedes in Sumskii Ostrog and captured some cannons.

When Prince Grigorii Volkonskii learned that the Kayani brigands had torched the Kola, or Pechenga, Cloister on Christmas Day and vilely murdered 50 monks and 65 monastery servants, he wrought vengeance on them by laying waste to Kayani. He returned to the Solovetskii Monastery with rich booty. These hostile operations almost caused a rift with Lithuania as well – for a long time Sigismund had not wanted to ratify the truce concluded in Moscow without obliging us to refrain from menacing Sweden. Theodor's emissaries Saltykov and Tatishchev lost their patience from being repeatedly stopped on their way to Warsaw. They were angered by the rudeness and the lack of any comforts, or even necessities – to the extent that they quite indignantly offered the king's officers 50 silver vessels, instead of money, in exchange for food for their hungry men. After Sigismund was informed of the khan's expulsion from Russia, he finally ratified the Moscow treaty, but forced our emissaries to include a new provision – that for a period of 12 years, neither the tsar nor Lithuania would contemplate the conquest of Narva. Kissing the cross, he said to Saltykov,

"We shall be at peace with the tsar as long as he does not attack Sweden, for the son should support the father." However, this threat did not save Swedish territory from devastation.

1592-1596

In the winter of 1592, the tsar sent his eminent voivodes, the princes Mstislavskii and Trubetskii, two Godunovs (Ivan and Stepan Vasilievich) and the princes Nogotkov and Bogdan Yakovlevich Belskii to Finland, where they torched villages and towns, and took several thousand prisoners. The Swedes did not risk a battle – they just sat there in Vyborg and Åbo, which the Russians did not assault, but they left ashes and ruins all around. The campaign was over by the end of February and the voivodes arrived in Moscow, where they complained about each other. Prince Thedor Trubetskii accused the Godunovs, and the Godunovs accused Trubetskii of a lack of zeal to serve the tsar. The tsar declared all of them disgraced for their dissension, which was harmful to the nation. He ordered them not to leave the court from Palm Sunday until Easter, since Boris wanted a reputation for impartiality, and with this mild disgrace he could demonstrate that he would not spare even his close relatives if it was a matter of national welfare.

At the same time that we were uninhibitedly laying waste to Finland, the Crimean khan's emissary was in Stockholm: the Circassian Antonii was demanding gold from the Swedes for Kazy-Girei's invasion of Russia.

"Gold is for the victor," King Johan replied. "The khan laid eyes on Moscow, but he did not spare our land from the Russian sword."

Realizing that not even Sigismund could be a reliable protector of Sweden, King Johan sincerely wanted peace with Russia in the final days of his life. In August 1592 he sent Marshal Fleming, General Boe and other officials to the Plyusa River, where in January 1593 they concluded a two-year truce with the okolnichii and Suzdal deputy Mikhail Saltykov in the name of the new Swedish monarch.

Johan had died on 25 November and his son Sigismund had succeeded to the Swedish throne, thereby joining under his power two puissant kingdoms hostile to Russia. This was a cause for rejoicing in Warsaw and Stockholm, and fear in Moscow – but not for long. There was an unexpected consequence, more to the benefit of Russia than its detriment: instead of close ties, Sigismund was the cause of mutual grievances between his two states. While fawning on the royal and the Lithuanian nobles, he tried to be autocratic in Sweden, to change the religion to Roman and to give Estonia to Poland. He saw the Swedes' displeasure and open resistance, and had barely managed to flee Stockholm for Warsaw, leaving the supreme power in the hands of the senate.

Under these unhappy circumstances, with dissension and disarray, Sweden could not consider a war with Russia. It sought a firm and permanent peace and, to please the tsar, agreed that its emissaries Sten-Baner, Horn and Boe should meet with Moscow's: Prince Ivan Turenin and Pushkin in Russian territory, at Tyavzin, near Ivangorod. At the same time, however, he assembled troops in Vyborg and Narva to lend greater force to his requests and refusals. The much more numerous Russian forces were stationed from Novgorod to the Estonian and Finnish borders, quiet and inactive, awaiting the conclusion of the negotiations.

Both sides presented their demands: we insisted on Estonia; the Swedes Ivangorod, Yam, Koporye, Oreshek, Ladoga and Gdov, or else money to defray the expenses of their protracted war, but in fact, Sweden only wanted peace without concessions on its part, while Russia wanted the Korela district. The emissaries of both sides complained of obstinacy and in their irritation would strike their tents and disperse, only to meet once again. Finally, Moscow gained the upper hand.

On 18 May 1595 the following agreement was signed:

"1) There is to be permanent peace between Sweden and Russia;

2) the former is to peacefully control Narva, Revel and the whole Estonian principality;

3) Russia will not aid Sweden's enemies, nor Sweden Russia's, with either men or money;

4) prisoners of war are to be released without ransom or exchange;

5) Österbotten and Varanger Lapps are to pay tribute to Sweden, those to the east (Kola and those neighboring the [Northern] Dvina lands) are to pay Russia;

6) Swedes are to be free to trade in Moscow, Novgorod, Pskov and other places, likewise for Russians in Sweden;

7) in the case of shipwrecks and any other unfortunate disasters, each are to diligently assist the other; and

8) Moscow's emissaries are to be free to travel through Swedish territory to the emperor, the Pope, the king of Spain and to all other great European sovereigns; similarly for Swedish emissaries

going to Moscow, and the same for businessmen, healers, artists and craftsmen."

This peace agreement gladdened both countries: Sweden was saved from a destructive war, while its reliable control of Estonia and Narva was confirmed, while Russia gained back old Novgorod territory, where our brothers and churches had been suffering under the domination of foreign conquerors. Along with some voivodes, Theodor also sent a prelate to Kexholm to purify Orthodoxy from traces of a foreign creed there.

Although Sten-Baner, Horn and Boe had been bargaining with us in the name of King Sigismund, in fact he took no part. He was little concerned with obstinate Sweden, and in some sort of spiritual somnolence, rarely dealt with Moscow regarding Lithuanian affairs either.

> CORRESPONDENCE
> WITH
> LITHUANIAN NOBLES

Our National Duma tried all the harder to surreptitiously instill in the noble pans a distrust for their negligent king. They feigned surprise in letting the pans know that he had placed the name of Sweden before the Polish kingdom in his title, asking,

"Are they aware he has deprecated the famous Jagellonian crown in favor of the Gothic, so new and insignificant? Until recently Sweden was subject to Denmark, and instead of sovereigns, had rulers who dealt only with the Novgorod deputies."

The masterful pans, however, still recalled Batory's imperious resolve with vivid displeasure; they preferred weak Sigismund and boasted of his good fortune in obtaining a victory over the Crimean khan. The new king had hopes of getting Estonia without a war and of enjoying a temporary peace with Russia, which was also not displeased with him.

Weakened by his unsuccessful Moscow campaign, the khan obviously had not yet halted strenuous operations against neighboring Christian powers. He needed to find loot in order to keep the respect of his grasping princes and so as not to be deprived of his power by an angry Murad – the sultan had heaped cruel reproaches upon him for his cowardly flight from Russia, since the shame also fell on Ottoman banners. Desiring to lull Theodor, Kazy-Girei wrote to him about restoring their mutual friendship. He apologized for his gullibility and for the slanders of bad people who wanted them to quarrel. A Crimean herald secretly disclosed to Godunov that the khan knew that the

---
A
CRIMEAN RAID
---

sultan was planning to give the Crimea another ruler, and that he intended to leave the Turks and wholeheartedly join with the tsar. He would pull all of his uluses out of the peninsula and lay waste to the Crimea, then found a new state and fortress at Koshkin Perevoz on the banks of the Dnieper, which would serve as an unconquerable bulwark for Russia. If Theodor would provide him several poods* of silver to construct this fortress, it would menace the hateful Ottomans. To attest to his friendship towards us and as an earnest of his future great services, Kazy-Girei was once again on the move to lay waste to Lithuania.

The khan was dissembling, as usual. Whether we believed him or not, we sent a herald to the Taurid with the response that we would forget all his crimes if he would sincerely make peace with us – that friendship between the great Christian monarch and the Moslems was preferable to the Ottoman yoke. Even though we were not at war with Lithuania, we *would not be angry* at the khan for the devastation of this hostile coalition (perfidy, thy name is politics!).

However, before Moscow's official arrived in the Taurid, he learned that its crown prince, the kalga Feti-Girei and Nuradin Bakhta, were ravaging the environs of Ryazan, Kashira and Tula with fire and sword. There, hardly to the credit of our vigilant ruler, everything had become a victim of their vengeance and greed – there was no defense. They had no plans to move on to Moscow and withdrew, destroying settlements and capturing a lot of nobles with their wives and children. Russia's negligence merited a sarcastic laugh from the khan, who, seemingly surprised, asked Theodor's herald,

"Where was Moscow's army? Our princes did not draw their sabers from their scabbards or their arrows from their quivers. They drove thousands of prisoners with the lash, and heard that your valiant voivodes were hiding in the forests and thickets."

---

* [A pood is 16.38 kg, or about 36 lbs.]

As a token of his graciousness, the khan gave our official a gold caftan to wear and ordered him to assure Theodor that the princes had acted on their own and that it was up to us to purchase peace with the Taurid with silver and valuable furs!

Obstinate in his desire for peace, Theodor now decided to renew relations with the sultan and sent the court noble Nashchokin to Constantinople via Kaffa in order to request

> EMBASSY TO
> CONSTANTINOPLE

that Murad, out of gratitude for our true friendship, forbid the khan, Azov and Belgorod from making war on Russia.

"For we," as the tsar wrote to the sultan, and Godunov to the grand vizier, "do not wish to heed the emperor, nor the kings of Spain and Lithuania, nor the Pope or the shah, who have been trying to convince us to join them and draw our sword on the chief of the Moslems."

Showing courtesy to the envoy, the vizier said, "The tsar offers us friendship. We will believe it when he agrees to hand over Astrakhan and Kazan to the great sultan. We fear neither Europe or Asia. Our army is so innumerable the earth cannot support it. It is ready to strike by land at the shah, Lithuania and the Kaiser, and by sea at the kings of Spain and France. If you indeed do not wish to join them, then we praise your wisdom. The sultan will order the khan not to harass Russia if the tsar will remove his Cossacks from the Don area and destroy the four new forts he has built on the banks of that river and on the Terek to block our route to Derbent. Either do this or, I swear to God, we shall not only order the khan and the Nogai to wage constant war with Russia, but we ourselves will move on Moscow by land and by sea. We shall fear neither hardship nor peril, nor will we stint treasure or blood. You are peace-loving, but why have you entered into close ties with [Caucasian] Iberia, which is subject to the sultan?"

Nashchokin replied that Astrakhan and Kazan were inseparable from Moscow and that the tsar had ordered the Cossacks expelled from the vicinity of the Don, where we had no fortifications whatever. Our ties with Georgia were with a coreligionist and we were sending priests there, not troops, and were permitting their residents to travel in Russia for commerce. Nashchokin proposed that the vizier communicate with the tsar through the sultan's emissary. At first the vizier did not want this, saying, "We do not have this custom. We permit foreign emissaries to come to us, but we send none of our own."

However, he finally consented to send an official, the emissary Rezvan, with the requests he had disclosed to Nashchokin. The tsar replied with gifts (a black fox coat for Murad, and sable furs for the vizier) and sent the court noble Isleniev to Constantinople in July of 1594, promising to suppress the Cossacks and to allow the Turks free access to Derbent, Shamakha and Baku if Murad would clamp down on Kazy-Girei.

"We commanded," wrote Theodor to the sultan, "that fortresses be built in Kabardia and the Shavkala lands, not in order to aggravate you, but for the safety of the inhabitants. We have taken nothing from you, because the Mountain, Circassian and Shavkala princes have long been tributaries to our Ryazan region. They fled to the mountains and submitted there to my father and myself, their legitimate rulers for a long time now."

This novel history of Kabardia and Daghestan did not convince the sultan that its princes were émigrés from Ryazan. He saw the Russian thrust to gain possessions in the East and could not approve. He was not contemplating cooperating to bring peace to Russia, i.e., reconciling it with the khan.

The embassy to Constantinople did not gain us anything except some interesting information about the current situation of the Ottoman Empire and of the Greeks.

"Everything has changed in Turkey," reported Nashchokin. "The sultan and the pashas concern themselves solely with greed. The former, to augment his treasury – but his motive is obscure; he hides gold in trunks and does not pay his army, which, in a terrible mutiny, recently assaulted the palace demanding the heads of the finance minister or the treasurer. There is no order or justice in the country: the sultan fleeces the officials, the officials fleece the people. Everywhere there is robbery and murder. There is no safety for travelers on the highways, nor for merchants doing business. The land has been emptied due to the Persian war and violence, especially in Moldavia and Wallachia, where the sovereigns are constantly being replaced because of bribery. The Greeks are terribly oppressed: they are impoverished and have no hope for the future."

The tsar's envoy Isleniev was detained in Constantinople, where Mehmet III came to power in 1595 – this new sultan, the vile murderer of 19 of his brothers, was only waiting for a favorable opportunity to declare war on Russia. Meanwhile, although in Constantinople we were calling the Don Cossacks a gang of brigands, we were in fact sending them materiel, lead and saltpeter. They increased their numbers by incorporating the Dnieper Cossacks and all freebooters; they were engaging in constant warfare with Azov, the Nogai, Circassia and the Taurid, and bands of them roved the sea seeking loot and paying little attention to the tsar's edicts. Nashchokin wrote to Moscow from Azov that the Cossack

> WILLFULNESS
> OF THE
> DON COSSACKS

villages in the lower reaches of the river had robbed him of the sovereign's gifts and would not release their prisoners without ransom. These included the sultan's emissary and six Circassian princes. In vexation, one of them cut off his hand and shouted in a noisy meeting,

"We are loyal to the white tsar, but without payment we do not release someone we have taken with a saber!"

While this willfulness earned them disgrace, the Cossacks also earned the sovereign's favor because they were implacable foes of those who were plotting and acting against Russia.

Having had no success in restraining the khan through the Turks, we finally gained our goal without their cooperation. We disarmed them not so much by favors

> BUILDING
> TOWNS

and negotiations as by taking prudent measures for the defense of Russia's southern districts. We restored ancient Kursk, long abandoned and founded fortresses in Livny, Kromy and Voronezh.

At the end of 1593 the tsar ordered still more to be built, on all the Tatar roads from the Donets to the banks of the Oka, at

Belgorod, Oskol and Valuiki, and settled them with military personnel – musketeers and Cossacks – so that the khan's brigands would no longer easily skirt our formidable fortifications, from which in summer we constantly sent out cavalry detachments for reconnaissance, and deafened the barbarians with the thunder of our cannons. In one hand the tsar held a sword, in the other, gold, and he laid down the law to the khan,

"The Roman Pope, the Kaiser, the kings of Spain, Portugal, Denmark and all of Germany are trying to persuade me to eradicate your uluses while they simultaneously take action against the sultan with all their forces. My own boyars, princes and voivodes, especially residents of the Ukraine, are petitioning me to remember all your injustices and crimes, to mobilize my army and not to leave one stone standing on another in the bowels of your horde. However, I wish your friendship and the sultan's. I am not heeding the emissaries of the European sovereigns or the cries of my own people. I offer you brotherhood and rich gifts."

The khan was constantly being ordered about by the sultan, from country to country, now to Moldavia and Wallachia, now to Hungary, to put down rebellions of Ottoman tributaries or to fight the Austrians, exhausting his troops in campaigns and obtaining only scanty booty, while losing many men in battle. He implored the sultan to permit him to deceive Russia with a false reconciliation, one formal and elaborate, such as we now had not had with the Taurid in 75 years. In November 1593 distinguished emissaries met for preliminary negotiations on the banks of the Sosna, below Livny. They were the khan's Akhmet-Pasha and Moscow's Prince Thedor Khvorostinin and Bogdan Belskii. This river was then the boundary of Russia's settled territory. Farther to the south the steppes began; this was Tatar space. Kazy-Girei's nobleman feared to come over to the left bank of the Sosna lest he fall into our hands and injure the khan's dignity.

Meeting on the bridge, the emissaries of both sides agreed to cease hostilities, release prisoners and establish peace and a permanent alliance. To this end the Crimea's Shirinskii prince Ishimamet was obliged to travel to Moscow, and our Prince Merkurii Shcherbatov, to the Taurid. The new grand emissaries met on this same bridge, greeted each other kindly, and then each proceeded to his own destination. As a token of friendship Theodor released the widow of Prince Murat, who had been killed in Astrakhan, to go to the khan. The tsar provided Kazy-Girei with 10,000 rubles, in addition to valuable furs and fabrics, and promised to send the same annually.

> PEACE WITH
> THE KHAN

Ultimately, in the summer of 1594, he had the satisfaction of receiving from him a sworn document with a gold seal. In its conditions and expressions, this document recalled the old, genuine treaty of alliance by which the good and wise Mengli-Girei had assured Ivan III of his amity and brotherhood. Kazy-Girei promised to be the enemy of our enemies, to punish the men of his own uluses without mercy for attacking Russia, to return their booty and prisoners, to protect the tsar's emissaries and tradesmen, not to detain foreigners en route to Moscow, etc. For about three years the Crimeans did not disturb our borders, since they were being energetically assisting the sultan in his Hungarian war, yet Moscow's army was always stationed on the banks of the Oka, prepared for battle.

During this time of utter peace for Russia, its foreign policy was hardly somnolent. We boldly informed the sultan that out of friendship with him, we would not befriend his enemies; more sincerely than before, the Moscow court wanted an alliance with him. In September 1593, the Kaiser once again sent his official, Nikolai Varkoch, to Moscow. He argued eloquently for the necessity of a unanimous uprising of Christian powers against the sultan, and requested monetary assistance, or valuable furs, towards a war with the infidels.

In a secret talk he told Godunov that Rudolf was planning to marry the daughter of King Philip of Spain and take over France with the consent of thousands of local nobles who hated Henry IV. He said that Sigismund, offended by the willfulness and impudence of the pans, wanted to take off the Jagellonian crown and return to Sweden. Varkoch also reported that the emperor's brother Maximilian once again hoped to become the king of Poland. He entreated Theodor to assist him with all our forces, and promised to yield Russia part of Livonia. Our boyars replied in the name of the tsar,

"Theodor's grandfather, father and Theodor himself have repeatedly declared to the Viennese court their readiness to fight the Ottomans alongside Europe, but we waited in vain for embassies from the emperor, Spain and Rome to come to Moscow to reach an agreement. We are still waiting. We are not worried about the expense: this great affair would be the beginning of glory and salvation for Christians. The tsar wishes the emperor success in all things. He will act diligently to get the Polish crown for Maximilian, and in the event, will cede him all of Livonia except Derpt and Narva, which are essential to Russia."

Varkoch was sent off with letters for Rudolf, Philip and the Pope, concerning the immediate dispatch of emissaries to Moscow, and also to Prince Gustav of Sweden, Erik's son, to whom Theodor offered asylum with these words:

"Our fathers had friendship and an alliance. I know that you are in exile in Italy and I invite you to Russia, where you will have a proper salary and many towns as an inheritable estate, a peaceful life and the liberty to leave whenever and to wherever you wish."

It will be explained later why we invited Gustav.

Meanwhile, the careless Rudolf, now fighting the sultan in Hungary, was still in no hurry to conclude an alliance with Russia. His herald came to Moscow in August 1594 with a strange letter (in Latin, with a broken seal), addressed to Theodor as well as the Moldavian sovereign Aaron, the Bryaslav voivode Zbarezhskii and the Dnieper Cossacks, containing the following:

"The bearer of this letter, Stanislav Khlopitskii, commander of the Zaporozhskie troops, has declared to us his good intention to serve the emperor against the infidel sultan with eight to ten thousand Cossacks. We willingly received him and gave him our banner, a black eagle, so that with it he can lie in wait along all routes to the Danube from the Crimea, and take fire and sword to the sultan's territory, but spare Lithuania and other Christian lands. To this end we entreat you to assist this, our diligent servant."

It was clear that the signature on Theodor's copy was fraudulent: the emperor would not be able to use the same language with the Muscovite tsar and the Cossacks. However, in his [own] words, in the name of Rudolf, Khlopitskii informed the boyars of his victories, of his alliance with the prince of Sedmigrad (i.e., Batory) and the Moldavian and Wallachian sovereigns, assuring them that the Zaporozhskie warriors, who considered Russia to be their true homeland, would not dare to operate without the tsar's consent, and entreated Theodor to ally some Muscovite units with them and order them to march against the Turks under Russian banners. Khlopitskii was not allowed to see the sovereign, and was told the Kaiser's letter was improper, but

"Out of respect for the emperor, the tsar dismisses you without prejudice and will write to the Zaporozhskii hetman Bogdan Mikoshinskii that they may serve Rudolf."

This was a noteworthy situation: the Dnieper Cossacks, who were Lithuanian subjects, but who, despite that, abjectly fawned on the sultan, were now entering into an alliance with the emperor to fight the Turks, while acknowledging themselves to be some sort of subjects of the Muscovite tsar! This illegitimate alliance did not have the results desired by Austria. The Lithuanian government punished the Cossacks for their willfulness and took away the cannons, banners, silver trumpets and the mace given them by Stefan Batory, and the emperor's black eagle as well. However, the recollection of their common ancient homeland, their same religion, the oppression of the Greek Church in Lithuania and the people's vengeance since that time had clearly prepared the hearts of these Dnieper warriors for the annexation of their blessed lands to the Muscovite state.

Theodor desired something decisive out of our protracted negotiations with Austria, and sent one of his heralds to Rudolf to find out the real reason for this strange procrastination in a matter so important. He learned that on leaving Russia, Nikolai Varkoch had found the emperor in Prague, but for a long time could not get to see him because this indolent monarch *was usually too busy.* Rudolf had finally communicated Theodor's amicable response to the Council of Electors, and they, valuing Russia's friendship highly, had convinced him to send a new embassy to us. A few months later, in December 1594, this same Varkoch arrived in Moscow with the information that the Turks in Hungary were becoming stronger and stronger: he requested immediate financial assistance. We astonished the Austrian court with our generosity: we sent the emperor, for his military expenses, the pelts of 40,360 sables, 20,760 martens, 120 black foxes, 337,235 squirrels and 3,000 beavers, valued at 44,000 contemporary Moscow rubles. The Duma noble Velyaminov accompanied them and was shown uncommon honors in Prague: troops stood at arms along all the streets as he rode to the palace in the imperial carriage. There was no end to greetings, entertainments and favors; he was given dinner after dinner, always with music, even though this official had not sought gaiety and said,

| ASSISTANCE FOR THE EMPEROR |

"The Orthodox tsar mourns the death of your dear daughter, and all Russia weeps with him."

Theodor's gifts were placed in 20 rooms of the palace, before the eyes of the emperor and his nobles. [Velyaminov] pleased them with his description of Siberia and its rich furs, but did not want to divulge how much the sovereign's shipment had cost. Bohemian Jews and merchants valued it at eight casks of gold. Velyaminov told the Austrian ministry that such significant assistance demonstrated the full sincerity of Theodor's friendship despite the baffling delay of the emperor and his allies in concluding a formal treaty with them.

It is indeed difficult to understand why the Viennese court seemed to be avoiding this treaty, which was more fraught with peril and difficulties for us than for them, since it would draw peaceful Russia into a war with the sultan, who was already fighting Austria. The response to the tsar was that long distances, the enmity of Spain with England and France, the rebellion in the Netherlands, the senile infirmity of King Philip and the newness of Pope Clement VIII were all hindering a general alliance of the Christian powers against the Ottomans. However, to express his gratitude, the emperor sent Theodor his eminent noble, baron Abraham of the Danube, the councilor Georg Kalem and 90 council servitors.

| A DISTINGUISHED AUSTRIAN EMISSARY |

This embassy at least satisfied the expectations of the Moscow court with its opulence, demanding something similar from it in return. The Austrian nobleman had traveled from Livonia by way of Pskov and had seen in all the towns and camps a vast number of neatly dressed people, assembled by order of the tsar from the most distant places to show him how populous and rich Russia was. From the border to Moscow, everywhere he was met and accompanied by detachments of troops on beautiful steeds, everywhere he found tranquility and splendor. All he lacked was freedom, since he was watched vigilantly to keep the truth from him, which would have been injurious to Russians' self-esteem. In the capital, this distinguished guest was taken along the best streets and past the best buildings. He was allocated Prince Nozdrovatii's beautiful home, provided with royal service, brought all the delicacies of the Russian table on silver and gold, as well as the most costly wines of southern Europe.

On 22 May 1597, the day of his presentation, the Moscow court radiated extraordinary splendor. The baron, who had gout, rode not on a horse, but in an open German carriage, preceded by 120 equestrians – court nobles and centurions – in glittering armor. Theodor received him in the great *painted* Faceted Palace, sitting on his throne with diadem and scepter. Godunov stood next to him, with an orb. Seated on the right bench were Kaibul's son Araslan-Alei, Mametkul of Siberia and Prince Theodor Mstislavskii; on the left was Uraz-Mahmet, the Kirghiz prince; farther off were the boyars and the sons of the Moldavian and Wallachian sovereigns, the service princes, the okolnichie, the royal carver, the armorer Belskii, the Duma nobles, the chamberlain, the scrivener [*stryapchii*], 13 stewards and 200 princes and court nobles; the Duma secretaries, however, were in the *golden* Faceted Palace.

The emperor had sent the tsar a gift of relics of St. Nicholas, bound in gold, two carriages, 12 sleigh horses, a striking clock with a musical organ and some crystal vessels. Godunov received a precious goblet with emeralds, a standing clock and two stallions with velvet horsecloths; his son Theodor Borisovich got a monkey and some parrots. With equal grace the baron thanked both the tsar and the ruler, who had allowed him to stay for a few days in his own home. He spoke graciously with the great monarch and allowed the courtiers to kiss his hand.

Nothing important came of this splendor or these favors, however. When the Austrian nobleman got down to important business, he announced that Rudolf was expecting further services from us: we should interfere with the khan's invasion of Hungary and the shah's peace with the sultan. We should first augment the emperor's treasury, within a certain period and with a designated amount of silver or gold, but not with furs, which he could not sell profitably in Europe. The boyars now declared decisively that without a mutual commitment in writing on the part of Austria, Theodor did not intend lavish Russian treasure on it. They said the tsar's envoy Isleniev had been detained in Constantinople because of our financial assistance to Rudolf, we had always restrained the khan and would have long ago ratified an alliance of Christian Europe with Persia had not the emperor deceived us with empty promises. Along with this emissary, there was also a herald from Maximilian with us who wanted Theodor to provide him monetary assistance in seeking the Polish throne. We wanted Maximilian to get the throne, but refused him money. The baron departed Moscow in July with honor and rich gifts, but nothing more.

LEGATE OF
CLEMENT VIII
IN MOSCOW

Most surprising of all, Rudolf excused his delay by the *newness* of the Pope, Clement VIII, yet this Pope had sent the eminent legate Alexander Comuleus, the Monenskii[*] abbot, to him via Lithuania on the same matter: he tried to convince the tsar to free the Christian states from the Moslem yoke. Comuleus and the Austrian nobleman scarcely saw each other in Moscow. In any case, they spoke and acted quite independently of each other. The Pope flattered Russia and the tsar with the usual subtlety of the Roman court. He argued that the Ottomans might, after conquering Hungary, also take Poland and Lithuania, and that, since they had subdued part of Georgia and Persia, they were now in contact with our borders from the other side.

---

[*] [Possibly a misspelling of the adjectival form for *Modena*.]

The Byzantine state and many others had fallen from an excessive love of peace, from inactivity and a failure to foresee danger. Theodor might easily send troops into Moldavia to capture the sultan's road to the shores of the Black Sea, where glory and rich booty awaited. There we could better learn the arts of war, since we would see how the Germans, Hungarians and Italians were battling and defeating the Turks. It would be up to us to annex to Russia these fortunate lands with invigorating climates, natural advantages and natural beauty. Through Thrace we could open a path to Byzantium itself and make it a hereditary possession of the Muscovite sovereigns. Religious ardor makes distances closer, and although Rome and Madrid are far from the Bosporus, Constantinople would see the apostolic banner, and Philip's as well. Peoples oppressed by the Turks were our brothers by language and religion. The time was ripe: Ottoman armies had been defeated in Persia and Hungary, and there was widespread rebellion inside Turkey, which had lost half of its populace. The following excerpts from the instructions given the papal legate are worthy of note:

"We hear that the tsar likes to boast of his fanciful descent from the ancient Roman emperors and gives himself overblown titles. Explain to Moscow's boyars that the grades of distinction or majesty of a sovereign must be confirmed by us. In your example mention the Polish and Bohemian kings – they owe their crowns to the archprelate of the Universal Church. Try to impress into their hearts veneration for the leader of the Christians, who are tranquil and happy under our spiritual power. Show them that the true church of Christ is in Rome, not Constantinople, where the infidel sultan bargains over the position of the slave-patriarchs, who are strangers to the grace of the Holy Spirit. To depend on the false pastors of Byzantium is to depend on the enemies of the Savior: Russia's eminence deserves better.

"As a scholar, you are aware of the discord between Roman teachings and the Greek faith: try to convince the Russians of the truth of our orthodoxy, forcefully, but cautiously, for they are sticklers for accuracy, and you, who speak their language, will not be able to make the excuse that you do not understand their words. On the other hand, what an advantage you have over all the other scholars, who have been sent to them over the course of seven centuries, unfamiliar with either the language or customs of Russia! If the Lord blesses your enterprise with success, if you open a way to our neighbor faith, then our hearts will be comforted, both by the glory for our Church and by the salvation of innumerable souls."

We know that Clement's emissary was twice in Russia with these instructions (in 1595 and 1597), but we do not know of his negotiations, which had no significant consequences, but probably diminished, at least for the time being, Rome's hopes of a political and ecclesiastical alliance with Russia.

THEODOR'S FRIENDSHIP WITH SHAH ABBAS

We had promised the emperor, and no doubt the Pope as well, that the Persian shah would be a loyal comrade-in-arms, and we were indeed able to keep this promise by renewing friendly ties with him. The eminent Shah Abbas was now prepared for the glorious deeds which would provide him with the name *the Great* in the chronicles. He succeeded to a state disordered by the weakness of Tahmasp and Khodabanda and disturbed by the intrigues of local khans. He was pressed by Turkish conquests and wanted at least a temporary peace with them to consolidate his rule and put down the internal rebels.

He tried to establish mutual relations with the most distant countries and welcomed the king of Spain from across the seas as a good ally, but he saw an even more reliable one in the powerful Russian monarch, whose territory now adjoined the Persian and Ottoman. In 1593 Shah Abbas's new emissary, Azi Khosrev, presented the shah's gracious letter to the tsar, and flattered the ruler even more in secret conversations with him. Using the luxuriant locutions of the East, he told him,

"You rule the Russian land with a single hand. Raise the other in friendship towards my shah and establish permanent amity between him and the tsar."

Boris modestly replied, "I only carry out the will of the autocrat. His word is my life."

Yet he undertook to become an ardent intermediary for the shah. The emissary explained to him that the truce Persia had concluded with the Turks was only a military ruse, and said,

"In order to lull them, the shah gave them his six-year-old nephew as a hostage – or a victim. Let them kill the child at the first flash of our saber! So much the better! For the formidable Abbas does not love his nephews or his brothers and is preparing the eternal peace of the grave for them, or the gloom of blindness in a dungeon."

Azi was not slandering the shah – this remorseless exterminator of his own kin knew how to appear a great monarch to the eyes of Theodor's emissary, Prince Andrei Zvenigorodskii, whose task it was to learn all about the situation in Persia and about Abbas's plans. In 1594, Prince Andrei traveled through Gilan, now under the control of the shah, who had expelled its ruler Akhmet, accusing him of perfidy. It was quiet and orderly everywhere, demonstrating the vigilant activity of the government, and everywhere our emissary was honored as the bearer of tidings of Theodor's friendship towards the shah.

Abbas received him at Kashan surrounded by his glittering court, his princes and nobles. He had a saber covered with diamonds on his thigh, and a bow and arrow next to him. He gave the emissary his hand, and did not suggest kissing his foot; he showed the liveliest pleasure and praised the tsar and Godunov. Feasts and entertainments preceded business: during the day, walks in the garden, music, dancing and martial games, in which Abbas himself showed rare skill, racing like a whirlwind on his fast horse and shooting arrows at a target. In the evening there were fireworks, brilliantly lit gardens, fountains, squares and beautiful shops, which were crowded with people and where the treasures of Asia were laid out to entice the eye. The shah boasted of his army, the flourishing state of commerce and the arts, of his splendor and majesty, and showed Prince Zvenigorodskii his new palace, saying,

"Neither my father nor grandfather ever had anything like this."

He also showed the prince his rare treasures: a yellow gem weighing as much as 100 zolotniks [a bit more than an English pound], which he was going to give the tsar, and Tamerlan's rich saddle, cuirass and helmet, of Persian workmanship. Sitting next to him after dinner, the shah asked,

"Do you see the Indian emissary sitting below you? His monarch, Jelladin Aiber, rules a boundless realm, almost two-thirds of the inhabited world, but I esteem *your* ruler even more."

When he began to discuss business with Prince Andrei, Abbas assured him that he firmly intended to expel the hated Ottomans from the western districts of Persia, but first he would take Khorasan from Abdula, the ruler of Bukhara, who had controlled it since Khodabanda's unhappy time and had also conquered Khiva.

"I live with but one thought," said Abbas, "to restore the integrity and distinction of ancient Persia. I have 40,000 cavalry, 30,000 infantry and 6,000 musketeers with firearms. I shall subdue my closest enemy, and then the sultan. On that I give my oath, for I am satisfied with the Muscovite sovereign's sincere promise to cooperate in this great exploit when the time comes. Let us share its glory and its spoils!"

Abbas agreed to enter into relations with Austria by way of Moscow (where his emissary would meet with Rudolf's). He would yield us [Caucasian] Iberia without argument, but said,

"Its ruler Alexander is deceiving Russia, insulting me and secretly paying tribute to the sultan."

Alexander's son Constantine was a hostage in Persia, and, willingly or not, had accepted the Mohammedan faith and taken a Moslem wife. To please Theodor, the shah released him to go to Moscow, but the young prince did not want to go there, and through his tears told our emissary,

"It is my destiny to die here in honorable servitude!"

To demonstrate his excellent friendship with Moscow, Abbas came unexpectedly to Prince Zvenigorodskii with Azim, the exiled ruler of Khiva and with his prime minister Ferhat-Khan. There he drank wine and mead with him (since he often liked to drink to excess, despite Mohammed). He attentively examined icons of the Virgin Mary and St. Nikolai and received a black fox hat as a gift from his host. In return he generously gave him a handsome steed and an image of the Virgin Mary painted on gold, [copied] from a foreign icon that had been sent to the shah from Hormuz.

To confirm everything said to Andrei Zvenigorodskii, Abbas sent Kulyi, one of his nobles, with him to Moscow, while Theodor sent Prince Vasilii Tyufyakin to the shah with a specimen of the treaty document, which said that they would be faithful allies and brothers, and with their joint forces would expel the Turks from the Caspian lands. Russia would get Derbent and Baku, while Persia would receive the Shirvan region. However, Tyufyakin and his secretary died en route, which fact for a long time was not known in Moscow, so that relations with Abbas, who was now engaged in a successful war with Bukhara, were interrupted until a new reign in Russia.

At any rate, the shah yielded us Iberia. While not clashing openly with the sultan over it, Theodor wanted to confirm his right to be its supreme ruler by subduing Alexander's cruel enemy, Shavkal. He sent his emissaries, the princes Grigorii Zaseknin and Andrei Khvorostinin, twice more against him. Shavkal fled from the former into the inaccessible mountains; it remained for the latter to complete the pacification of this Daghestan territory, to join up with Iberian troops inside it, and with Alexander's son George then take its capital, Tarki, in order to hand it over to George's father-in-law, another Daghestan prince.

> CAMPAIGN
> AGAINST
> THE SHAVKAL

Prince Khvorostinin advanced and took Tarki, but did not encounter either the son or the father of Alexander's daughter-in-law. He waited for them in vain, constantly battling the mountain-dwellers, his forces losing strength by the day. He was obliged to pull back to the Terek fort after laying waste to Tarki. It is written that no fewer than 3,000 Russians died in the mountains and thickets. Blame for this incident can be placed on Alexander: the tsar expressed his bewilderment as to why the son and his father-in-law had not linked up with our voivodes. Alexander's excuse was the impassibility of the mountains, but Theodor reasonably remarked to him that if the brigand Shavkal found his way to Iberia, then Iberian troops could have found a path to Shavkal's land. Nevertheless, this vexation did not change our cool and patient policy, nor did Alexander's stinginess in paying us tribute.

"My treasury is exhausted," he said, "from my daughter's wedding to Prince Dadyanskii, and from the many gifts that the powerful Moslem rulers demanded of me."

When he learned that Alexander had become reconciled with his in-law Simeon, supposedly in Russia's service, the tsar wrote to the former, "I trust in your zeal, and will do so even more if you persuade Simeon to become our vassal."

Was Alexander deceiving Russia, as Shah Abbas had told Prince Zvenigorodskii? No, he was only a weakling amongst strongmen. No doubt he sincerely preferred Russian dominion over Ottoman or Persian. He had hoped, and had been encouraged, but when he saw that we were unwilling or unable to send troops sufficient for Iberia's defense, his ardor toward us cooled. He did not reject the status of Russian tributary, but in fact continued to pay tribute to the sultan (silk and horses), while trying to persuade Theodor to protect Iberia at least from the Daghestan side, where Moscow's voivodes were building new forts on the banks of the Koisa in order to pressure Shavkal and to make up for Prince Khvorostinin's lack of success.

In addition to Iberia and the Circassian and Kabardian princes subject to Russia, and also in addition to the Nogai, who were our vassals, albeit not always loyal, Theodor in 1595 declared himself lord of the populous Kirghiz horde. Its Khan Tevkel, who called himself ruler of the Kazaks and Kalmyks, willingly submitted to him, asking only for the release of his nephew Uraz-Mahmet, whom we had captured along with the Siberian prince Seidyak. Theodor promised Tevlek favor, defense and artillery. He agreed to free his nephew, but demanded his son as a hostage.

Apart from the honor of being a ruler of rulers [*tsar tsarei*], Theodor also expected to make use of this new Russian servitor. Our enemy, the fugitive Siberian prince Kuchyum, was roaming the Kirghiz steppes. We wanted Tevkel to eliminate him or bring him to Moscow, and also fight Bukhara, since its ruler, Abdula, was protecting Kuchyum and insulting Theodor in his letters. This was the manner in which our policy was operating in Asia in order to establish Russian power over the East.

I n Europe we continued to deal with Denmark and England; with the former over the boundaries of Lapland, and with the latter over trade. Frederik of Denmark wanted to define a firm boundary between his territory

> RELATIONS WITH
> DENMARK
> AND ENGLAND

and ours in the depths of the North, between Kola and Vardø, and dispatched his official, Kersten Fris, there. However Fris returned because he was unwilling to wait for Moscow's emissary, Prince Ivan Boryatinskii. The new king, Frederik's son Christian IV, declared to Theodor his desire to be his firm friend, and also agreed to a meeting of their emissaries in Lapland, which also turned out to be fruitless.

In 1592 our voivode Prince Semyon Zvenigorodskii and the Volkhov deputy Grigorii Vasilchikov had sojourned a long time in Kola, but were unable to wait long enough for Christian's delegates. Both sides blamed the distance and unreliable roads, storms and snows, but both sides at least learned from old timers in Kola and Vardø, the ancient border between Norway and Novgorod's Lopya [Lapland, possibly]; they ordered the inhabitants to cease quarreling and to trade peacefully and freely pending a written agreement between the tsar and the king.

To please Christian, Theodor gave his word to release some prisoners of war the Russians had taken in a Danish raid on the Kolmogory uezd. He wrote of this to his deputies in Astrakhan, the Terek fort and Siberia, whither the prisoners had been sent. In brief, Denmark once again was seeking our friendship and was no longer contemplating interfering with Russia's maritime commerce with England.

T his important commerce was almost interrupted by mutual exasperation on the part of the English government and our own. We complained that the London merchants were cheating and demanded about half a million of today's rubles from them, for which they were in debt to the tsar's treasury, and to Godunov, boyars and court nobles. The merchants denied the debt while blaming each other, and complained of harassment. In 1588 the tsar again sent Bekman to London to clarify the matter with Elizabeth. For a long time she would not see him, being in mourning for the Earl of Leicester, who was once close to her heart.

At last she very graciously received the Russian interpreter, went with him to a corner of the room and conversed quietly with him. She reproached him, but without anger, for the fact that four years previously, after he had walked and talked with her in the garden, in a report to the tsar, he had called this delightful place a vegetable garden. She inquired about Godunov's health and made assurances that everything would be done out of friendship for Theodor. However, she had new requests, which Doctor Fletcher took with him to Moscow. This envoy, more learned than well known, proposed the following items to our Duma in Elizabeth's name:

66The queen would like to conclude a close alliance with the tsar, but there is an ocean between them. While distance hinders an alliance, it does not prevent heartfelt friendship. Theodor's father, a sovereign glorious and wise, always showed himself to be a true brother to Elizabeth, who wishes to be a kind sister to his son as well. This friendship, while unselfish, is nourished by frequent communications between the monarchs regarding commercial matters. If there were no English merchants in Russia, then the queen would not hear about the tsar, and would not this protracted lack of news cool their mutual friendship?

66To consolidate these relations, which are dear to her heart, the queen entreats the tsar to decree the following:

1) to more thoroughly investigate the matter of the controversial debts of the London merchants;

2) they are to be adjudicated only by Grand Boyar Godunov, a benefactor to Englishmen;

3) to give the merchants, as in Ivan's reign, free passage from Moscow to Bukhara, Shamakha and Persia, without restraint and without any inspection of goods in Kazan or Astrakhan;

4) the tsar's officials are to seize nothing from them without monetary payment;

5) to remove all restrictions on goods purchased by Englishmen in Russia;

6) to assist them in finding a route to China, by providing guides, boats and horses on all roads;

7) to forbid all merchants from entering harbors between Vardø and the mouth of the Dvina, and Novgorod as well, without a written visa from Elizabeth;

8) Russian coiners are to cast silver thalers [*Efimki*] for London merchants duty-free;

9) no matter what the crime, Englishmen are not to be tortured; they are to be sent instead to the elder or commissioner, or to England for punishment;

10) none of them are to be harassed with regard to religion. This will demonstrate the tsar's friendship for Elizabeth."

The boyars wrote in reply: "Our sovereign thanks the queen for her kindly disposition towards him, and like his great father, sincerely desires her friendship. However, he cannot agree that mutual friendship is nurtured by commerce, and that without trade they would no longer have the means to communicate with one another. Such expressions are improper. The tsar desires to live in brotherhood with eminent monarchs: with the sultan, with the emperor, with the kings of Spain and France, with Elizabeth and everyone, not for commercial profits, but because it is his administrative custom. To please Elizabeth, he granted favors to the London merchants, but they forgot this and began to live by deception, to travel secretly to other lands as spies, to malign Russia in their letters and to bar foreign ships from the mouth of the Dvina. In short, they deserve punishment by the laws of any nation. However, out of respect for the queen, he has pardoned these criminals and has written to her concerning their doings. Even now he pardons them – that is his will!

"1) Although the debts of the London merchants are beyond doubt, and although this matter has been thoroughly investigated in the tsar's Council, the sovereign is magnanimously cancelling half the debt, but demands that they immediately pay 12,000 rubles.

2) It is not fitting for such a great and intimate boyar and brother-in-law to the tsar to judge merchants: he has been entrusted with the state. Nothing is done without his knowledge. However, ministerial personnel will judge Englishmen, and then report to him.

3) Out of his special friendship with his sister Elizabeth, the sovereign permits Englishmen to travel through Russia to Bukhara and to Persia without paying duties on their goods, even though other foreigners have been commanded not to travel more than a verst from Moscow.

4) In his country, he does not tolerate the forcible taking of foreigners' property, no matter whose it is.

5) There is no prohibition, nor will there be, preventing London merchants from purchasing our goods, except wax, which in Russia is only traded for saltpeter, gunpowder or sulfur.

6) The tsar cannot permit foreigners [to travel] through Russia to reach other countries.

7) It is surprising that the queen once again makes demands so unreasonable and inimical: we have said before and repeat now that we will not close our ports to please England and will not change our laws regarding commerce – it is to be free.

8) Englishmen are free to mint coins on payment of duties, as are Russians.

9) No foreigners whatever are tortured in Russia. Englishmen accused of the severest crimes are handed over to their elders.

10) Religion is not a concern of our sovereign. Each person lives peacefully and quietly according to his own faith, as has always been and shall be the case amongst us."

The emissary was still not satisfied with these replies to each item in his document. He asked for an audience with Godunov and wrote to him:

"Your serene Highness! My queen has ordered me to petition you from our hearts. She knows of your good will towards her people and loves you more than any other Christian sovereign. I do not dare to importune the one upon whom the whole nation rests, but my soul would be overjoyed if you would allow me to see your radiant eyes, for you are the honor and glory of Russia."

Despite his flattery, Fletcher did not have complete success, and in a new open letter that was given to the London merchants, he now wrote of duties, albeit lighter ones. Godunov did not accept the queen's gifts,

"This is because you," as he wrote to Elizabeth, "apparently as a token of disrespect for our great tsar, sent him a gift of small gold coins."

To the greatest displeasure of our court, Jerome Horsey, Elizabeth's new emissary, now appeared in Moscow. He had once been a favorite of Ivan and Boris, but was expelled in 1588 for a scheme to prevent Germans from trading at Arkhangelsk. Neither the tsar nor the ruler wanted to see him, and the queen wrote to Boris that she did not recognize her former friend in him and that the Englishmen harassed by Andrei Shchelkovich no longer had an intercessor in Russia and should leave permanently. This threat may have had an effect, for Godunov was fully aware of all the benefits of the English trade for Russia, for our enrichment and for our national development. He knew that Ivan III had been unable to rectify his error after, with extraordinary severity, he had expelled the Hansa merchants from Novgorod.

Godunov, we are assured, liked the English more than any other Europeans, and especially respected Elizabeth's cunning. While complaining and threatening, she never ceased to express friendship for Theodor. As a demonstration of that, she suppressed a book about Russia published by Fletcher in 1591 that was offensive to the tsar and generally written with an animosity towards our homeland.

Perhaps the death of one of the tsar's eminent officials, who was hated by the English, also furthered their cause. By about 1595, Privy and Great Secretary Andrei Shchelkalov was no more. He had been a major operative in Russia for 25 years, favored by Ivan and Boris for his exceptional abilities: a mind flexible and crafty, a supple conscience, with a mixture of the laudable and evil qualities needed in a servitor of such rulers.

By the beginning of 1596 Elizabeth was thanking the tsar for his virtuous love for her and for a new letter of preference that he had given the London merchants granting them free, unrestricted, duty-free trade all over Russia. She also praised the wisdom of our National Duma (in which Vasilii Shchelkalov had replaced his brother Andrei and from now on called himself Privy Secretary and Keeper of the Seal). In another letter to Godunov, Elizabeth denied a slander that was hurtful to her, explaining herself in these words:

"You, a true benefactor of the English in Russia, the sole person responsible for the rights and privileges given them by the tsar, have secretly informed me that the emissaries of the emperor and the Pope concocted a vile lie when they were in Moscow, concerning my supposed alliance with the Turks against the Christian powers. You did not then believe it. Indeed, believe it not. I am pure before God and in my conscience, and have always sincerely desired good for Christendom. Ask the king of Poland: who gave him peace with the sultan? It was England. Ask the emperor himself if I did not try to avert the calamities of war from his realm. He thanked me, but desired war anyway. Now he regrets this, but unfortunately too late! My officer in Constantinople is there solely to facilitate our commerce and to free Christian prisoners. The Pope hates me because the Spanish king, an irreconcilable foe of England, powerful in fleets and the riches of both Indies, was humbled by me before the eyes of all Western Europe. I continue to place my hopes in the grace of God, and may He prosper Russia as well!"

Such were the last acts of Theodor's foreign policy, marked by Godunov's intellect. The following are some of the noteworthy domestic policies of this time.

| LAW ABOUT PEASANT AND SERVANT CONTRACTS |

We know that from time immemorial peasants in Russia have had civil liberties, but no real estate: the liberty to move from one place to another and from lord to lord during a certain period set by law under the condition that they work part of the land for themselves and the rest for their lord, or else pay him quit-rent. The ruler perceived the disadvantages of these movements, which often cheated the hopes of farmers seeking a better master. It did not give them time to establish roots or get used to a place and its people so as to promote better farming and community spirit. It also increased poverty and the number of vagabonds by emptying villages and towns as they were abandoned by these nomadic residents; habitable homes or shacks would fall into disrepair due to neglect by these temporary residents.

The ruler boasted of the improvements given farmers with regard to their situation on the tsar's patrimonies and, perhaps, on his own. There is no doubt that he wanted good things not only for lords but also for rural workers; he wanted to establish permanent ties between them, as in a family, based on a unity of benefits and on their common, integrated welfare. In 1592 or 1593 he made a law forbidding peasants free movement from volost to volost and from village to village, and permanently fixed them to their lords.

But what was the result? The better part of the populace and many of the rich owners were displeased. The peasants lamented their former liberty even though it had often caused them to wander homeless from childhood to the grave, and although the law had not protected them from the violence of a temporary master who was merciless toward apparently transient people. The rich landowners who had considerable vacant land were now deprived of the benefits of settling it with free plowmen whom they could entice from other patrimonies or estates.

The less well-off owners, however, were more grateful to Godunov, since they no longer feared the desertion of their towns and fields due to an exodus of residents and workers. It was later revealed that the good-intentioned legislator had probably foreseen that some would be pleased and others not, but he had not foreseen all the important effects of this new statute, which was then supplemented in 1597 by the mandated return of fugitive peasants with their wives, children and possessions to their masters if they had fled to escape involuntary bondage during the previous five years.

Now a law was issued that all boyars, princes, court nobles, military personnel, civil servants and businessmen must show a deed of purchase for all their serfs, whether in active service or fugitive so they could be registered in the books of the Ministry for Serfdom. This ministry had been ordered to give contracts of servitude to owners and also to freemen if they had served them no less than six months. That is, the legislator wanted to please the owners and was not afraid to offend against poor servants, or justice. However, he established permanent liberty for freedmen, their wives and children of either sex.

NEW FORTRESS IN SMOLENSK	Having protected southern Russia with new strongholds, in 1596 Boris founded a stone fortress in Smolensk to secure our Lithuanian border. He went there himself to designate the sites for the moats, walls and towers.

This journey also had another goal: Boris wanted to captivate the residents of western Russia with his generosity. He stopped everywhere, in towns and villages, patiently satisfied complaints, distributed money to the poor and entertained the rich. When the ruler returned to Moscow, he told the tsar that Smolensk would become *the breastplate of Russia.*

"But this *breastplate*," objected Prince Trubetskii, "might become infested by insects that we would not soon get rid of."

A memorable phrase, says the chronicler. *It might have happened that Smolensk, which we had fortified, would become a Lithuanian stronghold.* Theodor sent masons there from all towns near and far. Construction was completed in 1600.

Moscow was being beautified by durable buildings. In 1595, while Theodor was out of town at the St. Pafnuti Cloister in Borovsk, all of Kitaigorod burned. A few months later it had risen again from the ashes with new stone shops and homes, but it almost succumbed once more to fire and crime: a planned crime that astonished Muscovites with its godless audacity. The

INCENDIARIES	miscreants were found out, people of high rank: Prince Vasilii Shchepin, the court noble Lebedev, two Baikovs – father and son – as

well as others. They had secretly arranged to torch the capital in various places by night, and in the general confusion to rob the rich treasury kept at the Church of Vasilii the Blessed. Fortunately the ruler found out about the plot; the perpetrators were seized and punished – Prince Shchepin and the Baikovs were beheaded at the place of execution, while others were hanged or given life imprisonment. The executions made a powerful impression on the people of Moscow, who were no longer accustomed to sanguinary spectacles. Though repelled by this infernal plot, they felt a vivid and salutary fear of the laws for the restraint of criminals.

The supreme power was zealously and beneficially active in the circumstances occasioned by various calamitous events. Many towns destroyed by fire were rebuilt at the tsar's behest. In places where no grain had grown, it was immediately provided by places that had it in abundance. Laws were established for times of epidemic diseases. The chronicles around 1595 mention a severe plague in Pskov that left so few people alive that the tsar ordered townsmen neighboring to move there from elsewhere. Russia's internal peace was disrupted by raids by Crimean brigands in the districts of Meshchersk, Kozelsk, Vorotynsk and Peremyshl. The Kaluga voivode Mikhailo Beznin engaged them on the banks of the Vysa and soundly defeated them.

The Moscow court was distinguished by its grandeur. Not just a few favorites of the ruler, as in Ivan's days, but all the boyars and government personnel gathered daily, morning and evening, in the Kremlin palaces to see the tsar and to pray with him and to attend the Duma (three times a week – except in extraordinary circumstances – on | MOSCOW COURT | Monday, Wednesday, and Friday: from seven in the morning till ten or later), or to receive foreign emissaries, or just to converse with one another. They would return home to eat, except for two or three nobles who would occasionally be invited to the tsar's table.

Theodor, feeble and ailing, had eliminated the tiring and crowded meals of his father's, grandfather's and great-grandfather's time, nor did he often dine with emissaries either. The splendor of his court was enhanced by the presence of eminent exiles from Asia and Europe: the prince of Khiva, the Moldavian sovereigns

Stefan and Dimitrii, the sons of the Wallachian sovereign, Manuil Muskopolovich, related to the Byzantine emperors, the Selunskii noble Dimitrii and a host of noble Greeks came to Theodor's throne, along with other foreign officials seeking service in Russia. In front of the palace there were usually 250 musketeers stationed with loaded arquebuses and glowing matches. For the internal guard of the Kremlin palaces there were 200 eminent boyar cadets, called residents [*zhiltsy*]. In rotation, they would spend the night in the third room off the sovereign's bedchamber. In the first and second rooms were the closest palace courtiers, the chamberlains and their comrades, called keepers of the bedchamber. A stove-tender guarded every door and knew who was authorized to enter each room. Everything was arranged in order and by importance.

A s he neared his goal, Godunov more and more tried to beguile people with a semblance of administrative and humanitarian virtues – but, if tradition does not lie, he continued to add to his secret crimes. The so-called tsar and grand prince of Tver, Simeon, had married a sister of the boyar Fedor Mstislavskii and had gained Ivan's favor by loyal service and the acceptance of the Christian religion. He had a splendid court in Tver and a deputy's authority as well as some of the rights of an appanage prince. During Theodor's reign he was obliged to leave all this and go live in isolation in his village of Kushalino. Undistinguished either by intellect or manliness, he nevertheless had a reputation for piety, for humility in good fortune and magnanimity in exile.

Because he carried the imposing title of tsar and was the son-in-law of one of the foremost nobles, he seemed dangerous to the ruler. As a token of kindness, Boris sent him for his name-day some Spanish wine. Simeon drank a goblet of it, toasting the tsar's health. A few days later he went blind, apparently from some toxic potion mixed with his wine. So says the chronicler, and so said

TSAR SIMEON BLINDED

the unfortunate Simeon to the Frenchman [Jacques] Margeret. In any case, this blindness might have benefited Boris, since government documents of later times show that the idea of placing Monomakh's crown on the head of a Tatar had not seemed absurd to all Russians.

We turn our gaze for the last time on Theodor himself. Even in the bloom of youth he had had no other significant concern except for the salvation of his soul, and now cared even less about the world and his realm. He would walk and ride from cloister to cloister, dispensing charity to the lowly and the priesthood, especially to monks from Greece, Jerusalem, the Peloponnese and elsewhere who had brought us precious sacred objects (those not stolen by the Turks!), such as crosses, icons and relics. Many of these unfortunate exiles remained in Russia: Archbishop Ignatios of Cyprus lived in Moscow; Arsenios of Oloosson, who had visited us with the patriarch Jeremy, had returned and was in charge of the Eparchy of Suzdal. Theodor was happy to learn of the appearance in Uglich of some imperishable relics of Prince Roman Vladimirovich (grandson of Konstantin*), and was sincerely grieved by the disaster that befell Nizhnyi-Novgorod's Pecherskii Cloister:

GREEK PRELATES
IN
MOSCOW

where the saints Dionisii of Suzdal, his disciple Evfimii and Makarii Zheltovodskii (or Unzhenskii) had once found refuge. With a shuddering crash, the mountain above the monastery slid toward the Volga, burying and destroying the church, cells and fence. This destruction of a holy place staggered the imaginations of superstitious folk, and in the chronicle was called a great portent of what awaited Russia and Theodor, who was in noticeably failing health. It is written that in

DESTRUCTION
OF THE
PECHERSKII CLOISTER

a formal ceremony in 1596 he transferred the relics of the metropolitan Aleksii to a new silver shrine. He then ordered Godunov to take them in his hand and sorrowfully said,

"Feel these sacred relics, ruler of a Christian people! Henceforth care for them diligently. You will attain what you desire, but all is vain and transitory on this earth!" Theodor had foreseen his approaching end, and the hour was at hand.

We do not believe the frightful tradition that Godunov hastened this hour with poison. More reliable chroniclers are silent about this, while describing Boris's other

THEODOR'S
WORDS TO
GODUNOV

* [Vsevolodovich, 1186-1218.]

crimes with justified loathing. Gratitude humbles even a raging lion.* But if neither the sanctity of the monarch nor the sanctity of his benefactor could have stayed this monster, then he at least might have been halted by seeing that frail Theodor would clearly soon be a victim of an early natural death. Meanwhile, the longer Boris ruled, the more he consolidated his power, like an inalienable possession. Yet history reveals even the slanders earned through criminality.

Theodor became seriously ill at the end of 1597 and on 6 January, to the horror of the capital, he was found to have clear symptoms of approaching death. The people loved Theodor like an earthly angel, illumined by rays of sanctity, and they ascribed the prosperity of their homeland to the efficacy of his fervent prayers. They loved him with great feeling, as the last tsar of Monomakh's blood, and while they prayed in the open

THEODOR'S
DEATH

cathedrals, still hopeful that their kind sovereign be cured, the patriarch, the nobles and the officials, who had already lost hope stood by his sickbed awaiting the last act of Theodor the Autocrat: his testament regarding the fate of orphaned Russia. But just as during the course of his life, so at its end: Theodor had no volition aside from Boris's, and in this momentous hour, still had unbounded trust in his preceptor. As his vision and hearing was fading, he fixed his darkening gaze on Godunov and strained to whisper that he should do as he thought best. The boyars were silent, while the archprelate Iov said in a shaking voice,

"The light in our eyes becomes dark; this just man is going to God . . . Sovereign! To whom do you leave the nation, us orphans and your tsaritsa?"

Theodor softly replied, "To the realm, to you and to my Irina, God willing, I leave my will and testament."

His will was already written: Theodor entrusted the state to Irina and his *soul* to the archprelate Iov, to his cousin Thedor Nikitich Romanov-Yuriev (nephew of the tsaritsa Anastasiya) and to his brother-in-law Boris Godunov, i.e., he chose them to be the principal advisors to the throne. He desired to say goodbye to his

---

* [Karamzin's endnote cites the story of Androcles.]

dear wife alone, and spoke to her without earthly witnesses, so that content of this conversation remains unknown. At the eleventh hour, Iov anointed the tsar with oil; Theodor made confession and partook of the holy sacrament. At one in the morning of 7 January, Theodor released his soul, without convulsion or shuddering, imperceptibly, as if falling into a deep, sweet sleep.

In this moment of numbness produced by sorrow, Irina appeared and fell, fainting, on the body of the deceased. Now Godunov, expressing deep sorrow and an unusual firmness of spirit, reminded the boyars that since they no longer had a tsar, they must swear allegiance to the tsaritsa. They all diligently performed this sacred ceremony, kissing the cross in the patriarch's hands. This was an unprecedented situation, for Ivan's mother Elena had ruled only in the name of her infant son, while Irina had been given Monomakh's scepter with all its rights to

> OATH TO
> TSARITA IRINA

pristine, unbounded power. At dawn the great bell of the Cathedral of the Dormition was rung, informing the people of Theodor's passing; wailing reverberated in Moscow from palace to shack. Every home, in the expression of a contemporary, became a *house of lamentation.* The palace could not hold all the people, of high and low estate, straining towards the deathbed. Tears flowed, but officials and citizens, like the boyars, fervently swore allegiance to their beloved tsaritsa-mother, who was saving Russia from complete orphanhood. The capital was in despair, but calm. The Duma sent couriers to the districts and ordered that the roads to foreign lands be closed pending new instructions, and that the peace be strictly kept everywhere.

Theodor's body was placed in a coffin in Irina's presence; the frenzy of her indescribable grief frightened everyone. She was thrashing and hurting herself, and would not listen to either her brother or the patriarch. From her mouth, red with blood, burst the words,

"I am a childless widow; the royal line ends with me!"

In the evening the coffin was taken to the Church of the Archangel Michael, accompanied by the patriarch, the prelates, the boyars and the people: there was no distinction in rank – in the common grief, all were made equal. The funeral was held on 8 January, memorable not for its splendor, but for its touching disorder. Overcome by tears and weeping, the clergy interrupted the service and the assembly fell silent. No one had been able to hear the hymns over the wailing of the people. Irina was the only one no longer crying: she had been brought to the cathedral like a dead person. Without wiping the tears from his eyes, Godunov looked at Irina, but he was giving all the orders.

The grave was opened for Theodor's coffin, next to Ivan's. The people loudly expressed their gratitude to the deceased for the happy days of his reign and ardently praised the personal virtues of this angel of meekness, whom they had inherited from the unforgettable Anastasiya, calling him not tsar, but a loving father, forgetting, in their heartfelt sorrow, Theodor's weakness of spirit. As his body was committed to the earth, the patriarch and all the people raised their arms to Heaven to pray that the Lord save Russia, and that although it had lost its shepherd, that it not lose His grace. Following the sorrowful rite, a great deal of money was distributed to the unfortunate, to churches and monasteries. Prisons were thrown open and all the inmates freed, even murderers, so as to crown the earthly glory of Theodor's virtues by this act of mercy.

Thus, on the throne of Moscow, the renowned Varangian line ended, to which Russia was obliged for its existence, its name and its greatness. From such small beginnings, through the stormy centuries, through fire and blood, it had achieved dominion over northern Europe and Asia through the martial spirit of its rulers and its people, its good fortune and God's efforts!

Soon the sorrowing capital learned that together with Irina, Monomakh's throne was also widowed, that the crown and scepter lay idle upon it, and that Russia, which no longer had a tsar, no longer had a tsaritsa either.

It is written that pious Theodor, in bidding farewell to his wife, notwithstanding his will, had secretly commanded her to scorn earthly majesty and devote herself to God. Perhaps Irina, a childless widow, in sincere despair, had come to hate the world, and had found no comfort in royal splendor.

It is much more likely, however, that this is what Godunov intended as he looked to his tender sister's heart and fate. He could no longer advance himself in Irina's reign after his unbounded rule in Theodor's time; at the end of his fifth decade, he could neither wait nor postpone any longer. He had entrusted the reign to Irina so that he could take it for himself, from the hands of a blood relative, as if by right of succession. On the throne he would take a Godunov's place, and not that of one of Monomakh's line, and thus seem less like a usurper in the eyes of the people. This cunning and ambitious man had never been so busy, openly and clandestinely, as in the last days of Theodor's reign and the first days of Irina's, illusory as it might have been. It was clear that the people had no idea of the possibility of a governmental system without Boris's zeal. He operated under cover, so as to give a semblance of liberty and love to actions of force, seduction and perfidy. It was as if an invisible hand had taken hold of Moscow: he controlled all its operations through his innumerable servitors. From the Church to the council, to the army and the people, everyone heeded and followed his suggestions. This promoted diffidence on the one hand and genuine gratitude for Boris's services and favors on the other. His operatives promised and threatened; by whispers and shouts they showed that Russia's salvation was integrally linked with the authority of its ruler.

On the ninth day after the death of the tsar, having prepared minds and emotions for this magisterial stroke of theater, it was formally announced that Irina was renouncing her position as sovereign and permanently retiring to a monastery to take on the angelic form of a nun. This news stunned Moscow. The prelates, the Duma, the court nobles, the officials and the citizens all fell before the crowned widow, weeping inconsolably, calling her *mother* and entreating her not to leave them in terrible orphanhood, but the tsaritsa, tenderhearted till now, was unmoved by their tearful supplication. She replied that her mind was made up, that the country would be for the boyars to govern, along with

> IRINA TAKES
> VOWS

the patriarch, until such time as all ranks of the Russian state could manage to gather in Moscow to decide, with divine inspiration, the fate of their homeland. That same day Irina left the Kremlin palace for the Novodevichii Monastery to become a nun with the name of Aleksandra. Russia was left without a leader, and Moscow was apprehensive and disturbed.

Where was Godunov and what was he up to? He had shut himself up in a monastery with his sister, weeping and praying with her. It seemed as if he, like she, had renounced the world, majesty, power and the helm of state and had consigned Russia to be the victim of storms. Yet the helmsman was indefatigably vigilant: from a close monastery cell, Godunov was ruling the realm with a firm hand!

After they were informed that Irina had taken vows, the clergy, the officials and the citizens gathered in the Kremlin, where the state secretary and keeper of the seal Vasilii Shchelkalov warned them of the calamitous consequences of anarchy and demanded that they kiss the cross in the name of the boyar Duma. No one wanted to hear of this, and they all shouted,

"We do not acknowledge princes or boyars. We acknowledge the tsaritsa alone. We gave her our oath and will not give it to another. Even amongst nuns, she is still the mother of Russia."

Shchelkalov consulted with the nobles and then came out to the citizens and said that the tsaritsa had left the world and was no longer concerned with the affairs of state, and that the people should swear to the boyars if they did not want to see governmental collapse. The unanimous reply was,

SELECTION OF GODUNOV AS TSAR

"So let her brother rule!" No one dared to speak against this, or to remain silent; they all shouted, "Hail to our father, Boris Theodorovich! He will succeed our mother, the tsaritsa!"

They all proceeded immediately to the Novodevichii Monastery, where the patriarch Iov, speaking for the nation, implored the nun Aleksandra to bless her brother's accession to the realm, which she had renounced out of love for her immortal bridegroom, Christ the Savior. She would thereby satisfy the will of God and the people, quiet the vacillation in hearts and in the nation, dry the tears of miserable, orphaned, helpless Russians and restore the sorrowing nation before the enemies of Christianity found out that Monomakh's throne was vacant. Everyone was weeping, including the nun-tsaritsa, as they listened to the eloquent archprelate. Iov turned to Godunov and humbly offered him the crown, saying that he had been chosen by God to restore a royal line to Russia. He would be the natural successor to the throne after his brother-in-law and friend, who was indebted to Boris's wisdom for all the successes of his reign.

Thus were the desires of this ambitious man fulfilled! But he knew how to dissemble, while not forgetting the joy in his heart, and because seven years previously he had boldly thrust an assassin's knife into the throat of the saintly youth Dimitrii in order to steal the crown. This he now rejected in horror as it was formally and unanimously offered to him by the priesthood, the Council and the people. He swore that he, who had been born a loyal citizen, had never dreamed of such a lofty rank and would never dare to take the scepter consecrated by the hand of the late tsar-angel, his father and benefactor. He said that there were many princes and boyars in Russia who had greater renown and personal merits than he, but out of gratitude for the people's love, he promised to work with them to look after the nation even more zealously than before.

To this speech, which had been composed beforehand, the patriarch replied in like manner, and very floridly, full of oratorical gestures and historical examples. He accused Godunov of excessive modesty and even of disobedience to God's will, which was so evidently the people's will as well. He argued that the Most High had long since prepared him and his line for perpetual control of the power [which had been held] by Vladimir's line and which had been terminated by Theodor's untimely death.

He mentioned David, king of the Jews, Theodosius the Great, Marcianus, and Michael Stumbletongue [Paleologus], Vasilii the Macedonian,* Tiberius and other Byzantine emperors who had

---

* [Basil I. died 886.]

been elevated from obscurity to the throne by inscrutable divine destiny. He compared their virtues to Boris's; he tried to persuade, he demanded, but could not shake Godunov's resolve, either on this day or the next ones; neither before the people, nor in the absence of witnesses; neither in his entreaties, nor in his priestly threats. Godunov decisively disavowed the crown.

But the patriarch and the boyars had not yet lost hope: they were waiting for the Grand Assembly, which was supposed to take place in Moscow six weeks after Theodor's death, i.e., select men from all the district towns and cities had been ordered to meet there. This meant churchmen, military and civil officials, merchants and tradesmen. Godunov intended that not just the capital, but all Russia call him to the throne, and he took measures to insure its success, sending his diligent servants and minions everywhere. This appearance of unanimous, free choice seemed to him to be essential – but was it for easing his conscience, or for the stability and security of his rule?

Meanwhile, Boris stayed at the monastery and the Duma ran the country, consulting with the patriarch on important matters. Edicts, however, were issued in the name of Tsaritsa Aleksandra, and the reports of the regional voivodes were addressed with this name. In the meantime, there was disobedience and disorder. In Smolensk, Pskov and other cities the voivodes heeded neither each other nor the instructions of the Duma. Meanwhile, there were rumors that the khan of the Crimea was attacking across Russia's borders and frightened people were saying,

"The khan is coming to Moscow and we are without a tsar or defender!" In brief, everything favored Godunov – because he had set it all up!

The Duma of the Land, or National Council, opened on Friday, 17 February, in the Kremlin. Besides all the eminent churchmen, councilors and courtiers, there were no less than 500 officials and selectmen from every district for this great event, the like of which had not been seen since Ryurik's time. They were to appoint a Russian monarch. Hitherto the descendants of the Varangian princes had ruled without interruption, by right of inheritance. The sovereign was the state and all legal rights flowed from his single, pristine right: to judge and order the land according to the law of conscience. A perilous hour was at hand: those who made the choice would give the power, and therefore have it. No laws or examples could assure the tranquility of the populace during such an important action, and the Kremlin sejm might come to resemble Warsaw's – a stormy sea of passions destructive of the order and power of the state.

However, Boris's long time skills of seeming submissiveness and cunning produced a surprising spectacle: there was quiet, unanimity and courtesy in this diverse crowd of people, in this hodge-podge of ranks and vocations. It seemed that everyone wanted the same thing: as orphans, to quickly find a father – and they knew where to find him. The citizens looked to the courtiers, the courtiers looked to the nobles and the nobles looked to the patriarch. After the council was informed that Irina did not want to rule or bless her brother to rule, and that Godunov would not accept Monomakh's crown, Iov said,

"Russia is in anguish without a tsar and impatiently awaits one to be produced out of the wisdom of this council. You, prelates, archimandrites and abbots; you, boyars, courtiers, ministerial personnel, boyar cadets and all ranks of people in the ruling city of Moscow and in the entire Russian land! Declare your thoughts and give us counsel as to who should be our sovereign. We, however, witnesses to the passing of Tsar and Grand Prince Theodor Ivanovich, think that we need not look past Boris Theodorovich to find another autocrat."

Now all the clergy and boyars, the military and the people unanimously responded, "Our counsel and desire is the same: to immediately petition the sovereign Boris Thedorovich and seek no further for an autocrat for Russia."

Diligence turned into gaiety, and for a long time it was impossible to hear anything except Boris's name being repeated by the whole crowded assembly. There were princes of Ryurik's tribe there: the Shuiskiis, Sitskiis, Vorotynskii, Rostovskiis, Telyatevskiis and so many others, but they had so long been deprived of the dignity of ruling princes, had so long been servitors of the Muscovite sovereign on the same level as the boyar cadets that they did not dare to consider their hereditary right or to contest the crown with him who, without the title of tsar, had ruled Russia as an autocrat for 13 years. Although he was a descendant of a mirza,* he was the tsaritisa's brother. After quiet had been restored, to honor Boris the nobles told the clergy, the officials and the citizens about the following circumstance.

"The tsaritsa Irina Theodorovna and her distinguished brother grew up in the palace of the great tsar Ivan Vasilievich and ate at his table from their earliest childhood. But after the tsar deigned to make Irina his daughter-in-law, Boris Theodorovich lived with him continuously, practicing his administrative expertise. One time, after the tsar learned of his young favorite's illness, he went with us to him and graciously said,

'Boris! I feel for you as if my son were sick, for my son as if my daughter-in-law were sick, for my daughter-in-law as if I myself were sick.' He raised three fingers of his right hand and added, 'Here are Theodor, Irina and Boris – you are not a slave, but my son.'

"In the final hours of his life, when everyone had left him so he could make confession, Ivan detained Boris Theodorovich by his bedside and told him,

'To you I have opened my heart. To you I commend my soul, my son, my daughter and my entire realm. Guard them, lest you be answerable to God.'

"Recalling these unforgettable words, Boris Theodorovich protected, like the apple of his eye, the young tsar and this great realm."

The nobles then described how the ruler, with his indefatigable and wise actions raised up the nation, pacified the khan and the Swedes, restrained Lithuania, expanded Russia's territory, increased the number of its vassal princes and servitors. They told how the most eminent monarchs of Europe and Asia declared their respect and friendship, and how there was tranquility within the realm, favors for the troops and the people, justice in the courts, protection for the poor and for widows and orphans. The boyars then concluded with this:

---

* [The Godunovs were supposedly of Tatar origin. Mirzas were Tatar gentry.]

"We shall remind you of a memorable event: when Tsar Theodor, with the benefit of the ruler's mind and courage, gained a most glorious victory over the khan, he feasted happily with the clergy and the Council and then, with touching gratitude, took the royal *grivna* from his neck and placed it around the neck of his brother-in-law.* The patriarch explained to the gathering that the tsar, filled with the Holy Spirit had by this mysterious act designated Godunov to be the future holder of supreme power, something that had long been predestined by Heaven. Cries again rang out:

"Hail to our sovereign, Boris Theodorovich!"

The patriarch shouted to the assembly, "The voice of the people is the voice of God: hearken to what is pleasing to the Most High."

At the first hour of the morning the next day, February 18th, the Church of the Dormition was filled with people. All of them: clergy, councilors and the people were on their knees, fervently praying to God that the ruler would relent and accept the crown. They kept praying for two more days, and on February 20th Iov, the prelates and the nobles announced to Godunov that he had been chosen as tsar, not just by Moscow, but by all of Russia. But Boris once again replied that the height and radiance of Theodor's throne terrified his soul. He swore once more that in his secret heart he had never dared to even think of such a thing. He saw their tears; he listened to their heartfelt pleading, but was unmoved. He sent away these *tempters*: the clergy and the councilors from the monastery and ordered them not to return.

A more efficacious method of persuasion was needed: they thought it over – and found one. In a joint council with the boyars, the prelates decreed that on 21 February there would be holiday services in all the churches, with solemn rites, including the sacred objects of the nation and the faith, to attempt one last time to win over Boris's heart with forceful persuasion and tears. Secretly, however, amongst themselves, Iov, the archbishops and the bishops agreed on the following:

"If the sovereign Boris Theodorovich takes pity on us, then we shall absolve him of his oath not to be the tsar of Russia. If he

---

* [A grivna usually denotes a coin, but in this case, it is a neck ornament.]

does not do so, then we shall excommunicate him, and there in the monastery we shall remove our own sacred regalia, crosses and pectorals. We shall relinquish our wonderworking icons, and forbid services and hymns in all the holy churches. We shall consign the people to despair, the country to death, rebellion and bloodshed – and the cause of this unfathomable evil will answer before God on the Day of Judgment!"

That night the lights did not go out in Moscow; everything was in readiness for a great event. At dawn, the city roused itself to the sound of all the bells ringing. All the churches and homes were opened. The clergy emerged from the Kremlin singing hymns and the people gathered silently in the squares. The patriarch and the lords carried famous icons with glorious memories, of Vladimir and Donskii, like national banners.

Following the clergy came the Council, the Court, the military, ministry personnel and delegates from the cities, and after them came all the residents of Moscow, citizens, laborers, women and children to the Novodevichii Monastery, from which, likewise to the sound of bells ringing, the icon of the Virgin of Smolensk been brought out to meet the patriarch, and behind the icon, came Godunov, seemingly bewildered by such an unusually solemn religious procession. He prostrated himself before the icon of Vladimir and weeping, cried out,

"Oh Divine Mother! What is the reason for this movement of yours. Protect me beneath the shade of your veil!" He turned to Iov and with an expression of reproach, said, "Great Pastor! You will make answer to God!" Iov replied, "Beloved son! Do not consume yourself with sadness, but put your faith in Providence! The Virgin is doing this out of love for you and that you may be ashamed!"

He entered the church of the holy cloister with the clergy and the most eminent people. Others stood within the enclosure and the whole vast field before the monastery was filled with people. They recited the liturgy together and the patriarch once more tried in vain to persuade Boris to accept the crown. He ordered the icons and crosses be taken to the tsaritsa's cell, and there with all the prelates and nobles he bowed his head to the ground – and at that very moment, as a signal was given, the whole number-less crowd of people, in the cells, in the enclosure and outside the monastery, fell on their knees and with an unprecedented cry demanded their tsar, their father, Boris! Mothers put babes at the breast on the ground, nor did they heed their cries.

Sincerity won out over pretense, the indifferent and even the hypocritical were filled with inspiration. The patriarch, weeping, kept entreating the tsaritsa in the name of the holy icons that stood before her, and in the name of Christ the Savior, the Church and Russia to give the millions of Orthodox people a steadfast sovereign – her great brother! Finally, these gracious words were heeded; the tsaritsa's eyes, heretofore impassive, filled with tears. She said,

"By the will of almighty God and the most holy Virgin Mary, take my brother from me for the nation so that the people's lamentations may be soothed. Let your hearts' desire be done – for Russia's good fortune! I bless your choice and hand him over to our Heavenly Father, the Virgin, the holy saints of Moscow and to you, patriarch – and to you, prelates – and to you, boyars! Let him take my place on the throne!"

Everyone fell at the feet of the tsaritsa, who, after sadly looking at meek Boris, gave him the command to rule over Russia. But he still showed unwillingness, was frightened by the weight of the burden that was being placed on his frail shoulders and asked to be delivered of it. He told his sister, that simply out of char-ity, she should not commit him to be sacrificed to the throne, and once again swore that in his tremulous mind he had never dared to ascend such heights, which are terrifying for a mortal man. He testified by the All-Seeing Eye and by Irina herself that he only wanted to live beside her and gaze on her angelic face. The tsar-itsa resolutely insisted. Then Boris, as if sad at heart, cried out,

"Let your sacred will be done, Lord! Put me on the right path and enter not into judgment with thy servant. I obey You, in fulfill-ment of the will of the people."

The prelates and nobles fell at his feet. Covering Boris and the tsaritsa with the life-giving cross, the patriarch hastened to inform the nobles, the ministerial personnel and all the people that the

Lord had given them a tsar. It is impossible to describe the general rejoicing. People raised their hands to Heaven, praised God, wept and embraced one another. From the tsaritsa's cell to all corners of the monastery field roared the cry,

"Glory! Glory!"

Surrounded by nobles, pressed and kissed by the people, Boris followed the churchmen into the cathedral of the Novodevichii Monastery, where the patriarch Iov, before the Vladimir and Donskii icons, blessed his elevation to head the Muscovite state and all Russia; he named him tsar and loudly wished him many years.

What indeed could have been more solemn, unanimous and legitimate that this nomination? And what more prudent? Only the name of the tsar had changed. Power remained in the hands of him who had long possessed it and had ruled with good effect for Russia's integrity, for its internal organization, for its external honor and its security. So it seemed. Yet this ruler, endowed with human wisdom, had reached the throne through criminality. The grim punishment of Heaven was in store for this criminal tsar and his unfortunate realm.

CHAPTER IV

REIGN OF TSAR BORIS GODUNOV

1598-1604

Moscow welcomes the tsar. Oath to Boris. Council document. Boris's activism. Triumphal entry into the capital. Significant mobilization. Khan's embassy. Entertaining the army. Patriarch's speech. Supplement to electoral document. Tsar crowned. Royal favors. New ruler in Kasimov. Events in Siberia. Death of Kuchyum. Foreign affairs. Fate of Swedish Prince Gustav in Russia. Truce with Lithuania. Relations with Sweden. Close ties with Denmark. Danish duke affianced to Kseniya. Negotiations with Austria. Persian embassy. Events in Georgia. Russian calamity in Daghestan. Friendship with England. The Hansa. Embassies from Rome and Florence. Greeks in Moscow. Affairs among the Nogai Tatars. Internal affairs. Letter of preference granted to patriarch. Law concerning peasants. Public houses. Boris's love of education and for foreigners. Panegyric for Godunov. Boris's ardor towards his son. Calamities commence.

The priesthood, Council and state officials returned to the Kremlin with the gonfalons of the Church and the nation, to the sound of all the bells of Moscow and the shouts of the people, intoxicated with joy. They had given Russia an autocrat, but left him in his cell. On 26 February, during Cheesefare Week,* Boris entered the capital. He was met before the

| MOSCOW WELCOMES |
| THE TSAR |

walls of the wooden fortress by all the rich Moscow merchants with bread, goblets of silver and gold, sable pelts, pearls and many other royal gifts for the tsar. He thanked them graciously but did not want to take anything other than the bread, saying that he preferred leaving these riches in the hands of the people rather than the treasury. After the merchants, Iov and all the clergy greeted the tsar, and after the priesthood, the Council and the

---

* [The week before Lent.]

people. A service was held in the Cathedral of the Dormition and the patriarch once more blessed Boris's accession to the throne underneath the cross of the life-giving tree. The choir sang for long life for the tsar and also for the ruling house: for the tsaritsa Mariya Grigorievna and their young son Theodor and daughter Kseniya. Then all the Russians hailed the new monarch while the patriarch raised his hands to Heaven, saying,

"We praise you, Lord, for you have not ignored our prayers. You have heard the weeping and wailing of Christians; you have transformed their grief into joy and have given us the tsar for whom we have entreated you day and night with our tears!"

After the liturgy, Boris expressed his gratitude to the memory of the two men primarily responsible for his prominence. In St. Michael's Cathedral he fell down before the tombs of Ivan the Terrible and Theodor. He also prayed over the remains of the oldest and most renowned monarchs of Russia – Kalita, Donskii, Ivan III – that they would be his heavenly helpers in the worldly affairs of the realm. He stopped by the palace and then went to visit Iov at the Chudovskii Monastery. He conversed with him alone for a long time and informed him and all the bishops that he could not leave Irina alone in her grief before Easter. He returned to the Novodevichii Monastery after directing the Boyar Duma to deal with the affairs of state, with his knowledge and authorization.

Meanwhile, all the service people eagerly kissed the cross as a token of loyalty to Boris, some of them before the famous Vladimir icon of the Virgin Mary, others at the grave of the saintly metropolitans Pyotr and Iona; they swore not to betray

| OATH TO BORIS |

the tsar by word or deed, nor to plot against the life or health of the reigning sovereign, nor to harm him with a poisonous potion, nor by sorcery; not to consider elevating former Grand Prince Simeon Bekbulatovich of Tver to the throne, nor his son; nor to have secret relations or correspondence with them; to report all criminal activities or plots without compassion for friends or relatives, and not to leave for another country: Lithuania, Germany, Spain, France or England. In addition, boyars and Duma and diplomatic officials were enjoined to be discreet with regard to national affairs and state secrets. Judges were bound not to act against their consciences in lawsuits, the treasurer not to embezzle the tsar's property and secretaries not to take bribes. Letters of notification of the auspicious selection of a sovereign were sent to the districts, with orders that they be read publicly, bells be rung for three days and prayers be offered in the cathedrals, first for the tsaritsa-nun Aleksandra, then for her reigning brother, for his family, for the boyars and the troops.

On 9 March the patriarch in council solemnly decreed that God be asked to ensure that the blessed tsar take the crown and the purple; he also decreed that henceforth and for all time, 21 February would be celebrated in Russia as the day of Boris's coronation. Finally, he proposed that the Duma of the Land confirm the oath given to the monarch by a council document

> COUNCIL
> DOCUMENT

with the obligation that no official would refuse any service nor request anything more than what he merited by birth or service and to always and in every way obey the tsar's edicts and the boyars' resolutions so that in matters of rank and state the official would not cause the sovereign grief. All the members of the Grand Duma replied with one voice,

"We give our promise to put our lives and souls at the disposal of the tsar, the tsaritsa and their children!" The foremost scribes of Russia were ordered to draw up a charter to this effect.

This extraordinary matter did not interfere with the course of ordinary governmental affairs, which Boris engaged in with notable diligence, both in his monastery cell and in the Duma, for he was going to Moscow frequently. No one knew when he found quiet time to relax, sleep or eat. He was constantly seen in council with the boyars and with the state secretaries, or by the unhappy Irina's side, comforting and commiserating with her day and night. It seemed that Irina was indeed in need of his presence, for he was still dear to her heart. Crushed by the death of her husband, who had sincerely and tenderly loved her, she

> BORIS'S
> ACTIVISM

grieved and wept inconsolably, to exhaustion; she was clearly failing, torn apart by grief, and now carried death in her breast.

The prelates and the nobles tried in vain to persuade the tsar to leave his mournful monastery, move into the Kremlin palace with his wife and children, and show himself to the people, wearing a crown and on the throne. However, Boris answered,

"I cannot be separated from her majesty, my ill-starred sister." He continued to assert with indefatigable hypocrisy that he did not want to be tsar. But Irina once more *ordered* him to fulfill the will of the people and of God, to take the scepter and rule, not from his cell, but on the throne of Monomakh. Finally, on April 30th, the capital came out to meet their lord.

<table>
<tr><td>TRIUMPHAL ENTRY
INTO THE
CAPITAL</td></tr>
</table>

This day was one of the grandest days in Russia's history. At the morning hour, everyone was waiting for the tsar at the stone bridge near the Church of St. Nikolai Zaraiskii: the priesthood with crosses and icons, the Council, the court, the ministries, the troops and all the citizens. Boris was traveling from Novodevichii Monastery with his family in a splendid carriage. When he caught sight of the church gonfalons and the people, he got out, bowed to the holy icons, graciously greeted everyone, whether eminent or otherwise, and presented the tsaritsa to them – she who had long been known for her piety and sincere virtue. He also introduced his nine year old son and 16 year old daughter, both angels of beauty. The people exclaimed,

"You are our sovereign; we are your subjects!"

Hearing this, Theodor and Kseniya, together with their father, charmed the officials and the people; like him, the children accepted bread and salt from them,* but turned down the gold, silver and pearls that had been brought as gifts for them, and invited all to dine with the tsar. Unrestricted by a heterogeneous crowd of innumerable people, Boris followed the clergy with his wife and children, like a good father to his family and his people, to the Cathedral of the Dormition. There the patriarch placed on his chest the life-giving cross of St. Pyotr the Metropolitan (this was the beginning of the tsar's coronation ceremony) and for a third time blessed his accession to the great state of Muscovy.

---

* [A token of hospitality.]

After hearing all of the liturgy, the new autocrat, accompanied by his boyars, walked around to all the important Kremlin churches, praying at all of them with warm tears. He heard the joyous cries of the citizens everywhere, and, holding his young heir by one hand and guiding the charming Kseniya with the other, he entered the tsars' palace with his wife. On this day the people dined with the tsar. The number of guests was not known, but everyone was invited, from the patriarch down to the lowly. Moscow had not seen such splendor even in Ivan's time. Boris did not want to live in the apartments in which Theodor had died; he occupied that part of the Kremlin palace in which Irina had lived and ordered a new, wooden palace annex be constructed for himself.

He now ruled as tsar, but still without crown or scepter, nor could he yet call himself *the tsar crowned by God, anointed by the Lord.* One would think that Boris would have immediately had himself crowned with all the formal ceremonies that consecrate a ruler in the people's eyes – this is what the patriarch and the Council requested, in the name of Russia. Doubtless it is also what Boris wanted as well, in order to establish the throne for himself and his line by a significant ecclesiastical act. However, a cunning mind controlled the actions of his heart: he had thought up a new diversion: instead of a scepter, he took a sword in his right hand and hastened to the field, to show that the security of the country was more important to him than a crown or his life. And so a very pacific reign began with a mobilization that recalled memories of Russians rising up to do battle with Mamai.

> SIGNIFICANT
> MOBILIZATION

Back in March, from his cell in the Novodevichii Monastery, Boris had sent a herald to the khan with a letter of friendship. On 1 April he learned from the report of his voivode Oskolskii that a prisoner captured by Cossacks in a skirmish with Crimean brigands on the other side of the Donets had spoken of Kazy-Girei's intention to invade Muscovy with his entire horde and 7,000 of the sultan's troops. Boris had no doubts as to the truth of such unreliable information and decided to lose no time in

> KHAN'S
> EMBASSY

moving the whole mass of our forces to the banks of the Oka. He wrote of this to his voivodes in a persuasive and flattering manner, requesting their zeal in this first important threat of his reign, and to show their love for him and for Russia.

This directive had a surprising effect: there were none who were disobedient or sluggardly. All the boyar cadets, both young and old, willingly saddled up and urban and rural units hastened without stopping for rest to the assembly points. The main camp was to be in Serpukhov, the right wing in Aleksin, the left in Kashira, the vanguard legion in Kaluga and the reserve legion in Kolomna. On 20 April news arrived from Belgorod that a Tatar captured by the Don Cossacks at a ford had told them about the khan's massive mobilization: small bands of Crimeans had appeared on the steppes and were everywhere driving out our sentries.

Boris now ordered everyone to prepare for a *tsar's campaign*. On 2 May he left Moscow in his armor with five crown princes, a Kirghiz, a Siberian, one from Shamakha, one from Khiva and Kaibula's son. Also with him were his boyars, Prince Mstislavskii, the Shuiskiis, Godunov and Romanov princes and others, including many noted officials such as Bogdan Belskii, the keeper of the seal Vasilii Shchelkalov, court nobles, Duma secretaries, 44 stewards, 20 junior stewards and 274 resident boyar cadets. In short, everyone who would be needed for war, for advice and for court splendor. Remaining in Moscow with the tsaritsas – the nun Aleksandra and Mariya – were young Theodor, the boyars Dmitrii Ivanovich Godunov and the princes Trubetskii, Glinskii, Cherkasskii, Shestunov and others. Theodor was with his tutor, Ivan Chemodanov. Arrangements were also made in the capital in case there was a siege: voivodes were appointed for defending the walls and towers, patrolling the city, scouting and fighting within the fortifications.

On 10 May in the village of Kuzminskoe two prisoners – a Lithuanian and one of the khan's men, who had come from the Crimea. They asserted that the khan had taken the field and was indeed headed for Moscow. Boris now sent couriers *with gracious words* to all the commanders of fortifications in the steppes – to Tula, Oskol, Livny, Elets, Kursk and Voronezh. These couriers were ordered to inquire after the health of the voivodes, as well as the court nobles, centurions, boyar cadets, musketeers and Cossacks. They were to hand the tsar's letters to the voivode and request that the following be read out in public:

"I am standing on the banks of the Oka {Boris had written} and watching the steppes. Wherever the enemy appears, there you will see me."

In Serpukhov he organized the voivodes' commands, giving honorary titles to the crown princes and real ones to five of his most distinguished princes: to Mstislavskii in the main legion, Vasilii Shuiskii in the right legion, Ivan Golitsyn in the left, Dmitrii Shuiskii in the vanguard, and Timothei Trubetskii in the reserve legion. The old fences and walls against the khans' attacks, in addition to forts, abatises* served to defend Old Russia** in places difficult to go around, near Peremyshl, Likhvin, Belev, Tula, Borovsk and Ryazan. The sovereign inspected their plans and then sent special voivodes with Mordvi and musketeers to these places. He also formed a water-borne force, or flotilla, on the Oka to better harm the enemy in battles on its banks. We saw what had never been seen before: we are assured it was a half million troops in rapid, ordered movement, with inexpressible enthusiasm and boundless confidence.

This all affected men's minds powerfully, and so did the newness of the reign, which promoted optimism, as well as high opinion of Boris, whose wisdom had been seasoned by long experience. Even the struggle for precedence vanished: the voivodes asked only where they were to be stationed and then proceeded to their banners, nor did they consult the Book of Ranks about the service of their fathers and grandfathers. The tsar had declared that the Grand Council defer to him in prescribing for the boyars and court nobles *service without regard to station.* This enthusiasm, which promoted necessary subordination, also had another important effect: it increased the number of troops and improved their discipline. Court nobles and boyar cadets took the field on the best horses, in the best armor and with all their servants who were fit for military duty. This greatly pleased the tsar, who knew no bounds in expressing his favor. Every day he inspected the

---

* [Defensive obstacles made of felled trees.]
** [Not a currently recognized term. From the towns and cities mentioned, evidently an area centered about 100 km south of Moscow.]

legions and the guard units, inviting their commanders and rankers to dinner, no less than 10,000 people at a time under canvas with silver dinnerware.

These truly royal entertainments continued for six weeks. Rumors of the enemy had suddenly gone quiet; our mounted patrols no longer encountered them and silence reigned on the banks of the Donets. Nowhere did the guards see dust clouds, nowhere did they hear horses' hooves; they just dozed in the silent steppes. Had false reports deceived Boris, or had he deceived Russia with his feigned credulity, in order to appear to be the tsar not only of Moscow, but of all the armed forces as well? They were fired with love for their new autocrat who in a perilous time preferred a war helmet to Monomakh's crown, which would perhaps double the luster of his formal coronation. This would be cunning worthy of Boris, and scarcely to be put past him. Instead of a cloud of enemies, peaceful emissaries of Kazy-Girei appeared in southern Russia with our herald. On 18 June the voivodes in Elets reported this to Boris, who rewarded the courier with money and a promotion.

Did this unprecedented mobilization, which had cost great effort and expense, seem to have been in vain? We are assured that it saved the country and struck fear into the khan; that the Crimeans had really been on the march, but when they learned of Russia's mobilization, had retired hastily. In any case, the tsar wished to instill fear in the khan's emissaries, of whom the most important was Mirza Alei. They had entered Russia as if into an armed camp. On the way they had seen the flash of swords and lances and the numerous horsemen of the guards' units, handsomely uniformed and meticulously equipped, and in the forests and abatises they could hear calls and the firing of weapons. They were halted near Serphukhov, seven versts from the tsar's tents on the meadows by the Oka where the army had now been gathering from all over for several days. There, before dawn on 29 June, 100 cannons roared and the first rays of the sun illuminated an innumerable host prepared for battle.

The Crimeans, astonished by this terrible volley and by the menacing spectacle, were ordered to proceed to the tsar through close ranks of infantry and surrounded in the distance by dense groups of cavalry. They were led into the tsar's tent, where everything was glittering with arms and splendor. There Boris, wearing a golden helmet instead of a crown, was foremost among a throng of crown princes and princes not so much due to his rich dress, but also because of his imperious mien. The mirza Alei and his companions were silent for a long time, unable to find words, due to their amazement and confusion. At last they said that Kazy-Girei wanted a permanent alliance with Russia and a renewal of the negotiations concluded during Theodor's reign. He would be *of one will* with Boris and prepared to march with all his horde against Moscow's enemies. The emissaries were feted sumptuously and some of ours were sent back with them to the khan for ratification of the new treaty document with his oath.

O n this same Day of Sts. Peter and Paul, the tsar took his leave of the army after giving them a lavish meal in the field: 500,000 guests feasted in the meadows by the Oka.

Viands, mead and wine were distributed from carts and the officers were given velvet, brocade and damask. The tsar's parting words were,

"I love this Christian army and I am relying on it."

Loud blessings accompanied Boris far along the Moscow Road. The voivodes and the troops were delighted that their sovereign was so wise, gracious and fortunate – he had without bloodshed, but by threats alone, given the nation the eminently desirable fruits of the most glittering victory: tranquility, security and honor! The chronicler says that Russians hoped Boris's whole reign would be like its beginning and earnestly praised the tsar. Part of the army was left on the Oka to keep an eye on things; another part marched to the Lithuanian and Swedish borders. The greater part was dismissed, but the most senior officers sped after the sovereign to the capital.

T here a new triumph awaited Boris: all of Moscow greeted him as it once had Ivan, the conqueror of Kazan. In a welcoming speech, the patriarch told him,

<table>
<tr><td>PATRIARCH'S SPEECH</td></tr>
</table>

"Great autocrat, chosen by God and beloved of God! We see your glory; you give thanks to the Most High, and we thank Him with you. But rejoice and celebrate with us after this immortal victory! The nation and its people's lives and property are intact, while the fierce enemy has knelt down and sued for peace. *You have not hidden, but rather have multiplied your talents** in this amazing exploit, which is marked by more than human wisdom . . . Greetings O lord, tsar beloved of Heaven and your own people! We weep for happiness and bow down to you."

The patriarch, clergy and the people all bowed to the ground. Expressing emotion and humility, the sovereign hastened to the Cathedral of the Dormition to praise the Most High and then to the grieving Irina in the Novodevichii Monastery. Every home was decorated with greenery and flowers.

<table>
<tr><td>SUPPLEMENT TO ELECTORAL DOCUMENT</td></tr>
</table>

But Boris still put off his coronation until 1 September so as to perform this important rite in the New Year, on a day of general good will and hope that is charming to the heart. Meanwhile a letter of election was written in the name of the Duma of the Land, with the following appendix:

"Upon all those disobedient to the tsar's will: anathema and excommunication from the Church, and vengeance and punishment from the Council and the nation. Curses and punishment upon any rebel or disputatious schismatic who dares to speak against the action of this council or to trouble people's minds with evil words, be he priest or boyar, citizen or noble, of the Duma or the army. May his memory be expunged for all time!"

This document was ratified on 1 August with the signatures and seals of Boris and young Theodor, by Iov and all the prelates, archimandrites, abbots, archpriests, cellarers and ranking elders, boyars, okolnichie, eminent court officials, the keeper of the seal Vasilii Shchelkalov, the court nobles and secretaries of the Duma, stewards, ministerial secretaries, court nobles, assistant stewards and selectmen from the cities, resident boyar cadets, low level secretaries, merchants and centurions – about 500 in all. One

---

* [The reference is to The Parable of the Talents (Matthew 25:14-30).]

scroll was placed in the tsar's archives, where the national statutes of former monarchs also lay, the other was placed in the patriarch's vestry in the Cathedral of the Dormition. It seemed that human wisdom had done all it could to ensure a firm bond between the sovereign and the state.

Finally Boris's coronation took place, even more splendid and ceremonious than Theodor's, since he received Monomakh's

TSAR CROWNED

regalia from the hand of an ecumenical patriarch. The people stood in reverent silence, but the tsar, beneath the archprelate's right hand, exclaimed in a burst of feeling, as if he had forgotten the Church rules in the midst of the liturgy, loudly shouted,

"Father, great patriarch Iov! God is my witness that during my reign there will be no orphans or poor people." Adjusting his collar, he added, "We shall provide for even these last people."

Shouts of emotion and gratitude were all that could be heard in the cathedral. The boyars praised the monarch; the people wept. We are assured that the new monarch, moved by these tokens of popular love for him, then also declared another important promise: to spare the lives and blood of criminals as well, and exile them to the wastes of Siberia instead. In short, no other coronation of a Russian tsar had ever made a more powerful impression on the imaginations and sentiments of the people than Boris's. Showered with gold coins from Mstislavskii's hand at the church entrance, Boris, wearing his crown, with his orb and scepter, hastened to the tsar's palace to take the place of the Varangian princes on the throne of Russia and to celebrate this great day with favors, generosity and good works for the nation.

ROYAL FAVORS

It began with the court and the Council: Boris promoted the Kirghiz crown prince Uraz-Mahmet to become a ruler of Kasimov, Dmitrii Ivanovich Godunov to become equerry, Stefan Vasilievich Godunov to become majordomo in place of Grigorii Vasilievich, who was the only one unhappy about the elevation of his clan, and who died

NEW RULER IN KASIMOV

in secret sorrow. Promoted to boyar were the princes Katyrev, Cherkasskii, Trubetskii, Nogotkov and Aleksandr Romanov-Yuriev. Promoted to okolnichii were Mikhail Romanov, Belskii (a favorite of Ivan and at one time Boris's friend), Krivoi-Saltykov (also a favorite of Ivan) and four more Godunovs. Many others were promoted to steward or other ranks. He ordered the salary doubled for soldiers and citizens in his service and that Moscow's merchants and others be permitted to trade without duties for two years. Government farmers and the very primitive inhabitants of Siberia were to be exempt from taxes for a year. To these extraordinary benefactions he added another for estate serfs: he decreed how much they were to work for, and to pay their lords legally and satisfactorily. After promulgating these benefactions from the throne, Boris invited the people to 12 days of feasting.

EVENTS IN SIBERIA

It seemed as though fate itself favored the new monarch. The beginning of his reign was marked by a both a longed-for peace and a fortunate feat of arms in a battle with an insignificant number of troops, but memorable for its circumstances, consequences, the site of this victory at the ends of the world, and in the man who was defeated. We had left Kuchyum, the exiled ruler of Siberia, in the Barabinskaya Steppe, adamant against Theodor's charitable proposals, indefatigable in his raids on lands that had been taken from him, and still dangerous.

On 4 August 1598 the Tara voivode Aleksandr Voiekov set out with 397 Cossacks, Lithuanians and native auxiliaries to the banks of the Ob. There, amidst fields of grain and surrounded by distant swamps, Kuchyum was holed up with the miserable remnants of his realm: his wives and children, as well as princes and troops loyal to him, numbering upwards of 500. He was not expecting his enemy. Meanwhile, hearty Voeikov was marching day and night, having left his baggage train behind. He had scouts out taking prisoners, and before sunrise on 20 August, he assaulted this khan's fortified camp. The battle lasted all day, which was Kuchyum's last. His brother and sons, the crown princes Iliten and Kan, six princes, 10 mirzas and 150 of his best warriors perished from our volleys, which by evening had forced the Tatars out of their fortifications and pressed them into the river, drowning more than 100 of them. We took 50 prisoners, but a few escaped in boats in the dark of night.

Thus did Voeikov exact vengeance on Kuchyum for the death of incautious Yermak. The victors captured eight wives, five sons and eight daughters of the khan, as well as five princes and considerable riches. Voeikov did not know the fate of Kuchyum and figured he, like Yermak, had drowned in the depths of the river. He considered it pointless to proceed farther – he burned everything he could not take away and returned to Tara with the most eminent of his prisoners. He reported to Boris that Siberia now had no other ruler than the Russian one. Yet Kuchyum still lived: two diligent servitors had taken him down the Oka in a boat during the battle to the Chatskaya land. Once again our voivodes proposed that he go to Moscow to join his family and live out his days on the charity of a magnanimous sovereign. The *seit*,* Tul-Mehmet, sent by Voeikov, found Kuchyum in the forest on the banks of the Ob near a place where there were many corpses of Tatars killed by the Russians. The blind old man, indomitable in adversity, was sitting under a tree surrounded by his three sons and 30 loyal retainers. He heard out the *seit*'s speech about the benevolence of the Muscovite tsar and calmly replied,

"I did not want to go to him of my own free will in better times, whole and rich; why would I go there to die? I am blind and deaf, poor and orphaned. I do not regret the loss of my wealth, only of my dear son Asmanak, taken by the Russians. With him alone, without my realm or wealth, without my wives or other sons, I would be able to continue to live in this world. Now I am sending the last of my children to Bukhara and I myself will travel to the Nogai."

He had neither warm clothing nor horses, and requested them as a favor from his former subjects, the inhabitants of the Chatskaya volost, who had now promised to be Russian subjects. They sent him a single horse and a fur coat. Kuchyum returned to the scene of the battle and there, in the presence of the seit, was busy for two days burying the dead. On the third day he mounted his horse,

---

* [A distinguished official of the sultan's court; from Arabic *sayyid*, a male descendant of Mohammed.]

and vanished from history. Only unreliable rumors about his miserable end remain. It is written that while roaming the steppes of the Upper Irtysh, near the lake of Zaisan-Nor in the land of the Kalmyks, he had stolen some horses and had been pursued by the inhabitants from wilderness to wasteland. He was defeated on the shores of Lake Kurgalchin and made it to a Nogai ulus almost alone. There the blind old refugee was pitilessly murdered by its residents:

> DEATH OF
> KUCHYUM

"Your father pillaged us and you are no better than your father."

Moscow and Russia were cheered by the news of this event. Boris sped by night with Voeikov's report to the monastery to see Irina, since he loved to share the pure pleasures of his lofty rank with her. The destruction of Kuchyum, the first and last khan of Siberia – who was memorable, if not for his puissance, then for his intransigent steadfastness in misfortune – seemed to put the seal on our rule over northern Asia. In the capital and all the cities and towns, the victory over this boundless realm was celebrated once again to the sound of church bells and with church services. Voeikov was awarded a gold medal and his comrades in arms received money.

The eminent prisoners were ordered brought to Moscow and it gave the people great pleasure to see their formal entrance into the capital in January 1599. Kuchyum's wives, daughters, daughters-in-law and sons (the youths Asmanak and Shaim, the boy Babadsha and the young boys Kumush and Molla) rode in rich, carved sleighs. Kuchyum's wives and daughters wore fur coats with velvet, satin and damask trim and adorned with gold, silver and lace. The crown princes wore velvet robes lined with precious furs. There were a great number of horsemen fore and aft: boyar cadets two-by-two, all in sable fur coats with arquebuses. The streets were filled with spectators, both Russian and foreign. The wives and princes were quartered in private homes belonging to merchants and court nobles and given a proper, but very modest allowance.

> 1599

Ultimately the khan's wives and daughters were sent off to Kasimov and Bezhetskii-Verkh, to the ruler Uraz-Mahmet and the

Siberian prince Mametkul in accordance with the wishes of both parties. Kuchyum's son Abdul-Khair, who had been captured back in 1591, now accepted the Christian faith and was named Andrei.

There were no wars after this, just a rather effortless mellowing of the obduracy of our Siberian subjects. Whether by fear or by the peaceful benefits of an active authority, their numbers increased, while we were busy quietly establishing new

1598-1604

towns there: Verkhoture in 1598, Mangazeya and Turinsk in 1600 and Tomsk in 1604. They were settled by military personnel and their families, especially Cossacks, Lithuanians and Little Russians. Even the native Siberians were employed for military purposes. They became imbued with an enthusiasm for service with benefits and honors, so that they were very eager to cooperate with us in the pacification of their fellow countrymen. In brief, if chance had given Ivan Siberia, then Boris's wise policies made it a reliable and indefeasible part of the Russian state.

Nothing changed in Russia's foreign policy, neither in its spirit or appearance. We wanted peace everywhere; we wished to gain territory without war, although we made ourselves ready for a defensive one. We had no faith in the good will of those whose benefit was incompatible with our own, and we

FOREIGN AFFAIRS

did not overlook the chance to harm them if it could be done without a clear violation of treaty.

The khan, while assuring Russia of his friendship, deferred formally concluding a new treaty with the new tsar. Meanwhile, the Don Cossacks harassed the Taurid with their raids and Crimean brigands did the same to the Belgorod district. Finally, in June 1602, Kazy-Girei, after receiving gifts valued at 14,000 rubles, handed a sworn treaty document over to our emissary, Prince Grigorii Volkonskii, with all the formalities. However, he still wanted 30,000 more rubles and complained that Russians were encroaching on the khan's uluses by building new forts in steppes that had hitherto been Tatar space.

"How can we not see," he said, "your intent, which is so un-friendly? You want to fence us in. You do not have many friends like me. The sultan lives with the thought of marching on Russia, but he always hears a single word from me: 'Back off! There are wastelands, forests, watercourses, swamps and impassable mud there.'"

The tsar replied that his treasury was exhausted from the favors that he had shown to his army and his people, that these forts were built only to ensure the safety of our embassies to the khan and to restrain the predatory Don Cossacks. We had a powerful army and did not fear the sultan's. One of Kazy-Girei's favorites, Akhmet-Chelibei, was sent to the tsar with a treaty document to get his oath that he would faithfully fulfill its mutual obligations. Boris took a book in his hand (certainly not the Gospels) and said,

"I promise sincere friendship to Kazy-Girei: here is my *great oath*."

He did not want to kiss the cross or show the book to Chelibei, who was assured that out of special love for the khan, the Russian sovereign had orally recited the sacred treaty obligations and that treaties with other monarchs were affirmed with only a boyar's word. And so Boris, despite this ancient custom, avoided the vain abasement of a sacred object in dealings with barbarians, while respecting only greed and power. He honored the khan with moderate gifts and most of all relied on his army, which was prepared to defend southwestern Russia's borders and to keep the peace there. There were mutual irritations, but no hostile action. In 1603 Kazy-Girei angrily expelled the sovereign's new emissary, Prince Vorotynskii, from the Taurid because he would not try to restrain the Don Cossacks from attacking the Karasanskii ulus. The prince rudely responded,

"You have a saber. My business relates only to the khan, not Cossack thieves."

This event did not produce a rift, however: the khan complained without threatening, and affirmed his obligation to die our friend. He was afraid of the sultan and thought to find a protector in Boris.

In Lithuanian and Swedish affairs, Boris likewise tried to increase Russia's prestige, making use of time and opportunity. Sigismund was still king of Sweden in name but was now fighting with its ruler, his uncle, Duke Karl. He had persuaded the noble pans to participate in this internal strife by yielding Estonia to their country [i.e., Poland]. These circumstances favored us: Lithuania wanted a firm peace and Sweden an alliance with Russia. Boris expressed readiness for either. He had conceived an easy way to recover from them territory that had once been ours, that we had yielded to them involuntarily. This was the territory of the old [Teutonic] Order, which Ivan so regretted, as did Russia. It had been bought with protracted sanguinary efforts and given away to power-hungry foreigners for nothing.

We have previously mentioned the son of King Erik of Sweden, the exiled Gustav. Wandering from country to country, he had lived for a while in Thorn on a scanty allowance from his brother Sigismund. In 1599 he decided to seek his fortune in our country, to which both Theodor and Boris had invited him. They had offered him not only temporary shelter, but also a rich estate or appanage. The tsar's officials were waiting to greet him on the border, in Novgorod and Tver, with greetings and gifts. They dressed him in gold and velvet and took him to Moscow in a rich carriage; he was presented to Boris in a quite magnificent gathering of the court and kissed the hands of Boris and young Theodor. He made a speech (he knew the Slavic language) and then sat on a golden pillow. He dined with the tsar at a special table with a special carver and cup-bearer. He was given a huge house with officials and servants, a great many precious vessels and bowls from the tsar's pantry and ultimately an appanage in Kaluga with three towns and their volosts to provide him with income.

> FATE OF SWEDISH PRINCE GUSTAV IN RUSSIA

In brief, except for Boris's family, Gustav appeared to be the first man in Russia, with daily favors and gifts. He had merits: a nobility of spirit, sincerity, uncommon knowledge of the sciences, especially of chemistry, so that he had earned the sobriquet of a second Theophrastus Paracelsus. He knew languages in addition to Swedish and Slavic: Italian, German and French. He had seen much of the world, had an inquiring mind and was a pleasant conversationalist. However, it was not his merits or knowledge that were the cause of the tsar's favor: Boris intended to employ him as an instrument of his policy, like a second Magnus, as a bugbear for Sigismund and Karl. He beguiled Gustav with the hope of ruling Livonia with Russian help and cunningly set about beguiling Livonia as well.

There were still a lot of officials from Derpt and Narva living with their wives and children in tolerable captivity in Moscow, but they were sad at losing their homeland and wherewithal. Boris gave them their liberty on condition that they swear inalienable loyalty to him. They could go wherever they wished: to Riga, Lithuania or Germany to trade, but they would everywhere be his diligent servants. They were to observe and find out things of importance to Russia and secretly report them to the keeper of the seal, Shchelkalov. These people, at one time wealthy merchants, no longer had any money, so the tsar ordered them given up to 25,000 of today's silver rubles so that they could more diligently serve Russia and attract their fellow countrymen to it.

The tsar knew the dissatisfaction of the residents of Riga and of other Livonians, whose government was oppressing them with regard to both their civil life and religion. He ordered them to be told secretly that if they wished to save their liberty and the faith of their fathers, if they were afraid of permanent servitude under the heavy Lithuanian yoke and of becoming papists or Jesuits, then the Russian shield had them covered and its sword was poised above their oppressors. The most puissant of monarchs, equally famed for his wisdom and humanity, wished to be their father more than to be sovereign of Livonia, and was waiting for delegations from Riga, Derpt and Narva to conclude an agreement that would then be ratified by the boyars' oaths. Their liberty, laws and faith would remain untouchable under his supreme power.

Meanwhile, the Pskov voivodes were to artfully spread the word in Livonia that Gustav, who had been so graciously received by the tsar, would be crossing their borders with our troops to expel the Poles and the Swedes, and he would then govern as its proper, hereditary ruler, albeit with the obligation to be a Russian vassal. Gustav himself wrote to Duke Karl:

"Europe is aware of the miserable fate of my father, and you know its perpetrators and my persecutors. I am leaving vengeance to God. Now I am in my quiet and secure haven with a great monarch who is gracious towards my unfortunate ruling house. Here I can be of use to our beloved homeland if you will yield me Estonia, which is menaced by Sigismund's love of power. With the help of God and the tsar, I shall not only stand up for its towns, but I shall also take all of Livonia, my legitimate patrimony."

We note that in this letter no mention is made of our negotiations with Sweden, but this information would hardly have been provided to the duke. This letter, which had probably been composed in a Moscow ministry, traveled only in the form of scrolls, to be passed from hand to hand amongst the citizens of Livonia in order to arouse them to abet Boris's plan. This is how we schemed while we were at peace with Sweden and had a truce with Lithuania!

Yet this cunning, no different from perfidy, remained without fruit – for three reasons:

1) The Livonians had long feared and been hostile to Russia; they remembered the story of Magnus and still saw traces of Ivan's ferocity in their country; they heard our promises but did not believe them. Just a few residents of Narva, who were in secret correspondence with Boris, were plotting to hand over the city to Boris, but they were convicted of treason and publicly executed.

2) We had spies, but Sigismund and Karl had an army in Livonia. How could Narva, even if it wanted to, even consider sending an embassy to Moscow?

3) Gustav fell out of favor with Boris, who had been thinking of marrying him to Princess Kseniya on condition he convert to her faith, because Gustav would not agree to betray his own religion, nor to abandon the sweetheart whom he had brought with him from Danzig. It is written that he also did not want to be a blind instrument of our hostile policy, toward Sweden. He asked leave to depart, and, inflamed with wine, in the presence of Boris's physician Fiedler, threatened to torch Moscow if he was not permitted to leave Russia. Fiedler informed the boyar Semyon Godunov of this and the boyar informed the tsar, who angrily took away both

treasure and towns from the ingrate and ordered him held under house arrest. However, he soon relented and gave him, instead of Kaluga, the ruins of Uglich.

In 1601 Gustav was once again a guest of the tsar, but no longer dined with him. He retired to his estate and there, amidst the sad ruins, quietly busied himself with chemistry until the end of Boris's life. He was then involuntarily moved to Yaroslavl, and later to Kashin. This unfortunate prince died in 1607, complaining of the inconstancy of the woman for whom he had sacrificed a glittering destiny in Russia. His solitary grave in a beautiful grove of birches on the banks of the Kashenka was visited by the eminent Swedish commander Jacob De la Gardie and Karl IX's emissary Petrei during Shuiskii's reign.

TRUCE WITH LITHUANIA

Meanwhile, we had the chance to proudly repay Sigismund for the abasement endured by Ivan from Batory. The Lithuanian grand emissary, Chancellor Lew Sapieha arrived in Moscow and spent six weeks in idleness, because, as he was told, the tsar was suffering from gout. Presented to Boris on 16 December 1600, Sapieha disclosed the conditions that had been drawn up by the Warsaw Sejm for the conclusion of a permanent peace with Russia. They were listened to and rejected, and for several more months Sapieha was held in tedious solitude to the point that he threatened to get on his horse and depart Moscow with his business unfinished. Finally, supposedly out of respect for the gracious intervention of Boris's young son, the sovereign ordered the Duma councilors to conclude a truce with Lithuania for 20 years.

A document was drawn up on 11 March 1601, but there was no desire to name Sigismund therein as *King of Sweden*, on the sneaky pretext that he had not informed Theodor or Boris of his elevation to his father's throne, but in fact we were using this occasion to take revenge for Lithuania's earlier obstreperousness in calling Russian sovereigns only grand princes. Thereby we would still give ourselves a claim to the gratitude of the Swedish ruler for the right to enter into negotiations with him as if with a legitimate monarch. Sapieha objected, demanded, entreated and even wept to get all the king's titles inserted into the document, but in vain. The document was sent to Sigismund for ratification with the boyar Mikhail Glebovich Saltykov and the Duma secretary Athanasii Vlasiev, who despite their poor reception in Lithuania, managed to succeed in their primary task, to the honor of the Muscovite court. Sigismund was then commanding his army in Livonia and summoned our emissaries to Riga. They replied,

"We will wait for the king in Vilnius."

They stuck it out: in late autumn they remained for some time in tents on the banks of the Dnieper, enduring cold and want, but they forced the king to come to them in Vilnius, where a heated dispute commenced. The Lithuanian nobles told Saltykov and Vlasiev,

"If you really desire peace, then acknowledge our king as Sweden's and Estonia as a Polish possession." Saltykov replied,

"You need peace more than we. Estonia and Livonia have been Russian territories since the time of Yaroslav the Great, while the Swedish kingdom is now ruled by Duke Karl. Our tsar does not give anyone empty titles." The pans retorted,

"Karl is a traitor and a usurper. Will your tsar stop using the titles *of Astrakhan* or *of Siberia* if some brigand temporarily conquers those lands? The best part of Hungary is now in the sultan's hands, but the Kaiser titles himself *of Hungary* and the Spanish king *of Jerusalem.*"

These arguments were ineffective, but on 7 January 1602 Sigismund kissed the cross in the presence of our emissaries, promising to keep the agreement sacred and adding,

"I swear in the name of God to die with my hereditary title of king of Sweden, to yield Estonia to no one, and in the course of this 20-year truce to obtain Narva, Revel and its other cities from whomever has occupied them."

At this point Saltykov broke in, saying loudly, "King Sigismund! Kiss the cross for the great sovereign Boris Theodorovich according to the exact wording of the document, without any additions, or your oath will be invalid!"

Sigismund was obliged to rephrase his speech as the boyars and the sense of the document demanded. Evidently in both Moscow and Vilnius, Russian policy had gained the upper hand over Lithuanian. The king yielded, for he did not want to fight both the Swedes and us at the same time. He stood his ground only in his refusal to name Boris *Tsar* or *Autocrat*, which is something we had demanded both in Moscow and Vilnius. However, we were satisfied with his word that this title would indisputably be given to Boris on conclusion of a permanent peace treaty.

"Very well," said the pans. "Christian blood will not be spilled for 20 years. Still, it would have been better for both powers to have a permanent peace. Twenty years will pass quickly, and no one knows who will then be the sovereigns of Lithuania and Russia."

We note another memorable event: on the day of their sendoff, Moscow's emissaries were feasting at the royal court and caught sight of Sigismund's young son Władysław. As if they had a premonition of the future, they offered to kiss his hand. The seven year old boy, who was to play such an important role in our history, greeted them wisely and graciously. He got up from his place, took off his hat, and told them to give his greetings to Crown Prince Theodor and to tell him that he wished to be his sincere friend. By retaining a pleasant recollection of young Władysław, the eminent boyar Saltykov and the Duma secretary Vlasiev, who had replaced Shchelkalov in the government, might have imbued many Russians with a favorable opinion of this truly gracious heir-apparent. On their return, the emissaries reported to Boris that he could be assured of security and tranquility on the Lithuanian side for a long time. The king and the pans knew of and could see Russia's power directed by such a wise sovereign and would naturally not consider violating the treaty under any circumstances. Inwardly they were praising the peace-loving tsar as a divine gift for their homeland.

We have said that the Swedish ruler was seeking an alliance with Russia. Boris was trying to persuade the duke not to make peace with Sigismund. He gave the

RELATIONS WITH SWEDEN

Swedes permission to pass through Novgorod territory when traveling from Finland to Derpt and desired to cooperate with them in expelling the Poles from Livonia. The king's officials came to Moscow and ours went to Stockholm with declarations of mutual friendship. As a token of his special esteem for Boris, the duke secretly asked him if he would fulfill the wish of his government officials and call him the Swedish *king*? The tsar advised that this should be done immediately, to benefit Sweden, thereby earning much gratitude from Karl. His counsel was sincere, for Russia's security demanded that Lithuania and Sweden have separate rulers.

We wanted Narva, however, and to that end, in February 1601, the sly tsar announced to the Swedish emissaries, Karl Hendrikson and Georg Klauson, who happened to be in our capital at the same time as the Lithuanian chancellor Sapieha, that the peace treaty of 1597, written in the name of Theodor and Sigismund, be re-examined and formally ratified. He said it was inoperative, since Sigismund had not ratified it – circumstances had changed, and the king was ready to cede us part of Livonia if we would assist him in his war against the duke. The emissaries were astounded:

"We concluded the treaty," they told our boyars, "between Sweden and Russia, not between Theodor and Sigismund, for all time and in the name of God, and have been fulfilling its conditions in good conscience: we handed over Kexholm despite Sigismund's objection. No, Duke Karl will not believe that the tsar is thinking of violating his promise, sealed by kissing the cross on the Holy Gospel. If Sigismund is ceding you cities in Livonia, then he is ceding that which is not his – half of Livonia has been conquered by the duke. And has the tsar secured a reliable alliance with Lithuania? Is the dispute over Kiev and Smolensk at an end? An agreement to the advantage of Sweden and Russia can be reached far sooner. The principal advantage would be to have a good, peaceful neighborhood. Was it not the tsar himself who tried to persuade Karl not to make peace with Sigismund? We are at war and capturing cities. What hinders you from taking up arms also and dividing Livonia with us?"

However, while Boris was pleased to see the flame of war between the duke and the king, he was not considering joining in, at least for the time being. He concluded a truce with Lithuania and delayed ratifying an equitable treaty with Karl; he dismissed the latter's emissaries empty-handed and was covertly trying to get the Estonians to betray Sweden and join it to Russia. This deviousness irritated the duke, but at the same time, Boris was sincerely favoring him in the war over Livonia, since a victory by Sigismund would threaten us with the union of the Swedish crown and the Polish, while a victory by Karl would permanently split them apart. Boris was the first, and most willing of all the European sovereigns to acknowledge the duke as king of Sweden, and in his relations with him he already used that title, even though the duke did not yet call himself king, but just ruler.

| CLOSE TIES WITH DENMARK |

The new and significant tie between Boris and Sweden's hereditary enemy must also have discomfited Karl. After he had informed neighboring and other monarchs, the emperor and Elizabeth of his coronation, Boris long delayed in showing this courtesy to King Christian of Denmark. However, in 1601 he commenced a very amicable relationship with him. Christian's emissaries Eske-Brok and Karl Briske set out for Moscow at the same time that ours – the distinguished court noble Rzhevskii and the secretary Dmitriev – set out for Copenhagen, to exchange greetings and resolve the old, endless disputes over the Kola and Vardø wildernesses. In arguing that all of Lapland belonged to Norway, Christian cited Saxo Grammaticus' history and even the Münster Cosmography. He also said that Russians themselves had long called Lapland *Murmansk* or Norwegian land.[*] We retorted that there was no doubt it was ours, since in the reign of Vasilii Ivanovich of Novgorod, the priest Iliya had baptized its primitive inhabitants. They also asserted right of ownership with the following tale, based on traditions of the local elders:

"There once lived in Korela, or Kexholm, an eminent ruler named Valit or Varent, a tributary of Great Novgorod. He was a man of unusual courage and strength: he fought, conquered and wished to rule over the Lapp or *Murmansk* lands. The Lapps requested protection from their Norwegian German[**] neighbors. Valit conquered the Germans, as well, and there at the current site of the Varengskii summer parish, with this own hands he placed

---

* [Murmane is the Old Russian word for a Norwegian.]
** [Russians used *German* in an extended sense, to denote foreigners speaking Germanic languages, e.g., Swedish.]

an enormous rock more than a sazhen* in height as a monument to the ages and built a sturdy enclosure around it with *12 walls* and named it *Vavilon* [Babylon]. This rock is even now now called *Valit's Rock*. The same sort of enclosure once existed at the Kola stockade. In the Murmansk land it is still known as Valit's Homestead or Valit's Town. It is amidst islands or high crags, where Karelian knights could safely take their ease. The defeated Germans ultimately concluded a peace treaty with him, ceding him all of Lapland to the river Ivgei. Long praised and fortunate, Valit died with the Christian name Vasilii and is buried in Kexholm, at the Church of the Savior. Since that time the Lapps have paid tribute to Novgorod and the Muscovite tsars."

These historical arguments from either side were not very persuasive, and the Danes, as a token of their desire for peace, wanted to divide Lapland with us, lengthwise or crosswise, into two equal portions. Boris, out of fondness for Christian, ceded him all the land north from the Pechenskii Monastery, while recommending that Danish and Russian officials fix the boundary between the two powers at a future meeting in Kola. Meanwhile, negotiations were renewed concerning free trade for Danish merchants in Russia, and an agreement was also reached on this very important matter.

Boris was seeking a suitable husband for his charming tsarevna amongst the princes of the ruling houses of Europe so as to thereby increase the glory of his own house in the eyes of the Russian boyars and princes,

DANISH DUKE AFFIANCED TO KSENIYA

who until quite recently had viewed the Godunovs as beneath them. After failing in his plan to give his daughter's hand together with Livonia to Gustav, this tender father and slick politician hoped to provide Kseniya with happiness and Russia with advantages by marrying her to Duke Johan, Christian's brother. He was young, intelligent and pleasant, and might serve as an instrument of our power-hungry designs on Estonia, at this time a Danish possession. The tsar made the offer and the king, undaunted by Magnus's fate, was happy at the prospective honor of becoming

---

* [A sazhen is 2.13 meters, or about 7 feet.]

brother-in-law to the renowned Muscovite autocrat, in hopes of his earnest assistance in dealing with hostile Sweden.

Unfortunately the interesting documents concerning this match have been lost: we do not know the conditions relating to religion, dowry or of the other mutual obligations. We do know that Johan agreed to give up his homeland for Kseniya and become an appanage prince in Russia. Might the reason for this match also have been so that in the case of possible misfortune – the premature death of the tsarevich – the Muscovite throne would have a successor from Boris's line? The farseeing tsar ardently loved his son, but may also have loved the idea of an unbroken succession to the throne for his house over the centuries.

The prospective groom was then fighting under Spanish banners in the Netherlands. He hurried back, boarded a flagship and on 10 August 1602 arrived at the mouth of the Narova with five friends. The tsar's boat was awaiting the guests there, covered with velvet, and as soon as the duke set foot on Russian soil, cannons roared. The boyar Mikhailo Glebovich Saltykov and the Duma secretary Vlasiev greeted him in the name of the tsar. They conducted him to a rich tent and brought him 80 sable pelts. Johan rode in a carriage glittering with gold and silver past Narva to Ivangorod, where banners fluttered from the towers and walls covered with curious spectators. He had also been greeted this way in Sweden, which inwardly feared this journey whose goal they already knew or had guessed.

The duke was honored much more sincerely in Russia, however. Traveling with him were Christian's emissaries, three senators (Gildenstern, Brahe and Holk), eight eminent officials, several court nobles, two physicians and a plethora of servants. At every stage, even the poorest villages, they were treated as if they were in the Moscow palace, and music was played at dinner. In the towns, cannons were fired, soldiers stood at arms and official after official was presented to *his serene majesty*. They traveled slowly, no more than 30 versts a day, through Novgorod, Valdai, Torzhok and Staritsa. The traveler was not bored: during rest periods, he rode around on horseback or took boats on the rivers. He amused himself with hunting and fowling, and conversed with the boyar Saltykov and the secretary Vlasiev about Russia, wishing to know its national laws and its people's customs. Christian's emissaries advised him not to immediately adopt our customs, but to keep his German ones.

"I am going to see the tsar," he replied, "and therefore I must acquaint myself with everything Russia."

As it was 1 September in Bronnitsy, Johan told Saltykov,

"I know that on this day you celebrate the New Year, that the clergy, Council and court now formally wish the tsar long life. I have not yet had the good fortune to see his face, but I, too, earnestly pray for his health."

He asked for wine and stood drinking *the tsar's cups* along with the Muscovite officials and the Danish emissaries. In brief, Johan wanted Boris's love and the love of the Russian people. Saltykov and Vlasiev wrote to the tsar about the health and merry disposition of the prince and informed him of everything Christian said and did – even of what he wore: the color of his satin caftans, decorated with gold or silver brocades. The tsar had asked for these details, and sent the traveler new gifts: rich Asiatic fabrics, hats embroidered with pearls, valuable sashes and waistbands, gold chains, sabers studded with turquoise and rubies. At last, Johan expressed his impatience to be in Moscow. He was told in reply that the tsar feared to tire him with rapid travel, but their speed increased. On 18 September they spent the night in Tushino and arrived in the capital on the 19th.

It was not just troops and eminent people, members of the Council and ministerial secretaries, but also the citizens who met him in the field. After listening to the boyars' flattering speeches, he got on a horse and rode around Moscow with Danish and Russian officials to the sound of the giant Kremlin bell. He was taken to the best house in Kitaigorod and the next day he was sent dinner: a hundred heavy gold platters with viands as well as a great many goblets and cups, along with wine and mead. His formal audience was on 28 September. Richly dressed soldiers were lined up from his house to the Red Porch. On Red Square, citizens, Germans and Lithuanians were in their best attire. At the

Porch, Johan was met by the princes Trubetskii and Cherkasskii, on the stairway by Vasilii Shuiskii and Golitsyn, and in the hall by the First Noble, Mstislavskii, along with okolnichie and secretaries. The tsar and the crown prince were in the Golden Palace, dressed in purple velvet embroidered with huge pearls; on their crowns and chests shone diamonds and huge gemstones of extraordinary size.

Boris and Theodor stood up when they saw the duke and tenderly embraced him, then sat down next to him and conversed for a long time in the presence of nobles and royal courtiers. Everyone looked on young Johan with affection, captivated by his good looks. Boris now viewed him as a future son. They dined in the Faceted Palace; the tsar sat on a golden throne before a silver table beneath a crown with a striking clock, between Theodor and the duke – he was already considered one of the family.

The reception concluded with gifts: Boris and Theodor took off diamond-studded chains and put them around Johan's neck, while the royal courtiers brought him two golden ladles adorned with precious gems, some silver vessels, valuable fabrics: English wool, Siberian furs and three sets of Russian clothing. The groom had not yet seen Kseniya, however, believing only rumors of her charms, amiable qualities and merits. He had not been deceived.

Contemporaries write that she was of medium stature, full-bodied and well built; she had a milky white complexion, black hair, dense and long, lying in coils on her shoulders. Her face was fresh and pink, her brows joined, her eyes large, black and bright – they had an ineffable beauty, especially when tears of tender compassion glistened in them. Her personality was no less captivating: she was mild, well-spoken, intelligent, with cultivated tastes, and loved books and sweet hymns.

Strict custom forbade such a bride from being shown prematurely, but Johan's traveling companions thought that Kseniya and the tsaritsa could see him, secretly and at a distance. The betrothal and wedding were deferred until winter, and in preparation there were prayers instead of banquets: the parents, the princess and her brother traveled to the Trinity Monastery. Eyewitnesses say the following about this lavish royal outing:

"There were 600 horsemen in front and 25 spare horses, glittering in their tack, with silver and gold. Next were two carriages: the empty crown prince's, upholstered in crimson fabric and the other in velvet, occupied by the sovereign. They each were pulled by six horses. The first was surrounded with horsemen, the second with courtiers on foot. Farther back, young Theodor rode on horseback, his steed led by eminent officials, and followed by boyars and courtiers. There were many people running after the tsar, holding up papers. These petitions were taken from them and placed in a red box for presentation to the sovereign. The tsaritsa came out a half hour later, in a splendid carriage; in a second, concealed from every angle, sat the tsarevna. The first carriage was pulled by 10 white horses, the second by eight. There were 40 spare horses in front and a contingent of horsemen – old men with long, gray beards. To the rear there were 24 boyars on white steeds. Surrounding them were 300 constables with staffs." There in the quiet and sanctity of the cloister, Boris and his wife and children prayed for nine days over the tomb of St. Sergii that Heaven bless the union of Kseniya and Johan.

Meanwhile, the groom was honored by dinner in his house every day. He was sent velvet, watered silk and brocades for Russian clothing. He was also sent a bed with linens embroidered in silver and gold. It is written that he was eager to learn our language and even to convert to our faith, so that he would have the same religion as his future wife. In general, he conducted himself prudently and everyone was pleased with his courteous deportment. But that which was sincerely desired by both Russians and Danes, that which the parents and bride prayed for – did not please Providence.

On 16 October, in the village of Bratovshchino, during the return trip from the monastery, the sovereign learned of the groom's sudden illness. Johan was still able to write to him and sent one of his officials to reassure him. The illness kept getting worse and a fierce fever developed, but neither the Danish nor Boris's physicians lost hope. The tsar implored them to use all their skills, promising unheard of favors and rewards. On 19 October, young Theodor visited Ivan, and the tsar himself on the 27th, with the patriarch and some boyars. When Boris saw the mute and feeble patient, he was horrified, and angrily blamed those who had concealed the seriousness of Johan's condition. On the evening of the next day, he found the duke already at death's door. He wept: he was devastated, saying,

"Oh, unfortunate youth! You have left your mother, your kinfolk, your homeland and come to me, only to die an untimely death!"

Not yet willing to give up hope, the sovereign swore to release 4,000 prisoners if Johan recovered and requested the Danes to pray fervently to God. But at 6 o'clock on that same evening, 28 October, Johan died in the bloom of youth, in his 20th year. Not just the royal family, the Danes and the Germans, but also the whole court and all the citizens of the capital were in mourning. Boris went to Kseniya himself and said, "Beloved daughter! Your happiness and my consolation has perished!" She fell senseless at his feet.

Orders were given for all the obligate honors for the deceased. The tsar's treasury was opened for poor people, widows and orphans; the lowly were fed in the house in which Johan had expired. Distinguished officials attended the body. An autopsy had been forbidden and his body placed in a wooden coffin full of fragrances, and later, inside a copper one while still in the oaken one, upholstered in black velvet and silver with a depiction of a cross in the center and a Latin inscription of the merits of the deceased, the good will of the tsar and the Russian people towards him and of their inconsolable sorrow. On 25 November, the day of the funeral, Boris tearfully bade farewell to the deceased and rode after the coffin through Kitaigorod to White Town. The coffin was carried in a carriage under three black banners with the crests of Denmark, Mecklenberg and Holstein. Soldiers of the tsar's guard marched on either side with their sharp lances lowered. The carriage was followed by boyars, officials and citizens, to German Town, where, in a new church of the Augsburg confession [i.e., Lutheran], Johan's remains were buried in the presence of the Moscow nobles. They wept together with the Danes, even though they did not comprehend the touching eulogy, in which the duke's pastor thanked them for their sensitivity.

Is the tale of our chronicler probable: that Boris inwardly did not regret Johan's death because he supposedly envied his wide popularity with the Russian people and feared to leave him as a rival for young Theodor; that the physicians, knowing the tsar's secret thoughts, did not dare to heal the patient? Yet the tsar wanted Russians to love his intended son-in-law. That was why he had advised him to be courteous and to follow our customs. No doubt he also desired Kseniya's happiness as well. This marriage would have given new brilliance and stability to his house, and he could not have changed his mind in only three weeks, to come to fear that which he had desired, to see that which he had not foreseen, or to entrust such a vile and evil secret to his foreign court physicians, whom he, on Johan's death, would not allow into his sight for a long time, and who had treated the duke right along with the duke's own Danish physicians. Officials of Christian's court who witnessed the illness published their faithful description of it, showing that every means of their art had been employed to save Johan, albeit without success.

No, Boris was not feigning his devastation and perhaps felt the punishment of Heaven in his conscience. He had been preparing happiness for his beloved daughter, but saw her widowed while still a bride. He now rejected royal regalia and put on a chasuble of sorrow; for a long time he showed the signs of deep depression. All that he had given to the duke was sent to Copenhagen and all of Johan's companions were sent off with generous new gifts: not even the least of their servants was forgotten. Boris wrote Christian that Russia would remain in indissoluble friendship with Denmark. And indeed, this friendship remained intact, seemingly strengthened for both countries by the sorrowful memory of the fate of the young duke. After lying beneath the vault of the Lutheran Church in Moscow for a long time, his remains were transported to Roskilde. To honor Johan's memory, Boris donated a bell to this church and permitted it to be rung during Easter week.

Sorrow, however, neither interfered with Boris's attention to affairs of state with his usual diligence, nor from considering another groom for Kseniya. Around 1604 our emissaries were again in Denmark. With Christian's collaboration, an agreement was reached with Duke Johann of Schleswig that one of his sons, Filipp, would go to Moscow to marry the tsarevna and become an appanage prince there. These conditions were not fulfilled, but only due to disastrous events in our homeland.

NEGOTIATIONS
WITH AUSTRIA

Russian relations with Austria were, as in Theodor's time, very amicable and not unfruitful. In 1599 the Duma secretary Vlasiev had been sent to the emperor with the news of Boris's coronation. He embarked on a London ship at the mouth of the Dvina and disembarked on the coast of Germany. There in Lübeck and Hamburg the eminent citizens received him with much graciousness, with cannon salvos and music. They praised Boris's known favor towards the Germans and hoped to enjoy new benefits from their trade with Russia. Rudolf had fled Prague due to a pestilent epidemic and was staying in Pilsen, where Vlasiev was having talks with the Austrian ministers. He assured them that our army had set out to fight against the Turks, but that Sigismund had blocked its passage through Lithuanian territory to the Danube. He said that the tsar, as a true brother of the Christian monarchs and eternal enemy of the Ottomans, was trying to convince the shah and other Asiatic princes to make strenuous efforts to counter the sultan, and that he himself was prepared to march against the Crimeans should they assist the Turks. We were constantly trying to get the Lithuanian pans to establish an alliance with the emperor and by the elevation of Maximilian to the Jagellonian throne.

Boris was peace-loving, but would not hesitate to fight for this goal if the emperor were to take vengeance on Sigismund for the dishonor done his brother. Rudolf expressed his gratitude, but requested gold, not troops, from us to make war on Mehmet III; he only wanted us to pacify the khan.

"The emperor," the ministers said, "loves the tsar and does not want him to subject himself to *personal* danger in battles with the barbarians. You have many brave voivodes who could easily pacify the Crimeans even without the tsar – that is the main task! If it please Heaven, then the Polish crown, with the good offices of your magnanimous tsar, will not escape Rudolf. But now is not the time to multiply the number of our enemies."

Naturally we were not considering taking up the sword to put Maximilian on the Polish throne, since Sigismund, already a foe of Sweden, would be no more dangerous to us than an Austrian prince wearing the Jagellonian crown. And despite Vlasiev's assurances, we were not considering doing battle with the sultan unless it was necessary. We could see that it might be necessary, however, since we knew that Mehmet had malice towards Russia and was in fact ordering the khan to lay waste to our territory. Boris earnestly wished Austria well in its war with this enemy of Christendom. Between 1598 and 1604, various Austrian officials visited us, including the eminent Baron Logau, and the Duma secretary Vlasiev went to see the emperor again in 1603. We have no information concerning their talks; we know only that the tsar assisted Rudolf from his treasury and restrained Kazy-Girei from a new invasion of Hungary.

He also tried to establish friendship between the emperor and the shah of Persia, who was putting up a glorious fight against the Ottomans, and to whom the Austrian emissaries traveled after visiting Moscow. The renowned Abbas had flatteringly congratulated Boris on becoming tsar and expressed his readiness to conclude a close alliance with him, and in his behalf with the emperor. In 1600 he had send his envoy Isenalei by way of Kolmogory to Austria, Rome and to the king of Spain. As a token of his special love, in August 1603 he had sent his nobleman Lachin-Bek to

PERSIAN
EMBASSY

his *Muscovite brother* with a golden throne of the ancient Persian sovereigns. However, now he suddenly became hostile to us over poor Georgia: he had neither quarreled with Theodor nor with Boris over the right to call himself its supreme sovereign. He now also wanted to rule over it in the same way – indisputably – and clutch it, like a feeble victim, in his bloody hands.

The ruler Alexander had not ceased complaining to Moscow about the miserable fate of Iberia. His emissaries told our boyars,

"We were weeping because of the infidel and therefore entrusted ourselves to the Orthodox tsar to protect us, but we are weeping still. Our homes, churches and monasteries are in ruins, our fami-

EVENTS IN
GEORGIA

lies in captivity, our shoulders under the yoke. Is this what you promised? And the infidels laugh at the Christians and ask, 'Where is the White Tsar's shield? Where is your protector?"

Boris ordered that they be reminded of Prince Khvorostinin's campaign, in which they were supposed to link up with our troops, but failed to do so. He sent two officials, Nashchokin and Leontiev, to Iberia to thoroughly investigate the situation there, however, and to get an agreement with the Terek voivodes regarding defense measures.

Changes had taken place there: while Alexander had been seriously ill, his son David had declared himself ruler. The father recovered, but his son did not want to return the tokens of power to him: the royal gonfalon, hat and saber with belt. That was not all: he murdered all those close to Alexander. The unfortunate father ran, half-dressed and barefoot, to the church. Weeping, streaming tears, he publicly pronounced anathema and divine vengeance on his son. This fate indeed caught up with the monster: David expired from a sudden, painful illness.

Our envoys returned with the news that Alexander was once again ruling in Iberia, but was unworthy of the sovereign's favor, since he had become an ardent slave of the sultan and dared to reproach Boris for cupidity with regard to gifts.

"Why," the tsar said indignantly, "why would I be attracted by gifts from a pauper, when I could fill all of Iberia with silver and shower it with gold?"

He had not wanted to see the new Iberian envoy, the archimandrite Kirill, but the wise old man showed him clearly that Nashchokin and Leontiev had been slandering Alexander. Kirill did still more: he entreated the sovereign not to punish them and also suggested to him that, for a reliable future union of Iberia with Russia, he should build a stone fortress at Tarki, a place that was inaccessible, abundant and beautiful, and another in Tuzluk, where there was a great salt lake with sulfur and saltpeter, and a third on the river Buinak, where there had once been a town, supposedly founded by Alexander the Great, and where there still was an old tower standing in the midst of some vineyards.

For this rather significant undertaking, the sovereign chose two distinguished voivodes, the okolnichie Buturlin and Pleshcheev, who were to get troops from Kazan and Astrakhan, coordinate with the Terek voivodes and await the Iberian auxiliaries that had been promised under oath in Alexander's name by their emissary. They wasted no time and were unsparing of money: no less than 300,000 rubles were allocated from the treasury for this very remote and difficult campaign. A rather large army set out from the banks of the Terek in 1604 for the Caspian Sea, but only caught sight of the enemy's rear. Shavkal, now a decrepit old man and blind, fled to a canyon in the Caucasus, and the Russians occupied Tarki.

It was impossible to find a better place to build a fort: on three sides high cliffs could serve instead of sturdy walls. It was only necessary to fortify the slope heading down to the sea, which was covered by forest, gardens and grain fields. There were springs in the mountains that provided the inhabitants with fresh water through a series of pipes. There, on the heights, where Shavkal's palace stood with two towers, the Russians immediately began to build a wall. They had everything necessary: timber, stone and lime. They called Tarki *New Town,* and also sited a fort at Tuzluk. Some built while others fought, as far as Andria or Endren and Warm Waters without encountering any significant resistance. They captured the people in the settlements, took their grain and drove off their flocks and herds.

They were afraid of shortages, however, and therefore, late in autumn, Buturlin sent about 1,500 troops to winter in Astrakhan. Fortunately they proceeded cautiously, since Shavkal's sons and the Kumyks were awaiting them in the wilderness. These made a bold assault, fought manfully all day and fled at night, leaving 3,000 dead. The voivodes wrote to Moscow and to the Iberian ruler about this sanguinary fray. They expected the latter's troops by spring, at least, to clear the mountains of the enemy, complete the conquest of Daghestan and build new forts there unhindered. But there was no word of the auxiliary troops, nor any news from unhappy Georgia. Alexander was no longer deceiving the Russians – he was fated to die, and for *us*!

In March 1604 our sovereign sent Kirill off from Moscow with a court noble from the Inner Duma, Mikhail Tatishchev, firstly, to confirm Georgia as our vassal, and secondly, for a family matter, still secret. In August 1604 this official failed to find the Iberian ruler in Zagem – he was with the shah, who had strictly enjoined him to appear in the Persian camp with his troops despite his being a Russian tributary; he was unafraid of offending his friend, Boris. Alexander's son George received Tatishchev not only graciously, but slavishly; he praised the majesty of the Muscovite tsar and wept for his poor homeland.

"Never," he said, "has Iberia been more terribly miserable than now. We are under the knives of both the sultan and the shah. Both want our blood and all that we have. We have handed ourselves over to Russia. Now let Russia take us, not in word, but in deed! There is no time to lose, for soon there will be no one left here to kiss the cross in futile loyalty to its autocrat. He could save us. The Turks, Persians and Kumyks are bursting in on us in force. We are inviting you of our own free will. Come and save us! You see Iberia – its cliffs, canyons and thickets – if you build forts here and man them with Russian troops, we shall genuinely be yours, and intact, and will fear neither the shah nor the sultan."

When George was informed that the Turks were marching on Zagem, he tried to convince Tatishchev to give him his musketeers to fight them, but the astute emissary vacillated for a long time, fearing that this would be tantamount to declaring war on the sultan without the tsar's orders. Finally, he decided to ensure Boris's right to call himself Iberia's supreme ruler by giving George 40 Muscovite troops under command of the doughty centurion Mikhail Semovskii. They joined with five or six thousand Georgians and on 7 October, they moved forward, engaging the Turks with a powerful volley.

This first sound of our arms in the Iberian wilderness astounded the enemy. Their closely packed vanguard suddenly began to thin as they saw a new formation, new troops. Recognizing them as Russian, they shuddered, for they were unaware of our small numbers. George and his troops struck valiantly and did more pursuing than fighting, for the Turks fled without looking back. It seemed that the ancient glory of Iberia had been reborn on this day – its troops captured four of the sultan's gonfalons and a great number of prisoners. The next day George gained victory over the predatory Kumyks. He displayed his trophies to the people, who had long been unknown to him and ascribed all honors to his comrades-in-arms, a handful of Russians, praising them as heroes.

A lexander finally returned from Persia with his son Constantine, who had adopted the Mohammedan faith there, as we mentioned previously. Abbas, treating Iberia autocratically, had ordered Constantine to assemble its troops, all of them, without exception, and to march on Shamakha immediately. He gave him 2,000 of his best troops, some khans and princes, and also gave him secret orders, which the clever Tatishchev managed to guess. The latter warned Alexander and George in vain, telling them that the Persian troops were more a danger to them than for the Turks. He said that Constantine, who had betrayed the Christian God, could also betray the sacred ties of kinship. They did not dare show any suspicion, lest they incur the wrath of the powerful shah. They fulfilled his commands, assembled their troops and handed themselves over to their murderers.

On 12 March, Tatishchev was about to have dinner with Alexander when he suddenly heard a volley of shots in the palace, shouting and the sounds of battle. He sent his interpreter to find out what was going on. The interpreter entered the palace and saw the Persian troops with drawn sabers, blood on the floor, corpses and two severed heads lying before Constantine – the heads of his father and brother! The Moslem Constantine, who had already been declared ruler of Christian Iberia, indicated to Tatishchev that Alexander had been killed by accident, but George deservedly, as a traitor to both the shah and the Muscovite sovereign, and as a friend and lackey of the hated Turks. He said that this execution would not alter Iberia's relations with Russia, that he was fulfilling the orders of the great Abbas, Boris's brother and ally, and that he was prepared to make every effort on behalf of the Christian tsar.

Tatishchev, however, had already learned the truth from Georgian nobles. Abbas had long endured Alexander's ties with Russia in hopes of getting the tsar's cooperation in the war with the Ottomans. He was now the victor and no longer wanted to put up with our suzerainty, albeit fictitious, over a land which had been considered a possession of his predecessors. He understood Boris's policy and had seen that we were rejoicing in the bloodshed between him and the sultan, while avoiding it ourselves. He had ordered the son to kill the father, supposedly because of his partiality towards the Turks, but in fact for his submission to Russia, which had been both audacious and imprudent of the unfortunate Alexander.

The latter's quest for a remote and unreliable patron had irritated two more proximate oppressors. Constantine had been only a tool of Abbas's vengeance and had wept the whole night before the scene of this vile patricide. He assured Boris's emissary that the shah had had no part in it.

"My father," he said, "was the victim of strife between his sons – a very familiar misfortune in our land! Alexander himself eliminated his father and murdered his brother. I did the same, not knowing whether it would be good or bad for the world. In any case, I will be true to my word and better earn the favor of the Russian sovereign than Alexander or George. I am grateful to him for the forts which he built in Shavkal's land, and will soon send rich gifts to Moscow."

Tatishchev did not want carpets or fabrics; he wanted submission, and requested an oath of allegiance to Russia from him. He argued that the Iberian ruler could only be a Christian. Constantine replied that for the time being he would remain a Moslem and a subject of the shah, but would be a defender of Christianity and a friend of Russia, adding,

"Where is your sturdy backbone, on which we can rely in case of need?"

With this, Tatishchev was obliged to depart Zameg, after formally declaring that Boris would not cede Iberia to the shah and that Abbas had imperiously executed Alexander by Constantine's hand and destroyed the happy amity that up till now existed between Persia and Russia. To summarize, we had lost one realm, that is the right to call it our own, but Tatishchev, without leaving Georgia, would gain another for Boris's title.

Boris saw that young Theodor was now almost a grown man; he once again offered his daughter's hand to a Danish prince, but he wanted in any event to have another prospective husband ready for her. He quickly began searching for both a prospective bride and a groom in the homeland of the famous Tamara, the distinguished wife of Georgii Andreevich Bogolyubskii. Alexander's emissary Kirill had praised the good looks of the Iberian crown prince Teimuras, David's son, to our boyars, and the beauty of the Kartaliniya princess Elena, a granddaughter of Simeon. Tatishchev was ordered to see them: he could not find Teimuras, who had been handed over to the shah as a hostage, but rode to Kartaliniya to visit the family of its ruler. This district of ancient Iberia was less subject to the raids of the Daghestan Kumyks and also had fewer ravines than eastern Georgia, or Kakhetia. Elena's father, Prince George, ruled there after Simeon, who had been taken captive by the Turks. He had his own vassal princes (Sonskii and others), a great number of courtiers, boyars and priests.

He entertained Tatishchev in his tents and seemed grateful to hear his proposals. The first was that George become a vassal of Russia, the second, that he send Elena to Moscow with his close relative, Prince Khozdroi, on condition that they have all the requisite merits for the honor of entering Boris's family.

"This is a great honor," our earnest emissary said. "The emperor and the kings of Sweden, Denmark and France have ardently sought it."

George was horrified at Alexander's fate, but Tatishchev replied that this unfortunate had perished through his own duplicity – he had tried to serve a Christian and an infidel sovereign at the same time, to the irritation of both.

"Wishing to please Abbas," he said, "Alexander did not give us troops to destroy Shavkal. He left a son in Persia and permitted him to become a Mohammedan, that is, to whet his knife at his father and Christendom. He also sent a grandson there after he learned of the [Russian] sovereign's intention to give the tsarevna Kseniya to that grandson in marriage, since he was afraid that Teimuras might give Georgia as a bride-price for the tsarevna. But how could our great tsar leave Kseniya to go to the miserable throne of Zagem, since he had many more distinguished principalities [to serve] as an appanage for his dear future son-in-law? Alexander fell because he was not honest with Russia and was unworthy of its powerful assistance."

Forty musketeers had saved Zagem. Tatishchev had then been obliged to immediately dispatch 150 of his bravest soldiers from the Terek fort as an advance guard to protect Boris's future son-in-law, and George had declared himself Russia's tributary in holy ceremonies. Wanting all the more to have a familial tie with the tsar, he presented the prospective bride and groom to Tatishchev for his appraisal, saying,

"I hand them over to Russia with my country and my life. Prince Khozdroi was raised by my mother, together with me, and serves me with his right hand in martial matters; when he is in the field, then I can be at ease at home. I have two children: the son is my eye and the daughter is my heart: I delight in them even in the midst of our country's calamities, but I will not stand in the way of Elena if this is pleasing to God and the Russian sovereign."

In his report to the tsar about the prospective groom and bride, Tatishchev writes,

"Khozdroi is 23; he is tall and well-built. His face is handsome and clear, but dark; his eyes are light brown and his nose is aquiline. His hair is dark blond, his mustache thin and he already shaves his beard. In conversation he is clever and voluble. He knows Turkish and is literate in the Iberian language. In short, he is well-qualified, but not outstanding. It is likely that he will catch [her] fancy, but not certain . . . I saw Elena in the tent of the ruler's wife: she was sitting between her mother and grandmother on a pillow embroidered with pearls on a golden carpet. She was wearing an embroidered velvet dress with a hat adorned with precious stones. Her father bade her stand and take off her coat and hat. He measured her height with a pole and gave me the measurement to check with that given by the sovereign. Elena is charming, but not extraordinarily so. She is pale, but even so, uses white makeup. Her eyes are dark, her nose not large, and her hair is dyed. She has an erect figure, but is too thin, due to her youth: she is only 10 years old. Her face is not yet filled out. Her older brother is much better looking."

Tatishchev wanted to bring the two to Moscow, saying that the former would live to adulthood with tsaritsa Mariya and be taught the Russian language and customs. George sent Khozdroi off with him, but retained Elena until the arrival of a new embassy from the tsar and thereby saved himself the tears of a futile separation, for Elena would not find her ill-fated groom in Moscow. Tatishchev also had to leave Khozdroi in the Sonskii territory for his safety when he learned what had taken place in Daghestan, where the Turks had taken vengeance with interest for the heroism of Moscow's musketeers in Iberia – in a few days there we lost everything but our reputation as soldiers.

R ussia's relations with Constantinople were odd. In Ivan's time the Turks had attacked Astrakhan without a declaration of war, and during Theodor's, even Moscow, under Crimean banners. Yet the tsars still assured the sultans of their friendship. They were surprised by these hostilities, but seemed to ascribe them to mistakes or misunderstandings. Shavkal, under pressure from us, waited in vain for help from Abbas and then

> RUSSIAN CALAMITY
> IN DAGHESTAN

sought protection from Mehmet III, who ordered the pashas of Derbent and other Caspian districts to expel the Russians from Daghestan. The Turks joined with the Kumyks, Lezgians and Avars, and in the spring of 1605 they approached Koisa, where Prince Vladimir Dolgorukii was commanding. He had few troops, since the legions he had sent to winter in Astrakhan had not yet returned. Dolgorukii torched the fort and took boats by sea to Terek Town.

Meanwhile, the pashas laid siege to Buturlin in Tarki. This voivode, already old in years, was praised for his courage. Poorly protected by the wall, which was still incomplete, he lost many men, but repelled several assaults. Part of the wall was destroyed and the stone tower was mined by the besiegers and blown to bits along with the best Muscovite musketeers. Buturlin still fought bravely, but saw the impossibility of saving the town. He listened to the offers of the sultan's officials, vacillated, and finally, contrary to the opinion of his comrades, decided to save just the troops. The chief pasha himself visited his headquarters; he feasted and swore he would release the Russians honorably with their armor and share all needed provisions with them. The perfidious Kumyks, however, after giving us free passage from the fort to the steppes, suddenly encircled them and commenced a terrible bloodbath.

It is written that the good Russians unanimously decided on a glorious death. They fought hand-to-hand with the numerous and nefarious enemy, man-to-man, one against three, fearing not death, but capture. Among the first to fall was the son of the commander Buturlin, right before his eyes, a handsome youth, then his elderly father. Likewise the voivode Pleshcheev and his two sons, the voivode Polev, and everyone except for the severely wounded Prince Vladimir Bakhteyarov and a few others, who were taken unconscious by the enemy, but later freed by the sultan. This unsuccessful battle, although glorious in its valor, cost us five to seven thousand troops and effaced Russian control from Daghestan for 118 years.

Tatishchev would return to a new reign, and Boris, who would not live to learn of the accession of the patricide Moslem to the Iberian throne, remained friends with Abbas to the end of his days, regarding him as an enemy of our dangerous foe, the sultan, against whom we were diligently rousing all of Asia and Europe.

Even in his negotiations with the English, Boris had expressed the desire that all the Christian powers rise up against the Ottoman.

FRIENDSHIP
WITH ENGLAND

"It was not just the emissaries of the emperor and of Rome," he wrote to Elizabeth, "but other foreign travelers, who assured us that you seem to be in a close alliance with the sultan. We were astonished and did not believe them. No, you will never befriend the malefactors against Christendom, and will of course join in a common alliance with the sovereigns of Europe to bring low these high-handed infidels – it is a goal worthy of you and of all of us!"

But Elizabeth was concerned only with the profits of her commerce and to that end flattered the tsar's pride with extraordinary tokens of respect for him. Our emissary, the court noble Mikulin, met with an unusual honor in London when on 18 September 1600 he sailed up the Thames and rode in Elizabeth's carriage through the city to cannon salutes from the harbor and the Tower, accompanied by 300 mounted officers, aldermen and merchants in their finery, with gold chains. The streets were dense with spectators. Royal servants waited on the distinguished guest in one of the best homes in London; Elizabeth sent him silver dishes, cups and goblets from her treasury. They anticipated and hastened to fulfill his desires, but he comported himself wisely and modestly: he expressed gratitude for everything and requested nothing.

His audience was in Richmond on 14 October. Elizabeth arose from her seat and walked a few paces to meet our emissary. She praised Boris's elevation to tsar, *her brother of the heart, who had long been solicitous of Englishmen.* She said that she daily prayed to God on his behalf and that she had friends among the sovereigns of Europe, but was not as fond of any of them as the Russian autocrat, and that one of her chief pleasures was to fulfill his wishes. Mikulin dined with the queen and was the only one to sit with her – the lords and eminent officials did not sit. She stood and drank a toast to Boris. Our emissary was invited to a most interesting spectacle: on her Coronation Day he viewed knightly tournaments; on the Feast of the Order of St. George, religious services in St. Paul's Cathedral and Elizabeth's formal entry into London. At night he also witnessed, by the light of torches and to the sound of trumpets, all the peers and royal courtiers, amidst a huge number of citizens, filled with fervor and love for their queen.

Elizabeth everywhere thanked Mikulin for his presence, and in her flattering conversations with him, never forgot to praise Boris and Russia. Captivated by her favors, our emissary had an occasion to show her his earnestness. 18 February 1601 was a terrible day for London, when the unfortunate Essex, who had dared to declare himself a rebel, marched with 500 of his adherents to take control of the Tower. All the streets were closed off with chains and filled with troops and citizens in armor, Mikulin took up arms along with loyal Englishmen to save the queen. After the insurrection was put down, she herself wrote to the tsar to praise the valor of his official. In a word, this embassy established a personal friendship between Boris and the queen.

Although Elizabeth, as an enemy of Spain and Austria, could not accept Boris's idea of a new crusade, or an alliance of all the Christian powers to expel the Turks from Europe, she assured him that she never considered helping the sultan and fervently wished for the success of European arms. The tsar had other misgivings, however: he had heard that England favored Sigismund in his war with the Swedish ruler. She tried to demonstrate to him that both religion and politics required her to zealously support Karl. Satisfied with this explanation, Boris granted a new letter of preference to the English permitting free trade in Russia without duties. He received Elizabeth's envoy, Richard Lee, with especial good will. Lee's main task was to assure the tsar of her friendship and to extol his virtues.

"The world is full of praise for you," Lee wrote to him as he was leaving Russia, "for you, most puissant of monarchs, are satisfied with what you have and do not want others'. Your enemies wish to be at peace with you out of fear, and your friends, in alliance, due to their love and trust. If all Christian monarchs thought as you, then tranquility would reign in Europe, and neither the sultan, nor the Pope could disturb its quietude."

Knowing that Boris intended to see his son married, in 1603 the queen offered him the hand of a distinguished 11-year-old Englishwoman adorned with rare charms and qualities. She proposed to immediately send him portraits of her and other London beauties and did not want the tsar to seek another bride for young Theodor in the meantime. But Boris wanted to know beforehand who the prospective bride was and whether she was related to the queen. He assured her that many great monarchs were requesting the honor of joining their children in marriage to his family.

The death of Elizabeth, who was so renowned in British chronicles, and also memorable in our history for her longtime friendship with Russia, put an end to matchmaking, but did not interrupt friendly ties between England and the tsar. The new king, James I, did not delay in notifying Boris of the union of Scotland with England, and wrote, "I have inherited the throne of my aunt, and hope likewise to inherit your love for her."

In October 1604 James's emissary, Thomas Smith, presented Boris with the gift of a splendid carriage and several silver vessels, saying,

"The king of England and Scotland, strong in land and sea forces and more powerful because of the love of his people, requests only friendship of the Muscovite monarch. Since all the other sovereigns of Europe are seeking it of James, he therefore has a double right to such friendship, requesting it in memory of great Elizabeth and her unforgettable brother-in-law, Danish Duke Johan, whom the tsar loved so tenderly and whom he has so sorrowfully mourned."

Boris replied that there was no other monarch for whom he had such heartfelt love as for Elizabeth, and that he wanted always to have friendship with England. In addition to the right to trade duty-free in all of our cities, James also asked for free passage for Englishmen through Russia to Persia and India to seek a route to China and other eastern lands that was shorter and safer than the one by sea around the Cape of Good Hope and which would be to the mutual benefit of both England and Russia. He explained that valuables transported by merchants from country to country leave wealth in their wake.

The boyars assured the emissary of the immutable force of the letters of preference that the tsar had given to the merchants, but explained that a fierce war was raging on the shores of the Caspian Sea; Abbas was assaulting Derbent, Baku and Shamakha so that for the time being, for their safety, the tsar could not permit Englishmen to go there. With this response, Smith departed Moscow on 20 March 1605. There was no longer any talk of an alliance between England and Russia; trade alone served as a firm tie between them, since it was advantageous to either party.

While favoring the facilitation of this commerce as most important for Russia, Boris did not hesitate to give the

| THE HANSA |

German merchants new rights as well. The Hansa was still dissatisfied with Theodor's letter of preference and so it sent the Lübeck burgomaster Germers to Moscow with three aldermen and the city secretary. On 3 April 1603 they presented the sovereign and his son with cast silver gilded representations of Fortuna, Venus, two large eagles, two horses, a lion, a unicorn, a rhinoceros, a deer, an ostrich, a pelican, a griffin and a peacock. The merchants were received as if they were the most eminent of nobles and were served dinner on gold tableware.

In the name of 59 allied German cities, they submitted a petition to the boyars that was written humbly and persuasively. In it they said that the antiquity of their commerce with our homeland was measured not in years, but centuries; that in the most remote ages, when England, Holland and France hardly knew the name of Russia, the Hansa had provided them with everything necessary and pleasant for civic life and thus had enjoyed the favor of the tsar's reigning forebears since time immemorial, with exclusive rights and privileges. The Hansa was entreating Boris for the restoration of these rights, and praised him. They desired duty-free commerce and permission to trade freely in the ports of the Northern Sea, in Kolmogory and Arkhangelsk, and to give them merchants' courts in Novgorod, Pskov and Moscow with the right to have churches there, just as it was long ago. They also requested post horses to transport their goods from place to place, etc.

The tsar said that in Russia customs duties were exacted from merchants of the emperor and the kings of Spain, France, Lithuania and Denmark. The residents of the free German cities should pay it, just like everyone else, but as a token of favor, half of these duties would be waived for the Lübeckers – for other Germans, who were subjects of various rulers, nothing obliged us to be so unselfish. Only the Lübeckers would be exempt from customs inspection: they would declare the value of their goods according to their own consciences. The Hansa would be permitted to trade in Arkhangelsk and also to buy or build merchants' courts in Novgorod, Pskov and Moscow at their own expense, not the sovereign's.

All faiths were tolerated in Russia, but neither Catholics nor Lutherans were permitted to build churches – this was also denied to the most distinguished monarchs of Europe: the emperor, Queen Elizabeth, and so on. The postal stages had been established in Russia solely for government couriers and foreign emissaries, not merchants. A letter of preference was written to this effect on 5 June, with the addition that the property of merchants who died in Russia would be inviolable by the treasury and would be turned over intact to their heirs. Germans might keep Russian wine, beer and mead in their own homes for their own consumption, but only sell foreign wine by the cask or barrel, not by the pail or by the measure.

The emissaries departed for Novgorod with this letter of preference, presented it there to the voivode, Prince Buinosov-Rostovskii, and requested sites to build homes and shops. However, the voivode was waiting for his own instructions, and waited so long that they lost patience and went to Pskov, where things were happier. The city governor immediately allotted them the site of the old German merchants' court on the banks of the Velikaya River, outside of town. That is, the ruins thereof, a memorial to the ancient flourishing trade in the homeland of the renowned Olga. The residents rejoiced no less than the Lübeckers, recalling the traditions of a happy alliance between their city and the Hansa. The past, however, could not return, due to the changed relations of the Hansa with Europe, and Pskov with Russia. Leaving agents behind to make everything ready for the establishment of offices in Novgorod and Pskov, Germers and his comrades hurried home to gladden Lübeck with the progress of their affairs. By 1604, ships from Hamburg were already arriving at Arkhangelsk.

A mongst the European embassies we also note the Roman and Florentine. In 1601 Clement VIII's nuncios Francisco Costa and Didak Miranda were in Moscow, and others in 1603, requesting permission to travel to

> EMBASSIES FROM ROME AND FLORENCE

Persia. The tsar ordered them to be given boats to sail the Volga to Astrakhan. In March 1602 Grand Duke Ferdinand of Tuscany and Florence, one of the most eminent rulers of the renowned house of Medici and a magnanimous friend of Henry IV [of France], sent his official, Abraham Lyusa, to Boris to offer his services in recruiting scholars, artists, artisans and craftsmen to Russia and through our port on the Dvina to provide by sea the rich natural products of Italy, especially marble and valuable timber.

<table>
<tr><td>GREEKS IN
MOSCOW</td></tr>
</table>

Since we had relations neither with Mehmet III or his successor Ahmet I, we learned about events in Constantinople from the Greek prelates, who were constantly coming to Moscow for alms with icons and blessings from the patriarchs. Ivan had given the Athonskaya Vvedenskaya Cloister a court at the Epiphany Monastery in Kitaigorod. Pilgrim monks and other Greeks who were seeking service in Russia would stay there. The news from our ardent coreligionists of the troubles and poor internal situation in the Ottoman Empire assured Boris of the lack of danger from that direction, at least for a while.

<table>
<tr><td>AFFAIRS
AMONG THE
NOGAI TATARS</td></tr>
</table>

According to the chronicler, the cunning of Boris's statecraft was most successful of all in the Nogai uluses, which had been weakened and devastated by internal strife amongst its rulers, who were supposedly quarreling with the Astrakhan deputies. Contrary to the chronicler, state papers show Boris as a peacemaker for the Nogai, or at least for its main ulus. This was the Volga or Ural ulus, which from the time of the renowned Syuyunbek's father Yusuf, had had a single prince and three ruling officials: Nuradin, Taibug and Kokubat, but then obeyed two princes: Ishterek, son of Tin-Akhmat, and Yanaraslan, son of Urus, who were filled with mutual hatred. To Boris's edict that they live in love and brotherhood, Yanaraslan replied,

"The Muscovite tsar desires a miracle: he orders the sheep to befriend the wolves and drink water out of the same hole in the ice!"

The boyar Semyon Godunov, with full powers from the tsar, now traveled to Astrakhan. In November 1604 he gathered the nobles together and announced that Ishterek was the first, or senior prince and took from him a sworn document to the effect that he and all the Ismailov tribe would serve Russia and fight its enemies to their last breath; would not give property belonging to the prince or Nuradin to anyone without the tsar's confirmation; nor carry on civil war; nor have relations with the shah, the sultan, the Crimean khan, the rulers of Bukhara and Khiva, Tashkent, the Kirghiz Horde, Shavkal or Circassia. They were to roam the

Astrakhan steppes by the sea, along the Terek, Kuma and Volga near Tsaritsyn, and either to call on Kazy's ulus to join them, or conquer them, so that from the Black Sea to the Caspian and farther to the east and north there would be no other Nogai horde except that of Ishterek, who was loyal to the Muscovite tsar. Kazy's ulus had separated from the Volga ulus and was pasturing near Azov with its Prince Barangazy. It was subordinate to the Turks and the Crimeans, but often sought favors from the tsar, promising to serve Russia, breaking its word and pillaging our territory.

In order to weaken or completely exterminate it, Boris ordered the Don Cossacks to assist Ishterek. They sent him the gift of an expensive saber, writing, "It will either be on the neck of Russia's malefactors or on your own." The prince fulfilled the conditions and constantly pressed on the Azov Nogai so that many of them became pauperized and were selling their children in Astrakhan. The third Nogai ulus, called the Altaulskii occupied the steppes near the Aral Sea. It had close ties with Bukhara and Khiva. Ishterek was also supposed to convince its mirzas to become Russian subjects – it would be a union with great commercial advantages. Boris now permitted the loyal Nogai to peacefully trade in Astrakhan, exempt from all duties.

We have presented in this survey Boris's most important policies with regard to Europe and Asia – policies that were in general prudent, not incompatible with the love of power, but moderate, and more preservative than acquisitive. Now we shall present Boris's actions inside the country, in legislation and the civic development of Russia.

> INTERNAL AFFAIRS

In 1599 Boris had, as a token of his love for the patriarch Iov, renewed a letter of preference issued by Ivan to the metropolitan Athanasii to the effect that all of the archprelate's people, monasteries, officials, servants and peasants would be exempted from the jurisdiction of the tsar's boyars, deputies, volost administrators and tiuns and would not be judged by them in any case except homi-

> LETTER OF PREFERENCE GRANTED TO PATRIARCH

cide; they would only be subject to the Patriarch's justice. They would also be exempt from any treasury imposts. These ancient rights of our priesthood were to remain unchanged through the reigns of Vasilii Shuiskii, Mikhail [Romanov] and his son.

LAW CONCERNING
PEASANTS

We have already spoken of the law regarding enserfment of rural workers – its goal was to improve things for middle-level owners or those not so well off, but it had pernicious consequences for them as well, with the frequent flight of peasants, especially from the villages of the lesser nobility. Owners were chasing fugitives, accusing each other of hiding them, going to court and ruining each other. The evil was so great that Boris, who did not want to completely repeal his well-intentioned law, decided to declare that it would be temporarily rescinded.

In 1601 he once again allowed farmers belonging to petty officials, boyar cadets and the like to transfer during a certain period from one owner to another of the same status, but they could not do so all at once – no more than two at a time. This would be in effect everywhere but the Moscow uezd. As for the peasants of boyars, court nobles, eminent secretaries, the government, prelates or monasteries, they were ordered to stay where they were during the aforesaid year of 1601. We are assured that the change in the old law and the inconstancy of the new one aroused the displeasure of numerous people and had an effect on Godunov's miserable fate, but this interesting interpretation by historians of the 18th century is not based on information from contemporaries, who are unanimous in praising Boris's wisdom in the affairs of state.

PUBLIC
HOUSES

He is also praised for his diligence in getting rid of rude popular vices. An unfortunate passion for strong drink is more or less a characteristic of all northern peoples. In Russia it had long been condemned, but only by Christian preceptors and moralists. Ivan III and his grandson had wanted to place legal limits on immoderation: they punished it as a civil crime. Ivan IV imposed a duty on brewing beer and mead, perhaps not so much as to increase the tsar's revenues as to restrain the intemperate.

In Theodor's time there were government drinking houses in the larger cities where they also sold *grain wine* [vodka], which was unknown in Europe until the 14th century [possible typo for 17th century], but many private individuals also dealt in strong liquors, thereby spreading drunkenness. Boris strictly forbade this free sale, declaring that he would sooner pardon a thief or brigand than a purveyor of spirits. He tried to convince them to find another way of making a living, through honest labor, promising to give them land if they wanted to engage in tillage. It is written that the tsar wished thereby to restrain people from a passion as injurious as it was vile, but he was unable to eliminate the sale of alcoholic beverages, and even the government drinking houses, which kept paying stiff bribes, became places of depravity for weak people.

B oris surpassed all the old Russian monarchs in his fervor for education. He intended to establish schools and even universities to teach young Russians European languages and sciences. In 1600 he sent the German, Johann Kramer, to Germany, authorized to seek out professors and doctors and bring them to Moscow. This scheme cheered the many ardent friends of education in Europe. One of them, a professor of law named Tobias Lontsius, wrote to Boris in January 1601,

BORIS'S LOVE FOR EDUCATION AND FOR FOREIGNERS

"Your royal majesty wishes to be a true father of his country and earn universal, undying glory. You have been chosen by Heaven to perform a great task, a new one for Russia: to enlighten the minds of your uncountable population, and thereby elevate its spirit along with national power, following the example of Egypt, Greece and Rome, and of the renowned states of Europe, which are blooming with the arts and noble sciences."

It is written that this great intention was not fulfilled due to strong objections from the clergy, which submitted to the tsar that Russia was prospering in the world solely due to its creed and language. Different languages might promote different ways of thinking, which would be dangerous to the Church, and in any case, this would imprudently entrust the education of our youth to Catholics and Lutherans. After abandoning the idea of establishing universities in Russia, however, he sent 18 young boyar cadets to London, Lübeck and France to study foreign languages even as young Englishmen and Frenchmen traveled to Moscow to study Russian.

With his native intelligence, the tsar understood a great truth: that public education is a national strength. With the view of definitely surpassing other Europeans, he invited not only physicians, artists, artisans, craftsmen, but also officials into his service from England, Holland and Germany. Thus our envoy in London, Mikulin, told three traveling German barons that if, out of curiosity, they wished to see Russia, the tsar would receive them with pleasure and send them back with honors; but if, loving glory, they wished to serve him with their minds and swords in military affairs on a level with sovereign princes, they would be amazed by his kindness and his favors.

In 1601 Boris received 35 Livonian court nobles and citizens in Moscow with exceptional kindness – they had been exiled from their Polish homeland. They did not dare enter the palace because they were poorly dressed. The tsar ordered them to be told,

"I wish to see people, not clothes."

He dined with them, comforted them and moved them to tears with the assurance that he would be as a father to them. He made the court nobles into princes and the tradesmen into court nobles. In addition to rich fabrics and sable furs, he gave each a proper salary and estate, asking nothing in exchange but their love, loyalty and prayers for the prosperity of his house. The most distinguished of them, Tiesenhausen, swore on behalf of all of them to die for Boris and we shall see that these fine Livonians did not deceive the tsar. They eagerly joined his German guards unit.

In general, Boris was favorable disposed towards educated people, but especially towards his foreign physicians. He saw them every day and conversed with them about governmental affairs and religion. He often asked them to pray for him, and just to please them, agreed to restore the Lutheran Church in Yauza Town. The pastor of this church, Martin Berg, to whom we are indebted for his interesting history of Godunov's times and later, writes:

"While peacefully obeying Christian teachings and solemnly praising the Most High in their services, the Germans of Moscow wept for joy to have lived to see such happiness!"

Foreigners' gratitude for the tsar's favors was not deleterious to his glory: in 1602 the scholar Fiedler, a resident of Königsberg, and brother to one of Boris's physicians, com-

PANEGYRIC FOR GODUNOV

posed a eulogy in Latin for him that was read by all Europe. In it the orator likens him to his hero Numa,* praising him for his legislative wisdom, love of peace and *pure morals*. Boris actually deserved the last of these, for he was a diligent observer of all religious precepts and rules of decorum; he was sober, restrained, industrious, an enemy of idle amusements and an exemplar in his family life, a tender husband and parent, especially to

BORIS'S ARDOR TOWARD HIS SON

his beloved son, whom he loved to excess. He fondled him constantly, called him his commander, never let him out of his sight and put a great deal of effort into educating him, even teaching him science.

An interesting memento of this crown prince's geographical knowledge is the map of Russia published under his name in 1614 by the German, Gerard. Preparing his son to be a worthy monarch of a great power and accustoming the people to love Theodor in advance, Boris gave him the right to intercede, support and conciliate in all domestic and foreign affairs. He awaited Theodor's word before showing favor or indulgence, acting in every case as an indubitably skillful politician, but even more as a passionate father and showing by his family happiness such an inexplicable mixture of good and evil in the same human heart!

Yet the time was approaching when this wise ruler, worthy of Europe's praises for his prudent policies, love of education and fervor to be a true father of his country, and ultimately for his morality in his social and family life, should have to taste the bitter fruit of his criminality

CALAMITIES COMMENCE

---

* [Numa Pompilius, the legendary second king of Rome.]

and to become one of the more astounding victims of the judg-ment of Heaven. There were precursors in the internal unease of Boris's heart and the various disastrous events against which he still fiercely struggled with all the resolve of his soul, only to sud-denly be revealed as weak and helpless in the final scenes of his amazing destiny.

CHAPTER V

CONCLUSION OF THE *R*EIGN OF *B*ORIS.

1604-1605

Godunov's brilliant rule. Prayer for the tsar. Boris's suspicions. Persecution. Famine. New buildings in the Kremlin. Brigandage. Depraved morals. Imaginary marvels. Death of Irina. Appearance of the Pretender. Conduct and appearance of the deceiver. Jesuits. The False Dimitrii meets with Polish king. Letter to the Pope. Gathering of troops. The False Dimitrii's pact with Mnishek. Measures taken by Boris. First betrayal. Knight-hero Basmanov. Godunov's timidity. Tenor of public opinion. Boris's courage. A battle. Poles desert the Pretender. Basmanov honored. Victory of Boris's voivodes. Kromy besieged. Pretender's letter to Boris. Death of Boris.

Having achieved his goal, having risen from servile insignificance to autocratic heights through indefatigable efforts, unremitting cunning, perfidy, intrigue and criminality, was Godunov able to enjoy in full measure the majesty his soul had craved,

1600-1605

a majesty bought at so dear a price? Could he enjoy the purest pleasure, that of benefiting his subjects and thereby gaining their love? In any case, it would not be for long.

The first two years of this reign seemed the best time for Russia since the 15th century or its restoration: it was at the height of its new powers, secure due to its own strength

GODUNOV'S BRILLIANT RULE

and fortunate external circumstances, while internally it was governed with firm wisdom and surprising mildness. Boris was fulfilling the promises he had made at his coronation and could justly wish to be called the father of his people: he had diminished their burdens; he was a father to orphans and the poor, having conferred unheard-of generosity upon them. He was philanthropic:

he did not interfere with people's lives or stain the Russian land with a single drop of blood, and punished prisoners solely with exile. The merchants were less restricted now in doing business; the army, in the quiet of peacetime, was showered with awards. Court nobles and ministry personnel were awarded tokens of favor for diligent service.

The Council was esteemed by a tsar who was energetic and eager for advice, and the priesthood was honored by a tsar who was devout. In brief, all segments of society could be pleased on their own behalf, and even more so on behalf of their homeland, seeing that Boris had exalted the name of Russia in Europe and Asia without bloodshed or seriously straining its powers, and had taken care of the common welfare, justice and development. Thus it was not surprising that Russia, according to contemporaries, *loved* its monarch, and wanted to forget about Dimitrii's murder, or to doubt it.

But the monarch was aware of own his secret, and did not have the comfort of trusting in his own popularity. While doing good for Russia, he soon became alienated from the Russians. He rescinded laws from ancient times; he did not want to go out to the people at a prescheduled time and place to hear their grievances and receive their petitions with his own hands. He appeared rarely, and then only in unapproachable splendor. He avoided people, seemingly lest their monarch's face remind them of Ivan's former slave. He wished to be an invisible presence in their dwellings and in their thoughts. Unsatisfied with the conventional prayers in churches for the sovereign and the nation, he ordered skilled scribes to compose a special reading, to be recited in all of Russia, in all homes, at meals and toasts for the spiritual salvation and corporeal health of

PRAYER FOR THE TSAR

"The servant of God, the tsar chosen and extolled by the Most High, autocrat of all the lands of the East and the North; for the tsaritsa and their children; for the prosperity and tranquility of the nation and the Church under the scepter of a single secular Christian monarch, so that all other rulers might bow down before and humbly serve him, magnifying his name from sea to sea as long as the world shall last, so that Russians might always fervently praise God for such a monarch, whose mind is a vast chasm filled with wisdom and whose heart is filled with love and forbearance; so that all lands will tremble before our sword and Russia will continue to rise and spread; and so that the young, blooming scions of Boris's house grow up with Heaven's blessing and continuously protect that house until the end of time."

That is to say, Boris dared to profane the sacred agency of the human soul and its mysterious relation with Heaven with his vainglory and hypocrisy, compelling the people to bear witness before the All-seeing Eye to the virtues of a murderer, destroyer and thief! While Godunov did not seem to fear God, he more and more feared the people, yet prior to the impending blows of fate – the mutiny by fortune and his subjects – he was at ease on the throne and was sincerely praised and loved, even though he no longer knew spiritual peace. He now felt that if it was possible to attain greatness by a criminal path, then greatness and earthly happiness were not the same thing.

This inner unrest of his soul, unavoidable for a criminal, was revealed in the tsar by the unfortunate effects of his mistrustfulness, which threatened him, and soon threatened Russia. We have seen that when he laid his hands on the crown of Monomakh, he began to imagine secret plots against him, of poison

> BORIS'S SUSPICIONS

and sorcery. He naturally believed that others like himself might thirst for the highest power, might be hypocritical and audacious. He indiscreetly revealed this fear when, after he took shameful oaths from Russians, he naturally did not believe them: he tried to be constantly on guard, to see and hear everything, to anticipate evil thoughts. Accordingly, he revived Ivan's calamitous system of informants and entrusted the fate of his citizens, courtiers and nobles to a vile throng of informers.

The first notable victim of suspicion and informants was someone who had once lived very closely with Godunov, who had willingly shared Ivan's favor with him and who had suffered for it during Theodor's reign. This was Belskii, one of Tsaritsa Mariya's in-laws. Godunov had saved him from the people's malice during the Moscow insurrection, but for a long time Belskii had been relegated to honorable exile. He was recalled to the court, but without any distinction. During Boris's reign he was deemed worthy only of second-class Duma rank. He had been Ivan's prime favorite and considered himself Godunov's benefactor, and might have been or seemed to be dissatisfied, and therefore guilty in the tsar's eyes. He had another, more important fault: he knew better than others the depths of Boris's heart. In 1600 Boris dispatched him to build the new fortress of Borisov on the banks of the Northern Donets. This assignment could hardly be considered a token of favor, but Belskii was ashamed to appear humiliated and rode into the distant wilderness as if to the most distinguished command, with unusual pomp, a rich treasury and a large number of servants. He ordered the town to be built by his own, not the tsar's people.

> PERSECUTION

Every day he entertained the musketeers and Cossacks, giving them clothing and money, and did not ask for anything from the sovereign. The result was that the new fortress was built faster and better than any of the others and that the builders did not tire of their labors, but rather loved and praised their commander. It was reported to the tsar that this commander, having enticed his troops with favors, was planning to declare himself independent, saying,

"Boris may be tsar in Moscow, but I am tsar in Borisov!"

This slander was probably based on Belskii's vainglory and one of his careless comments, but it was taken for the truth, since Godunov wanted to get rid of his old and disturbing friend. It was decided that he merited death, but the tsar, boasting of his mercy, only ordered that his property be confiscated and that his long, dense beard be plucked out; he ordered the Scottish surgeon Gabriel to carry out this novel punishment.

Belskii suffered disgrace and was confined to one of the Nizovye towns, where he lived for the chance of avenging himself on the ingrate, even if only from the grave. Intelligent and experienced in governmental affairs, this successor to Malyuta Skuratov was hated by Russians due to their horrible memories of his heyday, and by foreigners due to his cruel hostility towards them that could anger even Boris, their diligent protector. Few felt sorry for the old, homeless favorite, but his disgrace preceded another, much more poignant for the eminent noble houses and for the whole nation.

The memory of the virtuous Anastasiya and the relationship by marriage of the Romanovich-Yurievs to the royal house of Monomakh was [for these nobles] the right to general respect and even the people's love. The boyar Nikita Romanovich was also worthy of this love by virtue of his own noble qualities. He had five sons: Thedor, Aleksandr, Mikhail, Ivan and Vasilii, and in the last hour of his life had entreated Godunov to take the place of their father. While outwardly honoring them – he made the eldest, Thedor and Aleksandr, boyars, made Mikhail an okolnichii and married his close relative, Ivan Ivanovich Godunov, to their younger sister Irina – Boris inwardly feared the Romanovs as rivals of his young son – there were rumors that [Tsar] Theodor, some time before his death, had considered declaring the eldest of them as heir to the throne. These rumors were probably unfounded, but since these sons were of the same blood as Anastasiya and cousins to Theodor, they seemed to the populace to be closest to the throne.

This was sufficient to incur Boris's malice, which was strengthened by malicious gossip about the royal relatives. Yet persecution required a pretext, if not to soothe the conscience, then supposedly for the safety of the persecutor. The crime must be covered with a legal fiction, as Ivan and even Boris had previously done, thereby avoiding the people's hatred in Theodor's time. At this time, slaves were considered the most reliable informants, and to encourage them in this perfidy, the tsar was not ashamed to openly reward one of the servants of the boyar Prince Thedor Shestunov for a false denunciation of his lord as hostile to the monarch. Shestunov was left untouched so far, but the *charitable word of the sovereign* was pronounced upon the slanderer in a public square and he was given his liberty, rank and an estate.

Meanwhile it was whispered to the Romanov servants that for the same diligence, they might expect even greater favor from the tsar. The chief henchman of the new tyranny, the new Malyuta

Skuratov, was the nobleman Semyon Godunov, who contrived means to implicate the innocent in crimes, relying on general ignorance and gullibility. He bribed the Romanovs' treasurer, gave him bags full of roots and ordered him to hide them in the pantry of the boyar Aleksandr Nikitich. He was then to report that his lords were engaged in concocting poison and were plotting against the life of the monarch. Moscow was suddenly alarmed: the senate and all the eminent officials hastened to the patriarch. The okolnichii Mikhail Saltykov was sent to search the boyar Aleksandr's pantry. The bags were found there and brought to Iov, where the roots were emptied out in the presence of the Romanovs as supposedly magical preparations to poison the tsar. Everyone was horrified, and the nobles, fervid as the Roman senators of Tiberius' or Nero's time, fell howling on the alleged wrongdoers like wild beasts upon lambs. They menacingly demanded a reply and did not listen to it in the uproar. The Romanovs were placed under heavy guard and ordered to be tried as criminals.

This deed was one of the vilest of Boris's shameless cruelties. Not only the Romanovs, but all those close to them had to die, so that there would be no one left on earth to avenge these innocent martyrs. Princes were arrested: the Cherkasskiis, Shestunovs, Repnins, Karpovs and Sitskiis. The most prominent of the latter, Prince Ivan Vasilievich, governor of Astrakhan, was transported to Moscow in fetters with his wife and son. They were interrogated and terrorized by torture, especially the Romanovs. Their servants were unmercifully and futilely tortured and tormented: none of them gave comfort to the tyrant with denunciations of themselves or others. The loyal slaves died in agony, witnesses before the tsar and before God only to the innocence of their lords.

Yet the judges did not dare doubt the veracity of the crime, so basely plotted, and praised the tsar's unprecedented mercy when he ordered the Romanovs and those close to them merely imprisoned, being convicted of treason and the criminal intent to do away with the sovereign by means of sorcery. In June 1601 the *boyars' sentence* was carried out. Thedor Nikitich Romanov, the future hierarch, was tonsured and renamed Filaret and exiled to the Siskaya Antonieva Cloister. His wife, Kseniya Ivanovna, was likewise compelled to take vows, named Martha and exiled to one of the Zaonezhskie parishes. Thedor's mother-in-law, the court noble-woman Shestova, was sent to the Nikolskii Devichii Monastery in Cheboksary; Aleksandr Nikitich to Usole-Luda on the White Sea; the third Romanov son, Mikhail, to the Nyrobskaya volost in Great Perm; the fourth, Ivan, to Pelym; and the fifth, Vasilii, to Yarensk. Their brother-in-law, Prince Boris Cherkasskii, was sent to Belo-ozero with his wife and the children of her brother, Thedor Nikitich [a.k.a. Filaret]: six year old Mikhail (the future tsar) and his young sister. Boris [Cherkasskii]'s son, Prince Ivan was sent to Malmyzh in Vyatka; Prince Ivan Vasilievich Sitskii to the Kozheozerskii Monastery and his wife to the wilderness of Sumskii Ostrog.

The rest of the Sitskiis, Thedor and Vladimir Shestunov, the Karpovs and the Repnin princes were imprisoned in various cities. One of the latter, the Yarenskii voivode, was imprisoned in Ufa, supposedly for stealing royal property. The patrimonies and estates of those disgraced were distributed to others; their moveable property and homes were taken by the treasury.

This persecution, however, did not end with exile and confiscation of property. Boris did not have faith in the diligence or severity of the local deputies and sent Muscovite constables along with the unfortunates. These were supposed to watch tirelessly over them, provide them with the necessities and report to the tsar anything significant they said. No one dared to look at the declared *traitors*, nor go near the isolated houses where they lived, outside towns and settlements and far from the main roads, some of them in dugouts and even in fetters.

Pilgrims were not allowed in the Sitskii Monastery so that no one could bring letters to Thedor Nikitich [Romanov]. He was an unwilling monk, but fervent in his piety. The insidious constable schemed to talk with him about the court, his family and friends, and reported to the tsar that among the boyars and nobles Filaret had not found anyone very intelligent or able in governmental affairs except for disgraced Bogdan Belskii, and that he considered himself a victim of their malicious calumnies.

Although he was occupied only with the salvation of his soul, he pined for his wife and children. He did not know where or how they were getting on without him and prayed to God for the quick conclusion of their miserable lives (God did not heed this prayer, fortunately for Russia). It was likewise reported to the tsar that Vasilii Romanov, weighed down by illness and chains, did not care to praise Boris's mercy and said to the constable,

"True virtue does not know vanity."

Boris, however, as if to show the truth of his mercy to the prisoner, ordered his chains removed and that he be told of the tsar's anger at the constable for his excess fervor in mistreating those disgraced. The invalid Vasilii was conveyed to his brother in Pelym, Ivan Nikitich, who had lost the use of his arms and legs from a blow, and this gave them the sad comfort of suffering together. Vasilii died after prolonged illness on 15 February 1602, prayed over by his brother and his magnanimous slave, who had loyally served his master with honor and also diligently served his young son while in fetters.

Aleksandr and Mikhailo Nikitich likewise did not survive long in captivity, the victims of sorrow, or violent death, it is written. The former was buried in Luda, the latter seven versts from Chardyn in the wilderness near the village of Nyrob. Two cedar trees grew up over the grave. The church at Nyrob still conserves Mikhail's heavy fetters and elders there still tell of his courageous fortitude and marvelous strength, and of the love for him of all the residents, whose children would go to his prison to play pipes and would feed him the best that they had, through openings in his mud dwelling to soothe his hunger and thirst. For this love, they were persecuted in Godunov's time, but rewarded under the Romanovs with a letter of pardon and favor.

If the chronicler is to be believed, then Boris, after he ordered Prince Ivan Sitskii and his wife strangled in their monastery, also planned to starve to death the ailing Ivan Romanov, but ministerial papers show that the latter had quite good treatment: two or three plates of meat, fish and white bread daily, and that his guard had 90 (450 of today's silver) rubles in his cashbox to provide for his prisoner's needs. The situation of the disgraced was soon alleviated, either from the tsar's change in policy (because the people felt sorry for them) or due to the intercession of their brother-in-law, the royal carver Ivan Ivanovich Godunov. In March 1602 the tsar *graciously instructed* Ivan Romanov to go to Ufa *for service* (leaving him under surveillance, but no longer designated as a malefactor), thence to Nizhnyi Novgorod and finally to Moscow with his nephew, Prince Ivan Cherkasskii.

The Sitskiis were sent to be voivodes in the Nizovskie towns (whether the Shestunovs and Repnins were released is not known). The Cherkasskaya princess, Martha Nikitishna, widowed at Belo-ozero, was ordered to live with the daughter-in-law, sister and children of Thedor Nikitich on the Romanov patrimony, in the village of Klin in the Yurievskii uezd, where the seven year old boy Mikhail Romanov (the future monarch of Russia), deprived of his father and mother, but watched over by Providence, lived until the extinction of Boris's line.

The tsar also wanted to show mercy to Filaret: he allowed him to stand in choir of the church and to take a monk into his cell for service and conversation; he also ordered everybody to satisfy his *traitor* (for so he still called this man of clear conscience) and for pilgrims to be admitted to the Sitskii monastery, but not be allowed to see this disgraced priest. Finally, in 1605 he ordered Filaret ordained as a hieromonk and as an archimandrite, so as to remove him further from the world.

It was not just the Romanovs who were bogeys in Boris's imagination. He forbade the princes Mstislavskii and Vasilii Shuiskii from marrying, figuring that their sons might, due to the ancient distinction of their lines, contend with his son over the throne. Even while eliminating supposed future dangers to young Theodor, the timid murderer trembled before real and present ones. Agitated by suspicion, he constantly feared secret malefactors and also feared to earn the people's hatred as a torturer. He alternately persecuted and pardoned: he exiled the voivode Prince Vladimir Bakhteyarov-Rostovskii and then forgave him. He dismissed the eminent secretary Shchelkalov, but did not openly disgrace him; several times he also dismissed the Shuiskiis and then brought them back and favored them while at the same time threatening with disfavor anyone who dealt with them.

There were no formal executions, but many unfortunates died in prison while being tortured on the basis of informants' reports. Throngs of informers, while not always rewarded, were always exempt from punishment for lies and slander; they flocked to the tsar's palace from boyars' homes and from shacks, from monasteries and churches. Servants informed against their masters, monks against priests, the women who baked communion bread against people of any calling – even wives against husbands and children against their fathers, to the horror of humanity.

"Even among the savage hordes." adds the chronicler, "there has never been such evil: masters dare not look at their slaves, nor families speak freely amongst themselves. When they do talk, then they bind each other with terrible oaths not to violate confidence."

In brief, this sorrowful period of Boris's reign was second to Ivan's in bloodthirstiness, but did not yield to his in illegalities and depravity – a ruinous legacy for the future! But Russians still had magnanimity: it outlived Ivan and Boris and saved the country. They felt sorry for the suffering of the innocent martyrs and abominated the monarch's shameless favors to informers. Others feared for themselves and their relatives. The dissatisfaction soon became widespread. Many still praised Boris: adherents, flatterers, informants, those who grew rich off the property of the disgraced, and we are assured that even eminent churchmen maintained their fervor for a monarch who showered the clergy with tokens of his good will. But the voice of the country was no longer heard amidst this avaricious and self-seeking praise, and the people's silence served as a clear reproach to the tsar, informing him of a significant change within the hearts of Russians – *they no longer loved Boris!*

So says a contemporary, impartial chronicler, distinguished in our history for his national reputation for valor: the cellarer Palitsyn. The people were always grateful: they left it to Heaven to judge the secrets of Boris's heart. Russians sincerely praised the tsar when he seemed to them, with his mask of personal virtue, to be the father of his country, but when they perceived him as a tyrant, they hated him for both his present and his past, about which they perhaps were inclined to doubt, and then again to believe, and in which Dimitrii's blood was more clearly indicated on the royal robes of this murderer of innocents. They recalled the fate of Uglich and other victims of Godunov's vengeful lust for power.

They kept silent, but their feelings were all the more powerful in the presence of informers, and spoke out more strongly in sanctuaries inaccessible to the servants of tyranny, whose times are those of calumny, but also of inviolable discretion. There, in quiet conversations amongst friends, the inevitable truth was revealed and hatred blackened Boris's character, reproaching him not only for murder, persecuting eminent people, plundering their property, craving illegitimate gain, avariciously introducing tax farming, multiplying the number of government drinking house and ruining morals, but also for his partiality for foreigners, new customs (the shaving of beards particularly outraged fervent old-believers) and even a tendency to the Armenian and Latin heresies! Like love, hate is rarely satisfied with the truth, the former in praising, the latter in condemning. Godunov was even denounced for his fervor for education.

During this time of general unpopularity, Boris had the opportunity to show his sensitivity to the people's misery, to show

FAMINE

concern and extraordinary generosity, but even this no longer touched people's hearts, which had turned cold towards him. Amid the natural abundance and riches of a fertile land settled by industrious farmers up to a million people perished from a terrible scourge during a blessed period of protracted peace and an energetic and farsighted reign: in the spring of 1601 the sky darkened with dense clouds and the rains poured down for 10 weeks without respite. Rural residents were terrified; they could neither mow nor reap. On 15 August a cruel frost damaged the growing grain and the unripe fruit. There was still considerable old grain in granaries and barns, but unfortunately the farmers sowed their fields with new, spoiled, poor quality grain. They did not see it sprout either in the fall or the spring; it all decayed and became one with the earth. Meanwhile, reserve supplies had been exhausted and the fields remained unsown.

A disaster ensued, and the cries of the hungry alarmed the tsar. Not just the barns in the villages, but the markets in the capital were also empty, and the price of a chetvert* of rye rose from 12 or 15 dengas to three (15 of today's silver) rubles. Boris ordered the royal granaries opened in Moscow and other cities, and persuaded the clergy and the nobility to sell their grain reserves at a low price. He also opened the treasury: piles of silver for the distressed lay in heaps in four enclosures built near Moscow's wooden walls. Every day at the morning hour everyone was given two moskovki, a denga or kopeck,** but famine raged, since clever profiteers fraudulently bought up the cheap grain in the government, prelates' and boyars' granaries to resell it for unconscionable profits. The poor, who had received a daily silver kopeck could not feed themselves. The best of intentions went wrong in the capital as farmers from places near and far rushed with their wives and children into Moscow for the tsar's charity, thereby multiplying the number of beggars. The treasury was distributing several thousand rubles a day to no avail. The famine worsened to such a terrible extent that it is impossible to read the reliable descriptions of contemporaries without shuddering

"I testify to the truth even before God," writes one of them, "that in Moscow I saw with my own eyes people lying in the streets, biting off grass and eating it like cattle; the dead were found with hay in their mouths."

Horsemeat was considered a delicacy. They ate dogs, cats, dead animals and all kinds of unclean things. People became worse than wild animals, men left their wives and families so they would not have to share a last bite with them. They not only robbed and killed for a piece of bread, but also devoured each other. Travelers feared innkeepers, and inns became lairs for murderers: they strangled and cut up sleeping guests for a terrible repast! Human flesh was sold in pies in the markets and mothers gnawed on the bodies of their infants. Criminals were executed, burnt, hurled into the water, but these crimes did not diminish.

During this time, other monsters hoarded grain in hopes of selling it at a higher price. Many perished from the indescribable

---

* [See the footnote after next.]
** [100 kopecks equals one ruble.]

pangs of hunger. Everywhere half-dead people were staggering, falling and expiring in public spaces. Moscow would have been contaminated by the stench of decaying corpses had not the tsar ordered them buried at his own expense, exhausting his treasury even for the dead. In Moscow constables rode from street to street collecting corpses, washing them, wrapping them in white shrouds and putting red shoes or boots on them. The centurions would cart them out of town to three cemeteries, where, in the course of 28 months 127,000 bodies were buried, not counting those interred by good Christians at parish churches. It is written that 500,000 people died in Moscow alone, and incomparably more in the villages and other districts, from hunger and cold. In winter, large numbers of the poor died on the roads. Unnatural foods likewise produced sickness and death, especially in the Smolensk uezd, to which the tsar sent 20,000 rubles at one time for the poor. No town in Russia was left without assistance, and if many were not saved, at least everywhere there were fewer victims.

The Moscow treasury which had been full from Theodor's happy reign, seemed inexhaustible. All other possible measures were taken as well; Boris bought up all the grain supplies from the rich, willing or not, at a price he himself set, not just from neighboring towns – he also sent people to quite distant, more abundant places to examine the granaries. Enormous haystacks were found, untouched for half a century and overgrown with trees. He ordered the grain to be threshed immediately and transported to Moscow and other districts. Unavoidable, almost insurmountable difficulties were encountered in distribution; in many places there were neither carts nor fodder available en route – the drivers and all the rural residents had fled. Wagon trains traversed Russia as if in the African desert, guarded by soldiers' swords and lances in fear of attack by starving people, who were forcibly stealing edibles not just in the country, but also in the streets and markets of Moscow.

Finally the actions of higher authority eliminated all obstacles and in 1603, little by little, all signs of these terrible evils vanished. Abundance returned, and such that the price of a chetvert of grain fell from three rubles to 10 kopecks, to the delight of the people and the despair of profiteers who still had copious secret supplies of rye and wheat. A permanent memorial to this unprecedented rise in prices remains: the chronicles say that a new unit of [dry] measure was introduced – the *chetverik*. Before 1601 grain had been sold in Russia only by the *okov, bochka or kad* [barrel], the *chetvert* and the *osmina*.*

The calamity was at an end, but its traces lingered: Russia's population was noticeably diminished and many had fewer possessions. No doubt the treasury was also depleted, and although Godunov had magnanimously lavished it to save his people, he not only did not diminish the customary royal pomp, but wished it to be more conspicuous than ever in order to conceal the effects of Heaven's wrath, especially from foreign emissaries. He had them surrounded en route from the border to Moscow with apparitions of abundance and luxury. People would appear everywhere, richly and beautifully dressed; markets everywhere would be full of wares, meat and bread, and not a single beggar, while a verst to either side graves were filled with victims of starvation.

| NEW BUILDINGS IN THE KREMLIN |

Simultaneously, Boris was lavishly entertaining his intended son-in-law, the Danish duke, and also beautifying the ancient Kremlin with new buildings. In 1600 the great bell tower of Ivan the Great was erected, and in 1601 and 1602 two large stone palaces, the Stolovaya and Panikhidnaya, were erected on the site of Ivan's broken-down wooden palace, facing the Golden and Faceted palaces to provide work and subsistence for the poor, thereby joining charity with utility, looking toward future splendor in those days of sorrow. It is not Muscovite chroniclers, however, but foreign historians who reproach Boris for stubborn pride, vanity and vaingloriousness even in the midst of general catastrophe, saying that he forbade Russians from buying a large amount of quite moderately priced rye from Germans in Ivangorod because he was ashamed to feed his people with foreign grain. This information is of course false: our governmental papers testifying to the arrival of German grain ships in 1602 make no mention of this cruel prohibition. Boris, who had shown such energy and

---

* [A kad or okov was about 840 liters. A chetvert was a quarter of that, and an osmina an eighth. A chetverik (little quarter) was a quarter of an osmina, or about 26 liters, roughly three-quarters of a US bushel.]

generosity during this misfortune in order to assure Russia of its father-tsar's love, would not have so obviously sacrificed them to salvage an irrational vainglory.

However, Boris did not seduce Russians with his good deeds, since an idea, horrifying to him, ruled men's minds: the thought that Heaven was punishing the country for the tsar's crimes.

"Pouring out his generosity on the poor," say the chroniclers, "he was serving them the blood of innocents in a golden cup so they could drink to his health. He nourished them with impious favors, stealing the property of honorable nobles and defiling the old royal treasures with the fruits of plunder."

Russia did not prosper in this new abundance; there was no time to rest, since a new calamity now came to light, one for which contemporaries blamed Boris directly.

Ivan the Terrible had wanted to settle the Lithuanian Ukraine and the Severskii lands, with people fit for military service. He did not interfere with criminals who had escaped punishment from hiding and living quietly there, since he figured that they might be reliable defenders of the border in case of war. Boris, who liked to pursue many of Ivan's administrative ideas, pursued this one as well, although it was very mistaken and very unfortunate, for he thereby unwittingly prepared a large force of criminals to serve our country's enemies and his own.

"Ivan's great intellect and cruelty," in the words of the chronicler, "did not let these serpents get out of control, while meek and pious Theodor bound them with his prayers."

Boris, however, perceived the evil and yet magnified it with other fruits of his scheming, which were incompatible with the eternal precepts of justice. From ancient times our boyars had surrounded themselves with lots of servants, both free and enserfed. They had likewise long preferred to enserf the former. A law promulgated in Theodor's time solely to please the senior nobility allowed the enserfment of people who had served their lord no less than six months. This effectively put an end to free peasants in our country: boyars' homes were filled with serfs who had become so in violation of Ivan's Code. Due to poverty, even many military personnel and noblemen, served the eminent rich without shame.

This was a law unworthy of the name because of its glaring injustice! Not only that, compulsion abetted the effects of this law: eminent people and opportunists unscrupulously enserfed not just servants, but any defenseless persons who pleased them with their art, handicrafts, dexterity or beauty. In times of low prices, nobles willingly increased their serving staff, but in times of famine, they would begin to dismiss them, so that liberty became a sentence of torment and death. People who still had a conscience would at least dismiss servants from their homes with proper papers, but bad people would not provide any documentation, intending to falsely accuse them of flight or theft in order to ruin by false accusation anyone who might give them work or food out of charity. In times of misfortune this was a common and horrible perversion of justice.

BRIGANDAGE

The unfortunates either perished or became brigands, along with many exiled nobles: the Romanovs and others were condemned to spend their lives as vagabonds, since no one dared to take a disgraced person into their service. They were like Ukrainian fugitives, who would come out of their dens for booty inside Russia. Gangs appeared on the highways – they established lairs in quiet, forested places, and robbed and murdered right up to Moscow itself. The criminals did not even fear military patrols – they would boldly set out to do battle with them. They had a certain Klopko, or Kosolapo, as their ataman, an unusual daredevil. Our sovereign was obliged to make a significant effort, and in peacetime dispatched a whole army against the brigands.

The chief voivode was the okolnichii Ivan Thedorovich Basmanov, who had barely taken the field when he encountered Klopko, an evil, scornful enemy, who had unified his gangs and dared to contest victory with the voivode near Moscow. This stubborn conflict, inglorious and fierce, was decided by the death of Basmanov: when his troops saw him fall from his horse, they selflessly hurled themselves at the brigands and finally overcame the fury of the latter. Our troops wiped out most of them and captured their ataman, who was disabled by serious wounds. He was a criminal whose unusual courage was worthy of a better incentive and a better goal.

Surprised by the audacity of this gang, it seems that Boris began searching for Klopko's secret accomplices or advisors amongst eminent men, knowing that there were servitors of disgraced lords in his gang and suspecting that they might be out for vengeance against the persecutor of the Romanovs. An investigation was ordered: the captured brigands were interrogated and tortured, but apparently nothing was learned, except for the prisoners' own crimes. Klopko probably died from his wounds or under torture; all the rest were hanged – and Boris on this one occasion deviated from his humanitarian promise not to employ capital punishment. Many of Klopko's comrades escaped to the Ukraine, where in accordance with their sovereign's orders our voivodes tried to hunt them down and hang them, but were unable to exterminate this nest of criminals, who were waiting to provide a vanguard to march on Moscow to a new, much more dangerous ataman.

Thus was Russia made ready for the most terrible scenes in its history. The run-up was protracted: the towering tyranny of Ivan's 24 years on the throne, the hellish effects of Boris's love of power, the calamity of cruel famine and ubiquitous brigandage, the hardening of hearts and the depravity of the populace – all this presaged the overthrow of a state, condemned by Providence to either perish or to undergo a painful rebirth.

Eyewitnesses write that there was no justice or honor among the people. Protracted famine had not subdued and corrected them, but in fact had multiplied their vices – debauchery, avarice, bribery and insensitivity to the suffering of those closest to them. Even the best of the nobility and the clergy were infected with an epidemic of depravity: their patriotism had been weakened by a lawless tsar

| DEPRAVED MORALS |

who was now widely hated. With all this, how could there have been any other terrible portents for Russia? Yet the chroniclers, following the time-honored tradition of superstition, say,

"Frequently two or three moons now rose together, or two or three suns. Flaming columns burned by night in the firmament, in which rapid movements seemed like hosts doing battle, and a red glow illuminated the land.[*] Belfries and towers fell due to tempests and whirlwinds. Women and animals gave birth to many freaks; fish in the depths and beasts in the fields disappeared, or were eaten for food, despite having no flavor. Greedy dogs and wolves everywhere ran wild in the towns, devouring people and each other. Birds and beasts appeared that had never been seen before. Eagles soared over Moscow, and in the streets and in the palace itself, black foxes were hunted with bare hands. In the summer {of 1604} a comet shone in the heavens in broad daylight and the wise elder whom Boris had brought from Germany a few years previously declared to the state secretary {Vlasiev} that the realm was in great peril."

IMAGINARY MARVELS

We shall now leave superstition to our forebears: its fictitious horrors lack the variety of the real ones in the histories of nations.

DEATH OF IRINA

About this time, Irina died in her cell at the Novodevichii Monastery. For six years she had not broken her voluntary confinement to go anywhere except to the church attached to her humble habitation. She was a woman renowned for her spiritual qualities and her unusual destiny. Without a father or mother, sadly orphaned, she recovered a surprising degree of happiness. Raised and loved by Ivan, she was also virtuous, and the first reigning tsaritsa of Russia. She became a nun while still young; her heart was pure before God, but she was blackened in our history by her association with her evil, power-hungry brother for whom she pointed the way to the throne. She herself was innocent, blinded by her love for him and by the luster of his outward virtues. She was either ignorant of his crimes or gave them no credence.

How could Boris have disclosed his dark soul to a heart devoted to piety? He shared only his good impulses with his tender sister. He shared with her his joy at his country's triumphs and grieved over its calamities, perhaps reassuring her with his grand intention

---

[*] [Probably intense aurora borealis.]

of bringing enlightenment to Russia. He complained of evil ingratitude and evil plots – apparitions of his unquiet conscience – and of the sad necessity of punishing mutinous noblemen. He pretended to be virtuous when he was with his sister, and perhaps the only time he was not hypocritical was when he grieved over her passing.

Irina had not interfered with his rule, but served as a guardian angel, loved by all as the true mother of the people even in her monastic cell. This nun was buried in royal splendor at the Devichii Voznesenskii Monastery next to the grave of Ivan's daughter Mariya. Never had alms been distributed so lavishly as on this day of sorrow: the poor blessed Boris's generosity in all the towns of Russia. When she closed her eyes forever, Irina was fortunate that she had not lived to see the destruction of all that she still loved in life.

A time of real punishment began for this man who did not believe in divine justice in the secular world, who had hoped, perhaps, to save his soul from hell by humble repentance (as Ivan had also hoped) and to dim the people's memory of his criminality through praiseworthy deeds. A sudden peril now arose, but not one Boris had been on guard against. It was not Ryurik's descendants, not the princes and nobles he had persecuted, nor their children and their friends, armed for vengeance, plotting to dethrone him. No, this affair was planned and carried out by a contemptible vagabond in the name of a boy long in his grave. As if by a supernatural agency the shade of Dimitrii rose from the grave, to terrify and drive his murderer mad, and to throw all of Russia into disarray. We now commence a tale as true as it is incredible.

A poor boyar cadet, Yurii Otrepiev from Galich, had lost his father in his youth: Bogdan Otrepiev had been a centurion of musketeers, and had been stabbed to death in Moscow by a drunken Lithuanian. The son had served in the homes of the Romanovs and Prince Boris Cherkasskii. He was literate and had considerable intellect, but little prudence.

> APPEARANCE
> OF THE
> PRETENDER

He grew tired of his lowly status and decided to seek the care-free pleasures of idleness as a monk, following the example of his grandfather Zamyatin-Otrepiev, who had been a monk at the Chudovskii Monastery long ago. After being tonsured by the Vyatka abbot Trifonii and given the name of Grigorii, the young monk wandered from place to place. He lived for a while in Suzdal at the cloister of St. Efimii, in Galich at John the Forerunner's and other places, and at last at the Chudovskii Monastery in his grandfather's cell, under supervision.

There the patriarch Iov got to know him, ordained him as a deacon and took him on for literary work, since Grigorii knew not only how to copy well, but also how to compose canons of the saints better than many of the senior bookmen of the time. He gained Iov's favor and also traveled often with him to the palace. There he saw the royal splendor and was entranced by it. He displayed unusual curiosity and listened avidly to intelligent people, especially when in frank and secret conversations the name of Tsarevich Dimitrii was mentioned. He tried everywhere he could to find out about the circumstances of his unhappy fate, and wrote it down. A wonderful idea now lodged and ripened in the dreamer's soul, suggested, we are assured, by an evil monk. This was the thought that an audacious pretender might exploit the gullibility of Russians touched by the memory of Dimitrii and honor divine justice by punishing his killer. The seed had fallen on fertile ground: the young deacon read the Russian chronicles assiduously and indiscreetly, but as a joke, would sometimes ask the Chudovskii monks,

"Do you know that I shall be the tsar in Moscow?"

Some laughed, others spat in his eye as an insolent liar. These words, or something similar, reached the metropolitan Iona of Rostov, who reported to the patriarch and to the tsar himself that

"The disreputable monk Grigorii wishes to be a vessel of the Devil."

The good-natured patriarch did not pay much attention to the metropolitan's report, but the tsar ordered his secretary Smirnoi-Vasiliev to send the crazy Grigorii to the wastes of Solovki or Belo-ozero, ostensibly for heresy, to do a permanent penance.

Smirnoi told another secretary, Efimiev, but Efimiev was a relative of the Otrepievs and entreated him not to be hasty in carrying out the tsar's edict. He provided the disgraced deacon with a means to escape (in February 1602) with two other Chudovskii monks: the priest Varlaam and choir member Misail Povadin. No one thought to pursue them, and we are assured that no one informed the tsar of this escape, whose consequences would be so significant.

Vagabond monks were a common phenomenon then – monasteries served as their guest houses. In each of them they found peace and comfort, and when on the road, provisions and blessings. Grigorii and his comrades safely reached Novgorod Severskii, where the archimandrite of the Spasskaya Cloister received them very amicably and gave them a servant and horses so they could travel to Putivl. The monks, however, dismissed their escort and hastened to Kiev. The Spasskii archimandrite found the following note in the cell where Grigorii had stayed:

"I am the tsarevich Dimitrii, Ivan's son, and I will not forget your kindness when I sit on my father's throne."

The archimandrite was horrified, and not knowing what to do, decided to keep quiet.

Thus the Pretender was first discovered while still within Russian territory; the fleeing deacon was concocting base lies to overthrow a great monarch and sit on his throne in a state where the ruler counted as an earthly god – where the people had never betrayed their tsars and where the oath given to a *chosen* sovereign was no less than sacred for his loyal subjects. How, except for the action of inscrutable fate, except for the will of Providence, might we explain not only the success, but even the very idea of such an undertaking? It seemed crazy, but the madman chose a reliable path to his goal – Lithuania!

The ancient, natural hatred of Russia there had always vigorously favored our renegades, from princes Shemyakin, Vereiskii, Borovskii and Tverskii to Kurbskii and Golovin. The Pretender also hastened there, but not by the direct route: he went past Starodub to the Luevie Mountains, through dark forests and thickets, where a new traveling companion, the monk Pimen of the Dnieper Monastery, served as his guide. When he finally exited Russia territory near the Lithuanian settlement of Slobodka he gave fervent thanks to Heaven for his safe deliverance from all dangers. In Kiev, after he gained the favor of the eminent voivode, Prince Vasilii Ostrozhskii, Grigorii stayed at the Monastery of the Caves and later at the Nikolskii and in Derman. He performed services as a deacon everywhere, but led a dissolute life, scorning the precepts of temperance and chastity. He boasted of free-thinking and liked to discuss religion with people of other faiths; he even had close ties to the Anabaptists.

Meanwhile, this crazy idea was still alive in the vagabond's head: he spread dark rumors about Dimitrii's rescue and secret asylum in Lithuania. He made the acquaintance of another desperate vagabond, a monk from the Krypetskii Monastery named Leonid, and convinced him to assume his name, to wit, Grigorii Otrepiev. He himself took off his monk's habit and put on secular garb so as to more conveniently obtain the skill and knowledge necessary to bamboozle people. At this time bold gangs of Zaporozhie Cossacks had their lairs amidst the dense reeds of the Dnieper – they were alert guards and audacious plunderers of the Principality of Lithuania. It is written that while among them, the former monk Otrepiev learned how to handle swords and horses in the gang of Gerasim Evangelik, a distinguished elder. He learned to know and love danger and got his first military experience and his first spoils.

But the vagabond was soon seen in another theater: at a peaceful school for Polish and Latin grammar in the town of Gashcha [in the uezd of Lutsk] in Volhynia, since the bogus tsarevich needed to be able to use words as well as weapons. From the school he transferred to the service of Prince Adam Vishnevetskii, who lived in Bragin in all the splendor of a rich nobleman. There the Pretender set to his task, and if he had sought a good, reliable accomplice in an enterprise as bold as it was absurd, he was not mistaken in his choice. Vishnevetskii was powerful in the court and in the National Duma, with many friends and underlings. He also combined pride with a weak mind and the gullibility of youth.

The new servitor of the eminent pan[*] conducted himself discreetly: he avoided all base
amusements, but eagerly participated in military activities, and with notable skill. He was
hardly handsome in appearance: of middling

stature, with a broad chest, reddish hair, a round, pale and quite
unattractive face, light blue eyes without fire, a dull gaze, broad
nose, a wart below his right eye and another on his forehead, and
one arm was shorter than the other. Otrepiev made up for these
disadvantages with a bold and lively mind, eloquence and a noble
deportment. After gaining the attention and good will of his master, the sly fraud pretended to be ill and asked for a confessor. He
softly told him,

"I am dying. Commit my body to the earth with honor, as sons
of tsars are buried. I will not reveal my secret this side of the
grave, but when I close my eyes forever you will find a scroll under my couch and will learn everything, but do not tell others.
God has condemned me to die in unfortunate circumstances."

As the confessor was a Jesuit, he hurried to inform Prince
Vishnevetskii of the existence of the secret and the curious
prince hastened to find out what it was. He searched the bed of
the malingerer and found the scroll, which had been prepared
beforehand. He perused it and learned that his servitor was the
tsarevich Dimitrii, saved from assassination by his loyal physician.
It seemed that the criminals sent to Uglich had killed a priest's
son instead of Dimitrii, who had been hidden by kind nobles and
the Shchelkalov secretaries. Later they took him to Lithuania,
in fulfillment of the instructions Ivan had given them for this
eventuality. Vishnevetskii was astounded; he did not want to
believe it, but had to when the schemer, accusing his confessor of
indiscretion, bared his chest, revealing a gold cross covered with
precious stones (probably stolen from somewhere). He tearfully
told the prince that the relic had been given him by his godfather,
Prince Ivan Mstislavskii.

The Lithuanian nobleman was delighted: such glory had
seemed impossible to him – to see his former servitor

---

[*] [Member of the Polish gentry; also used as a title, like "Mr."]

on the throne in Moscow! He spared nothing to get the phony Dimitrii out of his deathbed. Soon after Otrepiev's pretended recovery the prince prepared him a sumptuous dwelling, splendid service and rich clothing, and managed to spread the word to all of Lithuania of the wondrous rescue of Ivan's son. Prince Adam's brother, Konstantin Vishnevetskii, and the latter's father-in-law, the Sandomir voivode Yurii Mnishek played a special role in the destiny of a fugitive so eminent, or so they thought, believing the scroll, the fraud's gold cross and the testimony of two servants. One was the convicted thief and fugitive Petrovskii, and the other, Mnishek's serf, who in Ivan's time had been our prisoner and had supposedly seen Dimitrii (then a boy of two or three years) in Uglich.

The former averred that the tsarevich really had the Pretender's features (up till now unknown by anyone): warts on his face and a short arm. The Vishnevetskiis reported to Sigismund that they had Theodor's true heir. Sigismund replied that he would like to see him – he had already been informed of this curious appearance

JESUITS

by others, who were equally enthusiastic partisans of the Pretender. These were the papal nuncio Rangoni and pushy Jesuits, who were dominant in Poland at this time, and governed the conscience of the weak-willed Sigismund. They easily convinced him of the significant consequences such an opportunity.

In fact, what could have seemed more propitious for Lithuania and Rome? What might they request from a grateful False Dimitrii if they helped him to gain a realm that had always threatened Lithuania and had always rejected Rome's spiritual authority? Sigismund might be able to find a friend and ally in this dangerous enemy, and the Pope to find an ardent son in this stubborn and disobedient child. This explains the credulity of the king and the nuncio: they were not concerned with the truth, but only of the possible advantages.

It was only Russia's misery, upheaval and internal strife that now captivated the imaginations of our natural enemies, and if the timid Sigismund continued to vacillate, then the earnest Jesuits would overcome his indecisiveness by presenting a means, beguiling to a weak spirit, of acting, not openly, not directly, but under the mask of a peaceful neighbor, to hurl the flame of war into Russia. Rangoni already had close ties with the Pretender, and his energetic Jesuits were serving as intermediaries between them. Both parties had presented their positions and concluded an agreement, and the False Dimitrii had promised in writing to convert himself and Russia to the Latin faith. Rangoni was to be his intermediary, not only in Poland and Rome, but in all of Europe. He counseled the Pretender to hasten to the king, and vouched for favorable consequences from their meeting.

In 1603 or 1604, Otrepiev appeared in Krakow together with the Sandomir voivode and Prince Vishnevetskii, and the nuncio immediately visited him.

"I myself was a witness to this," writes the king's secretary Cilli, putting his faith in the supposed tsarevich. "I saw how the nuncio embraced and treated Dimitrii kindly, conversing with him about Russia and telling him that for the success of his enterprise he needed to formally declare himself a Catholic. Dimitrii, seemingly with heartfelt emotion, swore to immediately carry out the promise he had given him and reaffirmed this oath in the nuncio's house in the presence of many nobles. After entertaining the tsarevich with a lavish dinner, Rangoni conveyed him to the palace. Sigismund, usually pompous and dignified, received Dimitrii in his office, standing, and with a kindly smile. Dimitrii kissed his hand and told him his entire story, concluding with,

THE FALSE DIMITRII
MEETS WITH
THE POLISH KING

'Sovereign! Recall that you yourself were born in fetters and saved only by Providence. As a sovereign exile, I request of you sympathy and assistance.'

"One of the king's officials motioned to the tsarevich that he should go into the next room, where the voivode of Sandomir and all of us were waiting for him. The king remained behind, alone with the nuncio and after a few minutes recalled Dimitrii. Placing his hand on his heart, the humble tsarevich tried to persuade Sigismund, more with sighs than words, to be charitable. The king then lifted his hat and with a merry expression said,

'May God assist you, Prince Dimitrii of Moscow! We, having heard and seen all your testimony, are not in doubt. In you do we see Ivan's son, and as proof of our sincere good will, are granting you 40,000 zlotys per annum {54,000 of today's silver rubles} for your maintenance and all expenses. In addition to that, as true friend of the republic, you are at liberty to communicate with our pans and to make use of their eager assistance.'

"This speech so delighted Dimitrii that he was unable to utter a word. The nuncio thanked the king and conveyed the tsarevich back to the home of the Sandomir voivode. He once again embraced him and counseled him to act at once, the sooner to achieve his goal: to take power from Godunov and with the Jesuits to permanently establish the Catholic faith in Russia."

Prior to this it had been necessary for the False Dimitrii to accept Catholicism himself (something devoutly desired by Rangoni), but on condition that this might not be made public for the time being out of fear of the inveterate hatred of Russians for the Latin Church. This action was performed at the house of the Krakow Jesuits. The former monk went to them secretly with a certain Polish nobleman, in miserable rags, with his face covered so that no one would recognize him. He chose one of them for his confessor, professed his faith, renounced our Church and as an eager new son of the Western Church accepted the body of Christ and unction from the Roman nuncio. So it is stated in *The Letters of the Society of Jesus*, which praised the supposed Dimitrii's

| LETTER TO THE POPE |

great *future* virtues in hopes that he would be diligent in subordinating *all the boundless lands of the East* to Rome. Following the nuncio's instructions, Otrepiev now wrote an eloquent letter in Latin and in his own hand to the Pope, so as to have a sincere protector in him – and Clement VIII lost no time in assuring him of his readiness to assist him with all the spiritual power of the Apostolic Deputy.

One must justly give credit to the former monk's intellect. After he committed himself to the Jesuits, he chose a more effective means to inspire the fervor of incautious Sigismund, who contrary to honor, conscience, civil law and the opinion of many eminent nobles, resolved to be a comrade-in-arms to this vagabond. Batory's renowned friend, Hetman Zamoiskii, still lived. The king wrote to him of his important undertaking, saying that after the republic provided Dimitrii with his crown, it would have the forces of the Muscovite state at its disposal and would easily check the Turks, the khan and the Swedes, take Estonia and all of Livonia, and open a route to Persia and India for their commerce. This important plan, however, would require secrecy and speed and could not be proposed to the Sejm lest Godunov have time to prepare a defense.

In vain did the elder Zamoiskii, the pan Zholkevskii, Prince Ostrozhskii and other prudent nobles try to restrain the king, advising him not to frivolously enter into the perils of such a war, especially without the knowledge or approval of government officials, and with small forces. In vain did the eminent pan Zbarazhskii try to show that the supposed Dimitrii was without doubt a fraud. The king had been convinced by the Jesuits but was afraid to autocratically violate the 12-year truce concluded between himself and Boris. He ordered Mnishek and Vishnevetskii to raise the banner against Godunov in the name of Ivan's son and form an army from volunteers, basing its salaries on the revenues of the Sandomir district. He intimated to the nobles that glory and riches awaited them in Russia and solemnly placed a golden chain from his own chest on the former monk. He then sent

> GATHERING OF TROOPS

him off from Krakow with two Jesuits to Galicia where, on the estate of the nobleman Mnishek near Lvov and Sambor, a large throng of gentry and rabble had gathered under unfurled banners to march on Moscow.

First and foremost of this campaign's zealots was the old man Mnishek, whose age did not interfere with his ambition or his irrational foolishness. He had a charming young daughter Marina, who was, like him, ambitious and flighty. The False Dimitrii, his guest at Sambor, declared himself, sincerely or otherwise, to be passionately in love with her and managed to turn her head with his title of tsarevich. The

> THE FALSE DIMITRII'S PACT WITH MNISHEK

proud voivode blessed this mutual attraction in hopes of seeing Russia at his daughter's foot: a hereditary possession of his descendants. In order to realize this enticing hope and slyly make use of the potential groom's still dubious circumstances, Mnishek offered conditions under which he would unhesitatingly accept the former monk if he gave him the following commitment (written 25 May 1604 by the Sandomir voivode's own hand):

"We, Dimitrii *Ivanovich*, by God's grace *crown prince* of Great Russia, Uglich, Dmitrovsk, etc., prince of his line and sovereign of all Muscovy, heir by divine law and exemplar of all Christian monarchs, have chosen a worthy bride, the noble Lady Marina, daughter of the right noble pan Yurii Mnishek. Having experienced his integrity and love for us, we consider him a father. However, we have put off the wedding until our coronation. Then, to which we swear by the Holy Trinity and our royal word, I shall wed Lady Marina, promising

"1) to immediately give a million zlotys {1,350,000 of today's silver rubles} to pay his debts and finance her journey to Moscow, in addition to valuables, which I will send her from our treasury in Moscow;

"2) to inform King Sigismund of this matter by formal embassy and to ask his favorable consent to it;

"3) to cede to our future wife the two great states of Novgorod and Pskov, with all their uezds and suburbs, and with their Duma personnel, court nobles, boyar cadets and clergy so that that she may administer and dispense justice within them autocratically, appoint deputies, distribute patrimonies and estates to her servitors, establish schools, build monasteries and churches of the Latin faith, to freely confess this faith, which we ourselves have accepted with the firm intention of introducing it into the whole state of Muscovy. But if – God forbid – Russia rises up against our intention and we are unable to fulfill our promises in the course of one year, then Marina shall be free to leave me or to delay doing so for another year, {and so on}."

As if this was not enough, in a transport of gratitude, the False Dimitrii, in another letter, written on 12 June 1604, gave Mnishek the principality of Smolensk and Severskii as a heritable possession, except for some uezds that he had given to King Sigismund and the republic as an earnest of permanent, inviolable peace between him and the Muscovite state. Thus did this fugitive deacon with the title of Russian tsar, as a miraculous instrument of Heaven's wrath, prepare to hand over Russia, with its majesty and Orthodoxy, as spoils for Jesuits and Poles! His means were not yet commensurate with the magnitude of his schemes, however.

He was in fact assembling not an army against Russia, but a rabble. Hardly any eminent court nobles showed up at Sambor or Lvov to answer the call of a king who was little respected, nor were they tempted to display valor for a fugitive crown prince. It was hungry and half-naked vagabonds who were rushing there, demanding arms, not for victory, but for pillaging or else for pay, which Mnishek was dispensing generously in hopes of the future – of a rich bride price for Marina and the income of the principality of Smolensk. The former monk and his friends felt the necessity of other, better comrades-in-arms and were naturally obliged to seek them in Russia itself. It is noteworthy that some of the fugitives from Moscow – boyar cadets filled with hate for Godunov and now hiding out in Lithuania – did not want to take part in this enterprise, for they saw its deceit and deplored its criminality. It is written that one of them, Yakov Pykachev, even testified publicly and before the king, about this crude fraud, together with Otrepiev's former comrade, the conscience-stricken monk Varlaam. But they were not believed and both were sent in fetters to the voivode Mnishek in Sambor, where Varlaam was imprisoned and Pykachev, accused of intending to murder the False Dimitrii, was executed.

Other fugitives, less conscientious – the nobleman Ivan Voroshin and 10 or 15 henchmen, fell at the bogus tsarevich's feet and became his first Russian detachment – which soon became much stronger. Knowing the nature of the rebellious Don Cossacks, and also knowing they were not fond of Godunov, who had executed many of them for robbery, the False Dimitrii sent the Lithuanian Svirskii to the Don with a letter: he wrote that he was the son of the first White Tsar to whom these free Christian knights had sworn allegiance. He summoned them to a glorious task: to depose the thrall and criminal from Ivan's throne. Two atamans, Andrei Korela and Mikhailo Nezhakozh, hastened to come see the False Dimitrii. They saw that he was honored by Sigismund and the noble pans and returned to their comrades with the assurance that the genuine tsarevich was summoning them. The bold Cossacks of the Don mounted their horses to join the Pretender's throngs.

Meanwhile, his diligent servitor, the pan Mikhailo Ratomskii, headman of Ostyor, was roiling our Ukraine with his spies and two Russian monks, probably Misail and Leonid, of whom the latter, assuming the name of Grigorii Otrepiev, could bear witness that this was not the name of the Pretender. They stealthily distributed letters from the False Dimitrii to the Russians in towns and villages, and on the highways, with the news that he was alive and would soon be with them.

People were bewildered, not knowing whether to believe them or not, while the vagabonds, scoundrels and robbers who had long made the Severskii land their lair, were overjoyed: their time had come. Some hastened to the Pretender in Galicia, some to Kiev, where Ratomskii had likewise planted his banner to assemble volunteers. He also roused the Zaporozhskie Cossacks with the enticing idea of taking their former apprentice to the throne of Muscovy. How could such commotion, such public events stay secret from Godunov?

Even before Vishnevetskii revealed the Pretender, rumors spread by him in Lithuania concerning Dimitrii had likely become known to Boris. In January of 1604 the Narva official Tirfeld had sent a letter by courier to the mayor of Abø, informing him that Ivan's supposedly murdered son was living among the Cossacks. The courier had been detained in Ivangorod and his letter reached the tsar. At the same time, news arrived from Lithuania, as well as the False Dimitrii's planted letters, sent by our Ukrainian voivodes. Simultaneously, on the banks of the Volga, the Don Cossacks defeated the okolnichii Semyon Godunov, who had been sent to Astrakhan, and captured some musketeers, whom they released to go to Moscow with the following instructions:

"Tell Boris that we are coming for him soon with the tsarevich Dimitrii!"

Only God knew what went on in Godunov's soul when he heard that fateful name, but the more he was frightened, the harder he tried to seem unperturbed. He had no doubts about the murder of Ivan's real son and interpreted such a brazen lie as a scheme of his secret enemies. He ordered spies to be sent

> MEASURES
> TAKEN BY BORIS

to Lithuania, to find out who this Pretender was, and also searched for plots in Russia, suspecting the boyars. Boris summoned the tsaritsa-nun to Moscow, Dimitrii's mother, and went with the patriarch to see her at the Devichii Monastery, probably imagining that she might be a participant in the supposed plot, and hoping by charm or threats to find out her secret. But the tsaritsa-nun, like the boyars, knew nothing and was astounded, albeit perhaps with a certain inner satisfaction, to learn of the False Dimitrii, who would not replace her son, but would frighten his assassin.

Boris finally found out that the Pretender was the former monk Otrepiev and that his secretary Smirnoi had not carried out his instructions to send him to the White Sea wilderness. Boris made an effort to pretend not to be angry, for he wished to assure Russians of the unimportance of this affair. Smirnoi trembled, expecting his doom, but he was executed later, supposedly for a different crime: theft of government property. The tsar doubled the number of pickets on the Lithuanian border to transmit news of the Pretender, but perceived the impossibility of concealing his appearance from Russia. Fearing that silence would promote harmful gossip, Godunov published the story of the Chudovskii fugitive along with the interrogations of the monk Pimen, the Smolensk monk Benedikt, the tradesman Yaroslavets and the icon-painter Stepan. The first declared that he had guided the vagabond Grigorii to Lithuania, but had not wanted to proceed farther with him and had returned. The second and third testified that they had known Deacon Otrepiev in Kiev and as a brigand among the Zaporozhie Cossacks; he said that this scoundrel, apostate and necromancer, with the connivance of the princes Vishnevetskii and the king himself, was bold enough to call himself Dimitrii in Lithuania.

In the name of the boyars, the tsar simultaneously sent the former monk's uncle, Smirnoi-Otrepiev, to Sigismund's nobles to unmask his nephew in their presence. He also sent the court noble Khrushchov to the Don Cossacks to prevent them from making a catastrophic error. But these letters and words had no effect: the king's nobles did not want to show the False Dimitrii to Smirnoi-Otrepiev and dryly replied that they had no dealings with the phoney Russian crown prince. The Cossacks, however, seized Khrushchov, put him in fetters and brought him to the Pretender. The former monk had now (on 15 August) moved with his troops to the banks of the Dnieper and encamped there in Sokolnikii for 17 months. When Khrushchov was presented to him in chains and saw him, he began weeping, fell to his knees and exclaimed,

> 1604

"I see Ivan in your face; I am your servant forever!"

At this his fetters were removed and this first traitorous official, blinded by fear or greed, reported to his new sovereign, mixing lies with the truth as a token of his zeal, that people in Russia were expressing their love for Dimitrii; that many eminent people – Menshii Bulgakov and others – had drunk to his health with their guests and had been condemned to death, based on denunciations by their servants. He said that Boris had also killed his sister, the widowed tsaritsa Irina, who had always regarded him as an illegitimate monarch, and that he, not daring to openly raise troops against Dimitrii, was gathering his legions in Livny, supposedly in case of an attack by the khan; Khrushchov said that their chief voivodes Pyotr Sheremetev and Mikhailo Saltykov had met with him and in a frank conversation had said,

"We are expecting not a Crimean, but a completely different war, but it is hard to raise one's hand against a natural sovereign."

Khrushchov also said that Boris was in ill health, could hardly walk due to weakness in his legs,[*] and was considering secretly sending Moscow's treasury to Astrakhan and Persia. Godunov certainly did not kill his sister, nor was he considering asylum in Persia. He had not yet seen any treachery among Russians and had not executed a single person for openly siding with the Pretender. He listened avidly to spies, informers and calumniators, but refrained from tyrannical acts for his own safety in such circumstances. Torn by suspicions yet unfounded, he wished to

---

* [Elsewhere it is reported that he suffered from gout.]

affect his boyars and officials with tokens of his magnanimous trust. Yet he actually delayed in moving a significant force to the Lithuanian border.

Was this to show his fearlessness, or did he fear that a large mobilization would give people ideas about the importance of his enemy, or was this to avoid war with Poland until the direst necessity? Yet this necessity was now obvious: King Sigismund was arming not only the Pretender against Boris, but also Crimean brigands, and trying to persuade the khan to attack Russia at the same time as the False Dimitrii. Knowing all this, Boris still sent the court noble Ogarev to Warsaw to see the king personally and appeal to his conscience – to tell him that it was degrading to Christian monarch to be the ally of a base fraud. He once more declared that this man was a phony crown prince and asked what Sigismund wanted: peace or war with Russia?

Sigismund tried to be sly and, like his nobles, replied that he was not supporting the False Dimitrii and was not thinking of violating the truce; he said that some Poles were helping this vagabond on their own. He had *fled* to Galicia and they would be punished as rebels.

"We wished to deceive God," writes a contemporary, an eminent Pole, "by brazenly asserting that the king and the republic had no part in Dimitrii's enterprise."

The Pretender had now commenced operations, but the tsar still ordered the patriarch Iov to write to the Lithuanian and Polish clergies that it would be good for both powers to try to avoid bloodshed on behalf of the apostate monk. All of our bishops affixed their seals to the patriarch's letter, testifying under oath that they had known Otrepiev as a monk. Iov wrote the same letter to the Kiev voivode, Prince Vasilii Ostrozhskii, reminding him that he himself had known this fugitive as a deacon and adjured him to be a worthy son of the Church, to denounce the former monk, seize him and send him to Moscow. But the patriarch's couriers did not return; they were detained in Lithuania and neither the clergy nor Prince Ostrozhskii made answer to Iov, since the Pretender was already achieving glittering success.

The menacing militia that was marching to depose Godunov consisted of barely 1,500 proper cavalry and infantry troops, apart from an almost unarmed, undisciplined rabble. The principal commanders were the False Dimitrii himself (accompanied by two Jesuits), young Mnishek (the Sandomir voivode's son), Dvorzhitskii, Fredro and Neborskii. Each of them had his own unit and gonfalon. The elder Mnishek was foremost in their council. Near Kiev they joined up with 2,000 Don Cossacks brought by Svirskii, along with groups of Kiev and Severskii volunteers raised by Ratomskii, and on 16 October they invaded Russia.

Only then did Boris initiate decisive preparations for defense. He sent reliable voivodes to the Ukrainian forts, along with commanders of musketeers, and dispatched the distinguished boyars Prince Dmitrii Shuiskii, Ivan Godunov and Mikhail Glebovich Saltykov to Bryansk to marshal a large field army there. Even now Boris might be ashamed of his fear when he saw before him only groups of Poles and disorderly volunteers, led by a fugitive former monk, but this man had adopted a name terrifying to Boris and beloved by Russia.

The False Dimitrii was marching with a sword and a manifesto. He declared to Russians that he had been saved from Boris's knife by the invisible right hand of the Most High, and had long been hidden in obscurity. That same hand had led him into the theater of the world under the banners of a brave and powerful army. He was hastening to Moscow to claim the legacy of his forebears: Vladimir's crown and scepter. He reminded every official and citizen of the oath they had given Ivan; he urged them to abandon the usurper Boris and serve their legitimate sovereign. He promised them peace, tranquility and prosperity, which they could not have during the reign of an impious criminal.

At the same time, the Sandomir voivode proclaimed in the name of the king and the noble pans that they had been convinced by the manifest evidence and had unhesitatingly acknowledged Dimitrii as the true grand prince of Muscovy. Accordingly they had given him an army and were prepared to provide one even more powerful in order to elevate him to his father's throne.

This manifesto complemented the action of the False Dimitrii's previous letters scattered about the Ukraine, where not only Khlopkov's comrades-in-arms and servitors of disgraced boyars who hated Godunov – not only base rabble – but also many military men believed the Pretender, not knowing that the fugitive deacon was in cahoots with King Sigismund and surrounded by eminent Poles. They believed in a nimble knight, skilled at the mastery of both sword and horse, in a commander hearty and intrepid, for Dimitrii was always in the van, scorning danger, seeking with his calm gaze, it seemed, not enemies, but friends in Russia. The misfortunes of Godunov's times, the hope for something better, the love of the extraordinary and for the gold showered by Mnishek and the Vishnevetskiis, all abetted people's gullibility. Boris's mayors tried in vain to hinder the spread of the Pretender's handbills: they rebutted them and burnt them, but the bills still went hand to hand, fomenting rebellion.

A secret correspondence between the Pretender and the Ukrainian towns started up. His scouts were acting with great zeal, beguiling people's minds and seducing their passions, while demonstrating that the oaths given Godunov were without force, since the people swearing to him were deceived, and believed Ivan's son to be dead and that Boris himself knew the truth. They thought him to be mad with fear and that he would not oppose the crown prince's entry into Russia. Even his officials were wavering or were numbly awaiting further developments; even his voivodes, seeing that the general commotion was to the False Dimitrii's benefit, were apparently afraid to employ strong measures, and did not exercise the necessary diligence. Conspiracies were hatched and rebellion broke out.

O n the left bank of the Dnieper, Otrepiev split his army: he sent part of it to Belgorod while he himself marched up the

> FIRST BETRAYAL

Desna, following a loose contingent of turncoats who served as his loyal guides, since they knew the territory and the people. He had barely set foot in Russia (on 18 October) at Sloboda Shlyakhetskaya, when he learned of his first success: the inhabitants and soldiers of Moravia had defected from Boris. They bound their voivodes and turned them over to the False Dimitrii, and they greeted him with bread and salt. Feeling the significance of the commencement of his undertaking, the clever vagabond conducted himself with notable skill. Solemnly praising God, he was gracious and majestic. He did not reproach the Moravian voivodes for loyalty to Boris; he merely regretted their error and gave them their freedom. He rewarded and flattered turncoats, citizens and soldiers, and in appearance and in conversation, skillfully presented the mien of a ruler, so that favorable word about the False Dimitrii spread with incredible speed from the Lithuanian border to the innermost districts of Russia.

The famous ancient capital of the Olgovichi did not hesitate to follow the Moravians' example. On 26 October Chernigov submitted to the Pretender; its soldiers and citizens likewise greeted him with bread and salt, and handed over their voivodes. One of these, Prince Ivan Andreevich Tatev, secretly hated Boris and like a second Khrushchov, shamelessly entered the fraud's service. Chernigov had a sizable treasury, which the False Dimitrii divided among his troops, thereby increasing their zeal. Their numbers also increased: 300 musketeer turncoats and residents joined them, enlisting out of enthusiasm for him or because of a violent disposition. After taking 12 cannons from the Chernigov fortress, the Pretender left a Polish commander there and hurried to Novgorod Severskii. He hoped to be victorious everywhere without bloodshed, and indeed, on the banks of the Desna, Svina and Snov he only saw people kneeling before him and hears their joyful cry,

"Hail to our sovereign, Dimitrii!"

There was no news from Novgorod, however; its residents had sent neither a letter of invitation to the False Dimitrii, nor their bound voivodes. One man was on guard there who was decisive, bold, and still loyal! This knight was

KNIGHT-HERO BASMANOV

Pyotr Theodorovich Basmanov, brother of Ivan Basmanov, who had been murdered by brigands in 1604. Pyotr had up till now been known only because of the extraordinary fates of his father and grandfather. They had sacrificed everything for Ivan's favor, so their deaths were a demonstration of divine justice. He had inherited their courtly spirit and combined great intellectual ability and even some noble qualities with a mild and evasive conscience; he was ready for either good or ill in order to gain precedence among men. Boris had seen only the young Basmanov's merits; he had raised him and his brother from his family's disgrace to eminent rank. In 1601 he promoted Pyotr to olkolnichii and had been about to send him with the boyar Prince Nikita Romanovich Trubetskii to save Chernigov, but 15 versts from the city learned that the Pretender was already there and so they ended up in Novgorod, where Basmanov was known.

The great peril gave him precedence over the boyar Trubetskii: he took command of a city in which everything was wavering due to fear and rumors of treachery. He employed threats and the truth to curb treachery. He himself was convinced of fraud, and persuaded others as well. He himself did not fear death, but he terrified the rebels with capital punishment. He torched the suburbs and with a contingent of 500 musketeers he shut himself up in the fortress along with the most eminent residents, willing or not. The False Dimitrii arrived outside Novgorod on 11 November: there, for the first time, Russians greeted him with cannonballs and bullets! He asked to parley. With a lit match* he stood on the wall and listened to the Pretender's henchman, the Pole Buchinskii, who said that tsar and grand prince, Dimitrii, was ready to be a father to their soldiers and residents if they surrendered, but if they resisted, he would not leave even a babe at the breast alive in Novgorod.

"The grand prince and tsar is in Moscow," Basmanov replied, "and your brigand Dimitrii will be impaled on a stake, along with you."

Otrepiev also sent Russian turncoats to try to persuade Basmanov, but it was no use. He tried to take the fortress by a bold assault, but was repulsed; he tried to burn down its walls, but did not succeed in that either. He was losing a lot of men and saw that he was facing disaster; his camp was despondent. Basmanov gave Boris's troops time to mobilize, and served as an example of intrepidity to the other city commanders.

---

* [He was presumably armed with a matchlock arquebus.]

However, the Pretender was comforted by good news. The eminent okolnichii Mikhailo Saltykov and Prince Vasilii Rubets-Mosalskii were in charge at strong Putivl. The prince was not without merits as a warrior, but as a citizen he was without honor or principle. With the secretary Sutupov, he declared himself for the bogus crown prince. He himself provoked the citizens and soldiers, and seized Saltykov. On 18 November he handed this important place over to the former monk and became one of his favorites and an advisor. No less important, Rylsk, the Komarnitskaya, or Severskii, volost, Borisov, Belgorod, Voluiki, Oskol, Voronezh, Kromy, Livny and Elets (where the monk Leonid was operating zealously under the name of Grigorii Otrepiev) all likewise submitted to the Pretender.

All of southern Russia was seething with rebellion. Everywhere officials barely loyal to Boris were seized and brought before the False Dimitrii, who would immediately release them and graciously accept them into his service. His army was being augmented by new bands of turncoats. After he seized a treasury that was being secretly transported in copper barrels by Moscow merchants to the Severskie lands, he sent most of it to Prince Vishnevetskii and the pan Rozhinskii in Lithuania in order to enlist new comrades-in-arms there. He himself stayed by Novgorod, firing large cannons and breaking down its walls. Basmanov did not lose heart, and bravely made some successful sallies. He could see the destruction of the walls, but knew Boris's troops were coming to his relief. He slyly concluded a truce with the Pretender, supposedly to await news from Moscow, but promising to surrender in two weeks in any event. The Pretender now considered Novgorod to be his, and Basmanov to be his prisoner.

The speedy successes of Otrepiev's scam staggered Godunov and all of Russia. The tsar had probably realized his error – but now made another. He could

GODUNOV'S TIMIDITY

see that he must not try to fool the people with hypocritical contempt for the former monk, but must be ready with a powerful army to repel him from our borders and keep him out of the Severskii land, where the old Lithuanian spirit was still alive and where criminals, fugitives and servants of those disgraced had gathered who would naturally expect good things from a rebellion. The people and even the military personnel there, amazed by the Pretender's unobstructed entry into Russia, might believe the insinuations of his scouts and believe that Godunov indeed would not dare resist Ivan's true son. This was new evidence how much the intellect, struggling with conscience, can be deceived, and how guile, a stranger to virtue, may be entangled in its own snare.

Boris might still have rectified his error: he could have mounted his war horse and personally led the Russians against this criminal. The presence of the monarch, his courageous audacity and confidence, would doubtless have had an effect. Although not born a hero, Godunov had known war since his youth; with his strong spirit he had been able to inspire valor in men's hearts and save Moscow when he was still acting only as regent. Going for him were the sanctity of the crown and of the oath of allegiance, the habit of obedience and the memory of his many good deeds for the nation – Russia might not have gone over to the former monk on the field of honor. But he was addled by fear and did not dare go out to meet Dimitrii's ghost. While suspicious of his boyars, he entrusted his fate to them, naming Mstislavskii his chief voivode. This man was a conscientious and personally courageous commander, but more well-known than skilled. He strictly ordered all troops, without exception, to hasten to Bryansk, while he himself seemed to be hiding in the capital.

To summarize, the thunder of God's judgment was rumbling above the reigning criminal. Before 1604 nobody had had any doubts about Dimitrii's assassination: he had been brought up before the eyes of all Uglich and all Uglich had seen his corpse. For five days they had bathed his body with their tears. Consequently, Russians could not prudently believe in the tsarevich's resurrection, but *they did not like Boris!* This unfortunate predisposition prepared them to be victims of the fraud. Boris himself had weakened the evidence of the truth by executing the principle eyewitnesses of Dimitrii's death and obviously false evidence had eclipsed its terrible circumstances. Many people in Uglich and Pelym still knew the truth, but hatred for the tyrant was still alive in their hearts. It is written that Prince Shuiskii testified loudest of all, in the capital, at the place of execution, about the certainty of the tsarevich's death: he had seen him in the casket and in the grave. The patriarch wrote the same to all corners of Russia, also quoting Dimitrii's mother, who had buried her son. But Shuiskii's unscrupulousness was still a fresh memory and Iov's blind devotion to Godunov was well known. Only the name of the tsaritsa-nun was heard. No one had seen or talked to her since she was once again confined in the Vyksa wilderness.

> TENOR OF
> PUBLIC OPINION

We did not have a historical example of a pretender – such a brazen fraud was incomprehensible. Russians loved the ancient lineage of the tsars and listened avidly to secret tales of the fictitious virtues of the False Dimitrii. They secretly passed the word to one another that God, by some sort of miracle worthy of His justice, might actually have saved Ivan's son to punish the hated usurper and tyrant. At the very least they had doubts, and did not seem eager to stand up for Boris. The former monk and his Poles were now ruling within our borders. The nation's soldiers were reluctant to serve and proceeded with their banners to Bryansk unwillingly, even more so as they heard of the False Dimitrii's successes, thinking that God Himself was helping him. Thus it was that the sovereign's unpopularity also gave rise to indifference to the national honor!

In this now evident peril, Boris resorted to two means: to the Church and to severity. He ordered the priests to intone the perpetual memory of Dimitrii in the cathedrals and to publicly curse, from ambos and in the marketplaces, the former monk and his present and future accomplices as evil heretics who were scheming to steal not only the country, but also to introduce the Latin faith. Evidently Boris was now aware of, or had guessed, the promise the False Dimitrii had given to the Jesuits and the papal legate. The people, who had seen the debility and connivance of the prelates in investigating Dimitrii's murder, had less than total faith in them, but the horror of anathema must touch the consciences of devout people and instill in them a loathing for a man cast out by the Church and consigned to the judgment of God.

The second method was also effective: an edict was issued that for every 200 chetverts of worked land a trooper must be provided, with horse, armor and provisions – evidently half the number of warriors set by Ivan's decree. Boris demanded speed, writing that rich landowners living in their homes did not care about the fate of their country or their Church. He promised cruel punishment for the indolent and unconcerned, let alone those with evil intentions, and indeed ordered the disobedient to be punished without mercy – by confiscation of property, by prison and the knout. He also ordered that all those fit for military service who were serving the patriarch, the prelates or in monasteries to hurry to the army under peril of the tsar's wrath if they tarried.

"There was a time," it says in this resolution of the national council, "when monks, priests and deacons took up arms to save the nation, sparing not their own blood. However, we do not want that – we are leaving them in their churches to pray for the sovereign and the state."

In about six weeks, these measures – threats and punishments – gathered upwards of 50,000 cavalry in Bryansk, instead of the half million summoned to duty in 1598 by a tsar *whom Russia had loved.*

B oris still displayed courage, however. When the Swedish king, Sigismund's enemy, heard about the Pretender and the perfidy of the Poles, he offered the tsar an alliance and auxiliary troops.

BORIS'S COURAGE

The tsar replied that Russia was not requesting the assistance of foreigners, and that during Ivan's reign it had simultaneously fought the sultan, Lithuania, Sweden and the Crimea and need not fear a contemptible rebel. Boris knew that if the Russians were loyal, he would have no use for a handful of Swedes, and if they were disloyal, the Swedes would be of no use to him, for they would not be able to save him.

The terrible hour of trial had arrived; there was no time to be lost, since the Pretender was daily increasing in strength and extending his peaceful conquests. The boyars: the princes Thedor Ivanovich Mstislavskii, Andrei Terlyatevskii, Dimitrii Shuiskii,

Vasilii Golitsyn and Mikhailo Saltykov, and the okolnichie Prince Mikhailo Kashin, Ivan Ivanovich Godunov and Vasilii Morozov set out from Bryansk to curtail the successes of this treason and save the citadel of Novgorod, which alone was holding out against the former monk in the middle of territory under his control. It was not just Godunov who followed Moscow's banners in his thoughts with agonizing agitation of the soul, but all of Russia was in anxious anticipation as to how fate would resolve this most significant dispute between Boris and Dimitrii, be he true or false, for there was no guarantee as to the loyalty of either the army or the country.

The question of whether to raise their hands against Ivan's true son or to surrender to a brazen fraud cursed by the Church frightened noble hearts equally. Many, including the noblest of Russians, did not like Boris, but abhorred treason. They wanted to hold to the oath they had given him; others, following only the promptings of their passions, either wanted or did not want, a change of tsars and cared neither about the truth nor their duty as subjects. Still others had no set opinion and were ready to decide as the situation dictated. Even if a perceptive observer could have discerned men's inmost thoughts, he would perhaps not have been able to resolve for himself the question of the probable success or lack of success of the Pretender's enterprise. The disposition of minds was partly discordant and partly unclear or irresolute. The army marched, obedient to the tsar, but was shaken by doubt, gossip and mutual distrust.

Approaching Trubchevsk, where Dimitrii's name was now famous, Boris's voivodes wrote to the Sandomir voivode that he should immediately depart Russia, which was at peace with Lithuania, and leave the criminal former monk to the punishment he had earned. Mnishek did not reply, hoping that Boris's troops would not draw their swords. The Pretender thought the same, for that is what he was told by turncoats who were in communication with their confederates in Moscow's legions.

A BATTLE

On 18 December on the banks of the Desna, about six versts from the False Dimitrii's camp there was the first exchange of fire

between detachments of the opposing armies, and on the third day a minor skirmish. No one from either side displayed any ardor. It appears that the Pretender was waiting for Boris's army to follow the example of the cities: to bind and hand over their commanders to him, while Mstislavskii, who expected the enemy, being weaker, with barely 12,000 troops, to withdraw without a fight. However, there was neither defection nor flight. Only three men from the boyar cadets went over to the False Dimitrii. After leaving Novgorod and his fortified camp, Otrepiev had deployed on a plain, very disadvantageous for a small force. Appearing calm and hearty, he made a speech to his comrades-in-arms, trying to ignite their valor. He prayed in a loud voice, raised his hands to Heaven and dared, we are assured, to pronounce these words:

"Most High! You see into the depths of my heart. If I draw my sword unjustly and illegally, destroy me with your heavenly thunder. {Wait till 17 May 1606!}. But if I am in the right and pure in heart, give my arm invincible strength in battle! And you, Divine Mother, be protectress of our army!"

On 21 December the engagement began, at first not heated, but then the Polish cavalry suddenly charged, yelling, at the Russian right wing, commanded by the princes Dimitrii Shuiskii and Mikhailo Kashin. The wing shuddered, and the center of the army was thrown into flight. There stood Mstislavskii, appalled by such spineless disorder, he held back both his own troops and the enemy's with his sword. He fought in the melee, bleeding, and fell to the ground with 15 wounds; a contingent of musketeers barely saved him from capture. It was the decisive hour: if the False Dimitrii had reinforced his bold Poles with a general attack, then the entire Muscovite army, as eyewitnesses write, would have presented a spectacle of shameful flight. But he gave them time to recover: 700 German cavalry loyal to Boris checked the enemy charge and our left wing remained intact.

Now Basmanov emerged from the fortress to harry the Pretender's rear; when the False Dimitrii heard firing behind him and saw his fortified camp in flames, he broke off the engagement. Both sides quickly fell back; the False Dimitrii boasted of victory and 4,000 enemy dead, while Boris's voivodes were shamed into silence, even though they had taken some prisoners. In order to lessen their shame, the Russians concocted a fable: they asserted that the Poles, dressed in bearskins fur side out had spooked their horses. But foreigners who had witnessed the flight write that the Russians seemed to have no swords or arms, only legs!

Yet the supposed victor was not rejoicing: although this odd battle showed that which the Pretender wanted – that the Russians fought poorly and without zeal – they fought, nonetheless. Although they had run *from* him, not *at* him, he knew that without their widespread defection neither his Poles nor his Cossacks would overthrow Boris. He was also frightened to find himself between two fires, two loyal voivodes: Mstislav and Basmanov. When the latter saw the former's withdrawal, he shut himself up in his fortress once more, prepared to die in its ruins. The next day 4,000 Zaporozhskie Cossacks joined the False Dimitrii. Boris's army had withdrawn to Starodub Severskii, but only to await fresh legions from Bryansk. In a few days they might return to Novgorod, which was so strongly defended. His mercenaries' and

POLES DESERT
THE PRETENDER

allies' morale had fallen: the Poles had hoped to take their tsar to Moscow without bloodshed, but had seen that they must engage in serious fighting. They had no fondness for winter marches or winter sieges, and so they frivolously concluded that which they had just as frivolously begun: they declared that they were going home, supposedly in obedience to Sigismund's order not to do battle with Russia if it stood up for Tsar Godunov.

In vain did the False Dimitrii try to persuade them not to lose hope, but no more than 400 bravos stayed; all the rest cut out for home, the disappointed Mnishek with them. Thinking that all was lost, both the Principality of Smolensk for himself, and Russia for Marina, the flighty old man still bade a fond farewell to his potential son-in-law, boldly promising to return with a more powerful force. But the Pretender, while hardly believing his potential father-in-law, still believed in luck. With holy rites, he committed the bodies of the fallen, both his and his enemy's, to the earth on the field of battle. He raised the siege of Novgorod and set up camp in the Komarnitskaya volost; he occupied the Sevsk stockade and hastened to arm everyone he could, both citizens and farmers. Boris's army, however, did not give him enough time.

The disarray of the Muscovite voivodes was so great that they even delayed informing the tsar of the battle; he learned all of its sorry circumstances from others. On 1 January, Boris sent Prince Vasilii Shuiskii to the army to be its second commander, and the court cellarer Veliaminov to the wounded Mstislavskii to salute

1605

him for the blood he had lost out of his zeal for his sacred homeland. In the name of the sovereign, Veliaminov told him,

"After you had performed this outstanding service, you saw the images of the Savior, the Virgin, the wonderworkers of Moscow and our tsar's eyes. Now we shall grant you more than you expect. We are sending a skilled physician to you, so that you may regain your health and once again ride your war horse."

The tsar ordered all the other voivodes to be informed of his displeasure for their criminal silence, but that the troops be assured of his favor. In order to inspire valor into the hearts of the Russians by a glittering award, Boris, who was sincerely pleased with Basmanov alone, summoned him to the palace. He sent the most eminent state officials out to meet the hero and his own sumptuous sleigh for his formal entry into Moscow with complete royal pomp. With his own hands he gave Basmanov a heavy gold dish heaped with chervontsty and 2,000 rubles, as well as a large number of silver vessels from the Kremlin treasury, a revenue-

BASMANOV HONORED

producing estate and the rank of Duma boyar. The capital and all of Russia turned their gaze on the new nobleman, suddenly brought to prominence by his glorious exploit and by the tsar's favor. They extolled his unusual merit, and the sovereign's favorite became the people's favorite, the foremost man of his time in public opinion.

However, such a glittering reward for just one man was a reproach to the many and naturally gave rise to indignant envy among the eminent. If the tsar had dared to scorn the principle of boyar precedence and given overall command to Basmanov, then perhaps he might have saved his house from destruction and Russia from calamity, but fate did not wish it. After receiving Basmanov in Moscow the tsar, perhaps intending to make use of his counsel in the Duma, had in fact removed his best voivode from the army and, it seems, then made another mistake in choosing

Shuiskii as supreme commander. This prince, like Mstislavskii, might not fear death in battle, but he had neither intellect nor a genuine, bold and decisive spirit of leadership. Shuiskii was convinced of the vagabond's fraudulence and would not think of handing the country over to him, but while this smooth-talking courtier indulged Boris, he recalled his disgrace and saw, perhaps with secret satisfaction, the torments of Godunov's tyrannical heart. Although the prince wished to save Russia's honor, he did not wish the tsar well.

S huiskii, accompanied by a lot of stewards and their assistants, found our army in the forest near Starodub, amongst abatises, where it, although reinforced by new units, seemed to be hiding from the enemy, in idleness and despond, with an ailing commander. Another, reserve army was assembling near Kromy under the command of Thedor Sheremetev, so that Boris had no less than 80,000 troops in the field. Shuiskii and Mstislavskii, who was still weak from wounds, immediately moved on Sevsk, where the False Dimitrii had no intention of waiting for them.

VICTORY
OF BORIS'S
VOIVODES

Bold in his despair, he removed from the town and engaged them in Dobrynichi. The forces were disproportionate: he had 15,000 cavalry and infantry, while Boris's voivodes had 60 or 70,000.

When he found out that our legions had crammed into the village, he tried to burn it down at night and catch them asleep. The local residents tried to get him into the settlement unnoticed, but guards noticed the movement, became alarmed, and the enemy pulled out. They waited for dawn (21 January). The Pretender prayed and made a speech to his troops, as he had on the day of the Novgorod battle. He divided his army into three parts, taking 400 Polish and 2,000 Russian cavalry for the first assault; they all wore white clothing over their armor so they could identify each other in the fray. Eight thousand Cossack cavalry were to follow them, and 4,000 infantry with cannons. A powerful barrage commenced in the morning. The Russians, although so numerous, did not advance. They were on both sides of the settlement, where their infantry was stationed.

The False Dimitrii observed the Muscovite voivode's dispositions, then mounted a swift, dark brown steed, and sword in hand, led his cavalry through a valley, cutting through Boris's army with a quick assault between the village and his right wing. Mstislavskii, weak and feeble, was on his horse: he had guessed the enemy's intent and moved his wing, along with a foreign contingent, to meet the enemy. The former monk, like a real knight, showed uncommon audacity: with a swift blow he threw his enemy into confusion and pursued them; he also smashed the foreign unit, despite its brilliant and valorous resistance, then charged at the Muscovite infantry, which was stationed with artillery in front of the village and did not move, as if in a stupor.

They waited and then a sudden salvo from 40 cannons and a volley from 10 or 12,000 muskets staggered our enemy: a great number of riders and horses fell. Those untouched fled to their rear in a fearful frenzy, and so did the False Dimitrii. His Cossacks had been about to pull off a quick victory for their hero, but seeing that it was not to be theirs, turned tail – first the Zaporozhie, then the Don Cossacks and then the infantry. Five thousand Russians and Germans with the cry *Hilf Gott* [God aid us], pursued, striking down the fleeing troops over an extent of eight versts. They killed about 6,000, captured a considerable number of prisoners, 15 banners and 13 cannons. It is written that they would have wiped them out to the last man had not our voivodes ordered them to stop, probably believing it was all over and that the False Dimitrii was dead. Our officer Shein galloped to Moscow with the happy news and found the tsar praying at the Monastery of St. Sergii.

Boris was thrilled: he ordered thanksgiving services held, the church-bells to be rung and the people to be shown the trophies: the Pretender's banners, trumpets and tambourines. He promoted the courier to the rank of okolnichii, sent his favorite steward, Prince Mezetskii, with gold medals for the voivodes and 80,000 rubles for the troops. He wrote to the voivodes that he was waiting to hear news of the end of the rebellion from them and was ready to give his loyal servitors his last shirt. He especially thanked the ardent foreigners and their two commanders: the Lithuanian court noble Walter Rosen and the Frenchman Jacques

Margeret. Finally, he expressed great pleasure that the victory had not cost us dearly: we only lost 500 Russians and 25 Germans in the battle.

But the Pretender still lived: the victors had celebrated their triumph prematurely and had let him get away. He had galloped on a wounded horse to Sevsk and fled farther that same night to Rylsk with several Poles, Prince Tatev and some other turncoats. The next day the scattered Zaporozhie Cossacks came to him, but the Pretender would not admit them to the city – he considered them to be faint-hearted cowards or traitors – and they left for home in shame and vexation. Seeing no security for himself in Rylsk, the False Dimitrii sought it in Putivl, which was better fortified, and closer to the border.

Meanwhile, Boris's voivodes were all still in Dobrynichi, busy with executions: they hanged all the prisoners, except for Lithuanians – Prince Tishkevich and others, who were sent to Moscow. They also tortured and shot the inhabitants of the Komarnitskaya volost for their treason. This was inhumane and imprudent, since it increased the rebels' fury, hatred of the tsar and good opinion of the fraud, who had been merciful with even the most ardent servitors of his enemy. This cruelty, together with our voivodes negligence, saved the malefactor. Having now lost all hope, soundly defeated, almost wiped out, with a handful of dispirited fugitives, he tried to secretly escape Putivl for Lithuania. The desperate turncoats detained him, saying,

"We have sacrificed everything for you, but all you are thinking of is a life of shame, while consigning us to Godunov's wrath. But we can still save ourselves if we hand you over to Boris alive!"

They offered him all that they had – their lives and property. They cheered him up by vouching for a great number of his confederates both in Boris's legions and in the nation. The Don Cossacks showed no less fervor: 4,000 of them came once more to the Pretender in Putivl. Others occupied the cities and swore to defend them to their last breath.

The False Dimitrii stayed, willing or not. He sent Prince Tatev to Sigismund, requesting immediate assistance. He fortified

Putivl and, following the advice of the turncoats, published a new manifesto, telling the tale he had fabricated concerning Dimitrii's rescue, giving as witnesses people no longer living, and citing the valuable cross [supposedly] given him by Prince Ivan Mstislavskii, and added that he (Dimitrii) had been secretly raised in Belorussia, but later was with Chancellor Sapieha in Moscow, where he saw the usurper Godunov sitting on Ivan's throne.

The second manifesto satisfied the curious with its hitherto unknown fables and increased the number of the Pretender's friends, even though he had been defeated. It was said that Russians marched against him only under coercion, with an inexplicable fear that was prompted by something supernatural, no doubt of Heaven; that the enemy had defeated him by chance and would not have withstood him without the blind fury of the Germans. Therefore it was obvious that Providence wished to save this knight even in the most unsuccessful battle. God had not abandoned him even in the greatest extremity, nor had he been abandoned by his loyal servitors, who had acknowledged him as the true Dimitrii and were ready to sacrifice themselves, their wives and children for him. They of course would not have had such great ardor for a fraud. This declaration had a powerful effect on the gullible, and many people, especially from the Komarnitskaya volost, where Boris's vengeance had raged, flocked to Putivl demanding arms and the honor of dying for Dimitrii.

Meanwhile, the tsar's voivodes, after learning that the Pretender had not been eliminated, got a move on and assaulted Rylsk. They did not promise mercy for anyone; they wanted the city to surrender unconditionally. Wicked turncoats were in charge there: Prince Grigorii Dolgorukii-Roshcha and Yakov Zmeev. Seeing the gallows before them, they ordered Mstislavskii be told,

"We serve Tsar Dimitrii."

A salvo from all their cannons announced their resolve. The voivodes invested the city for two weeks. Boasting of an untimely feeling of charity and a reluctance to shed blood, and, genuinely burdened by a winter campaign, they decided to give their troops a rest. They withdrew to the Komarnitskaya volost and reported to the tsar that they would await spring there, in peaceful camps. However, Boris, after short-lived joy, was alarmed by the news of the False Dimitrii's escape and his new enticements to treason. He was angry with Mstislavskii and all his comrades-in-arms and sent the okolnichii Pyotr Sheremetev and the Duma secretary Vlasiev to them in Ostrog Radogostskii with a contingent of Moscow court nobles and some angry words: he reproached them for negligence in letting the Pretender out of their hands, at their futile victory, and railed at their troops.

They in turn complained of the tsar's cruelty and injustice – they who up till now had loyally fulfilled their oaths, had been bloodstained in battle and debilitated by the rigors of army life. Malefactors complained even more in order to increase the tsar's unpopularity, and they could boast of success, for from this time on, according to the chronicler, many army officers became noticeably partial the Pretender, and the desire to *get rid of Boris* seized their hearts.

There were defections, but they did not yet ripen into a mutiny: legitimate orders were still obeyed, albeit reluctantly. Following the sovereign's strict orders, Mstislavskii and Shuiskii once more led their troops out into the field, only to amaze Russia by the insignificance of their operations: leaving the False Dimitrii at liberty in Putivl, they linked up with Thedor Sheremetev's reserve army, which had now been pressing Kromy for two or three weeks.

KROMY BESIEGED

During Lent, they began to lay siege to this fortress. It was an improbable affair: at least 18,000 troops with many siege engines assaulted the wooden town inside of which, in addition to the residents, there were 600 valorous Don warriors under the courageous ataman Korela. The besiegers torched the town at night and occupied the ashes and the ramparts, but with powerful and accurate fire, the Cossacks kept them out of the citadel. The boyar Mikhailo Glebovich Saltykov, either a coward or now on the other side, said not a word to his commanders, but ordered his troops to withdraw at the very moment they should have assaulted the turncoats' last barricade.

Mstislavskii and Shuiskii did not dare punish him, for they could see the bad mood of their comrades-in-arms, and from that day on they only fired their cannons, hoping to take the citadel by starvation. They did no harm to the besieged, who dug themselves earthworks and hid safely below their ramparts, occasionally crawling out of their holes to essay a daring sally. Meanwhile, the opposing army became victims of a lethal epidemic in the cold and damp. This calamity demonstrated the tsar's still praiseworthy concern: he sent medicine to their camp and everything necessary to save the sick men, but this increased the negligence of the siege so that, in broad daylight, 100 cartloads of grain and 500 of the False Dimitrii's Cossacks were able to get through from Putivl to burned-out Kromy.

Irritated at the delays in military operations, contemporaries write that Boris tried another method to rid himself and Russia of the malefactor. Three monks who had known Otrepiev as a deacon appeared in Putivl on 8 March with letters from the tsar and patriarch to the local residents: the first promised them great favor if they would hand over the Pretender, alive or dead; the second threatened the terrible action of the Church's anathema. The monks were seized and brought to the False Dimitrii, who employed cunning: instead of himself, he seated the Pole Ivanitskii on the throne in tsarish raiment. Pretending to be the Pretender, Ivanitskii asked,

"Do you recognize me?" The monks replied, "No. We only know that there is no way you are Dimitrii."

They were subjected to torture: two endured and remained silent, the third saved himself by declaring that they had poison, with which, to fulfill Boris's will, they intended to kill the False Dimitrii, and that some of those nearest him were traitors conspiring with them. Poison was indeed found in a boot belonging to the youngest of the monks and the Pretender discovered two traitors among his favorites – he consigned them to popular vengeance. We are assured that he boasted that Heaven clearly favored himself and wrote to the patriarch and to the tsar himself, reproaching Iov for misusing the Church's power to benefit the

> PRETENDER'S
> LETTER TO BORIS

usurper, and tried to persuade Boris to leave the throne peaceably and retire from the world, secluding himself in a monastery and live for the salvation of his soul. The False Dimitrii promised him that he would receive the tsar's mercy. Such a letter, if it really had been written and delivered to Godunov, would have been a further inducement to severity.

The soul of this power-hungry man was full of fear and dissembling. Deceived by the results of his victory, Boris agonized, seeing the inaction of his military and the negligence, incompetence or evil intent of his voivodes. He also feared to replace them, lest he choose worse. He suffered, perceiving the people's silence as propitious for the Pretender, but powerless to stop it, either by indulgent persuasion, or by excommunication, or by punishments, for the times were riven by indiscreet talk. Denunciations multiplied daily, but Godunov was afraid that cruelty would only fuel the rebellion. He was still the autocrat, but felt his power frozen in his hands; from the throne, still surrounded by fawning slaves, he saw an abyss yawning before him.

From the outside, the Duma and the court appeared unchanged: in the former, affairs took their usual course; in the latter, there was glittering splendor, as before. Hearts were closed: some hid fear, others, malicious delight. Godunov was more than anyone forced to shutter his own heart lest his despondency and weakness presage his doom. Perhaps he opened up his heart only to his loyal wife (he seemed to her to be bloodstained, deeply wounded) in order to groaningly unburden himself.

He did not have the purest comfort: he could not surrender to the will of Divine Providence, for he served only the idol of personal power. He still wished to enjoy the fruits of Dimitrii's assassination, and would of course dare to commit new crimes so as not to lose his ill-gotten gains. In such a spiritual situation, how can a mortal comfort himself with faith and hopes of Heaven? The churches were open, and Godunov prayed – to God, who is inexorable towards those who know neither virtue nor repentance! And yet there is a bound to suffering – in the transitory nature of our earthly existence.

Boris was now 53: in the bloom of his manhood he had contracted an illness – severe gout. Now that he was getting old, he might easily have exhausted his corporeal strength through spiritual torment. At the morning hour on 13 April Boris was rendering judgment and handling affairs with his nobles in the Duma, and receiving distinguished foreigners. He had been dining with them in the Golden Palace and had just gotten up from the table when he felt faint: blood gushed from his nose, ears and mouth

DEATH OF BORIS

like a river. His doctors, of whom he was so fond, were unable to stanch the flow. He was losing consciousness, but then managed to bless his son to take the Russian throne and he succeeded in donning a monk's habit, taking the name Bogolep. Two hours later he expired, in the same chamber in which he had been feasting with his boyars and with the foreigners.

Unfortunately, posterity knows nothing further of his shocking end. Who would not have wished to see and hear Godunov in the last moments of such a life, to read his gaze and see into his soul, disconcerted by the sudden approach of eternity? Before him were the throne, crown and grave – his wife, children and those closest to him, already doomed by fate – his ungrateful thralls, already ready for treachery in their hearts – and also before him the holy banner of Christianity – the image of Him who perhaps never rejects an overdue repentance! The silence of contemporaries, like an impenetrable curtain, conceals what would have been an important and edifying spectacle and allows only the imagination to operate.

Some assert that Godunov was a suicide, who took his own life by poison out of despair, but do the circumstances and nature of his death support this claim? And could this tender paterfamilias, this strong-spirited man, while saving himself from disaster by poison or flight, have so cowardly left his wife and children to their almost inevitable doom? While our army had not yet betrayed its tsar, and still stood, albeit unenthusiastically, beneath his banners, was the Pretender's triumph assured? It was only Boris's death that decided the success of the fraud; it was only turncoats, open or clandestine, who might have wished to *hasten* it.

Yet most likely of all is that it was a stroke, not poison, which ended Boris's stormy days, to the genuine regret of his country, for his untimely end was divine punishment for Russia even more than it was for Godunov. After all, he died on the throne and not in the fetters of the fugitive deacon – as if this were a reward for his good deeds for the country. Russia, however, deprived of a tsar wise and solicitous, was to become the spoil of villainy for many years to come.

The name of Godunov, however, one of the world's wisest rulers, was and will be, over the centuries, pronounced with loathing, to the credit of unflinching moral justice. Posterity sees the place of execution incarnadine with the blood of innocents, St. Dimitrii expiring under the knife of the assassin, the hero of Pskov in the noose, and so many nobles in gloomy dungeons or monastery cells. It sees the vile recompense offered by the monarch's hand to informers. It sees a system of cunning, deceit and hypocrisy before the people and before God. The mask of virtue is everywhere, but where is the virtue itself? Is it in the truth of Boris's judgments, in his generosity, in his love for civic development, in his zeal for Russia's greatness, or in his peaceful and sound policies?

But the bright spark of his intellect chills the heart when it is assured that Boris would not hesitate to act contrary to his wise administrative principles if his love of power demanded it. He was only sometimes a tyrant, and he was not insane, yet he committed crimes like Ivan: exiling rivals or executing those who wished him ill. If Godunov for a time developed the country, and for a time raised it in the eyes of Europe, did he not precipitate it into the abyss of almost unheard of misfortune? Did he not also cause it to become a spoil for Poles and vagabonds, summoning into the theater a throng of vengeance-seekers and pretenders because of his extirpation of the ancient line of tsars? Did he not, finally, more than anyone else, collaborate in the debasement of the throne, by occupying it as a saint-killer?

Glossary

Abatis: defensive obstacle made of felled trees.

Ambo: an elevated platform in front of the iconostasis (which is the screen separating the nave from the sanctuary in an Orthodox church).

Ataman: a Cossack chief.

Boyar: a member of the higher Russian nobility.

Chetverik: see kad.

Chetvert: see kad.

Cossack: semi-independent cavalrymen inhabiting southern European Russia.

Funt: a Russian pound: 409.5 grams, or about 14.5 avoirdupois ounces.

Gonfalon: a banner suspended from a horizontal crosspiece.

Kad: a kad or okov was about 840 liters. A chetvert was a quarter of that, and an osmina an eighth. A chetverik (little quarter) was a quarter of an osmina, or about 26 liters, roughly three-quarters of a US bushel.

Kalga: a Tatar official second in rank to the khan.

Kopeck: a hundredth part of a ruble.

Little Russia: roughly the same territory as the present-day Ukraine.

Mirza: a Tatar aristocratic title.

Oblast: see volost.

Okolnichii, -ie: a member of the nobility one rung down from boyar, *q.v.*

Okov: see kad.

Oprichnina: Ivan the Terrible's system of secret police, as well as the system it operated under.

Osmina: see kad.

Pan: a member of the Polish gentry.

Pood: 16.38 kg, or about 36 lbs.

Pyatina: an old territorial division in the Novgorod area.

Sazhen: 2.13 meters, or about 7 feet.

Seit: a distinguished official of the sultan's court; from Arabic sayyid, a male descendant of Mohammed.

Sejm: the Polish parliament.

Tiun: a low-level official.

Shavkal: Shavkal or shamkal was ruler's title in Daghestan. Karamzin seems to use the term ambiguously to refer to their territory, their title or as a personal name.

Tocsin: an alarm.

Tsarevich: a son of a tsar; a crown prince.

Tsarevna: a daughter of a tsar.

Uezd: see volost.

Ulus: a Tatar encampment or settlement.

Voivode: a senior military officer, like a general. Sometimes a military governor as well.

Volost: a low-level administrative unit subordinate to an uezd, which in turn is subordinate to a district (oblast).

MOSCOW AND EAST

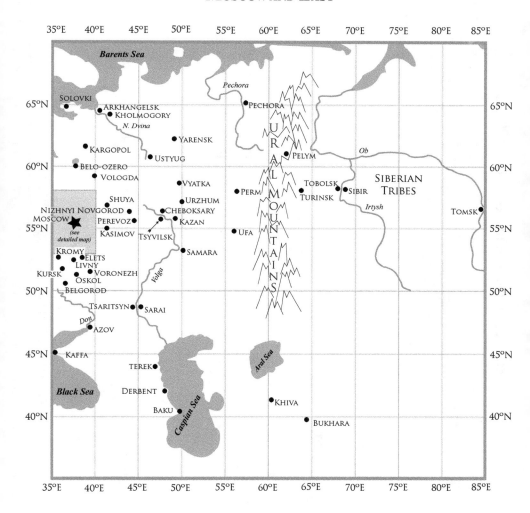

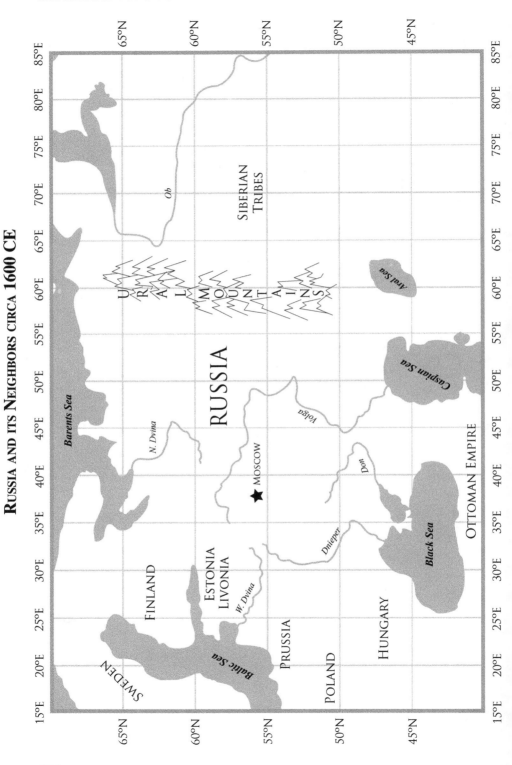

RUSSIA AND ITS NEIGHBORS CIRCA 1600 CE

GAZETTEER OF TOWNS AND CITIES

Aleksin	54.5°N	37.1°E
Arkhangelsk	64.5°N	40.5°E
Azov	47.1°N	39.4°E
Bakhchiserai	44.8°N	33.8°E
Baku	40.4°N	49.9°E
Belyov	53.8°N	36.1°E
Belgorod	50.6°N	36.6°E
Belo-ozero	60.0°N	37.8°E
Borovsk	55.2°N	36.5°E
Bukhara	39.8°N	64.4°E
Cheboksary	56.1°N	47.2°E
Cherni**g**ov	51.5°N	31.3°E
Derbent	42.1°N	48.3°E
Derpt (or Dorpat, Tartu, Yuriev)	58.4°N	26.7°E
Dmitrovsk	52.5°N	35.1°E
Dorogo**buzh**	54.9°N	33.3°E
Elets	52.6°N	38.5°E
Gdov	58.8°N	27.8°E
Gniezno	52.5°N	17.6°E
Grodno	53.7°N	23.8°E
Ivangorod	59.4°N	28.2°E
Kaffa	45.0°N	35.4°E
Kaluga	54.6°N	36.3°E
Kamenets	52.4°N	23.8°E
Kargopol	61.5°N	38.9°E
Kashin	57.4°N	37.6°E
Kashira	54.8°N	38.2°E
Kasimov	54.9°N	41.4°E
Kazan	55.8°N	49.2°E
Kexholm (see Korela)		
Khiva	41.4°N	60.4°E
Kholmogory	64.2°N	41.6°E
Kiev	50.4°N	30.5°E
Kitaigorod	55.8°N	37.6°E
Kola	68.9°N	33.0°E
Kolomenskoe	55.7°N	37.7°E
Kolomna	55.1°N	38.8°E
Königsberg	54.7°N	20.5°E
Koporye	59.7°N	29.0°E
Korela	61.0°N	30.1°E
Kozelsk	54.0°N	35.8°E
Krakow	50.1°N	20.0°E
Kromy	52.7°N	35.8°E

Krym	45.0°N	35.1°E	Oskol	51.3°N	37.8°E
Kursk	51.7°N	36.2°E	Ostrog	50.3°N	26.5°E
Ladoga	60.0°N	32.3°E	**Ostyor**	51.0°N	30.9°E
Livny	52.4°N	37.6°E	**Pechora**	65.1°N	57.2°E
Lübeck	53.9°N	10.7°E	**Pelym**	61.0°N	62.0°E
Velikie Luki	56.3°N	30.5°E	**Peremyshl**	54.3°N	36.2°E
Lutsk	50.8°N	25.3°E	**Perevoz**	55.6°N	44.6°E
Lvov	49.8°N	24.0°E	Perm	58.0°N	56.3°E
Marienburg	54.0°N	19.0°E	**Pilten**	57.2°N	21.7°E
Mecklenberg	53.6°N	12.4°E	**Polotsk**	55.5°N	28.8°E
Meshchovsk	54.3°N	35.3°E	**Poznan**	52.4°N	16.9°E
Mosalsk	54.5°N	35.0°E	Pskov	57.8°N	28.3°E
MOSCOW	55.8°N	37.6°E	**Revel** (or Reval, Tallinn)	59.4°N	24.7°E
Münster	52.0°N	7.6°E			
Murmansk	69.0°N	33.1°E	**Riga**	57.0°N	24.1°E
Narva	59.4°N	28.2°E	**Rostov**	57.2°N	39.4°E
Nizhnyi Novgorod	56.3°N	44.0°E	**Ryazan**	54.6°N	39.7°E
Novgorod	58.6°N	31.3°E	Rylsk	51.6°N	34.7°E
Novgorod Severskii	52.0°N	33.3°E	Rzhev	56.2°N	34.3°E
Oreshek (or Nöteberg)			Samara	53.2°N	50.2°E
	60.0°N	31.0°E	**Sambor**	49.5°N	23.2°E
Orsha	54.5°N	30.4°E	**Sandomir**	50.7°N	21.8°E

Sarai	48.7°N	45.3°E	Ufa	54.8°N	56.0°E
Serpukhov	54.9°N	37.4°E	Uglich	57.5°N	38.3°E
Sevsk	52.2°N	34.5°E	Urzhum	57.1°N	50.0°E
Shuya	56.8°N	41.4°E	Ustyug	60.8°N	46.3°E
Sibir	58.2°N	68.5°E	Vilnius	54.7°N	25.3°E
Smolensk	54.8°N	32.0°E	Vitebsk	55.2°N	30.2°E
Solovki	65.0°N	35.7°E	Vladimir	56.2°N	40.4°E
Staritsa	56.5°N	34.9°E	Vologda	59.2°N	39.9°E
Starodub	52.6°N	32.8°E	Voronezh	51.7°N	39.2°E
Stockholm	59.3°N	18.1°E	Vorotynsk	54.5°N	36.0°E
Suzdal	56.4°N	40.4°E	Vyatka	58.6°N	49.6°E
Tobolsk	58.2°N	68.2°E	Vyazma	55.2°N	34.2°E
Tomsk	56.5°N	85.0°E	Vyborg	60.7°N	28.8°E
Torzhok	57.0°N	35.0°E	Wesenberg	59.4°N	26.4°E
Trnovo	43.1°N	25.6°E	Yarensk	62.2°N	49.1°E
Trubchevsk	52.5°N	33.8°E	Yaroslavl	57.6°N	39.8°E
Tsaritsyn	48.7°N	44.5°E	Zvenigorod	55.7°N	36.8°E
Tsyvilsk	55.9°N	47.5°E			
Tula	54.2°N	37.6°E			
Turinsk	58.0°N	63.7°E			
Tushino	55.8°N	37.4°E			
Tver	56.9°N	35.9°E			

MOSCOW AND WEST
CIRCA 1600 CE

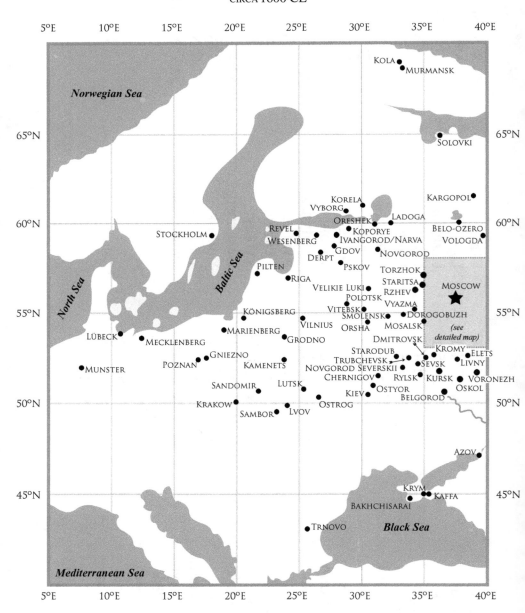

Moscow and Environs

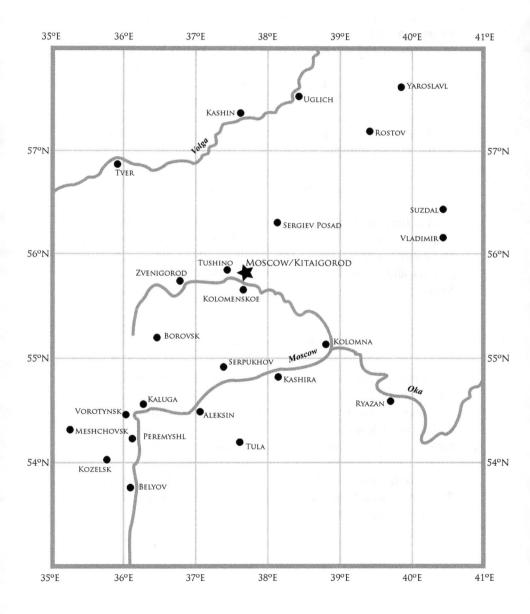

About the author

Nikolai Mikhailovich Karamzin was a major Russian literary figure – a writer, poet and critic. He was born in the province of Orenburg and when he was 14 he was sent to Moscow to an elite boarding school. In 1783, after brief service in the military, he began his literary efforts, which included some very popular, sentimental short stories. In 1803 he changed course: he was appointed historiographer to the Russian court and commenced work on his classic, monumental History, on which he labored until his death almost 23 years later.

About the translator

A retired systems software programmer, Geoff Baldwin is a graduate of the Army Language School and has worked as a translator for U.S. Intelligence agencies. He holds degrees in physics and mathematics from Reed College and San Francisco State.

Acknowledgments

I would like to express my appreciation to Kate Gladstone for copy editing, to Diane Moomey for consulting on publication, to Gwynne Stoddart for web page design, but last and most to Larissa Chiriaeva for her assistance on difficult Russian passages and her general encouragement over the years.

I should also note that Wikipedia (in both the English and Russian versions) has been an invaluable assistant, particularly with regard to annotation.

Index

CPSIA information can be obtained
at www.ICGtesting.com
Printed in the USA
BVHW052333140223
658548BV00012B/252